Ross Maddox
856-2612 (H)

MVS/VSAM
for the Application
Programmer

D1453305

Books from QED

Database

Managing IMS Databases
Building the Data Warehouse
Migrating to DB2
DB2: The Complete Guide to Implementation
and Use
DB2 Design Review Guidelines
DB2: Maximizing Performance of Online
Production Systems
Embedded SQL for DB2
SQL for DB2 and SQL/DS Application
Developers
How to Use ORACLE SQL*PLUS
ORACLE: Building High Performance Online
Systems
ORACLE Design Review Guidelines
Developing Client/Server Applications in an
Architected Environment

Systems Engineering

Software Configuration Management
On Time, Within Budget: Software Project
Management Practices and Techniques
Information Systems Architecture:
Development in the 90's
Quality Assurance for Information Systems
User-Interface Screen Design: Workstations,
PC's, Mainframes
Managing Software Projects
The Complete Guide to Software Testing
A Structured Approach to Systems Testing
Rapid Application Prototyping
The Software Factory
Data Architecture: The Information Paradigm
Software Engineering with Formal Metrics
Using CASE Tools for Practical Management

Management

Developing a Blueprint for Data, Applications,
and Technology: Enterprise Architecture
Planning
Introduction to Data Security and Controls
How to Automate Your Computer Center
Controlling the Future
The UNIX Industry
Mind Your Business

IBM Mainframe Series

From Mainframe to Workstations: Offloading
Application Development
VSE/SP and VSE/ESA: A Guide to
Performance Tuning
CICS: A Guide to Application Debugging
CICS Application and System Programming
CICS: A Guide To Performance Tuning
MVS COBOL II Power Programmer's Desk
Reference
VSE JCL and Subroutines for Application
Programmers
VSE COBOL II Power Programmer's Desk
Reference
Introduction to Cross System Product
CSP Version 3.3 Application Development
The MVS Primer
MVS/VSAM for the Application Programmer
TSO/E CLISTs: The Complete Tutorial and
Desk Reference
CICS: A How-To for COBOL Programmers
QMF: How to Use Query Management Facility
with DB2 and SQL/DS
DOS/VSE JCL: Mastering Job Control
Language
DOS/VSE: CICS Systems Programming
VSAM: Guide to Optimization and Design
MVS/JCL: Mastering Job Control Language
MVS/TSO: Mastering CLISTs
MVS/TSO: Mastering Native Mode and ISPF
REXX in the TSO Environment, 2nd Edition

Technical

Rdb/VMS: Developing the Data Warehouse
The Wonderful World of the AS/400:
Architecture and Applications
C Language for Programmers
Mainframe Development Using Microfocus
COBOL/2 Workbench
AS/400: A Practical Guide to Programming and
Operations
Bean's Index to OSF/Motif, Xt Intrinsics, and
Xlib Documentation for OSF/Motif
Application Programmers
VAX/VMS: Mastering DCL Commands and
Utilities
The PC Data Handbook
UNIX C Shell Desk Reference
Designing and Implementing Ethernet Networks
The Handbook for Microcomputer Technicians
Open Systems

---

*QED books are available at special quantity discounts for educational uses, premiums, and sales promotions.
Special books, book excerpts, and instructive materials can be created to meet specific needs.*

This is Only a Partial Listing. For Additional Information or a Free Catalog contact
QED Information Sciences, Inc. • P. O. Box 812070 • Wellesley, MA 02181-0013
Telephone: 800-343-4848 or 617-237-5656 or fax 617-235-0826

MVS/VSAM
for the Application
Programmer

Gary D. Brown
S.A.M. Smith

QED Publishing Group
Boston • London • Toronto

Many of the designations used by manufacturers and sellers to distinguish their products are claimed as trademarks. Where those designations appear in this book, and QED was aware of a trademark claim, the designations have been printed in initial caps or all caps.

This book is available at a special discount when you order multiple copies. For information, contact QED Information Sciences, Inc., POB 812070, Wellesley, MA 02181-0013 or phone 617-237-5656.

© 1993 QED Information Sciences, Inc.
P.O. Box 812070
Wellesley, MA 02181-0013

QED Publishing Group is a division of
QED Information Sciences, Inc.

All rights reserved. No part of the material protected by this copyright notice may be reproduced or utilized in any form or by any means, electronic or mechanical, including photocopying, recording, or by any information storage and retrieval systems, without written permission from the copyright owner.

Library of Congress Catalog Number: 92-14358
International Standard Book Number: 0-89435-423-X

Printed in the United States of America
93 94 95 10 9 8 7 6 5 4 3 2 1

Library of Congress Cataloging-in-Publication Data

Brown, Gary DeWard.
  MVS/VSAM for the application programmer / Gary D. Brown
and S.A.M. Smith.
    p. cm.
  Includes index.
  ISBN 0-89435-423-X :
  1. Virtual computer systems. 2. Application software.
I. Smith, S.A.M., 1937- . II. Title.
QA76.9.V5B76 1992
005.74—dc20   92-14358
                                                       CIP

Contents

Preface

VSAM dates back to a time when Watergate was just becoming a term that meant more than an upscale apartment. It was developed by IBM to provide a single, coherent file storage system for sequential, direct, and indexed files. Despite its age, VSAM has entered a second growth stage. The increasing demands of both online and database systems have brought VSAM into the mainstream for every programmer. Today, a knowledge of VSAM is as much a basic part of application programming as JCL, the linkage editor, Sort/Merge, and ISPF/PDF.

VSAM has been very successful for IBM. As a programmer, you access VSAM datasets at a high level without having to deal with the inner workings. This has allowed IBM to evolve VSAM over the years without impacting the programs that use it.

This book is a result of this evolution. A lot has happened to VSAM lately. IBM has introduced SAA (Systems Application Architecture), MVS/ESA (Multiple Virtual System/Enterprise Systems Architecture), DFSMS (Data Facility Storage Management Subsystem), VS COBOL II, CICS/ESA, and DFP/VSAM. These changes also reflect the evolution of the large mainframe computer. VSAM is at the heart of what it does best, which is to serve as a repository for corporate data. In a sense, the mainframe is becoming a VSAM machine. Even IBM's main database system, DB2, uses VSAM to store its data. Because there is so much new in VSAM, even experienced programmers can benefit from the material in this book.

This book explains VSAM with examples—*many* examples. People who use VSAM have programming experience. They prefer short examples to long explanations. They are concerned about performance. They are impatient to get things done. They are the people for whom this book is written.

The first two sections of this book describe everything you need to get started with VSAM. The third section becomes more technical, culminating in the final section that describes performance considerations. The emphasis is on today's programming environment, of which the PC is an inherent part. Although VSAM doesn't exist on the PC, you can write application programs in VS COBOL II that run on both the mainframe using VSAM and on the PC.

The authors would like to thank the following for their direction and guidance; Bob Lapin of R.B.L. Systems Inc., Steve Sword, and Willard Brocinton.

PART 1

Getting Started with VSAM

This first section of the book explains VSAM (Virtual Storage Access Method) concepts and introduces the terminology that is peculiar to this access method. It should be read by all beginning students for background information. Additionally, it may be read by experienced VSAM practitioners anxious to see how VSAM and its various dataset types have evolved in today's MVS (Multiple Virtual System) computing environment.

Upon completion of this part of the book, you should have an appreciation of the factors that influence your decision to choose one VSAM dataset type over another when designing and coding a programming application.

Introducing VSAM

VSAM, for Virtual Storage Access Method, is an IBM access method intended to provide, in one coherent system, most of the file organization needs for application programmers. As such, it provides sequential, indexed, relative record and linear datasets. In VSAM terminology, these four types of data organization are named with the following initialisms:

- *ESDS.* Entry-Sequenced Datasets. These are the familiar sequential datasets, and they can be read or written only in sequential order—that is, the order of entry.
- *KSDS.* Key-Sequenced Datasets. These are datasets stored in order of a key field in the record. Individual records can be accessed randomly by the record key. The keys are stored in a separate index so that record access is a two-stage process: first locating the key in the index and then using the information in the index for the key to locate the record.
- *RRDS.* Relative Record Datasets. These are datasets stored in some sequential order. The records have no internal keys, but individual records can be accessed randomly by giving the relative position of the record in the dataset, such as 1, 2, and so on.
- *LDS.* Linear Datasets. These are datasets that consist of a long stream of bytes. They aren't considered to have records.

IBM considers VSAM to have five main advantages over non-VSAM datasets:

1. Protection of the data against unauthorized access, including password protection for VSAM datasets. (RACF, Resource Access Control Facility, and similar products can do this for non-VSAM, but protection is not an inherent part of the dataset as it is with VSAM.)
2. Cross-system compatibility. There is less to this than might appear since it does not mean that VSAM datasets can be easily ported to CMS, the AS/400, the PC, or non-IBM computers. It means they can be exported and imported in MVS and VSE systems.
3. Device independence. There is no need to be concerned with block size and other control information. (DFSMS now does much the same for non-VSAM datasets.)
4. The JCL for COBOL programs using VSAM is simpler than that for non-VSAM datasets. Information needed by the system is available in VSAM or ICF catalogs. (The JCL is easier, but one generally must use the IDCAMS utility program to first create the dataset.)
5. VSAM processing is the only way your VS COBOL II programs can use indexed or relative file organization. This, of course, is an overwhelming advantage.

1.1.   DATA ORGANIZATION

The different data organizations are all rather standard and have been around in one form or another as long as data has been organized. Books make an excellent method of illustrating how data organization has evolved. The first books were essential sequential datasets. The author started writing on the first page (or scroll or clay tablet) and continued without any break until he or she had said all that needed to be said. This first data organization corresponds to what VSAM terms the linear dataset. Obviously, this presented some problems when one wanted to look something up in a book. One generally had to read the entire book from cover to cover or scroll to scroll.

Sentences and paragraphs were added to break up the contents of the book. In a computer, these segments would be equivalent to records. The book had now evolved into what in VSAM would be a sequential dataset. This helped readability, but it wasn't much help in looking things up. One still had to read the book cover to cover in search of specific information.

The next step was to add page numbers. This was great once you found what you were looking for because you could write down the page number and quickly find the reference again. In data processing, this would be the same as a relative record dataset. Each unit of data is assigned a relative record number. While this makes it easy to locate something once you have the number, it leaves unresolved the problem of how you find the number to begin with. Again, one was often forced to read the entire book.

The breakthrough with books came with the index. One could go to the index to find where the material is in the book, and then begin reading sequentially at that page number. This corresponds to what in VSAM is a keyed-sequenced dataset. This made looking things up in a book an order of magnitude easier.

Most of the materials we organize in our daily lives, such as file drawers and folders, use one or more of these four types of organizations. They all have one major problem: What happens when you want to add records?

With a sequential dataset, adding records is easy if you want to add them at the end of the dataset. If you want to insert records somewhere within a dataset, however, you generally have to copy it entirely and insert the records. The same is true with a linear dataset, and also for a relative record dataset. With a relative record dataset, you can leave empty slots for adding records, which sometimes helps. But generally, none of these three data organizations works well when you want to add data somewhere within a dataset.

The indexed or key-sequenced dataset works best when you need to add or delete records within a dataset. Since you access the records through an index that points to where the records are stored, you don't have to add new records where they should physically go in the dataset.

To illustrate the problem of adding records, let's use a library as an example. Most likely, the first library simply stacked all the books in order of title on the shelves. Maybe there were two books. Then a third book was published, and it was easy to insert it where it belonged. But one day there were hundreds of feet of bookshelves, and, whenever a new book was acquired, it had to be inserted where it belonged, and all the books following it had to be moved down on the shelves.

Libraries solved this problem with the card catalog and by leaving unused space on the shelves. If a book was added, the librarian only had to find the shelf where it belonged and insert it, moving down only the books on that shelf. If books didn't fit on the shelves, such as oversized books, they could be stuck somewhere else and the card catalog could direct people to them. Of course, when the shelves started to get full, it was time to reorganize. VSAM key-sequenced datasets use this same technique.

Key-sequenced datasets also encountered the same problem that libraries had with the card catalog. People often didn't want to access the books by title, but by author or subject. Libraries solved this problem by copying the card catalog and keeping one copy in order by author and another by subject. VSAM key-sequenced datasets allow this same facility, which it calls *alternate indexes*.

There are major differences between the way books are stored and accessed in a library and records are stored in a VSAM key-sequenced dataset, but the essential point is that there is really nothing mysterious, let alone new, about the way VSAM organizes data. The difficulty with VSAM isn't the concepts; it is the terminology. VSAM probably holds the modern record for the introduction of new initialisms.

1.2.   VSAM TERMINOLOGY

This book tries to minimize the use of unnecessary terms, but it is probably a lost cause. Let's examine some of the basic ones.

Just as the organization of a library is contained in its *catalogs,* so is the organization of VSAM datasets. The name of all VSAM datasets, along with necessary information about each dataset, such as where it is stored, how many records it contains, and what kind of records it contains, are kept in a catalog. VSAM can have two catalogs: a *master catalog* (there is one and it is mandatory) and *user catalogs* (created for individual applications to facilitate modularity, such as import/export operations).

In VSAM terminology, the logical dataset for storing records (a dataset in OS, operating system, terminology) is called a *cluster*. This new term is used because there are two components for many VSAM datasets, an *index component* (which contains the index) and a *data component* (which contains the actual data). (To use the library example, the card catalog and the stacks would both be clusters.) Individual records in a VSAM cluster are stored and accessed in what is termed a *control interval*. In OS terminology, a control interval corresponds to a block. The control interval is therefore the VSAM unit of work. In our library example, a shelf is a control interval.

This is enough terminology for us to limp along on until the next chapter. Chapters 2, 3, and 4 present more important concepts of how VSAM datasets are organized and stored.

1.3.   WHAT VSAM IS

An access method such as VSAM is not a database management system. The two are easily confused. An access method stores and retrieves data. It does not provide for a relationship among the data, aside from the fact that sequential datasets are in sequential order. A database system such as DB2 (Database 2) or IMS (Information Management System) is often implemented using VSAM. They differ in that the database also carries information that shows the relationship among the data. To use the book example, a book becomes a database when it references information in other books.

VSAM is not a programming language. It is used in conjunction with a programming language such as COBOL or PL/I to create applications. VSAM also has a set of utility programs called either AMS (Access Method Services) or IDCAMS (IDCAMS is the name of the actual program that is executed for the utility).

VSAM is not a communication system, such as VTAM (Virtual Terminal Access Method) or CICS (Customer Information Control System). VSAM is used by such systems as CICS to store and retrieve data.

The following gives a flavor of how VSAM is used by application programmers.

- Programmers write IDCAMS utility program commands and execute them to create VSAM datasets. Alternatively, they can also write JCL statements to create VSAM datasets, although this is not often done.
- Programmers write application programs in languages such as COBOL, PL/I, and Assembler language, using the statements provided by these languages to write and read VSAM datasets. The jobs can be run in batch or online. If run online, they are usually written as CICS applications.
- To access a VSAM dataset in a batch job, you write a JCL DD statement naming the dataset, as with any other dataset. In CICS online applications, you name the dataset as part of an online or macro resource definition.
- The IDCAMS utility program commands are often used to list, examine, print, tune, back up, and import/export VSAM datasets.

VSAM was introduced by IBM in 1973 as a replacement for several of its existing access methods. In particular, the key-sequenced datasets of VSAM replaced an old access method called ISAM (Indexed-Sequential Access Method). The VSAM relative record dataset replaced another old access method called BDAM (Basic Direct Access Method). VSAM also has entry-sequenced datasets that provide the same function as the normal sequential QSAM (Queued Sequential Access Method) datasets of the operating system. However, VSAM entry-sequenced datasets haven't replaced QSAM datasets because sequential datasets are inherently simple, and VSAM doesn't offer much of an advantage (except for CICS, which handles the ESDS better than its QSAM counterpart).

VSAM had many advantages over the old systems it replaced, which were often touted to encourage the use of VSAM. For example, there is an entire family of difficult to use utility programs for managing OS datasets, whereas VSAM has a single utility program (IDCAMS) for managing its datasets. VSAM gurus often object to the term "utility program" when referring to IDCAMS, but essentially that's what it is, and that's what we'll call it. VSAM advantages still exist, but since the old access methods have all but disappeared (except for QSAM) and VSAM is the only game in town, its advantages over them is of historical interest only.

One data organization missing in VSAM is the partitioned dataset (PDS). A partitioned dataset is a collection of named sequential datasets stored in a single dataset. In our library analogy, a PDS is like a set of encyclopedias. PDSs are extensively used for text files, such as programs, JCL, libraries, and so on. VSAM has no equivalent for a PDS.

Although VSAM is called *virtual* sequential access method, virtual is more of a marketing term than a description. There was nothing virtual about VSAM its first 15 years until recently with the advent of hiperspaces and data spaces. (Were VSAM being introduced today, it would probably be called the Enterprise Access Method—"enterprise" being the current hot term.)

1.4. VSAM HISTORY

VSAM is an alive and evolving system. As such, various versions of it exist, and sometimes an older version is retained even when a newer version is installed because not all versions are completely compatible, and there may be older applications that still need to be supported. The following summary shows the major VSAM versions:

- *1973.* First VSAM introduced—Standard VSAM. This version had only KSDS (key-sequenced datasets) and ESDS (entry-sequenced datasets).
- *1975.* Enhanced VSAM introduced. This added RRDS (relative record datasets) and alternate indexes for KSDS. It also provided for catalog recovery. Enhanced VSAM replaced Standard VSAM entirely.
- *1979.* DF/EF (Data Facility/Extended Function) VSAM introduced with ICF (Integrated Catalog Facility) to replace the old VSAM catalog of the previous VSAM versions. Because of the differences in the catalogs, Enhanced VSAM was often maintained along with DF/EF VSAM.

- *1983.*   DFP/VSAM Version 1 (Data Facility Product) introduced to replace DF/EF VSAM entirely and run under MVS/XA (Multiple Virtual System/eXtended Architecture). There were many changes, but they were compatible with DF/EF. However, enhanced VSAM was not impacted and many installations still maintain it.
- *1987.*   DFP/VSAM Version 2, Release 3.0 introduced to replace Version 1 entirely. Linear datasets (LDS) were added.
- *1988.*   DFP/VSAM Version 3 introduced to replace Version 2 entirely to run under MVS/ESA (Enterprise Systems Architecture). (DFSMS, Data Facility Storage Management Subsystem, support was incorporated into VSAM.)
- *1991.*   DFP/VSAM Version 3, Release 3 introduced to replace the other DFP/VSAM versions entirely. Under DFP/VSAM 3.3, relative record datasets can contain variable-length records, enhancements were made to DFSMS facilities, and support was discontinued for the IBM 3850 Mass Storage System (MSS).

Now that this is out of the way, we can begin to discuss the internals of VSAM.

2

It All Starts with the Catalog

The essence of VSAM is its catalog structure. That's because all VSAM objects must be cataloged, and any access to these objects is via the catalog. In VSAM terminology, an *object* is anything created by VSAM for storing data. An update activity against a VSAM object (say, a dataset) is reflected immediately in its catalog entry. For example, if a catalog entry for a VSAM dataset indicates that it contains 1000 records, and you add another 1000 records, the catalog entry is updated immediately with the new value of 2000 records. We refer to it as the *catalog structure* because, as you'll soon see, VSAM supports several different types of catalogs.

For an OS dataset, attribute information (such as number of records) is contained in the VTOC (Volume Table of Contents) for the volume on which the dataset is stored. However, for a VSAM dataset, this same attribute information is stored in its catalog entry and is easily accessible with a single LISTCAT command, which can be entered online or in batch mode.

2.1. VSAM OBJECTS

Besides several different types of datasets (as you saw in the last chapter), VSAM supports a plethora of other objects. For example, the VSAM catalog structure is itself an object (or more properly, multiple objects); a catalog or dataset alias is another object, as is an alternate index, which offers an alternate view of data and the path by which the alternate index is accessed. In the older versions of VSAM, even allocated space is an object. All of these objects must be defined to the VSAM catalog structure, and Part 2 of this book presents the commands to do this and how to use them in the most efficient way for your operating environment. (Even though the text in the rest of this chapter refers to datasets, the concepts apply to most VSAM objects.)

2.2. VSAM ADVANTAGES

There are several advantages to an access method such as VSAM that is totally catalog-driven. Here are just a few, and as you learn more about VSAM you'll discover many more on your own. For starters, the VSAM catalog structure has the following features:

- *Modular.* The catalog entry for a dataset contains all the information the system needs to know about the dataset: space allocation information, security and access criteria, attributes, and processing statistics.
- *Easily defined.* You use one utility to create and maintain a catalog entry versus multiple utilities for OS datasets.
- *Flexible.* You can define VSAM and non-VSAM datasets in the catalog structure, even Generation Data Groups (GDGs). OS datasets can coexist in the VSAM catalog structure, though they are defined in OS catalogs.
- *Easily used.* You can list dataset attributes or the records themselves online or in batch mode.
- *Portable.* When certain guidelines are met, you can transport an entire VSAM catalog from one system to another, for example from MVS to VSE, because VSAM catalogs have compatible structures.
- *Secure.* Catalogs are protected by internal VSAM security and add-on products like RACF (Resource Access Control Facility).
- *Controlled.* When processing a VSAM dataset with an application program, the access path is via the catalog entry. Since access to all VSAM datasets comes through this one point, access is easily controlled.
- *Adaptable.* VSAM uses two different types of catalogs, an older one aptly named *VSAM* and a newer one that supports the XA (eXtended Architecture) and ESA (Enterprise Systems Architecture) environments and is called the Integrated Catalog Facility (ICF). The newer catalog was developed to correct some of the technical shortcomings of the older VSAM catalog, including storage volume ownership restrictions and the inconsistencies imposed by two separate space managers. (More on this in the next chapter.)

While there are many operational differences between the two types of catalogs, they can co-reside within one computing environment. However, both types (VSAM and ICF) have the same generic structure.

2.3. GENERIC CATALOG STRUCTURE

The generic catalog structure of VSAM consists of one master and at least one (usually multiple) user catalog. Master and user catalogs are each defined separately and are considered separate VSAM objects. The master catalog has pointers to the various user catalogs, which contain application datasets and are typically allocated by function within an environment, say one for programmers, one for accounting—whatever is appropriate for the enterprise. A large installation may support hundreds of user catalogs. This is shown in Figure 2.1.

The master catalog typically contains system entries and should be kept small and compact to facilitate recovery if it becomes corrupted. In MVS systems, the master catalog also functions as the system catalog.

The catalog structure contains entries for both VSAM and non-VSAM datasets and other objects. While a VSAM dataset must be cataloged in either the master or a user catalog, a non-VSAM dataset can be cataloged in either the master or a user catalog, or in an OS catalog (CVOL, for Control Volume). You cannot catalog a VSAM dataset in a CVOL. Figure 2.2 illustrates the addition of a CVOL to the catalog structure.

The older VSAM catalog types actually own the storage volumes where they reside, meaning that no other VSAM catalogs can have datasets cataloged on that storage volume. That restriction does not exist with ICF-type catalogs, and multiple catalogs (up to 36) can share

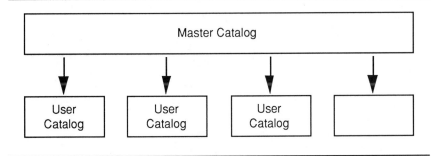

Figure 2.1.   VSAM catalogs.

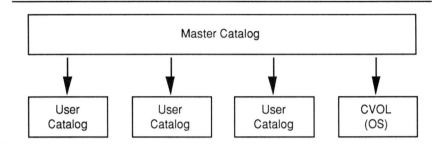

Figure 2.2.   Master catalog with a CVOL.

control in a given storage volume, resulting in better space utilization on that volume. There's more detail on ICF catalogs in Chapter 22.

Application programmers interact with the catalog using two basic Access Method Services (AMS) commands: DEFINE, which both allocates the dataset or other object and creates a catalog entry, and LISTCAT, which lists the attributes of the dataset or other object once it is defined. You can even list the contents of an entire catalog using LISTCAT. Both of these commands can be entered online or in batch mode. DEFINE and all of its many options are covered thoroughly in Chapters 6 through 9, and LISTCAT is the subject of Chapter 10.

In the next chapter, we'll look inside VSAM to see how its various components fit together.

Inside VSAM

This chapter takes you inside VSAM datasets to explain how they are stored on DASD (Direct Access Storage Device—a stuffy term for disk). VSAM datasets are usually allocated with the IDCAMS utility program as described in Chapter 6, but for now, let's just follow the process through.

3.1.   ALLOCATING VSAM DATASETS

When you allocate a VSAM dataset, you must provide the following information:

- A dataset name, which becomes the base cluster name (more on this later). If the dataset is a KSDS, you should assign a name to both the data and index components.
- The type of dataset: key-sequenced dataset, entry-sequenced dataset, relative record dataset, or linear dataset.
- The units of space in which you are allocating (tracks, cylinders, or records) and the amount of primary and secondary space to allocate. Unlike OS datasets (and *unique* VSAM datasets cataloged in the older VSAM catalogs), which can have only a primary and 15 secondary allocations on a volume, VSAM datasets can have one primary and 122 secondary allocations, which is a major advantage.
- The serial number of the volume or volumes on which to allocate the dataset.

- The length of the records and whether they are fixed or variable length.

There are a great number of other parameters that can be specified when creating a VSAM dataset, such as the data protection, the expiration data, and the buffering. However, the previous items are the essential ones.

The different components of a VSAM dataset, such as the catalog, the index component, the data component, and others, such as the alternate index component that is described later, are termed *objects*.

The IDCAMS command to allocate space is the DEFINE CLUSTER command. When this command is allocated, VSAM does the following:

- It records the dataset name and all the relevant information for the dataset in the catalog for VSAM.
- It then allocates the space for the dataset and then makes an entry in the catalog to point to the allocated space.

3.2.   CLUSTERS

It's time we defined the term *cluster*. Strictly speaking, a VSAM cluster is a named object that includes both the data and index components of a KSDS. It may help to think of the cluster as a *logical* dataset. The data component (which contains the actual data) and the index component (which contains the actual index) are each *physical* datasets.

The KSDS is the only type of VSAM dataset whose structure completely fulfills the cluster concept. But for consistency we refer to other types of VSAM datasets as clusters even though they contain only data. For this reason, you can refer to a cluster and a dataset synonymously. As you work with VSAM, you'll see that there are definite advantages to being able to work with a KSDS cluster as a whole, or the components separately.

3.3.   VSAM SPACE ALLOCATION

Space allocation for a VSAM dataset depends on whether the dataset is cataloged in an ICF or the older VSAM-type catalog. For VSAM datasets cataloged in the newer ICF-type catalogs, dedicated space is allocated dynamically when the cluster (dataset) is created with the DEFINE CLUSTER command. Space is managed by the OS space manager and, as such, does not provide any guaranteed space for the VSAM dataset. Each VSAM dataset cataloged in an ICF catalog has its own VTOC entry. These VSAM datasets can have one primary and 122 secondary allocations. For VSAM datasets cataloged in the older VSAM-type catalogs, space is either suballocated or unique.

Suballocation: Someone, often a systems programmer, allocates a large amount of OS space to VSAM. The space often consists of one or more entire DASD volumes. This is done with an IDCAMS DEFINE SPACE command. The DEFINE SPACE command causes OS to allocate this dedicated empty space to VSAM. This dedicated space pool is then suballocated to one or more VSAM datasets, perhaps for different users. The IDCAMS DEFINE CLUSTER command does this. All of the secondary space for the suballocated datasets is allocated on demand from the available space pool. The original space pool itself can have a secondary space—but only 16 total extents because it obtains its space from OS.

Suballocated datasets can be deleted, making space available within the space pool that can then be reallocated. The advantage of suballocation is that it makes efficient use of space as is shown in Figure 3.1. It also allows VSAM datasets to have 123 extents.

Suballocated space is managed by the VSAM Space Manager, which is actually a series of routines. A suballocated VSAM dataset does not have its own VTOC entry. Only the original space pool allocated by the DEFINE SPACE command has a VTOC entry.

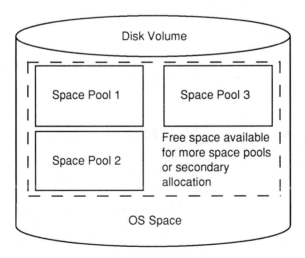

Figure 3.1.   Suballocation of VSAM space.

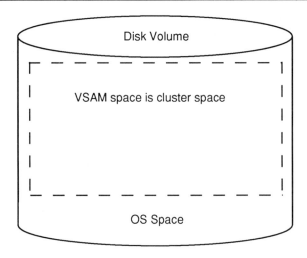

Figure 3.2.   Unique allocation of VSAM space.

Unique: With unique allocation, a dataset is suballocated directly from the OS disk space, and the dataset occupies the entire amount of space allocated. No DEFINE SPACE command is needed. Space for unique allocation can only be allocated in units of cylinders. Since the space is allocated directly from OS, a unique dataset can only have a primary and 15 secondary extents. A unique dataset can't be deleted and reused. When it is deleted, its space is released back to OS, which manages the space. Of course, one can always reallocate space again. Figure 3.2 illustrates unique space.

3.4.   CONTROL INTERVALS

Now with space allocation out of the way, let's see how the datasets are filled with records for VSAM. VSAM stores records in the data component in units called *control intervals* (CI). The control interval is VSAM's equivalent of a block, and it is the unit of data that is actually transmitted when records are read or written. You specify *control interval size* with a CISZ parameter of the IDCAMS DEFINE CLUSTER command when you create the VSAM dataset. This also specifies the buffer size. The DEFINE CLUSTER command is described in Chapter 6. Figure 3.3 illustrates records stored in a control interval.

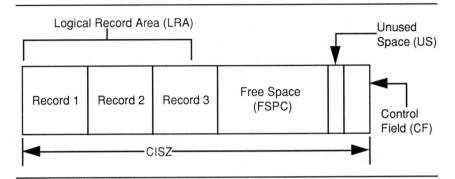

Figure 3.3.   A VSAM Control Interval (CI) for the data component.

The proper selection of the CISZ is important, both to minimize unused space and to provide an efficient unit for transmitting records. This gets tricky because the control field (CF) is not a fixed length. The control field actually consists of two subfields: one Control Information Definition Field (CIDF) and one or more Record Definition Fields (RDF). The length of the control field can affect the CISZ selected. Selecting the CISZ is described in Chapter 7.

For a KSDS, each record must have a primary key field containing a unique value. As described later in Chapter 11, there may also be alternate key fields, but these are less common. (ESDS and RRDS records may also have key fields, but VSAM doesn't use them or even have to know of their existence. VSAM doesn't consider an LDS to have records, let alone keys.) Figure 3.4 illustrates a typical KSDS record with a primary key field. The key fields in each record must occupy the same relative byte positions within the record. For variable-length records, this means that the key field must be in a contiguous, fixed portion of the record.

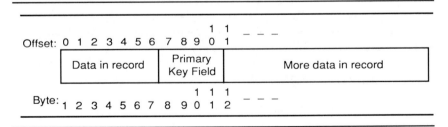

Figure 3.4.   Primary key field in a KSDS record.

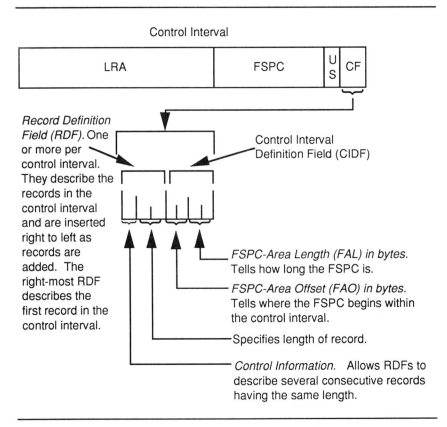

Figure 3.5.   The Control Field (CF) component of a control interval.

3.4.1.   Format of a Control Interval

You specify the key field in the IDCAMS DEFINE CLUSTER command by giving its offset in bytes (7 in Figure 3.4) and its length (4 in Figure 3.4). In VSAM, the position of fields is always given by the offset position (the first byte is 0) rather than the byte number.

Now back to the control interval. Notice that there are four separate areas within a control interval as shown in Figure 3.5.

1. The Logical Record Area (LRA) that contains the records.
2. The control interval Free Space (FSPC). You can specify the percentage of a control interval to reserve as free space when you create

a VSAM dataset. This is done with the FREESPACE parameter of the IDCAMS DEFINE CLUSTER command as described in Chapter 7. This area can then be used for adding records. It is like leaving space to add new books in the shelf of a library.

3. Unused Space (US). Because of the record length, the free space may not be a multiple of the record length, and there may be a small amount of space that cannot be used. This can be minimized (for fixed-length records) by selecting a proper control interval size.

4. The Control Fields (CF). This specifies the position and length of the free space within the record. It also contains one or more entries as necessary to specify the number of records contained in the control interval and their length.

This same structure is used for all four types of VSAM datasets. However, only KSDS can take full advantage of it by inserting and deleting records. Figure 3.6 shows how a record is inserted in a KSDS, moving records down to make room. Figure 3.7 illustrates a deletion with the records being shifted left. Exactly the same method is used to insert library books in shelves.

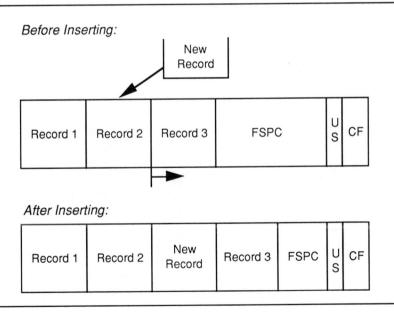

Figure 3.6.   Inserting a record in a control interval.

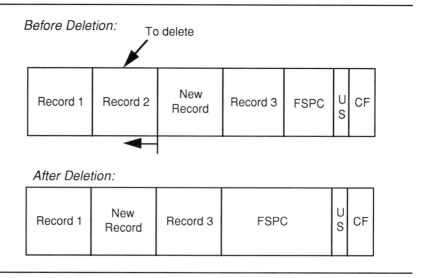

Figure 3.7.   Deleting a record.

3.4.2. Control Interval Split

Of course, there is always the problem of what to do when there is no room to add more records as shown in Figure 3.8. In this case, VSAM performs what is termed a *control interval split.* When you create a VSAM dataset, in addition to specifying a percentage of free space within each control interval, the FREESPACE parameter can also specify a percentage of control intervals to leave free as shown in Figure 3.9. The control interval split moves records off to one of the free control intervals as shown in Figure 3.8.

When a control interval split occurs, the inserted records may no longer be in sequential order. The control intervals in Figure 3.8 may not be in sequence, depending on where the next empty control interval is located. This is not a problem for a KSDS because it accesses the records through an index. (It is also not a problem for an ESDS, an RRDS, or an LDS because they can't have control interval splits.) However, from a performance point of view, control interval splits for a KSDS can cause big problems.

Before Control Interval Split:

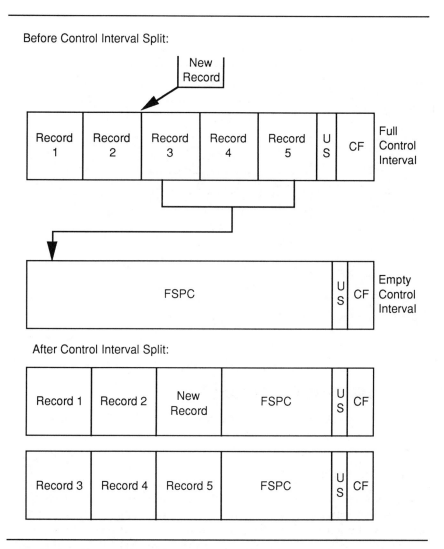

After Control Interval Split:

Figure 3.8.   Control interval split.

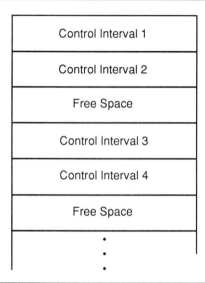

Figure 3.9.   Free space for control intervals.

3.5.   THE INDEX COMPONENT

VSAM creates an index component for a KSDS. It is actually a separate entity and is given a separate name.

3.5.1.   The Sequence Set

The first level of the index is called the *sequence set,* and it contains primary keys and pointers to the control intervals in the sequential order of the primary keys. Figure 3.10 illustrates the sequence set index pointing to control intervals. Notice that while the control intervals themselves may or may not be in sequential order, the sequence set indexes *are.* VSAM always uses the sequence set to access a KSDS sequentially so that the records are retrieved in their proper sequential order.

The index component is allocated as a separate entity from the data component. As such, it has a different CISZ, a different name, and might even be on a different volume. The index component is organized much the same as the data component we have been describing. The entries are stored in control intervals, and control interval splits can

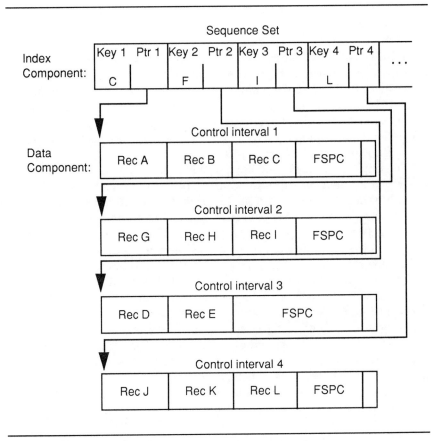

Figure 3.10.   Sequence set of a KSDS.

occur for the index entries just as they can for records. An index entry for a KSDS contains the following two items of information:

- A primary record key to indicate which control interval it points to. The record key must be contained within each record, it must be unique, and it cannot be changed once the records are written.
- A pointer to the control interval containing the records. The VSAM pointer is very simple. It is a Relative Byte Address (RBA) of the entry to which it points. VSAM treats the space allocation as a long string of bytes beginning at zero and going to *n,* and it points to the control interval with its byte address relative to the beginning of the

dataset. It doesn't depend on tracks, cylinders, or any device-dependent information.

VSAM uses a sophisticated method of compressing the index entries that needn't concern us here. There is only one index entry per control interval, and the RBA of the entry points to the beginning of the control interval. This way it need contain only one key and one pointer to locate all the records contained in a control interval. Once the control interval is located, VSAM must then look at each record within the control interval to find the actual record wanted.

To simplify the logic, the key stored in the index is not necessarily the key of the last record in the control interval. Instead, it is the highest value that any key within the control interval can have. That is, it is one less than the value of the first record in the next logical control interval. This simplifies searching as VSAM looks at each index entry only until the key it is looking for is less than or equal to the key of the index entry. Notice that in Figure 3.10, the second key of the index is "F," even though there is no record F in the control interval. VSAM stores the F because the first key of the next control interval is G, and F is one less than G. (The key values here are symbolic. The actual keys might be several bytes long.) Keeping the key this way also means that the index never has to be updated when records are inserted within a control interval. If a Record F is added to control interval 3 in Figure 3.10, the index entry doesn't need to be updated.

When a control interval split occurs, VSAM moves some of the records on the original control interval off to the new control interval, inserting the new record where it belongs. Then it updates the original entry in the sequence set and inserts a new index entry following it to point to the new control interval. This is shown in Figure 3.11.

3.5.2. Control Areas

Now the next inevitable problem. What happens when there are no more free control intervals to perform a control interval split? For this, VSAM uses something called a *control area* (CA). The control area is a fixed-length unit of contiguous DASD storage containing a number of control intervals as shown in Figure 3.12. The control area is VSAM's internal unit for allocating space within a cluster. That is, the primary and the secondary allocations consist of some number of control areas. You don't specify the control area size; VSAM computes it for you. The control area can range in size from one track to one cylinder. If you allocate storage in units of cylinders, a control area becomes a cylinder,

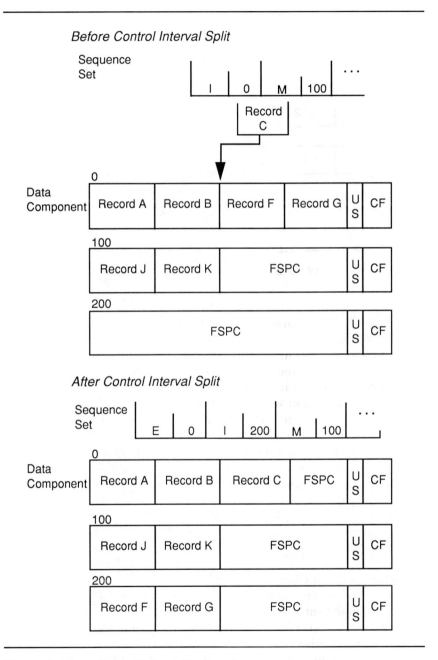

Figure 3.11.   Control interval split and sequence set.

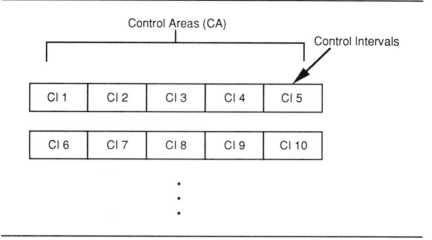

Figure 3.12. Control areas.

which allows VSAM to access all the control intervals without access arm movement.

Control areas are used internally by VSAM for storing the control intervals, and when you first load a dataset, VSAM stores the control intervals sequentially into the control areas, and the control areas are filled sequentially. But when a dataset is updated, all the control intervals within a control area may become filled. When this occurs, VSAM performs a control area split: It obtains a new control area, perhaps from a secondary allocation, moves half the control intervals from the original control area to the new control area, and updates the index pointers as needed. The control area split is performed the same as a control interval split. VSAM can continue control area splits until it exceeds its space allocation. Then it must abend (abnormally terminate).

3.5.3. The Index Set

Of course, when a control area split occurs, the control areas may no longer be in sequential order, as shown in Figure 3.13. VSAM solves this problem the same way it solves the problem of control intervals not being in sequential order—it creates an index of the control areas. This second level of index is called the *index set* to distinguish it from the first level of index, the sequence set. The index set contains primary keys and pointers to the sequence set in sequential order as shown in

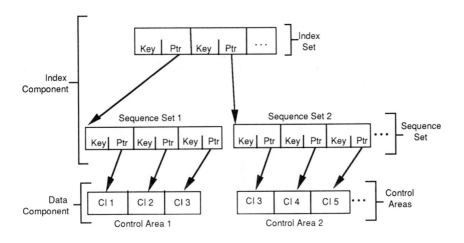

Figure 3.13.   Index set and control areas for a KSDS.

Figure 3.13. VSAM creates one sequence set for each control area and places one entry in the index set to point to each sequence set in its logical order.

3.5.4. Dataset Integrity

The weak point in all this is the inevitability of Murphy's Law. If the computer or system is going to fail, it will fail while a control interval or control area split is occurring. This could result in pointers not being updated. VSAM does all it can to minimize this, but it can occur. When it does, you can use the VSAM REPRO, VERIFY, and EXAMINE IDCAMS command described in Chapter 12 to restore things.

It is also apparent that it takes a lot less effort to insert a record within a control interval where there is free space than to have to perform control area and control interval splits. When a dataset uses up a significant amount of its free space, you should reorganize it to improve performance. You do this with the IDCAMS REPRO command as described in Chapter 12. To determine how the free space is faring, VSAM provides the LISTCAT command as described in Chapter 10.

To mark the end-of-file (EOF), VSAM maintains the last relative byte address used by the dataset and stores this in the VSAM catalog when the dataset is closed. This address is called the HURBA for High Used Relative Byte Address. If a dataset is updated but not closed properly, the HURBA may not be updated. The VSAM statements described in Chapter 12 explain what to do should this occur.

4

VSAM Dataset Organization

As described in the last chapter, the various components of a VSAM dataset, such as the data and index components (known collectively as the base cluster) are stored separately. (The terms cluster and dataset can be used synonymously.) Only a KSDS must have an index component. The other types of VSAM datasets, ESDS, RRDS, and LDS, need have only a data component. (An ESDS can also have an index component for an alternate index, but this is only supported in online CICS.) This chapter describes in more detail how the various types of VSAM datasets are stored.

4.1.   VSAM RECORDS

VSAM records can be fixed or variable length, the same as for normal OS dataset records. (VSAM doesn't have undefined-length records.) Records can also be spanned. Spanned records are records that are longer than a control interval.

You usually establish a control interval size that provides efficient I/O and contains one or more records with minimum unused space. Sometimes though, you may have very large records that are longer than the control interval. VSAM allows a maximum record length of 32,767 bytes. When a record is longer than a control interval, VSAM stores as much of the record as will fit in one control interval and spills over the remainder of the record into the next control interval. This results in what are termed *spanned records*. The records can span a

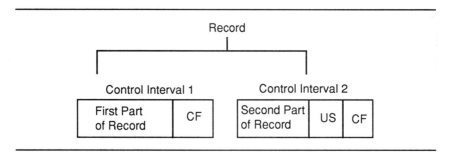

Figure 4.1.   Spanned records.

control interval but not a control area. Note also that the start of each spanned record begins in a new control interval and spills over into another control interval as necessary. The unused space at the end of the last control interval is wasted. Figure 4.1 illustrates a spanned record.

Obviously, spanned records have a large impact on performance when records are inserted or deleted because of the effort of dealing with multiple control intervals. No one uses spanned records unless they have to.

4.2.   ALTERNATE INDEXES

The data component, and for a KSDS the index component, are stored as two separate entities. These entities are called the *base cluster.* All VSAM datasets have a base cluster. The index component of the base cluster (KSDS only) is termed the *primary index,* and it contains the primary keys for the dataset. As described in the previous chapters, a KSDS (and as we'll see, an ESDS) can also have an alternate index.

An alternate index allows a dataset to be ordered on some other key. For example, the same personnel records could have the Social Security number as the primary key because each Social Security number is unique. It could also have the employee's last name as an alternate key, and there would likely be duplicate keys. One could then read the same physical dataset in Social Security number order by using the primary key, or in last name order using the alternate index. You can also have several alternate keys. For the personnel file, you might also set up the person's home telephone number as an alternate key.

A key for an alternate index must occupy the same bytes in each record. Unlike a primary key, the alternate keys do not need to be unique. Uniqueness is an option you specify as a part of creating the alternate index.

You use the IDCAMS utilities to build the alternate index as a separate step. You also build what VSAM calls a *path*. A path is the connection between the alternate index and the records in the base cluster. In languages such as COBOL, you in effect specify the path when you retrieve records to tell the system whether you are retrieving them based on the primary key or on some alternate key.

The alternate index is composed of both an index component and a data component. The index component contains the highest value a key can have within a control interval and a pointer to the control interval. This is shown in Figure 4.2. The control interval contains pointers to the data component control interval of the base cluster that contains the actual data records.

As shown in Figure 4.2, records in the control interval for an alternate index contain a header, the key of a record (not packed), and pointers to each data record containing that key value. (This is how VSAM allows duplicate key values.) The header contains, among other things, a count of the pointers that follow for the records with duplicate keys.

To access a record using the alternate index, VSAM first searches the alternate index component to get the pointer to the control interval

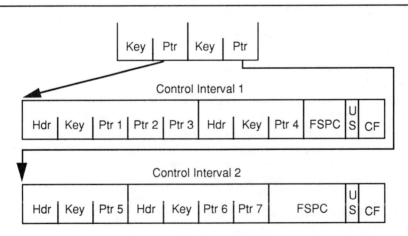

The pointers point to a control interval in the data component of the base cluster that contains the record.

Figure 4.2.   Organization of an alternate index.

of the data component in the alternate index. It then searches this data control interval to find the key and the pointer to the index component of the base cluster. It searches this index component to find the key and pointer to locate the record in the data component of the base cluster where the records are stored.

Even though an ESDS has no index component, VSAM can build an alternate index for this type of dataset by mapping one field to the record's Relative Byte Address. This is only used in online CICS applications, where it is sometimes useful. For example, you could set up an alternate index for a log file in which records are entered by time sequence and then retrieve them randomly based on the alternate index.

From Figure 4.2, it is clear that updating an alternate index when the base cluster is updated—records added or deleted—is a resource-intensive operation. The process of updating the index is called *upgrading*. It gets even worse when there are several alternate indexes. VSAM does this for you automatically unless you tell it not to.

The group of alternate indexes that VSAM automatically upgrades is called the *upgrade set*. When you create an alternate index, you can specify that the index not be upgraded automatically, and VSAM will not consider it part of its upgrade set. Of course, if VSAM does not upgrade the indexes, you must do it—or just live with them not being maintained.

4.3.   KEY-SEQUENCED DATASETS (KSDS)

A KSDS consists of both an index and a data component as described in Chapter 3. The index set of the index component points to the sequence set, which in turn points to the control intervals containing the records. Records can be added through a combination of free space within a control interval, empty control intervals through a control interval split, and empty control areas through a control area split. Records are deleted by simply shifting left all the records to the right of the deleted record, physically removing the deleted record and making the space it occupied available for inserting new records. Figure 3.13 illustrated a KSDS.

A KSDS has the following characteristics:

- The data and index components are separate entities with each given a different name.
- A KSDS is loaded with records by writing them in the sequential order of the primary record key. Each primary record key must contain a unique value and occupy the same contiguous bytes in each record. As directed by the IDCAMS DEFINE CLUSTER command,

free space is left within each control interval, and a percentage of free control intervals can be left with a control area.

- KSDS records can be fixed or variable length. They also can be spanned.

- A KSDS can be read and written sequentially. With *sequential access,* records are read and written in consecutive order based on the primary key. Sequential access is done through the index component so that the records are processed in the order of the primary keys, which is not necessarily the order in which the control intervals are physically stored.

- A KSDS can also be read or written randomly. With *random access,* records are accessed directly by providing VSAM the key of the record. VSAM uses the index to locate the control area and the control interval containing the record. It then reads that control interval and locates the specific record within it by examining the record keys.

- Records can also be accessed dynamically. With *dynamic access,* VSAM first uses random access to position to a specific record in the dataset and then shifts to sequential access to process the records sequentially thereafter.

- Records can be deleted or inserted in a KSDS.

- All KSDSs must have a primary record key. Optionally, they can also have one or more alternate keys. With an alternate key, VSAM creates a new index component for the alternate key. Like the primary key, an alternate key must occupy the same bytes in each record. Unlike a primary key, the alternate keys do not need to be unique. Uniqueness is an option you specify as a part of creating the alternate index. The alternate index is stored in a separately named cluster.

A KSDS is the most versatile type of VSAM data organization. It allows fixed- and variable-length records; it provides sequential, random, or dynamic access; it allows records to be inserted or deleted; and it allows spanned records. It also permits setting up an alternate index. (You can also have what is in effect an alternate index by making a copy of the entire dataset sorted on the alternate key. However, there are now multiple complete copies of the dataset with the problems of updating and storage space this represents.)

Generally a KSDS is used when random or dynamic access is needed. Sequential access for a KSDS is slower than it is for an ESDS because VSAM must access KSDS records sequentially through the index, and so the random access is the most important criteria for deciding whether to use a KSDS. The index component of a KSDS also occupies space, and it takes system resources to maintain the index.

4.4.   ENTRY-SEQUENCED DATASETS (ESDS)

An ESDS has no index component, only a data component. Records are stored physically in the order they are written. Often a dataset is sorted on some record key before being written so the records are stored in order of the key. But the sequence may also be in time order, as for a log or transaction file. Figure 4.3 shows how an ESDS is stored in VSAM. Note that you don't set aside free space for an ESDS.

Like a KSDS, an ESDS can have an alternate index. Records can be retrieved sequentially, randomly, or dynamically through the alternate index, which is constructed on the Relative Byte Address of the record. This gives an ESDS some of the capability of the KSDS. Surprisingly, the alternate index for an ESDS occupies less storage space and provides faster random access than the alternate index for a KSDS.

ESDSs have the following characteristics:

- There is only a data component, and it is given a name.
- Records may be fixed- or variable-length.
- New records can be added, but only at the end of the dataset. (This is like the DISP=MOD of an OS dataset.)
- Records cannot be inserted or deleted, except by copying the dataset.
- Records may be spanned.
- In CICS online applications records can be retrieved sequentially, randomly, or dynamically using an alternate index.

Control Interval 1

Record 1	Record 2	Record 3	Record 4	Record 5	Record 6	U S	CF

Control Interval 2

Record 7	Record 8	Record 9	Record 10	Record 11	Record 12	U S	CF

.
.
.

Figure 4.3.   Records in an ESDS.

ESDSs are the VSAM equivalent of regular OS QSAM datasets. They do not offer many advantages over QSAM, and since QSAM is simpler, it is more commonly used. The main application of ESDS datasets is for CICS transaction and log files.

4.5.   RELATIVE RECORD DATASETS (RRDS)

An RRDS is the VSAM dataset equivalent of a table or array. The records don't have keys (or if they have them, VSAM doesn't use them). Instead, each record has an implicit relative record number that represents its physical position in the dataset the same way a table entry is represented by its relative position within a table. Figure 4.4 shows how an RRDS is stored in VSAM. Note that you also don't set aside free space for an RRDS.

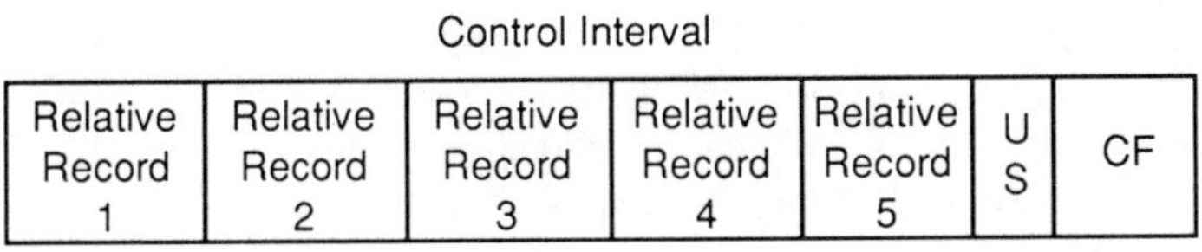

Control Interval

Relative Record 1	Relative Record 2	Relative Record 3	Relative Record 4	Relative Record 5	U S	CF

Figure 4.4.   Relative record dataset storage.

An RRDS has the following characteristics:

- The records must be fixed length. (Under MVS/DFP Version 3.3, they may also be variable length. You specify an RRDS, and then VSAM implements it using a KSDS.)
- The records may not be spanned.
- Space is allocated for a fixed number of records or slots. Records cannot be inserted—unless an empty slot has been reserved. Records can be deleted in that one can overwrite a record with another record or some indication that the record is deleted.
- Records can be written and read sequentially. They are stored in the physical order they are written.
- Records can be accessed randomly by their relative record number: 1 to n.
- There is no provision for an alternate index.

An RRDS is very fast because given the relative record number and knowing the length of the records, VSAM can quickly compute the relative byte address of the record. There is no index to search.

The main disadvantage of an RRDS is that many items do not readily lend themselves to retrieval by the relative record number. That is, the relative record number depends on the order the record is written. But once the record is written, how does one determine its relative record number to retrieve it later? For things such as years, months, and other items given consecutive numeric values, it is easy. There are hashing techniques for computing a number from a string of characters, and these sometimes work. Or you may need to keep a separate dataset that contains a record key and a relative record number. However, this is more or less reinventing the KSDS, and it might be better to just use a KSDS.

4.6.   LINEAR DATASETS

Linear Datasets (LDS) are the newest type of VSAM dataset, and they are also the least used. VSAM considers an LDS to be a long stream of bytes. The main use of linear datasets is to implement other data access organizations, such as a relational database system like DB2.

A linear dataset has no records. It is just a long string of bytes—nothing more. Linear datasets take advantage of the computer's very fast paging hardware for retrieval and storage. The bytes in an LDS are implicitly divided into 4K blocks or pages, and the paging hardware reads and writes blocks from disk.

As you manipulate the data in an LDS, the operating system automatically pages in and out the portions of the dataset you are working on. You address the dataset by the relative byte address as if it were in memory, and the system pages the needed pages in and out. Thus, it is both very simple and very fast. As an application programmer, you can

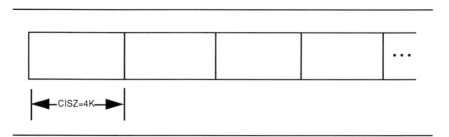

Figure 4.5.   Linear dataset.

treat an LDS as if it were a very long string or table resident in memory. You never have to read or write to get access to the data.

Linear datasets are mainly used for fast random access to data that has no hierarchical structure, such as for data that is a large flat file like a table or array. Chapter 27 describes linear datasets in more detail. Figure 4.5 illustrates an LDS. Note that since an LDS is a long string of bytes, there is no free space (FSPC), unused space (US), or control field (CF). The control interval size (CISZ) is always 4K.

4.7. SUMMARY

Selecting the type of VSAM to use may seem complicated, but in practice, it usually falls out as a simple choice:

- For log and transaction files where there is no need for random access and there is no need to add and delete records (other than adding them to the end of the dataset), you use an ESDS (or a QSAM dataset).
- Where you need fast random access and there is not much need to add or delete records, and you have some convenient means of determining a relative record number from the contents of a record, you use an RRDS.
- Where you need random access and the ability to add or delete records, you use a KSDS.
- Where you want very large work files or virtual storage for large tables or arrays with fast access, you use an LDS.

In practice, a KSDS is used about 90 percent of the time.

PART 2

Using Access Method Services

In Part 1 of this book, we introduced you to the various types of VSAM datasets and explained the factors that might influence your choice of one type over another for your programming application. In this part of the book, we'll show you how to create and manage these different types of datasets and make informed judgments when selecting parameters that influence performance and storage efficiency for your dataset.

Recall that VSAM datasets are created and managed by Access Method Services (AMS). Under MVS/DFP, however, VSAM datasets can be created and managed through the Data Facility Storage Management Subsystem (DFSMS), a plethora of complementary products that implement automated data placement and management services. Even in a DFSMS environment AMS is active under the covers.

In this section of the book, our approach will be to show you the basic format of each AMS command, then explain any DFSMS considerations that affect how the command is used in the DFSMS environment. Another thing—Chapter 9 is devoted entirely to creating and managing VSAM datasets with DFSMS, and so if your installation operates in that environment (or if planning to convert to that environment), you'll want to pay special attention to that chapter. Appendix A of this book also provides a handy reference summary for DFSMS-managed VSAM datasets.

5

Getting Started with Access Method Services

5.1.   THE IDCAMS PROGRAM

One of VSAM's strengths is that a single set of data management facilities called Access Method Services (AMS) manages both VSAM and non-VSAM datasets. AMS uses a command processor called IDCAMS to handle a variety of functions such as creating, reproducing, and printing datasets, and listing catalog contents. IDCAMS is a program, and, as an application programmer, much of your VSAM work will involve IDCAMS processing. Incidentally, IDCAMS is a name, not an acronym.

Because AMS is popularly known by its program name, it's perfectly okay to refer to AMS and IDCAMS (pronounced "EYE-D-CAMS" or "ĬD-CAMS") synonymously. Use the name and pronunciation with which you're comfortable.

IDCAMS can be invoked in the following three ways:

1. In batch mode with JCL statements.
2. Interactively with TSO (Time Sharing Option) commands.
3. Via calls from an application program.

If you enter IDCAMS commands with JCL statements, you can do the following:

- Print or display program and system messages and return codes.
- Code multiple IDCAMS commands per job.
- Specify IF/THEN/ELSE logic based on two special condition codes to selectively execute IDCAMS commands. (See LASTCC and MAXCC later in this chapter.)

TSO access does not support SYSOUT datasets, multiple IDCAMS commands, or IF/THEN/ELSE logic, so programmers generally execute IDCAMS via JCL statements (usually from within ISPF/PDF). There are exceptions for quick-and-dirty jobs (like VERIFY), and we'll point these out as we encounter them. We'll concentrate on JCL access since it is the most common usage. If you're interested in accessing IDCAMS in TSO or through subroutine calls, you can find more information in the Access Method Services reference manual.[1]

5.2.   IDCAMS JCL STATEMENTS

The JCL statements to invoke IDCAMS are as follows:

```
//MYJOB    JOB (ACCTNO),MYNAME
```

[The JOB statement contains installation-specific accounting information.]

```
//STEPA    EXEC PGM=IDCAMS
```

[The EXEC statement executes the program IDCAMS. Notice that we haven't specified a REGION parameter for either the JOB or the EXEC statement. Normally, the default REGION size will suffice. If not, you can always add a REGION parameter with a higher value; 350K should be sufficient.]

```
//SYSPRINT DD SYSOUT=*
```

[SYSPRINT directs error and other messages to your SYSOUT. IDCAMS error messages have the prefix IDC. IDC messages are explained in the system message reference manual for your operating environment.[2,3]]

```
//SYSIN    DD *
```

[SYSIN DD * tells the system that IDCAMS commands follow. You can also store IDCAMS commands in a dataset and point to the dataset with SYSIN. This dataset must have DCB attributes of RECFM=FB,LRECL=80. It can be sequential or partitioned.]

(IDCAMS commands go here, coded in columns 2 through 72.)

Here is an example:

```
//MYJOB    JOB (ACCTNO),MYNAME
//STEPA    EXEC PGM=IDCAMS
//SYSPRINT DD SYSOUT=*
//SYSIN    DD *
 DEFINE CLUSTER (NAME(A2000.LIB.KSDS.CLUSTER) -
   CYLINDERS(5 1) VOLUMES(VSO101))
```

You may use the following optional JCL statements:

JOBCAT or *STEPCAT:* Needed only if you are specifying a user catalog. JOBCAT and STEPCAT statements are not supported with DFSMS-managed datasets. JOBCAT names a user catalog that is available for the entire job. It is placed between the JOB and first EXEC statement. STEPCAT is placed following an EXEC statement and names a user catalog that is available only for the current job step, overriding any JOBCAT statement. (The master catalog is always open and should not be named in either a JOBCAT or STEPCAT statement.)

```
//MYJOB    JOB  (ACCTNO),MYNAME
//JOBCAT   DD   DSN=A2000.MY.CAT,DISP=SHR
//STEP1    EXEC PGM=ONE
//STEPCAT DD    DSN=A2000.OTHER.CAT.DISP=SHR
```

Input and output DD statements: Some commands (like REPRO to copy a dataset) need a named input and output dataset. Others, such as DEFINE CLUSTER, don't require them.

```
//INPUT  DD DSN=A2000.LIB.KSDS.CLUSTER,DISP=SHR
//OUTPUT DD DSN=A2000.NEW.KSDS.CLUSTER,DISP=SHR
```

When executing IDCAMS, valid DISP options are SHR or OLD. Always code DISP=SHR when reading a dataset because there is a possibility of sharing the dataset with another job. Code DISP=OLD when writing or updating a dataset so that you have exclusive control, for example, when you use REPRO to do an initial load of records.

5.2.1. Basic IDCAMS Commands

IDCAMS commands begin with a key word that describes the action of the command. Using basic verbs—which are really commands—the IDCAMS commands operate on a variety of VSAM objects, such as catalogs, clusters, and alternate indexes. The following list is a brief preview of basic IDCAMS commands and the objects upon which they usually operate.

- BUILDINDEX (alternate index)
- DEFINE (cluster, alternate index, catalog, etc.)
- IMPORT/EXPORT (cluster)
- LISTCAT (catalog entries)
- PRINT (cluster)
- REPRO (cluster)
- VERIFY (cluster)

5.2.2. General Structure of IDCAMS Commands

Since DEFINE creates such a wide variety of VSAM objects, we'll use it to demonstrate the general structure of all IDCAMS commands.

```
DEFINE CLUSTER -
  (NAME(A2000.LIB.KSDS.CLUSTER) -
   CYLINDERS(5 1) -
   VOLUMES(VS0101) -
   INDEXED)
```

This creates and names a basic cluster. First, we'll discuss IDCAMS parameters, which, like those of many utilities, can be either positional or keyword.

Note that the hyphen (-) denotes that the command is continued onto the next line. You could have coded the DEFINE CLUSTER command as:

```
DEFINE CLUSTER (NAME(A2000.LIB.KSDS.CLUSTER) -
CYLINDERS(5 1) VOLUMES(VS0101) INDEXED)
```

or as follows. Aligning the hyphens makes it easier to see when one is missing.

```
DEFINE CLUSTER                        -
  (NAME(A2000.LIB.KSDS.CLUSTER) -
   CYLINDERS(5 1)                     -
   VOLUMES(VS0101)                    -
   INDEXED)
```

The general form of IDCAMS commands is

```
verb object(parameters)
```

In the previous command, DEFINE is the command, CLUSTER is the object, and NAME, CYLINDERS, VOLUMES, and INDEXED are parameters.

The *verb* and *object* are positional parameters. They must be placed in their fixed positions as below:

```
DEFINE CLUSTER...     but not    CLUSTER DEFINE...
```

Note: The use of ellipses (. . .) in text indicates that an abbreviated form of the command or name is displayed due to space considerations.

Commands also contain parameters that can be coded in any order. Thus, one could code the previous command this way:

```
DEFINE CLUSTER (NAME(A2000.LIB.KSDS.CLUSTER) INDEXED -
   CYLINDERS(5 1) VOLUMES(VS0101))
```

Although keyword parameters (like CYLINDERS) can usually be placed anywhere in any order, NAME is an exception. It is a positional keyword parameter and must be coded first, immediately after the object.

Thus, you can have: But not:

```
DEFINE CLUSTER         -     DEFINE CLUSTER             -
   (NAME(A2000.LIB.KSDS...) -    (CYLINDERS(5 1)         -
   CYLINDERS(5 1)        -       NAME(A2000.LIB.KSDS...) -
   INDEXED)                      INDEXED)
```

Parameters consist of keyword parameters that are a string of characters that IDCAMS expects. Keyword parameters may themselves contain values that are actually positional subparameters. In the previous command, NAME contains a subparameter that is a user-supplied name. A keyword generally has some subparameters following it, but not always. (Note INDEXED in the example.) Subparameters allow for user-supplied values that must be enclosed in parentheses.

We can't make a blanket statement that all positional parameters are required (they're not) or that all keyword parameters are optional (they're not). Refer to the general format of the individual command in Chapters 6, 7, and 8 to see if a parameter is required or optional.

5.2.3. The Parameter Set

Subparameters are enclosed within parentheses. This is also true of something termed the *parameter set*, which consists of all the parameters that apply to a particular component, here NAME. In the following example, the parameter set begins with the left parenthesis before NAME and ends with the right parenthesis after INDEXED.

```
      DEFINE CLUSTER                        -
===>    (NAME(A2000.LIB.KSDS.CLUSTER)  -
        CYLINDERS(5 1)                     -
        VOLUMES(VS0101)                    -
        INDEXED)             <===
```

5.2.4. Continuing Commands

You can use a hyphen (-) or a plus sign (+) to continue command parameters onto a new line. The hyphen is more common. This is like other IBM command processors, such as CLIST. Stated another way, a hyphen indicates a new parameter on the next line; a plus sign indicates a continuation of the current parameter on the next line.

You can code this: Or this:

```
DEFINE CLUSTER            -      DEFINE CLUSTER              +
  (NAME(A2000.LIB.KSDS...) -        (NAME(A2000.LIB.KSDS...) +
    CYLINDERS(5 1)         -          CYLINDERS(5 1)         +
  . . .                           . . .
```

The hyphens or plus signs don't have to be aligned as shown, but it is a good practice because it is easier to spot when they are mistakenly omitted.

The hyphen or plus sign need not follow a blank:

```
DEFINE CLUSTER-              same as        DEFINE CLUSTER -
  (NAME...                                    (NAME...
```

The plus sign allows you to break a line for continuation within a field. The hyphen requires the command to be broken between fields.

```
DEFINE CLUSTER-          or          DEFINE CLUSTER -
  (NAME(A2000+        but not          (NAME(A2000-
   .LIB.KSDS) ...                       .LIB.KSDS) ...
```

Commands are easier to read if you break them between fields.

5.2.5. Terminating Commands

The most common command terminator is simply nothing. Just don't code a hyphen or plus sign on the last line. You can also use the semicolon (;) as in SQL if that's your preference, but it's more common to just leave the line blank.

You can code this: Or this:

```
DEFINE CLUSTER        -  DEFINE CLUSTER              -
  (NAME(A2000.LIB.KSDS...)-    (NAME(A2000.LIB.KSDS...)-
  CYLINDERS(5 1)      -    CYLINDERS(5 1)            -
  VOLUMES(VSO101)     -    VOLUMES(VSO801)           -
  INDEXED)                 INDEXED);
```

5.2.6. Comments

You can code any comments between fields or on a separate line by beginning the comment with /* and ending it with */.

```
/* This starts a DEFINE CLUSTER command. */
DEFINE CLUSTER /* Defining a KSDS dataset. */ -
  /* This name is subject to change.         -
     In fact, it always changes. */          -
  (NAME(A2000.LIB.KSDS...)                    -
  . . .
```

Notice that when you code comments between the fields of a command, you must code the continuation. If you continue a comment, you must also code a hyphen or plus sign for the continuation.

5.2.7. Guidelines for Coding Commands

Here are some miscellaneous syntactical rules:

1. You need at least one blank space between the command and the object and between subparameter values.

```
DEFINE CLUSTER  or  DEFINE  CLUSTER    not  DEFINECLUSTER

CYLINDERS(5 1)  or  CYLINDERS(5  1)    not  CYLINDERS(51)
```

(If you're confused about spacing, just look to see if the command might be misinterpreted by IDCAMS. Note the examples on the right above.)

2. A space is optional between a parameter and the parentheses enclosing its values:

```
CYLINDERS(5 1)  or  CYLINDERS (5 1)
```

3. You can separate subparameter values with a comma if you wish, but the space is more commonly used.

```
CYLINDERS (5,1)  or  CYLINDERS (5 1)
```

4. You can code multiple parameters on one line, but is it perhaps best to place each on a line by itself. This makes them easier to read and easier to change.

```
DEFINE CLUSTER (NAME(A2000.LIB.KSDS...) CYLINDERS(5 1) -
INDEXED)
```

Better as:

```
DEFINE CLUSTER                -
  (NAME(A2000.LIB.KSDS...)    -
   CYLINDERS(5 1)             -
   INDEXED                    -
   )
```

5. You cannot separate a parameter and a subparameter with a hyphen; use a plus sign for this. (But for clarity try to avoid this syntax.)

This:	Or this:	But not this:
`CYLINDERS(5 1) -`	`CYLINDERS +`	`CYLINDERS -`
	`(5 1)        -`	`(5 1)        -`

Within certain limits, IDCAMS syntax is quite flexible. You can also see that the possibilities for messing up are great, given the number and arrangement of spaces, hyphens, and right and left parentheses. Here are some tips to help you code IDCAMS commands that are easy to read and maintain, and free from structure errors.

- Code one parameter per line.
- Indent subordinate parameters and subparameters.
- Use the hyphen as a continuation character, and code each one on the far right of the line, aligning them all in the same column. (That way it is easier to see if one is missing.)
- Don't code anything in order to signify a command termination.
- Code the left and right parentheses, which delineate the parameter set, on the left side of the line for improved visibility. This will also make it easier to add parameters without rearranging the parentheses.

Here is an example of the application of these guidelines:

```
DEFINE CLUSTER                    -
  (NAME(A2000.LIB.KSDS...)    -
    CYLINDERS(5 1)                -
    VOLUMES(VS0101)               -
    INDEXED                       -
  )
```

5.3.   RETURN CODES AND THE LASTCC AND MAXCC REGISTERS

Each IDCAMS command returns a condition code after its execution that indicates the result of the command execution. You can then test the condition codes to selectively execute or skip subsequent commands. The condition code values are the standard values for all IBM programs:

  0 Command executed with no errors or warnings.
  4 Possible error (warning), but execution should be successful.
  8 Serious error detected, and execution likely to fail.
 12 Serious error detected and execution impossible.
 16 Fatal error detected and job step terminated.

IDCAMS stores the condition codes in variables named LASTCC and MAXCC as follows:

- *LASTCC:* Contains the condition code of the most recently executed IDCAMS command.

- *MAXCC:* Contains the maximum value of all the condition codes from the previously executed IDCAMS commands.

Both LASTCC and MAXCC are initialized to zero at the start of execution of IDCAMS. You can test the values of LASTCC and MAXCC at any point in the IDCAMS command stream with IF/THEN/ELSE commands, and then execute other IDCAMS commands with the IF/THEN/ELSE logic. You write the IF/THEN/ELSE command as follows:

```
IF LASTCC|MAXCC comparand value THEN command ELSE command
```

You must continue the IF should the THEN be continued on a following line, and continue the THEN if the ELSE is continued on a following line:

```
command
IF LASTCC [or MAXCC] comparand value  -
THEN                                  -
command
ELSE
command
```

The *comparand* must be one of the following:

=	*or* EQ	<	*or* LT
¬=	*or* NE	>=	*or* GE
>	*or* GT	<=	*or* LE

The *value* can be 0 through 16. (If you code a value greater than 16, it is set to 16.) Here is an example:

```
REPRO                     -
  INFILE(INDD)            -
  OUTFILE(OUTDD)
IF LASTCC EQ 0            -
THEN                      -
PRINT INFILE(INDD)
ELSE
PRINT OUTFILE(OUTDD)
```

The ELSE is optional. Notice that you still need to continue the THEN even if there is no ELSE.

```
IF MAXCC LT 4     -
THEN              -
command
```

If you forget the continuation for the THEN, and the command is on the following line, IDCAMS assumes a null command for the THEN and unconditionally executes the following command:

```
IF MAXCC LT 4     -
THEN
command                [Unconditionally executed]
```

The THEN can also specify a null command by immediately following it with the ELSE:

```
IF MAXCC LT 4     -
THEN              -
ELSE
command
```

A comment placed after a THEN or ELSE is assumed to be a null command. Since the THEN and ELSE expect to be followed by a single command, they assume the null command resulting from the comment is the command. This can lead to errors:

```
IF MAXCC LT 4        -
THEN                 -
/* some comment */
command                [Unconditionally executed]
ELSE                   [Error because no matching THEN]
command
```

You can solve the problem by continuing the comment.

```
IF MAXCC LT 4        -
THEN                 -
/* some comment */   -
command
ELSE
command
```

The THEN and ELSE can be followed by either a single command or a series of commands enclosed by a DO/END pair. Don't continue the DO/END, even if they appear on separate lines.

```
IF LASTCC GT 4    -
THEN              -
command
ELSE
DO
command
command
END
```

The command following the DO must begin on a separate line. The END must be on a line by itself.

DO	*but not*	DO *command* END
command	*or*	DO
END		*command* END
	or	DO *command*
		END

If you use comments in an IF/THEN/ELSE, it is best to use the DO/END pair so you don't have to worry about the continuation of comment lines:

```
IF MAXCC LT 4          -
THEN                   -
DO
/* some comment */
command
END
ELSE
command
```

You can nest the IF/THEN/ELSE commands to a maximum of ten levels but it's best not to. Each ELSE is paired with a THEN and each END is paired with a DO, working from the lowest nested level outwards.

LASTCC and MAXCC are set to zero at the start of the job step. You can set them to any value from 0 through 16 by executing a SET command:

```
SET LASTCC = 4
SET MAXCC  = 16
```

Setting MAXCC has no effect on LASTCC. However, setting LASTCC changes the value of MAXCC if LASTCC is set to a value larger than MAXCC.

The following example tells IDCAMS to set MAXCC to 16 (which causes the job to terminate) if LASTCC is set to a value greater than zero by the DEFINE command.

```
//SYSIN DD *
  DEFINE CLUSTER ...
  IF LASTCC > 0                -
     THEN SET MAXCC = 16       -
  ELSE
     REPRO ...
```

LASTCC and MAXCC are handy to use in a production environment where you wouldn't want an imperfectly defined cluster to be loaded with data. They are not supported under TSO.

REFERENCES

1. "MVS/ESA VSAM CATALOG Administration: Access Method Services Reference," Order No. SC26-4501, San Jose, CA: IBM Corporation, 1989.

2. "MVS/ESA Message Library: System Codes," Order No. GC28-1815, Poughkeepsie, NY: IBM Corporation, 1991.

3. "MVS/ESA Message Library: System Messages," Order Nos. GC28-1812, GC28-1813, Poughkeepsie, NY: IBM Corporation, 1991.

6

Defining a Basic VSAM Cluster with IDCAMS

6.1.   TYPES OF VSAM DATASETS

VSAM has four different dataset types, including the following:

- Key-Sequenced Datasets (KSDS)
- Entry-Sequenced Datasets (ESDS)
- Relative Record Datasets (RRDS)
- Linear Datasets (LDS)

This chapter shows how to code the basics—that is, the common IDCAMS parameters to define each of these types (except for linear datasets, which are treated separately in Chapter 27). If you want to review the characteristics of each VSAM dataset type, or if you need guidelines for selecting a specific type, review Chapter 4.

6.2.   ABOUT VSAM CLUSTERS

First, we need to get some terms straight. The *American Heritage Dictionary* refers to a cluster as, "A group of . . . similar elements gathered . . . closely together." VSAM uses the term *cluster* in this sense to name what is in essence a VSAM dataset. Strictly speaking, a VSAM cluster is a named object that includes both the data and index components of a KSDS. It may help to think of the cluster as a logical dataset. The data component (which contains the actual data) and the index component (which contains the actual index) are physical datasets.

Clusters are created and named with the IDCAMS DEFINE CLUS-

TER command. The following command creates a cluster named A2000. LIB.KSDS.CLUSTER with a data component named A2000.LIB.KSDS. DATA and an index component named A2000.LIB.KSDS.INDEX.

```
DEFINE CLUSTER              -
   (NAME(A2000.LIB.KSDS.CLUSTER)   -
```

[This names the cluster as A2000.LIB.KSDS.CLUSTER.]

```
   )                        -
   DATA                     -
```

[This tell VSAM that a data component is to be created.]

```
      (NAME(A2000.LIB.KSDS.DATA)    -
```

[The data component is named A2000.LIB.KSDS.DATA.]

```
      )                     -
   INDEX                    -
```

[This tells VSAM to create an index component.]

```
      (NAME(A2000.LIB.KSDS.INDEX)   -
```

[The index component is named A2000.LIB.KSDS.INDEX.]

```
      )
```

The KSDS is the only type of VSAM dataset whose structure completely fulfills the cluster concept. However, for consistency we refer to other types of VSAM datasets as "clusters" even though they contain only data. That's why, when "speaking" VSAM, you can refer to a cluster and a dataset synonymously.

At this point, you may be asking yourself, "Why use clusters at all?" As you work with VSAM, you'll see that there are definite advantages to being able to work with the cluster as a whole or the components separately. We'll point out these advantages as we encounter them.

6.3. GETTING STARTED

Before defining your first VSAM cluster, you'll have to gather some basic information—most of which is similar to the kind of information you need for a non-VSAM dataset. From your systems people, you'll need the following:

1. A list of general installation standards for defining and managing VSAM clusters.

2. Whether to catalog the cluster in a VSAM or an ICF catalog, and the name of the catalog. It's important to know if the high-level qualifier of the cluster name is an alias for the catalog in which it will be entered. Many installations use this technique to ensure that a VSAM cluster is cataloged in the appropriate user catalog.
3. The storage volumes that are available to VSAM and any considerations (like dataset size or volatility) for using one volume over another.
4. The names of any DFSMS classes you can use, but only if DFSMS is active at your shop. See Chapter 9 for more information on defining a VSAM cluster using DFSMS classes.

Then you'll need to study the application and talk to users in order to come up with the following:

1. The type of dataset you want to define. A KSDS is the most common choice, but sometimes you need an ESDS or an RRDS.
2. The name of the cluster and, optionally, the name of the data and index components for a KSDS.
3. The number of records that the dataset contains and how much you expect the dataset to grow over time. This determines how often you must reorganize the dataset to reduce split activity. Reorganization is done to improve performance, but frequent reorganization is expensive in computer resources.
4. The size of the records and whether they are fixed or variable length.
5. If creating a KSDS, you must specify the primary key. You need to know the length of the primary key and its offset (0 to n bytes) from the beginning of the record.
6. How often the dataset will be accessed. This makes a difference when specifying buffer space and whether or not the dataset should be assigned to a cached environment. There's more on buffer space in Chapter 24, and caching considerations are discussed in Chapter 26.

The previous example defined and named a cluster with separate data and index components. However, other parameters are required as well, and we'll expand this example to include them. Now, let's examine the DEFINE CLUSTER command in detail.

6.3.1. The DEFINE CLUSTER Command

This command tells IDCAMS to create and name a VSAM cluster. The DATA and INDEX parameters are needed only for a KSDS.

Format: DEFINE CLUSTER (NAME(*cluster name*)
                         parms) Note that NAME is required and must
                         be coded as the first parameter of DEFINE
                         CLUSTER. The NAME parameter is described
                         below, as are the *parms*.

Abbreviation: DEF CL

Used for: KSDS, ESDS, RRDS

Required: Yes

Default: None

Example: DEFINE CLUSTER   -
                           (NAME(A2000.LIB.KSDS.CLUSTER)   -
)   -
                           DATA   -
                             (NAME(A2000.LIB.KSDS.DATA)   -
)   -
                           INDEX   -
                             (NAME(A2000.LIB.KSDS.INDEX)   -
)

You can also define a VSAM cluster with the ALLOCATE command or through JCL statements (if DFSMS is active), but the IDCAMS DEFINE CLUSTER command is currently the only way to define and name separate data and index components.

6.3.2. The NAME Parameter

What's in a name? A lot, it turns out, if the name refers to the cluster component of a VSAM dataset. NAME, a required positional parameter placed right after DEFINE CLUSTER, tells VSAM that a cluster name follows.

Format: NAME(*cluster name*)
                         cluster name: The name to be assigned to the
                         cluster. The restrictions are described below.

Abbreviation: None

Used for: KSDS, ESDS, RRDS

Required: Yes

Default: None

Example: NAME(A2000.LIB.KSDS.CLUSTER)

The cluster name becomes the dsname in any JCL that invokes this cluster, either as an input or output dataset, for example:

```
//INPUT    DD DSN=A2000.LIB.KSDS.CLUSTER,DISP=SHR
```

In our example, we've assumed the MVS convention of a fully quali-fied dataset name. The rules for naming VSAM datasets are identical to those for naming their non-VSAM counterparts:

- Has 1 to 44 alphanumeric characters.
- Can include the national characters #, @, and $.
- Segmented into levels of eight or fewer characters, separated by periods (which count as alphanumeric characters).
- The first character must be either alphabetic or a national character.

The high-level qualifier is important because in most shops it is also an alias for the user catalog where the cluster is entered. As previously mentioned, this technique ensures that VSAM datasets are cataloged in the appropriate user catalog. Thus, A2000 in our example is not only the high-level qualifier for the cluster but an alias for a user catalog whose name is PRGMCAT.

```
A2000.LIB.KSDS.KSDS.CLUSTER              (cluster name)
  ↓
A2000                                    (user catalog alias)
  ↓
PRGMCAT                                  (user catalog name)
```

You're free to choose the mid-level qualifier (or qualifiers) that are important to you, but you may be bound by shop standards. Many shops adopt a low-level qualifier of .CLUSTER, which makes the name self-documenting.

```
NAME(A2000.LIB.KSDS.CLUSTER)
```

MVS/DFP supports multilevel aliases, which can be used for even more flexibility when assigning datasets to user catalogs. In this envi-ronment, for example, the high-level qualifier A2000 might be an alias for user catalog PRGMCAT, and the qualifiers A2000.TEST might be a qualifier for another user catalog, say one named PRGMCAT1.

When you code the DATA and INDEX parameters to create data and index components, you usually code a NAME parameter for them as well. Unless shop standards dictate otherwise, you should name any data and index components for a KSDS. If you omit the NAME parameter for DATA and INDEX, VSAM tries to append part of .DATA or .INDEX as appropriate as the low-level qualifier, depending upon how many characters the dataset name contains already and still staying within the 44-character limit. The results may not be what you want.

Another advantage of naming any data and index components is that you can apply parameter values separately. Often this can provide performance advantages, especially for large datasets.

There are several options for the DEFINE CLUSTER command, and we'll cover them next and in the following chapters.

6.3.3. The DATA Parameter

The DATA parameter tells IDCAMS that you are going to create a separate data component. DATA is optional, but if coded must follow all of the parameters that apply to the cluster as a whole. (This will make more sense later in this chapter when you see the cluster definition expanded with some common parameters.)

Format:	DATA(NAME(*data name*) *parameters*) The NAME parameter is optional, but you should usually code it. If coded, it must be the first DATA parameter.
	data name: The name you choose to name the data component. It must conform to the same rules and conventions as the cluster name.
Abbreviation:	None
Used for:	KSDS, ESDS, RRDS
Required:	No
Default:	None
Example:	DATA(NAME(A2000.LIB.KSDS.DATA))

There are several options for the DATA parameter, but NAME is most common. You don't have to code the NAME parameter, but you should for a KSDS so that you can operate on the data component by itself.

You can name a separate data component for an ESDS or a RRDS also, but it's not commonly done, because there's no index component.

6.3.4. The INDEX Parameter

The INDEX parameter creates a separate index component. INDEX is optional, but if coded must follow all of the parameters that apply only to the data component.

Format:	INDEX(NAME(*index name*) *parameters*)
	index name: The name you choose for the index component. It must conform to the same rules and conventions as the cluster name.
Abbreviation:	IX
Used for:	KSDS
Required:	No
Default:	None
Example:	INDEX(NAME(A2000.LIB.KSDS.INDEX))

6.3.5. Other Parameters

The next example expands the cluster definition to include some basic parameters. Not all of these are required, but it makes good sense to add them because the defaults are inappropriate for most datasets.

```
DEFINE CLUSTER                          -
  (NAME(A2000.LIB.KSDS.CLUSTER)         -
   CYLINDERS(5 1)                       -
```

[This allocates 5 cylinders of primary space and 1 cylinder of secondary space to the cluster.]

```
   VOLUMES(VS0101)                      -
```

[This allocates the space on disk volume VS0101.]

```
   RECORDSIZE(80 80)                    -
```

[This says that the average and maximum record length are both 80.]

```
   KEYS(8 0)                            -
```

[This tells VSAM that the key is 8 bytes long and begins in offset position 0 in the record, which is the first byte.]

```
INDEXED                                      -
```

[This tells VSAM that this is a KSDS.]

```
)                                            -
 DATA                                        -
(NAME(A2000.LIB.KSDS.KSDS.DATA)              -
)                                            -
 INDEX                                       -
(NAME(A2000.LIB.KSDS.KSDS.INDEX)             -
)
```

The space allocation parameter. The space allocation parameter specifies space allocation values in the units shown above. Note its similarity to the JCL SPACE parameter in that you specify both a primary and a secondary allocation.

Format:	Code only one of the following:
	CYLINDERS *(primary secondary) or*
	TRACKS *(primary secondary) or*
	RECORDS *(primary secondary) or*
	KILOBYTES *(primary secondary)* [MVS/ESA only] *or*
	MEGABYTES *(primary secondary)* [MVS/ESA only]
Abbreviation:	CYL, TRK, REC, KB, MB
Used for:	KSDS, ESDS, RRDS
Required:	Yes. (Can be specified in a DFSMS DATACLAS.)
Default:	None
Example:	CYLINDERS(5 1) TRACKS(140 6) RECORDS(10000 1000) KILOBYTES(5000 2000) MEGABYTES(10 2)

The parameters are as follows:

CYLINDERS: Allocate space in units of cylinders.

TRACKS: Allocate space in units of tracks.

RECORDS: Allocate space in units of number of records.

KILOBYTES: Allocate space in units of K (1,024) bytes.

MEGABYTES: Allocate space in units of M (1,048,576) bytes.

primary: Number of units of primary space to allocate. This amount is allocated once when the dataset is created.

secondary: Number of units of secondary space to allocate. This amount is allocated a maximum of 122 times as needed during the life of the dataset. That is, a VSAM dataset can have a primary allocation and 122 extents. Note, however, that if you create the dataset with the UNIQUE parameter in the older VSAM catalog structure, the dataset can have only 15 secondary extents.

For the best performance, assign enough primary space to accommodate the initial record load. However, you should be conservative when assigning the secondary allocation, and you can omit it entirely for datasets with no growth.

For datasets cataloged in an ICF catalog or those defined with the SUBALLOCATION parameter in an older VSAM catalog, VSAM space management routines allow a maximum of 123 extents, including one primary and 122 secondary (a good reason for conservatism). On the other hand, datasets defined with the UNIQUE parameter in a VSAM catalog permit a maximum of 16 extents, including one primary and 15 secondary.

VSAM calculates the control area size for you. A one-cylinder control area size, the largest permitted by VSAM, usually yields the best performance. For this reason you should try to allocate space in CYLINDERS because this ensures a control area size of one cylinder.

You may want to allocate space in units of RECORDS for small test datasets. However, you should avoid this for production datasets, because it can cause VSAM to calculate an inefficient control area size. If you allocate space in units of RECORDS, you must also specify the RECORDSIZE parameter (which makes perfect sense).

If you specify space allocation in units of KILOBYTES (thousand bytes) or MEGABYTES (million bytes), VSAM reserves space on the minimum number of tracks it needs to satisfy the request. This option is valid only under MVS/ESA, and the advantage is device independence.

It is best to apply space allocation to the entire cluster or to the data component, because VSAM then calculates the amount of space needed for the index, generally the most efficient technique; for example:

```
DEFINE CLUSTER       -              ... DATA            -
    (NAME( ... )     -      or          (NAME( ... )    -
    CYLINDERS(4 1)   -                  CYLINDERS(4 1)  -
```

At the cluster level, the amount calculated for the index is subtracted from the amount you specify; at the data level the entire amount is allocated to the data, and VSAM assigns additional space as needed for the index.

You can see that even though this parameter has a simple syntax, calculating the primary and secondary space allocation values can be somewhat complex. When testing your application, you can load a small subset of records, check the actual space used with the LISTCAT command described in Chapter 10, and then use this result to calculate the amount of space needed for the entire dataset.

LISTCAT also displays the control area size that VSAM has calculated. Refer to Chapter 10 for other LISTCAT parameters that you can monitor.

There are special space considerations if you specify the IMBED, REPLICATE, or KEYRANGES parameters. See Chapter 7 for more information.

The VOLUMES parameter. The VOLUMES parameter assigns one or more storage volumes to your dataset. Multiple volumes must be of the same device type (3390, for example).

Format:	VOLUMES*(vol ser)* or
	VOLUMES*(vol ser ... vol ser)* *vol ser*: The six-digit volume serial number of a volume.
Abbreviation:	VOL
Used for:	KSDS, ESDS, RRDS
Required:	Yes, except for DFSMS-managed datasets. A specific volume assignment may be ignored for DFSMS-managed datasets.
Default:	None

Example: VOLUMES(VS0101) [One volume]
                     VOLUMES(VS0101 VS0102 VS0103)
                     [Three volumes]

   You can store the data and index on separate volumes and this may
provide a performance advantage for large datasets.

The RECORDSIZE Parameters. The RECORDSIZE parameters tell
VSAM what size records to expect. The *avg* and *max* are the average and
maximum values for variable-length records. If records are fixed length,
avg and *max* should be the same.

Format: RECORDSIZE(*avg max*)

                     avg: Average length of records.
                     max: Maximum length of any record.

Abbreviation: RECSZ

Used for: KSDS, ESDS, RRDS

Required: No, but note the size of the default. (Can be
                     specified in a DFSMS DATACLAS.)

Default: RECORDSIZE(4086 4086)

Examples: RECORDSIZE(80 80) [Fixed-length records]
                     RECSZ(80 120) [Variable-length records]

   RECORDSIZE can be assigned at the cluster or data level. For a
KSDS, VSAM calculates the RECORDSIZE of the index based on the
KEYS parameter.

The KEYS parameter. The KEYS parameter defines the length and
offset of the primary key in a KSDS record. The *offset* is the primary
key's displacement (in bytes) from the beginning of the record.

Format: KEYS(*length offset*)

                     length: Length in bytes of the primary key.
                     offset: Offset in bytes of the primary key
                     within the record (0 to *n*).

Abbreviation: None

Used for: KSDS

Required: No, but note size of the default. (Can be
                       specified in a DFSMS DATACLAS.)

Default: KEYS(64 1) [Key is in bytes 2 through 65.]

Example: KEYS(8 0) [Key is in bytes 1 through 8.]

VSAM records begin in position zero. In our example, the primary key begins in position 0 for a length of 8 bytes (bytes 1 through 8).

KEYS(8 0) resolves to ===>   Record: 12345678
                              Offset: 01234567

Since an invalid primary key is a common VSAM error, be sure to check your values for this parameter carefully.

The dataset-type parameter. The dataset-type parameter specifies whether the dataset is KSDS (INDEXED), NONINDEXED (ESDS), or NUMBERED (RRDS).

Format: INDEXED | NONINDEXED | NUMBERED

Abbreviations: IXD | NIXD | NUMD

                       INDEXED: Specifies a KSDS and is the
                       default. When you specify INDEXED, VSAM
                       automatically creates and catalogs an index
                       (provided other parameters like KEYS are
                       valid). INDEXED is also used for a variable-
                       length RRDS.

                       NONINDEXED: Specifies an ESDS. No
                       index is created and records are accessed
                       sequentially or by relative byte address.

                       NUMBERED: Specifies an RRDS.

Used for: KSDS, ESDS, RRDS, respectively.

Required: No, because of default.

Default: INDEXED

Example: INDEXED
                       NONINDEXED
                       NUMBERED

Sample ESDS. The following example defines and names a sample ESDS. KEYS is omitted, and since there is no index, you don't code the DATA and INDEX parameters.

```
DEFINE CLUSTER                          -
   (NAME(A2000.LIB.ESDS.CLUSTER)        -
    CYLINDERS(5 1)                      -
    VOLUMES(VSO101)                     -
    RECORDSIZE(80 80)                   -
    NONINDEXED                          - [Makes it an ESDS]
   )
```

Sample fixed-length RRDS. The next example defines and names a sample fixed-length RRDS. DATA is optional and usually omitted. INDEX is not coded because there is no index component.

```
DEFINE CLUSTER                          -
   (NAME(A2000.LIB.RRDS.CLUSTER)        -
    CYLINDERS(5 1)                      -
    VOLUMES(VSO101)                     -
    RECORDSIZE(80 80)                   - [Fixed-length records]
    NUMBERED                            - [Makes it an RRDS]
   )
```

Sample variable-length RRDS. This example defines and names a sample variable-length RRDS. This is a hybrid-type available starting with MVS/DFP Version 3, Release 3. Although defined as a KSDS with a key length of 4 (always), it is processed as an RRDS.

```
DEFINE CLUSTER                          -
   (NAME(A2000.LIB.RRDS.CLUSTER)        -
    CYLINDERS(5 1)                      -
    KEYS(4 0)                           -
    VOLUMES(VSO101)                     -
    RECORDSIZE(80 204)                  - [Variable-length records]
    INDEXED                             -
```

[The maximum-size record is defined as the longest record in the dataset plus 4 bytes to accommodate the relative record number.]

```
   )
```

There's more on relative record datasets in Chapter 20. However, COBOL processing for a variable-length RRDS is beyond the scope of this book.

Be aware that all of the cluster examples in this chapter are "bare bones." We'll expand them further in Chapters 7 and 8 to include some parameters designed to enhance performance and add security.

7

Adding AMS Performance Parameters

The performance-related parameters described in this chapter are often coded in the DEFINE CLUSTER command in order to (1) reduce the amount of physical I/O, (2) make necessary I/O faster, and (3) optimize disk utilization.

In this chapter we'll see how to add parameters to a basic IDCAMS DEFINE CLUSTER command that can help you get "the most bang for your buck" in performance. The following example shows what we're working towards. The CISZ and FREESPACE parameters are new. We'll refer to this example as we discuss these and other performance-related parameters.

```
DEFINE CLUSTER                              -
  (NAME(A2000.LIB.KSDS.KSDS.CLUSTER) -
   CYLINDERS(5 1)                           -
   VOLUMES(VS0101)                          -
   RECORDSIZE(80 80)                        -
   KEYS(8 0)                                -
   INDEXED                                  -
  )                                         -
  DATA                                      -
  (NAME(A2000.LIB.KSDS.KSDS.DATA)    -
   CISZ(4096)                               - [new]
   FREESPACE(20 10)                         - [new]
  )                                         -
  INDEX                                     -
```

```
(NAME(A2000.LIB.KSDS.KSDS.INDEX)    -
)
```

7.1.   THE CONTROLINTERVALSIZE PARAMETER

The CONTROLINTERVALSIZE parameter specifies the control interval size. It is usually abbreviated CISZ, as in the previous example.

7.1.1.   Coding the CISZ Parameter

The control interval is the VSAM basic unit of work—that is, the minimum amount of data that is transferred, via buffers, between DASD and main memory. It corresponds to a block in a normal OS dataset. It is specified by the CISZ parameter.

Format:	CONTROLINTERVALSIZE(*bytes*)
	bytes: The size of the control interval in bytes. It should be a multiple of 512 or 2048 bytes, depending upon the type of catalog (ICF or VSAM) and the length of the record. VSAM rounds the CISZ value up to the next highest multiple of 512 or 2048 if necessary.
Abbreviation:	CISZ [commonly used]
	CNVSZ
Use:	KSDS, ESDS, RRDS
Required:	No, because of default.
Default:	Calculated by VSAM.
Example:	CISZ(4096)

In order to reduce I/O, the control interval needs to be an optimal size for the type of processing planned for the dataset. In most cases, it's more efficient to apply the CISZ parameter to the data component and let VSAM choose the index control interval size for you. Let's look at some control interval size considerations for the data component of a KSDS.

7.1.2.   Data Area CISZ Considerations

If you plan mostly sequential processing for a KSDS, a relatively large control interval size will reduce physical I/O by keeping more records accessible in the buffers. On the other hand, if you plan mostly random processing for a KSDS, a relatively small CISZ will require less data transfer time and fewer buffers, thus making I/O faster. But this raises the question, "Relative to what?" Well, a number of things, as it turns out.

First, you want to achieve optimal disk utilization by making sure that the control interval contains the maximum number of data records that it can hold, a "tight fit" in other words. To determine how many data records will fit within a given CISZ, you need to consider record length, the percentage of control interval FREESPACE you've allocated, and the CIDF and RDF control information that VSAM embeds at the end of every control interval.

We first introduced the CIDF (Control Information Definition Field) and RDF (Record Definition Field) in Chapter 3. Now we need to explain them further. The CIDF contains information specific to the control interval itself, such as the location and percentage of free space. It is four bytes long, and there is always just one CIDF per control interval. On the other hand, there can be one or more RDFs, depending on whether the record lengths are fixed or variable. The RDF contains information specific to the records and describes the length of the records and how many adjacent records are the same length.

For fixed-length records, there are only two RDFs per control interval; the first contains the number of records in the control interval and the second the length of the records. Things are more complex for variable-length records because RDFs can vary depending upon how many adjacent records are the same length in the control interval. If no two adjacent records are the same length, an RDF is needed to describe each record (a 1:1 ratio).

Control information occupies the following space:

- For fixed-length records with *multiple* records per control interval, *ten* bytes of every control interval.
- For fixed-length records with only *one* record per control interval, *seven* bytes.
- For variable-length records, a variable number of bytes that includes *four* bytes for the CIDF and *three* bytes for each RDF required. This last factor depends on the spread of the data records.

VSAM requires that the data CISZ be a multiple of 512 bytes, with a range of 512 to 32768 bytes for datasets cataloged in ICF catalogs. For datasets cataloged in VSAM catalogs, the data CISZ must be a multiple of 512 for records of 8192 bytes or less, and a multiple of 2048 for records larger than 8192 bytes. If you assign a CISZ that is not a multiple of one or the other, VSAM rounds the CISZ up to the next highest multiple of 512 or 2048. This will probably result in some amount of unusable space in each control interval. (This is not the same as planned, usable free space.)

Besides the type of processing planned and record length, you need to consider the buffering. The VSAM default is for two data buffers and one index buffer, but if you override this default with the BUFFERSPACE parameter, it may affect the CISZ.

To demystify all of this, let's look at an example. Notice that in the example at the beginning of this chapter we've assigned a CISZ of 4096, considered to be an optimal size for a combination of sequential and random processing with records in this length range. To determine how many 80-byte, fixed-length records will fit within the assigned CISZ, start with the planned CISZ (4096 here), and then

1. Reserve ten bytes for control information.   10
2. Reserve 20 percent of the assigned CISZ for
   FREESPACE. (4096 × .20) (VSAM rounds down.)   819
3. Add items 1 and 2 above.   829
4. Subtract 829 from 4096.   3267
5. Divide 3267 by 80 to obtain the number of data records   40
   per data control interval. (VSAM rounds down.)
6. The 67-byte remainder represents the portion of the   67
   control interval that will be unusable.

Things get more complicated if you have variable-length records because you have to calculate (or make a good guess at) the required control information.

For sequential processing with larger records, either fixed or variable length (say 1000 bytes or less), you may want to choose a CISZ of 8K (8192). For random processing of records in this range, a CISZ of 4K (4096) is still a prudent choice. Large SPANNED records represent a special case, which we discuss later in this chapter.

If your dataset will be processed randomly (say during the day) and sequentially (at night for backup and recovery) as is typical in a lot of shops, choose a CISZ for random processing and then allocate extra buffers for sequential processing with the AMP JCL parameter. We show you how later in this chapter and again in Chapter 24.

Another thing to consider: For CICS applications, larger control interval sizes can cause enqueue problems for datasets that are open for update. (Enqueue means that a dataset is waiting to be updated.)

Remember this is just a guide. We suggest that you load a small subset of records, enough to fill one or more control areas. Using LISTCAT, check the CISZ parameter to make sure that VSAM did not override your selection of CISZ. (If it did, one possibility is that you underestimated the amount of RDFs needed for variable-length record control information.)

You can always decrease the FREESPACE amount by some percentage in order to force a tighter fit for the records. You may have to do some experimenting in order to achieve the results you want. (You'll probably also learn a lot in the process.)

Since an ESDS is processed sequentially, the CISZ should be relatively large, depending on the size of the record. You do not assign FREESPACE to an ESDS, since all new records are added to the end of the dataset.

On the other hand, since an RRDS is usually processed randomly, the CISZ should be relatively small, again depending on the size of the record. You do not assign FREESPACE to a fixed-length RRDS, but you can do so for a variable-length RRDS, which is defined as a KSDS.

As stated earlier, it's generally best to let VSAM calculate the index component CISZ. For situations where you may want to calculate the index CISZ, see Chapter 23.

7.2. THE FREESPACE PARAMETER

The FREESPACE parameter, which applies to the KSDS and variable-length RRDS only, allocates some percentage of both the control interval and the control area for planned free space. This free space can be used for adding new records or for expanding existing variable records.

7.2.1. Coding the FREESPACE Parameter

FREESPACE applies only to the data component and should be coded there where one would expect it, even though it's syntactically correct to code it at the cluster level.

Format: FREESPACE(*ci*% *ca*%)

ci%: Percentage of control intervals to leave free for expansion.

ca%: Percentage of control areas to leave free for expansion.

Abbreviation: FSPC [commonly used]

Use: KSDS

Required: No, because of default.

Default: FREESPACE(0 0)

Example: FREESPACE(20 10)

Too much free space results in more I/O, especially when doing sequential processing. Too little results in excessive control interval and control area splits. Control area splits are especially detrimental to random processing.

You can allocate FREESPACE for the control interval or control areas only:

FREESPACE($ci\%$)   [Control interval only]

FREESPACE(0 $ca\%$)   [Control area only]

7.2.2.   FREESPACE Guidelines

If you expect even growth within the dataset, apply the desired percentage of FREESPACE to both the control interval and the control area. This option provides the most flexibility. If you expect uneven growth, apply FREESPACE only to the control area. This reserves a certain percentage of free control intervals within each control area. You can also apply FREESPACE in conjunction with the KEYRANGES parameter if you anticipate growth within certain key ranges. You can accept the default, which is FREESPACE(0 0), if you don't expect any growth within the dataset.

In order to effectively allocate FREESPACE, you need to know the following dataset characteristics:

- The expected rate of growth.
- The expected number of records to be deleted.
- How often it will be reorganized with REPRO. This procedure wipes out existing control interval and control area splits and restores the original FREESPACE allocation. If you reorganize the dataset frequently, you don't have to allow as much free space.
- The performance requirements. You may want to give a VSAM dataset used in CICS applications a large free space allocation in order to prevent split activity.

Be sure that your control interval FREESPACE allocation is enough to cover the length of one record plus any additional RDFs that may result from a variable record length.

In the example at the beginning of this chapter, FREESPACE was coded as

```
FREESPACE(20 10)
```

Notice that we've allocated 20 percent of a possible 4096 bytes for free space in each control interval (819 bytes). If you divide 819 by 80 (the record length), you can see that we have enough free space to add ten records per control interval with a 19-byte remainder of unusable control interval space. We've also allocated 10 percent of free control intervals within the control area. The resulting number of free control intervals within each control area will vary depending upon the storage device used.

When you list a dataset with the LISTCAT utility, the following LISTCAT fields provide FREESPACE-related information:

- *SPLITS-CI.* Shows the current number of control interval splits.
- *SPLITS-CA.* Shows the current number of control area splits.
- *FREESPACE-%CI.* Shows the original percentage of control interval free space allocated with the DEFINE CLUSTER command.
- *FREESPACE-%CA.* Shows the original percentage of control area free space allocated with the DEFINE CLUSTER command.
- *FREESPC-BYTES.* Shows the total number of bytes in all totally empty control intervals. You can divide this figure by the CISZ to determine the total number of empty control intervals.

You can revise the original percentage of control interval and control area FREESPACE allocation with the ALTER command, but this has no effect on current control interval and control area splits. A better technique is to reorganize the dataset, using REPRO to back up the data, redefining the cluster with a revised FREESPACE allocation, and finally, using REPRO again to reload the data.

7.3. THE BUFFERSPACE PARAMETER

Buffer space represents the amount of storage (in bytes) required to process the contents of a minimum of one control interval's worth of data. The BUFFERSPACE parameter, usually abbreviated BUFSP, overrides the VSAM default, which is to allocate two data buffers for all types of datasets, plus one additional index buffer for a KSDS. VSAM uses one data buffer for processing and reserves the second for potential split activity.

Format:	BUFFERSPACE(*bytes*)
	bytes: The number of bytes to allocate to each buffer.
Abbreviation:	BUFSP
Use:	KSDS, ESDS, RRDS
Required:	No, because of default.
Default:	Two data buffers for all types of datasets, plus one additional index buffer for a KSDS.
Example:	BUFSP(10240)

Buffering depends on the type of dataset as follows:

- *Sequential processing:* You'll typically want to allocate more data buffers. If enough data buffers are allocated and SHAREOPTIONS(1 3) (the VSAM default) are in effect, VSAM provides a read-ahead feature that can provide a significant performance advantage.
- *Random processing:* You'll want to allocate more index buffers, at least one buffer for each level of index. The ideal is to allocate enough index buffers to keep the entire index in virtual storage at all times, but this may not be possible in your environment. Read-ahead is not provided for random processing.
- *Dynamic processing:* You'll want to allocate additional data and index buffers in proportion to the ratio of sequential to random processing planned for the dataset.

Notice that the BUFSP allocation provides for one value in bytes. For an ESDS or RRDS, this value is translated into data buffers, but for a KSDS, VSAM decides on the number of data and index buffers based on the access method specified in the application program. Also, if you specify BUFSP in the DEFINE CLUSTER command, all applications that use the dataset are stuck with this buffer allocation, unless they override it.

There are several ways to override buffer space.

- Assembler programs can use the BUFSP/BUFND/BUFNI parameter of the ACB (Access method Control Block) macro.
- COBOL programs can use the AMP JCL parameter, which has subparameters also named BUFSP (total buffer space in bytes), BUFND (number of data buffers), and BUFNI (number of index buffers).
- CICS uses the RDO (Resource Definition Online) or a DFHFCT TYPE=DATASET macro to specify these same parameters.

For COBOL programs, the AMP parameter provides the most flexibility because it requires no internal program coding and can be tailored to fit the buffering requirements of each application. The following example shows the AMP parameter specifying additional data buffers to accommodate sequential processing.

```
//STEP1   DD DSN=A2000.LIB.KSDS.CLUSTER,DISP=SHR,
//           AMP=('BUFND=6')
```

Two things to note: The subparameter (BUFND above) must be enclosed within parentheses *and* single quotes. Also, values are only overridden if they represent values that are *larger* than those specified by the DEFINE CLUSTER command. Thus, given a data control interval size of 1024, the example that follows (which allocates ten buffers total) would *not* be overridden by the AMP parameter, which allocates only six data buffers. (We're assuming the program specifies sequential access mode for this example, so VSAM allocates only one index buffer.)

	DEFINE CLUSTER:	JCL:
	BUFSP(10240)	AMP=('BUFND=6')
Results in:	10 total buffers	6 data buffers

Notice that BUFSP coded for the DEFINE CLUSTER command and the AMP BUFND and BUFNI coded in the JCL express different values. (Interestingly enough, AMP BUFSP parameter values are expressed in bytes as are DEFINE CLUSTER BUFSP parameter values.)

The bottom line in all this is to ignore the DEFINE CLUSTER BUFSP parameter and override default buffering as needed at program execution time using BUFND and BUFNI. That way, you can tell VSAM exactly the number of data and index buffers that you want allocated for your application.

The following LISTCAT fields provide buffering information:

- *BUFSPACE.* Shows the number of bytes required to process the dataset. For default buffering, this figure represents two times the data control interval size plus the index control interval size. If you have not explicitly requested index buffering for this field, the index component will display zero.
- *LEVELS.* Displays the levels of index that VSAM has created for your KSDS—the smaller the better. If you have too many levels, performance will suffer.
- *SPLITS-CI/SPLITS-CA.* Informs you of split activity.

Refer to Chapter 10 to see these LISTCAT fields displayed.

7.4.   THE RECOVERY OR SPEED PARAMETERS

These two parameters are mutually exclusive. RECOVERY, the default, preformats the control areas during your initial dataset load, so that you can restart the job if it abends for some reason. That's the good news. The bad news is that unless you have written a recovery routine to restart the job, RECOVERY won't help you much. SPEED is the default and does not preformat the control areas.

Format:	RECOVERY I SPEED
	RECOVERY: With effort, allows you to recover if the job initially loading the dataset fails.
	SPEED: Faster, but you must reload the dataset from the beginning if the job fails during initial loading.
Abbreviation:	RCVY I None
Use:	KSDS, ESDS, RRDS
Required:	No, because of default.
Default:	RECOVERY
Example:	RECOVERY
	SPEED

We suggest instead that you override the RECOVERY default and add SPEED to your DEFINE CLUSTER command, because it will indeed speed up your initial data load. Notice in this example that we've done exactly that.

```
DEFINE CLUSTER                         -
  (NAME(A2000.LIB.KSDS.CLUSTER)        -
    CYLINDERS(5 1)                     -
    VOLUMES(VS0101)                    -
    RECORDSIZE(80 80)                  -
    KEYS(8 0)                          -
    INDEXED                            -
    SPEED                              - [this added]
  )                                    -
  DATA                                 -
  (NAME(A2000.LIB.KSDS.DATA)           -
    CISZ(4096)                         -
    FREESPACE(20 10)                   -
  )                                    -
  INDEX                                -
  (NAME(A2000.LIB.KSDS.INDEX)          -
  )
```

The following parameters may be used for large records.

7.5.   PARAMETERS FOR LARGE RECORDS

7.5.1.   The SPANNED Parameter

The SPANNED parameter allows large records to span more than one control interval. However, records cannot span control areas. The resulting free space in the spanned control interval is unusable by other records, even if they fit logically in the unused bytes. NONSPANNED is the default, and it means that records cannot span control intervals.

Format:	SPANNED I NONSPANNED
Abbreviation:	SPND I NSPND
Use:	KSDS, ESDS
Required:	No, because of default.
Default:	NONSPANNED

Example: SPANNED

                           NONSPANNED

Releases of CICS prior to 1.7 do not support spanned records. Likewise, an RRDS does not support this feature.

Use the SPANNED parameter with caution because it can affect your (or VSAM's) choice of CISZ and because it can result in some measure of unusable free space that will most certainly consume DASD and quite possibly degrade performance.

7.5.2. The KEYRANGES Parameter

The KEYRANGES parameter divides a large dataset among several volumes. If activity is evenly distributed, this may provide concurrent access, a definite performance advantage.

Format: KEYRANGES(*low key high key*)

                           low key: The low value for the range of keys to be placed on a volume.

                           high key: The high value for the range of keys to be placed on a volume.

Abbreviation: KYRNG

Use: KSDS

Required: No

Default: None

Example: KEYRANGES (00000001 2999999)
                           [You can specify one range.]
                           KEYRANGES ((00000001 2999999)   -
                                       (30000000 4700000)   -
                                       (47000001 9999999)) -
                           [You can also specify a series of ranges.]

You then specify the volumes on which you want the records placed with the VOLUMES parameter. Unless you specify the ORDERED parameter described next, the records are assigned randomly to the volumes. This is not usually what you want, and so ORDERED is usually coded with KEYRANGES.

As you might expect, KEYRANGES carries with it a few caveats—among them the following:

- The assigned volumes must be of the same device type (like 3390s).
- There must be enough space on each assigned volume to satisfy its initial primary space allocation or the request will fail. In the previous example, five cylinders per volume must be available.
- If subsequent dataset growth forces a lot of extents, performance will surely suffer.
- Any keyranges not explicitly included in the KEYRANGES values are ignored. This may not be what you want.
- An extra set of parentheses is required around the keyrange values, but not around the volume values. See the example in ORDERED.
- The dataset is not reusable. That is, it cannot be emptied of records and then reused. You must delete the cluster and then redefine it. (See the REUSE parameter following.)

7.5.3. The ORDERED Parameter

The ORDERED parameter tells VSAM to assign the KEYRANGES values to the volumes, one by one, in the order in which the KEYRANGES and VOLUMES values are specified.

Format:	ORDERED I UNORDERED
Abbreviation:	ORD I UNORD
Use:	KSDS
Required:	No, because of default.
Default:	UNORDERED
Example:	ORDERED
	UNORDERED

The following example illustrates the use of KEYRANGES with ORDERED. The arrows in the example show how the KEYRANGES values are assigned to the VOLUMES. UNORDERED, the default, causes VSAM to assign the specified volumes to the various keyranges in random fashion, usually not what you want. Note that ORDERED is ignored if the dataset is DFSMS-managed.

```
DEFINE CLUSTER                              -
  (NAME(A2000.LIB.KSDS.CLUSTER)             -
   CYLINDERS(5 1)                           -
   RECORDSIZE(80 80)                        -
   KEYS(8 0)                                -
   KEYRANGES ((00000001  2999999)           -
             (30000000  4700000)            -
             (47000001  9999999))           -
   VOLUMES (VS0101                          -
            VS0102                          -
            VS0103)                         -
ORDERED                                     -
NOREUSE                                     -
INDEXED                                     -
```

(more parameters would follow)

When you code ORDERED, you must code the same number of VOL-UMES as KEYRANGES.

7.5.4. The REUSE Parameter

The REUSE parameter specifies that a cluster can be opened a second time as a reusable cluster. NOREUSE is the default and specifies the cluster as nonreusable.

Format:	REUSE | NOREUSE
Abbreviation:	RUS | UNRUS
Use:	KSDS, ESDS, RRDS
Required:	No, because of default.
Default:	NOREUSE
Example:	REUSE
	NOREUSE

Reusable datasets may be multivolume, but they can have only 16 physical extents per volume if cataloged in a VSAM catalog. ICF-cataloged ones don't share that restriction. A cluster is not reusable under the following conditions:

- A KEYRANGES parameter is coded for it.
- You build an alternate index.
- The cluster has its own data space in both the VSAM and ICF catalog environments.

NOREUSE was coded in the previous example for documentation purposes. Many installations prohibit reusable clusters because of the alternate index restriction and because of the inherent problem of dataset fragmentation (a large number of extents) on high-growth datasets.

7.5.5. The IMBED Parameter

The IMBED parameter directs VSAM to place the sequence set (the lowest level of index next to the data component) on the first track of the data control area and duplicate it as many times as will fit. This process will reduce rotational delay because the desired sequence set record is found faster. NOIMBED is the default.

Format:	IMBED I NOIMBED
Abbreviation:	IMBD I NIMBD
Use:	KSDS
Required:	No, because of default.
Default:	NOIMBED
Example:	IMBED
	NOIMBED

7.5.6. The REPLICATE Parameter

The REPLICATE parameter directs VSAM to duplicate each index record as many times as it will fit on its assigned track. It applies to a KSDS index component only. The goal is to make I/O faster by reducing rotational delay (the amount of time it takes for a disk unit to complete one revolution under the read/write head—similar to the action of a needle on a phonograph record (remember those?)). NOREPLICATE is the default.

Format:	REPLICATE I NOREPLICATE
Abbreviation:	REPL I NREPL

Use:	KSDS
Required:	No, because of default.
Default:	NOREPLICATE
Example:	REPLICATE
	NOREPLICATE

IMBED and REPLICATE can be applied separately but are most often used together. They should never be used for control area sizes under one cylinder because of the extra tracks consumed. They can reduce I/O but DASD space increases. They can cause further performance degradation in the event of control interval and control area splits because of the extra time required to write the duplicate index and sequence set records.

IMBED and REPLICATE should not be used in a CACHE environment because you can actually waste CACHE memory with duplicate records. (CACHE is hardware that is used to retain frequently used data for faster access. CACHE is also discussed in Chapter 26.)

The following example illustrates the use of IMBED and REPLICATE for the index component.

```
DEFINE CLUSTER                              -
  (NAME(A2000.LIB.KSDS.CLUSTER)             -
   CYLINDERS(5 1)                           -
   VOLUMES(VS0101)                          -
   RECORDSIZE(80 80)                        -
   KEYS(8 0)                                -
   INDEXED                                  -
   SPEED                                    -
  )                                         -
  DATA                                      -
  (NAME(A2000.LIB.KSDS.DATA)                -
   CISZ(4096)                               -
   FREESPACE(20 10)                         -
  )                                         -
  INDEX                                     -
  (NAME(A2000.LIB.KSDS.INDEX)               -
   IMBED                                    -   <===
   REPLICATE                                -   <===
  )
```

You can use the VOLUMES parameter (described in Chapter 6) to assign different storage volumes to the data and index components. This may provide concurrency (and thus a performance advantage) because you have separate disk arms retrieving index and data records. However, any advantage may be neutralized by other system activity against the volumes, a situation that may be difficult to control. The following example illustrates the use of separate VOLUMES for the data and index components.

```
DEFINE CLUSTER                           -
   (NAME(A2000.LIB.KSDS.CLUSTER)         -
   CYLINDERS(5 1)                        -
   RECORDSIZE(80 80)                     -
   KEYS(8 0)                             -
   INDEXED                               -
   SPEED                                 -
   )                                     -
   DATA                                  -
   (NAME(A2000.LIB.KSDS.DATA)            -
   CISZ(4096)                            -
   FREESPACE(20 10)                      -
   VOLUMES(VS0101)                       - <===
   )                                     -
   INDEX                                 -
   (NAME(A2000.LIB.KSDS.INDEX)           -
   VOLUMES(VS0102)                       - <===
   )
```

One important guideline for applying performance parameters (or *tuning*) VSAM datasets: Never change more than one performance parameter before checking its intended effect on performance, storage, and other computer resources. That way you can monitor the effect of each change as it is implemented. As E. F. Schumacher noted in his book *Small Is Beautiful*, complex systems are counter-intuitive.

8

Adding AMS Security and Performance Parameters

This chapter shows how to protect your VSAM dataset by adding parameters that will ensure its security and data integrity. We'll begin with SHAREOPTIONS, an important parameter that protects data integrity.

8.1.   THE SHAREOPTIONS PARAMETER

SHAREOPTIONS specifies how a VSAM dataset can be shared.

Format: SHAREOPTIONS(*cr value cs value*)

cr value: Specifies the value for cross-region sharing. *Cross-region* sharing is defined as different jobs running on the same system, or on different systems using Global Resource Serialization (GRS), a resource control facility available only under MVS/XA and ESA.

cs value: Specifies the value for cross-system sharing. *Cross-system* sharing means different jobs running on different systems in a non-GRS environment.

The values specify read/write access as follows:

Value

1	Multiple read OR single write.
2	Multiple read AND single write.
3	Multiple read AND multiple write.
4	Same as 3, but refreshes buffers for each random access.

Abbreviation:	SHR [commonly used]
Use:	KSDS, ESDS, RRDS
Required:	No, because of default.
Default:	SHAREOPTIONS(1 3)
Example:	SHAREOPTIONS(1 3) or SHR(1)

The following example is used for the ensuing discussion of cross-region and cross-system sharing.

```
DEFINE CLUSTER                          -
  (NAME(A2000.LIB.KSDS.CLUSTER)  -
   CYLINDERS(5 1)                       -
   VOLUMES(VS0101)                      -
   RECORDSIZE(80 80)                    -
   KEYS(8 0)                            -
   SHAREOPTIONS(1)                      -  <===
   INDEXED                              -
  )                                     -
   DATA                                 -
  (NAME(A2000.LIB.KSDS.DATA)    -
   CISZ(4096)                           -
   FREESPACE(20 10)                     -
  )                                     -
   INDEX                                -
  (NAME(A2000.LIB.KSDS.INDEX)   -
  )
```

The details of the four SHAREOPTIONS values are as follows:

- A *1* specifies that any number of jobs can read the dataset, *or* one job can write to the dataset. This option provides complete data integrity and is only valid for cross-region sharing. It is the cross-region default and the one most commonly used.

- A *2* specifies that any number of jobs can read the dataset, *and* one job can write to the dataset. This option provides write (but not read) integrity. It is only valid for cross-region sharing.
- A *3* specifies that the dataset can be fully shared—in other words, no read or write integrity. It is valid for both cross-region and cross-system sharing and is the cross-system default.

Cross-region data integrity can be maintained for CICS applications using the ENQ and DEQ options, but no similar capability exists for batch COBOL applications.

Cross-system sharing for both CICS and COBOL requires the use of the Assembler RESERVE and DEQ macros to maintain data integrity. RESERVE carries with it a high penalty because it reserves the entire volume where the desired dataset is located.

- A *4* provides the same capabilities and responsibilities for cross-region and cross-system sharing as SHAREOPTIONS 3. Additionally, SHAREOPTIONS 4 forces a buffer refresh for each random access request, nullifying any gains produced by index buffering. The reason for this is that if one of the other jobs updated the dataset, a fresh copy is obtained reflecting the change. Needless to say, this can cause significant performance problems in online systems.

The following table shows a matrix of SHAREOPTIONS available for cross-region and cross-system sharing:

	Cross-region	Cross-system
SHAREOPTIONS 1	Y	N
SHAREOPTIONS 2	Y	N
SHAREOPTIONS 3	Y	Y
SHAREOPTIONS 4	Y	Y

Here are some things you should know about SHAREOPTIONS:

- For cross-region sharing, each batch job must have DISP=SHR coded in its JCL. DISP=OLD assumes exclusive control and nullifies sharing options.
- On the other hand, for cross-system sharing, DISP=OLD is ignored. You cannot force exclusive control across systems by coding DISP=OLD.
- For cross-system sharing, non-DFSMS managed systems cannot share DFSMS-managed datasets.

- SHAREOPTIONS can be included in a predefined DATACLAS.
- If you don't expect to share the dataset across systems, it's okay to ignore the cross-system value. In other words, you can code SHAREOPTIONS(1).
- You should apply SHAREOPTIONS to the entire cluster so that both the data and index components have identical sharing options.
- If operating in the XA or ESA environment, ask your systems people if the GRS facility has been enabled. Under GRS, you don't need RESERVE for cross-system sharing.
- You should also ask the person responsible for standards if there are any SHAREOPTIONS standards in effect at your shop.
- The LISTCAT field SHROPTNS displays the SHAREOPTIONS values that are currently in effect for the named dataset.

8.2.   THE ERASE PARAMETER

The ERASE parameter instructs VSAM to overwrite sensitive data with binary zeros when the cluster is deleted. NOERASE is the default and means that the deleted cluster is not to be overwritten with binary zeros.

Format:	ERASE	NOERASE
Abbreviation:	ERAS	NERAS
Use:	KSDS, ESDS, RRDS
Required:	No, because of default.
Default:	NOERASE
Example:	ERASE
	NOERASE

ERASE can be specified in one of several ways. It can be coded in the DEFINE CLUSTER command at the cluster or data level. Even if applied at the cluster level as in the following example, ERASE only applies to the data component, since the index component contains only keys and not data.

```
DEFINE CLUSTER                         -
   (NAME(A2000.LIB.KSDS.CLUSTER)       -
    CYLINDERS(5 1)                      -
    VOLUMES(VS0101)                     -
    RECORDSIZE(80 80)                   -
```

```
KEYS(8 0)                          -
SHAREOPTIONS(1)                    -
ERASE                              -  <===
INDEXED                            -
)                                  -
DATA                               -
(NAME(A2000.LIB.KSDS.DATA)         -
CISZ(4096)                         -
FREESPACE(20 10)                   -
)                                  -
INDEX                              -
(NAME(A2000.LIB.KSDS.INDEX)        -
)
```

ERASE can also be specified (or overridden with NOERASE) as part of the ALTER command when the cluster is modified, or as part of the DELETE command when the cluster is deleted. Thus you can have the following:

```
ALTER A2000.KSDS.CLUSTER   -        ALTER A2000.KSDS.CLUSTER   -
   ERASE                               NOERASE
```
                      or

```
DELETE A2000.KSDS.CLUSTER -         DELETE A2000.KSDS.CLUSTER -
   ERASE                               NOERASE
```
                      or

DELETE overrides both the DEFINE and any ALTER specifications. ERASE carries with it a performance penalty because it takes time and overhead to write binary zeros over the existing data.

For a dataset defined in an ICF-type catalog, your RACF administrator can impose the highest level of security by making ERASE part of the RACF profile. If ERASE is specified by RACF, it overrides any IDCAMS ERASE/NOERASE parameter. For a DFSMS-managed dataset ERASE should be specified by RACF.

The LISTCAT field ERASE/NOERASE displays the current status of this parameter for the named dataset.

8.3.   THE CATALOG PARAMETER

CATALOG names either a VSAM or ICF user catalog that will contain the entries for the VSAM cluster. If the CATALOG is password-protected, you must also name the password. Omit the /*password* if it is not password-protected.

Format:	CATALOG(*name/password*)
	name: The name of a catalog.
	password: The catalog's password—if there is one.
Abbreviation:	CAT
Use:	KSDS, ESDS, RRDS
Required:	No
Default:	None
Example:	CATALOG(VSAM.USER.CAT/BIGBLUE)
	CATALOG(VSAM.LIB.CAT)

You can use this parameter instead of the high-level qualifier technique described in Chapter 6 if you want to specify a different user catalog. The high-level qualifier technique designates the cluster's high-level qualifier as an alias for the user catalog where the cluster entry is defined.

```
A2000.LIB.KSDS.CLUSTER          (cluster name)
    ↓
A2000                           (user catalog alias)
    ↓
PRGMCAT                         (user catalog name)
```

You might want to use the CATALOG parameter as an addition to the high-level qualifier technique if you wanted to explicitly document the user catalog name for some reason. CATALOG requires that the catalog volume be physically mounted, but mountable DASD volumes are extremely rare today, so this is no great restriction. You can ensure this by using a JCL JOBCAT or STEPCAT statement, but be aware that these JCL statements are not valid for DFSMS-managed datasets. In fact, CATALOG should not be used at all under DFSMS, because datasets can be inadvertently cataloged in the wrong catalog, wreaking havoc in your DFSMS system.

In the following non-DFSMS-managed example, the CATALOG parameter specifies that the dataset entries will be contained in a user catalog named VSAM.USER.CAT, whose password is BIGBLUE. Notice that CATALOG forms its own parameter set.

```
DEFINE CLUSTER                          -
  (NAME(A2000.LIB.KSDS.CLUSTER)         -
   CYLINDERS(5 1)                       -
   VOLUMES(VS0101)                      -
   RECORDSIZE(80 80)                    -
   KEYS(8 0)                            -
   SHAREOPTIONS(1)                      -
   INDEXED                              -
  )                                     -
  DATA                                  -
  (NAME(A2000.LIB.KSDS.DATA)            -
   CISZ(4096)                           -
   FREESPACE(20 10)                     -
  )                                     -
  INDEX                                 -
  (NAME(A2000.LIB.KSDS.INDEX)           -
  )                                     -
  CATALOG(VSAM.USER.CAT/BIGBLUE)          <===
```

The LISTCAT field IN-CAT displays the user catalog containing the entries for the named dataset.

8.4.   PASSWORD PROTECTION PARAMETERS

VSAM allows you to specify various levels of passwords. You can specify the number of attempts to allow the operator in responding to a password, and you can also supply the name of an authorization routine.

8.4.1.   The Password Parameters

VSAM provides a hierarchical list of password parameters that you can specify for a non-DFSMS-managed VSAM dataset. (For DFSMS, you must use a security package like RACF.)

Format: MASTERPW(*password*)
                       Allows the highest level of access to all cluster
                       components, including DELETE and ALTER
                       authority.

CONTROLPW(*password*)
Allows control interval processing, generally only done by systems programmers.

UPDATEPW(*password*)
Allows write authority to the cluster.

READPW(*password*)
Allows read-only access to the cluster.

Abbreviation:	MRPW, CTLPW, UPDPW, RDPW
Use:	KSDS, ESDS, RRDS
Required:	No
Default:	None
Example:	MASTERPW(BIGBLUE)

Passwords are initially specified in the DEFINE CLUSTER command. To be effective, passwords should be applied at the cluster level. It's important to reiterate that the password coded in the CATALOG parameter specifies entry into the catalog and does not in any way password-protect the dataset. In fact, if the user catalog is protected with MASTERPW, only that password is needed to alter or delete any cluster in it.

At execution time, a password can be coded explicitly in the PASSWORD clause of a COBOL SELECT clause. However, the password's visibility here negates the security that it was intended to provide.

```
SELECT ...
   PASSWORD IS BIGBLUE
```

You can also have the operator or the user enter the password via the terminal. However, to employ this technique the operator or the user must *remember* the password. As you can see, either method has drawbacks.

Also, a password must be coded explicitly in any IDCAMS command that accesses a password-protected VSAM dataset. Thus, to ALTER or DELETE a password-protected VSAM dataset, you must specify the master password (MASTERPW). On the other hand, to LISTCAT a password-protected dataset, a read-only password (READPW) is sufficient.

A final word on passwords: RACF ignores VSAM passwords and imposes its own security, and for most VSAM datasets RACF security is sufficient. However, if you expect to export the dataset to another system that does not have RACF, you might want to set up passwords (even though they will be ignored on the current system) so they will be in place when the dataset is exported to the new system. In this case, see your security administrator for direction and guidance (not to mention authority). The following example sets up a hierarchy of passwords for our sample dataset.

```
DEFINE CLUSTER                              -
   (NAME(A2000.LIB.KSDS.CLUSTER)            -
     CYLINDERS(5 1)                         -
     VOLUMES(VS0101)                        -
     RECORDSIZE(80 80)                      -
     KEYS(8 0)                              -
     SHAREOPTIONS(1)                        -
     MASTERPW(HARVARD)                      -     <===
     CONTROLPW(PRINCETN)                    -
     UPDATEPW(YALE)                         -
     READPW(RADCLFFE)                       -
     INDEXED                                -
   )                                        -
   DATA                                     -
   (NAME(A2000.LIB.KSDS.DATA)               -
     CISZ(4096)                             -
     FREESPACE(20 10)                       -
   )                                        -
   INDEX                                    -
   (NAME(A2000.LIB.KSDS.INDEX)              -
   )                                        -
     CATALOG(VSAM.USER.CAT/BIGBLUE)
```

8.4.2. The ATTEMPTS Parameter

The ATTEMPTS parameter lets you specify the number of attempts to give the operator to enter the password before abending the step. ATTEMPTS is effective only if a MASTERPW has been assigned.

Format: ATTEMPTS(*tries*)

                          tries can be any number from 0 through 7.
                          A value of 0 results in the operator not being
                          prompted.

Abbreviation:	ATT
Use:	KSDS, ESDS, RRDS
Required:	No
Default:	2
Example:	ATTEMPTS(4)

8.4.3. The CODE Parameter

Normally when the operator is prompted for a password, the operator is prompted with the name of the entry, such as the cluster name. The CODE parameter lets you specify a code to display to the operator in place of the entry name.

Format:	CODE(*code*)
Abbreviation:	None
Use:	KSDS, ESDS, RRDS
Required:	No
Default:	The entry name
Example:	CODE(007)

8.4.4. The AUTHORIZATION Parameter

AUTHORIZATION provides additional security for a VSAM cluster by naming an Assembler User Security Verification Routine (USVR).

Format:	AUTHORIZATION(*entry point password*)
	entry point: The name of the entry point of a security verification routine written in Assembler language.
	password: The password the routine is to verify.
Abbreviation:	AUTH
Use:	KSDS, ESDS, RRDS
Required:	No

Default: None

Example: AUTH(MYRTN 'BIGGUY')

This parameter requires that both a master password and an additional authorization password be specified when the cluster is used in an application. If you're thinking that this can result in "password overkill," you're probably right.

8.5.   OTHER PERFORMANCE PARAMETERS

VSAM has several parameters that are rarely used because of their associated performance penalty. However, each provides a hefty measure of extra security for a VSAM dataset.

8.5.1.   The WRITECHECK Parameter

This parameter instructs VSAM to invoke a DASD verify facility whenever a record is written. NOWRITECHECK is the default and provides no DASD verification.

Format:	WRITECHECK I NOWRITECHECK
Abbreviation:	WCK I NWCK
Use:	KSDS, ESDS, RRDS
Required:	No, because of default.
Default:	NOWRITECHECK
Example:	WRITECHECK NOWRITECHECK

Because contemporary DASD devices are very reliable, and because of the high performance overhead associated with this parameter, we recommend strongly that you accept the NOWRITECHECK default. A better technique is to write image copies of data that would be difficult to recreate if lost. See your systems people about using dual copy for highly sensitive data.

8.5.2.   The EXCEPTIONEDIT Parameter

EXCEPTIONEDIT directs VSAM to transfer control to a user-written routine whenever an I/O error (exception error) occurs. You might want to do this if you were monitoring exception errors for some reason (and then again you might not).

Format:	EXCEPTIONEDIT(*entry point*)
Abbreviation:	EEXT
Use:	KSDS, ESDS, RRDS
Required:	No
Default:	None
Example:	EEXT(MYEXIT)

8.5.3. The REUSE Parameter

The REUSE parameter can be used to specify that a dataset can be reloaded a second time. REUSE is described in Chapter 7.

9

Defining a VSAM Cluster Under DFSMS

Data Facility Storage Management Subsystem (DFSMS), an optional MVS/ESA operating environment, provides automated, system-wide storage management. DFSMS liberates the programmer to concentrate on the programming needs of the application and leaves the vagaries of space management to the system.

Using predefined, named constructs (called classes), DFSMS tells the system where to store a dataset, what it looks like, how and when it will be available, how long it should be retained, when it should be backed up, and when and if it can be migrated to another system.

DFSMS classes are designed, created, named, and managed by a person who works in the systems group, usually the storage adminis-trator. DFSMS classes, especially so-called "data classes," are used by programmers to create VSAM and non-VSAM datasets. The program-mer becomes the user of DFSMS services in this environment.

The secret to successful implementation of system-managed storage is communication, communication, and more communication among the storage administrator, systems people, application programmers, and the users. The storage administrator should distribute to the program-mer a description and usage guideline for each named DFSMS class. Generally, only data classes are explicitly coded. Other classes that specify availability, performance attributes, and backup and migration information are controlled by the storage administrator through Auto-matic Class Selection (ACS) routines. The programmer should follow data class guidelines. When an exception occurs (and it will), the programmer needs to talk with the storage administrator so that a new class can be created, or an old one modified if that's more appropriate.

Programmers specify DFSMS data classes in one of three ways:

1. As part of an IDCAMS DEFINE CLUSTER command.
2. In the JCL statements that reference the application program that creates the dataset.
3. As part of the ALLOCATE command.

9.1. SPECIFYING DFSMS CLASSES WITH DEFINE CLUSTER

In the example following, we've added a DATACLAS and two other constructs (MGMTCLAS and STORCLAS) to our sample VSAM DEFINE CLUSTER command. At first glance it may also appear that we've removed some parameters, but actually they've just been "folded in" to the new DATACLAS. We'll use this example as we discuss these three new parameters.

```
DEFINE CLUSTER                              -
   (NAME(A2000.LIB.KSDS.CLUSTER)            -
    DATACLAS(KSDSDATA)                      -
    MGMTCLAS(VSAMGMT)                       -
    STORCLAS(SWIFT)                         -
   )                                        -
    DATA                                    -
   (NAME(A2000.LIB.KSDS.DATA)               -
   )                                        -
    INDEX                                   -
   (NAME(A2000.LIB.KSDS.INDEX)              -
   )
```

9.2. THE DATACLASS PARAMETER

The DATACLASS parameter, usually abbreviated DATACLAS to agree with JCL, can assign generic dataset attributes such as organization, record format and length, allocated space, and retention values. VSAM attributes can include the data CISZ, key length and offset, free space, and share options.

Format:	DATACLASS(*name*)
	name: one- to eight-character name chosen by system administrator. The name usually reflects an installation standard.
Abbreviation:	DATACLAS [commonly used]
Use:	KSDS, ESDS, RRDS
Required:	No
Default:	Depends on installation.
Example:	DATACLAS(KSDSDATA)

The DATACLAS named KSDSDATA in the previous example implicitly assigns the following parameters and values to the sample KSDS. Recall that previously these values were explicitly assigned.

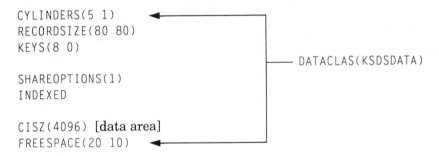

```
CYLINDERS(5 1)
RECORDSIZE(80 80)
KEYS(8 0)
                                        ── DATACLAS(KSDSDATA)
SHAREOPTIONS(1)
INDEXED

CISZ(4096) [data area]
FREESPACE(20 10)
```

Note: Under DFSMS, volume information, specified in previous examples as VOLUMES(VS0101), becomes part of a storage grouping. See the ensuing discussion on DFSMS storage groups in this chapter.

Some parameters are better candidates for a DATACLAS definition than others. For example, space allocation, RECORDSIZE, and KEYS are normally highly variable. We show them as part of our sample DATACLAS, but they may also be explicitly coded. Also, you can override any parameters that you want to change for the individual dataset by coding the parameter explicitly.

DATACLAS is the DFSMS construct that programmers relate to best, because it represents parameters and values that they generally code themselves. Here are some miscellaneous things you should know about DATACLAS:

- A named DATACLAS can be used to define datasets that are either non-DFSMS managed or non-VSAM as well.
- DATACLAS can only be specified at the cluster level. However, the CISZ specified in a DATACLAS applies to the data component.
- DATACLAS can default through ACS (Automatic Class Selection) routines written by the installation. In fact, it's possible to refine the DATACLAS construct to the extent that DFSMS will assign the dataset to a default DATACLAS based on the dataset name alone. For example, the DATACLAS named KSDSDATA could be set up as the default DATACLAS for any datasets with the low order qualifier of ".CLUSTER."
- If a DATACLAS is explicitly coded and DFSMS is not active, the DEFINE CLUSTER command will fail.

9.3.   THE MANAGEMENTCLASS PARAMETER

The MANAGEMENTCLASS parameter, usually abbreviated MGMTCLAS to agree with JCL, works with Data Facility Hierarchical Storage Manager (DFHSM) to automate dataset migration and backup, as well as the deletion of expired datasets. The MGMTCLAS construct helps manage DASD in the most effective manner at the cluster level.

Format:	MANAGEMENTCLASS(*name*)
	name: one- to eight-character name chosen by storage administrator. The name usually reflects an installation standard.
Abbreviation:	MGMTCLAS [commonly used]
Use:	KSDS, ESDS, RRDS
Required:	No
Default:	Depends on installation.
Example:	MGMTCLAS(VSAMGMT)

MGMTCLAS is similar to DATACLAS in these ways:

- It can be *implicitly* assigned through ACS routines so that the programmer doesn't have to code it. In fact, this is a common technique for using MGMTCLAS, and the one that is normally implemented in DFSMS environments in order to enforce separation of DASD pools. We show it coded explicitly just so you can see its format.

- If explicitly coded, MGMTCLAS must be specified at the cluster level.
- If a MGMTCLAS is explicitly coded and DFSMS is not active, the DEFINE CLUSTER command will fail.

MGMTCLAS is different from DATACLAS in these ways:

- It does not replace parameters that are normally coded explicitly within the DEFINE CLUSTER command, like CISZ and share options. It adds additional attributes to the dataset.
- It cannot be specified for a non-DFSMS-managed dataset.
- Attributes cannot be overridden in the DEFINE CLUSTER command.

9.4. THE STORAGECLASS PARAMETER

The STORAGECLASS parameter, usually abbreviated STORCLAS to agree with JCL, controls both the availability of and performance attributes for the dataset. A STORCLAS assignment tells the system that the dataset is DFSMS-managed.

Format:	STORAGECLASS(*name*)
	name: one- to eight-character name chosen by storage administrator. The name usually reflects an installation standard.
Abbreviation:	STORCLAS [commonly used]
Use:	KSDS, ESDS, RRDS
Required:	No
Default:	Depends on installation.
Example:	STORCLAS(SWIFT)

STORCLAS is similar to DATACLAS in these ways:

- It can be *implicitly* assigned through ACS routines so that the programmer doesn't have to code it. Both MGMTCLAS and STORCLAS are most commonly used in this manner. Once again, we show STORCLAS coded explicitly so that you can see its format.
- If explicitly coded, STORCLAS must be specified at the cluster level.
- If a STORCLAS is explicitly coded and DFSMS is not active, the DEFINE CLUSTER command will fail.

STORCLAS is different from DATACLAS in these ways:

- It does not replace parameters that are normally coded explicitly within the DEFINE CLUSTER command, like CISZ and share options. It adds additional attributes to the dataset.
- It cannot be specified for a non-DFSMS-managed dataset.
- Attributes cannot be overridden in a DEFINE CLUSTER command.

9.5.   DFSMS STORAGE GROUPS

DFSMS also provides for storage groups that don't concern programmers directly. Instead, ACS routines use storage groups to place datasets within a group of storage volumes pooled by say, enterprise, function, dataset size, security requirements—whatever installation criteria dictate. Storage groups are always implicitly assigned, but the programmer needs to be aware of them and their attributes.

9.5.1.   Overriding DATACLAS Values

Data classes are created by storage administrators for programmers to use. If the DATACLAS assigned to your dataset is not a "perfect fit," you can override any implicitly defined parameter with an explicit definition. In the following example, we've overridden the implicit SHAREOPTIONS value (SHAREOPTIONS 1) with an explicit definition of SHAREOPTIONS (2 3).

```
DEFINE CLUSTER                         -
   (NAME(A2000.LIB.KSDS.CLUSTER)       -
    SHAREOPTIONS(2 3)                  -  <===
    DATACLAS(KSDSDATA)                 -
   )                                   -
    DATA                               -
   (NAME(A2000.LIB.KSDS.DATA)          -
   )                                   -
    INDEX                              -
   (NAME(A2000.LIB.KSDS.INDEX)         -
   )
```

It's important to reiterate that you cannot override MGMTCLAS and STORCLAS attributes.

9.5.2. Creating a VSAM Dataset with JCL

If DFSMS is active, you can create a new VSAM dataset solely with JCL parameters. The main advantage is that you save a step because the same application program (say COBOL) can both load the input data and create the output dataset.

The disadvantage is that you can't name components separately, and so you can't specify parameters at the data or index level. Also, you can't specify (or override) every parameter with JCL, so you either have to take the VSAM (or an explicit or implicit DATACLAS) default.

The next example creates our sample KSDS once again, this time using JCL parameters.

```
//STEP1 EXEC PGM=MYPGM
```

[The stepname indicates the name of the job step, STEP1. EXEC specifies that a program named MYPGM will be executed.]

```
//S1DD1 DD DSN=A2000.LIB.KSDS.CLUSTER,
```

[The DD statement indicates the ddname, S1DD1, and the dataset name (DSN), A2000.LIB.KSDS.CLUSTER.]

```
//      DISP=(NEW,CATLG),
```

[DISP specifies the disposition of the dataset. Under DFSMS, VSAM datasets can have a disposition of NEW, PASS, CATLG, UNCATLG, or DELETE. CATLG causes the dataset to be cataloged at the beginning of the step, rather than the end, which is normal with non-DFSMS-managed datasets. Both DFSMS-managed and VSAM datasets must be cataloged. For them, NEW also catalogs the dataset. If you want to delete the dataset at the end of the job, specify NEW,DELETE,DELETE.]

```
//      SPACE=(CYL(5,1)),
```

[SPACE specifies the space allocation, in cylinders, consisting of five cylinders primary and one cylinder of secondary space, for a total of 123 extents. SPACE can also be specified in tracks (TRK) or average records (AVGREC) to have the system calculate the space.]

```
//      LRECL=80,
```

[LRECL specifies the record length, fixed in this case. For variable-length records, you specify the maximum length here. LRECL is analogous to the DEFINE CLUSTER RECORDSIZE parameter.]

```
//        KEYLEN=8,KEYOFF=0,
```

[KEYLEN and KEYOFF are used together to specify the record key and its offset. These parameters are required for a KSDS only and together are analogous to the DEFINE CLUSTER KEYS parameter.]

```
//        RECORG=KS,
```

[RECORG specifies the dataset organization. Acceptable values are KS (Key-Sequenced), ES (Entry-Sequenced), RR (Relative Record), and LS (Linear Space). RECORG is analogous to the DEFINE CLUSTER INDEXED, NONINDEXED, NUMBERED, and LINEAR parameters, respectively.]

```
//        DATACLAS=KSDSDATA
```

As an alternative to specifying space in blocks, tracks, or cylinders, you can code the AVGREC parameter on the DD statement as follows:

```
AVGREC=type,SPACE=(rec length,(primary,secondary),...)
```

- *type* is one of the following:
  U—*primary* and *secondary* are the number of records.
  K—*primary* and *secondary* are the number of K (1,024) records.
  M—*primary* and *secondary* are the number of M (1,048,576) records.
- *rec length* is the record length (average record length for variable-length records). JCL uses it to compute the amount of space.

Here is an example:

```
//  AVGREC=U,SPACE=(500,(4000,600))
```

[Primary space is allocated for 4,000 records and each secondary for 600 records. The average record length is assumed to be 500 bytes.]

AVGREC doesn't request space in units of cylinders. To use AVGREC to allocate cylinders, code the CONTIG and ROUND options on the SPACE parameter.

```
//  AVGREC=K,SPACE=(500,(4000,600),,CONTIG,ROUND)
```

There is also a SECMODEL parameter to assign a RACF (Resource Access Control Facility) profile name to a new dataset for security. You code it like this:

```
SECMODEL=(profile)
```

[Gives the name of the *profile* assigned by the installation belonging to a discrete dataset profile.]

```
SECMODEL=(profile,GENERIC)
```

[Gives the name of the *profile* that refers to a generic dataset profile.]

9.6.   THE ALLOCATE COMMAND

The ALLOCATE command can be used to create a VSAM dataset. Actually, ALLOCATE comes in two flavors, the Access Method Services version and the TSO version.

9.6.1.   The AMS ALLOCATE Command

As an Access Method Services command, ALLOCATE causes the Terminal Monitor Program (TMP) to execute TSO commands in the background. You can use ALLOCATE to create and dynamically allocate a VSAM or non-VSAM dataset to a job step. We'll concern ourselves only with VSAM datasets.

You specify VSAM dataset attributes the same way you do for the DEFINE CLUSTER command;

- By coding the parameters (which are similar to JCL) and their corresponding values explicitly on the ALLOCATE command.
- By using some combination of DFSMS DATACLAS, MGMTCLAS, and STORCLAS parameters, either explicitly or implicitly on the ALLOCATE command.
- By using a DATACLAS on the ALLOCATE command and then overriding some values explicitly.

The next example uses the Access Method Services ALLOCATE command to allocate the sample KSDS. The coding is analogous to its DEFINE CLUSTER counterpart shown in the first example in this chapter.

```
//MYJOB     JOB ...
//ONE       EXEC PGM=IDCAMS
//SYSPRINT DD SYSOUT=*
//SYSIN     DD *
 ALLOC
```

```
DSNAME(A2000.LIB.KSDS.CLUSTER)            -
```

[DSNAME names the dataset, A2000.LIB.KSDS.CLUSTER in the example. Notice it is enclosed within parentheses.]

```
NEW CATALOG                               -
```

[NEW CATALOG indicates this new dataset will be cataloged at the beginning of the job step. Both DFSMS-managed and VSAM datasets must be cataloged. For them, NEW catalogs the dataset. If you want to delete the dataset at the end of the job, specify NEW DELETE DELETE.]

```
DATACLAS(KSDSDATA)                        -
MGMTCLAS(VSAMGMT)                         -
STORCLAS(SWIFT)
```

[DATACLAS, MGMTCLAS, and STORCLAS name the same DFSMS constructs as in the first example in this chapter.]

The following example overrides certain DATACLAS parameters, while retaining others.

```
//MYJOB     JOB ...
//STEPONE   EXEC PGM=IDCAMS
//SYSPRINT DD SYSOUT=*
//SYSIN     DD *
 ALLOC                                    -
   DSNAME(A2000.LIB.KSDS.CLUSTER)         -
   NEW CATALOG                            -
   SPACE(CYL,(5,1))                       -
```

[SPACE specifies the space allocation, in cylinders here, consisting of five cylinders primary and one cylinder of secondary space, for a total of 123 extents. SPACE can also be specified in tracks (TRK) or average records (AVGREC) to have the system calculate the space. See the JCL discussion for an explanation of AVGREC. SPACE is analogous to the DEFINE CLUSTER space parameter.]

```
LRECL(80)                                 -
```

[LRECL specifies the record length, fixed in this case. For variable-length records, you specify the maximum length here. LRECL is analogous to the DEFINE CLUSTER RECORDSIZE parameter.]

```
KEYLEN(8)                                 -
KEYOFF(0)                                 -
```

[KEYLEN and KEYOFF specify the record key length and its offset. The parameters together are analogous to the DEFINE CLUSTER KEYS parameter. (Required for a KSDS only.)]

```
RECORG(KS) -
```

[RECORG specifies the dataset organization. Acceptable values are KS (Key-Sequenced), ES (Entry-Sequenced), RR (Relative Record), and LS (Linear Space). RECORG is analogous to the DEFINE CLUSTER INDEXED, NONINDEXED, NUMBERED, and LINEAR parameters.]

```
DATACLAS(KSDSDATA)
```

Two things to note about using ALLOCATE versus DEFINE CLUSTER. With ALLOCATE you cannot:

1. Specify every parameter. You have to accept the VSAM (or a named DATACLAS) default for the unspecified ones.
2. Name separate data and index components.

9.6.2.   The TSO ALLOCATE Command

You can also use the TSO ALLOCATE command to create a VSAM dataset in the foreground of TSO. The following example creates the sample KSDS in this manner. As you can see, the parameters are similar to that of their Access Method Services ALLOCATE counterparts.

```
ALLOC DA(A2000.LIB.KSDS.CLUSTER) RECORG(KS) +
KEYLEN(8) KEYOFF(0) SPACE(5,1) CYL LRECL(80) NEW
```

9.6.3.   Temporary Datasets

Under DFSMS you can create a temporary VSAM dataset (say for a work file) using JCL, the Access Method Services ALLOCATE command, or the TSO ALLOCATE command. A temporary dataset is created and deleted within a job. However, it can be passed to different steps within the job.

Here is some general information that pertains to all VSAM temporary datasets:

• They are always DFSMS managed, that is, they have a STORCLAS assignment (usually implicit). MGMTCLAS attributes are not appropriate for a temporary dataset.

- You should name your temporary datasets using a valid DFSMS-managed dataset name, for example

  WORK.SAMPLE

- The RECORG parameter tells the system that the temporary dataset is VSAM. Valid values are KS, ES, LS, or RR. RECORG can be part of an explicit or an implicit DATACLAS assignment.
- If DFSMS is not active, DATACLAS, STORCLAS, and MGMTCLAS assignments are ignored. This could cause the job to fail.
- The disposition for a temporary dataset that is passed to different steps within the job would be NEW PASS. Even temporary datasets are cataloged.

The following examples create the same ESDS via four different techniques. Examples 1 and 2 use the Access Method Services ALLO-CATE command and examples 3 and 4 use JCL statements. Examples 1 and 3 assume an implicit DATACLAS assignment, and examples 2 and 4 show DATACLAS parameters coded explicitly.

1.
```
//MYJOB    JOB ...
//STEPONE  EXEC PGM=IDCAMS
//SYSPRINT DD SYSOUT=*
//SYSIN    DD *
 ALLOC                          -
   DSNAME(WORK.SAMPLE)          -
   NEW PASS
```

2. The AMS ALLOCATE command has parameters similar to JCL DD statements as shown in the following example.

```
//MYJOB    JOB ...
//STEPONE  EXEC PGM=IDCAMS
//SYSPRINT DD SYSOUT=*
//SYSIN    DD *
 ALLOC                          -
   DSNAME(WORK.SAMPLE)          -
   NEW PASS                     -
```

   [You code the same dispositions as JCL.]

```
   RECORG(ES)                   -
```

   [This specifies ESDS.]

```
AVGREC(K)                              -
```

[The AVGREC values are the same as for JCL. This requests space in units of K bytes.]

```
SPACE(80,5)                            -
```

[The space parameter is coded the same as JCL. The average record length is 80. The primary amount is for $5 \times 1{,}024 \times 80$ bytes with no secondary.]

```
LRECL(80)
```

[This is the same as for JCL.]

3. `//STEPONE DD DSN=WORK.SAMPLE,DISP=(NEW,PASS)`

4. `//STEPONE DD DSN=WORK.SAMPLE,DISP=(NEW,PASS),`
   `//          RECORG=ES,AVGREC=K,SPACE(80,(5)),`
   `//          LRECL=80`

Note the following about these examples:

- Examples 1 and 2 execute IDCAMS; examples 3 and 4 execute a user-written application program (not shown in the example).
- Examples 1 and 3 specify only the dataset name and disposition; VSAM assigns the parameters via an implicit DATACLAS and STORCLAS designation based on the dataset name, WORK.SAMPLE. Examples 2 and 4 specify parameters explicitly.

10

Using LISTCAT

You can learn a great deal about the inner workings of VSAM by studying the output of the LISTCAT command. And this won't be just an intellectual exercise; you can use this information to make informed decisions about your VSAM dataset. For example, you may want to adjust the dataset's allocated free space based on the values displayed in two LISTCAT output fields, the HI-ALLOC-RBA and the HI-USED-RBA. Or, you may decide it's time to reorganize the dataset based on information in the SPLITS-CI and SPLITS-CA fields.

With LISTCAT, you can also view dataset attributes, DFSMS classes, password and security information, usage statistics, space allocation information, creation and expiration dates, and much more. LISTCAT's basic function is to list information about VSAM and non-VSAM objects that have entries in either a VSAM catalog or an ICF catalog. You can even list information about the catalog itself.

10.1. THE LISTCAT COMMAND

The basic LISTCAT command has no parameters, being simply

```
LISTCAT
```

That's the good news. The bad news is that this basic form lists the entire contents of the master catalog, something you probably won't want to do (at least not often). You'll probably want to apply parameters to the LISTCAT command, and we'll show you how to do this in order to get the information you need from the output. The following is the usual format for LISTCAT:

Format: LISTCAT CATALOG(*name/password*) *options*

                         name: The name of the catalog containing the entry.

                         password: The password for the catalog if there is one. Omit the */password* if the catalog doesn't have a password or if it is DFSMS-managed.

                         options: The options are listed following this.

Abbreviation: LISTC CAT(*name/password*)

Use: KSDS, ESDS, RRDS, non-VSAM

Required: No, if the object you want to list has a high-level qualifier that is an alias for the catalog that contains the entry. Also, the use of CATALOG is actively discouraged for DFSMS-managed datasets.

Default: All catalogs.

Example: LISTCAT CATALOG(PRGMR)

The following command, which lists all entries in the PRGMR catalog with the high-level qualifier A2000, is a more typical application of the LISTCAT command. Notice it also has a basic format, consisting of the command itself and a couple of parameters.

```
LISTCAT                -
  CATALOG(PRGMR)       -
  LVL(A2000)
```

The LISTCAT command doesn't need a CATALOG parameter when the object you want to list (let's assume for discussion that it's a base cluster) has a high-level qualifier that is an alias for the catalog that contains the entry, as in the following example.

```
A2000.LIB.KSDS.CLUSTER      (cluster name)
  ↓
A2000                       (user catalog alias)
  ↓
PRGMR                       (user catalog name)
```

If you do use a CATALOG parameter and the dataset is password-protected, you'll have to specify the passwords as well. You can list all other passwords by entering the master password.

As you may suspect, the LISTCAT JCL also consists of just a few basic statements. It is not necessary to include a DD statement for the dataset that you are listing.

```
//LISTJOB  JOB ...
//STEPONE  EXEC PGM=IDCAMS
//SYSPRINT DD SYSOUT=*
//SYSIN    DD *
```

LISTCAT needs three things in order to display selected information for your datasets:

1. The entry name of the object that you want to list.
2. The name of the catalog that contains the entry. As stated previously, this name can be implicitly or explicitly defined.
3. The type of information that you want to see.

10.1.1. The Entry Name

First let's tackle the entry name, which can be specified in one of several ways using two similar, though mutually exclusive, parameters, ENTRIES or LEVEL. An entry name can specify a base cluster or its data or index component, an alternate index, a path connected to the alternate index, a master catalog (the default, as seen previously), a user catalog, a generation data group (GDG), a non-VSAM object, a page space, and an alias as in the previous example.

Format: LISTCAT ENTRIES(*entry name*) *options*

LISTCAT LEVEL(*level*) *options*

entry name: The generic name of each entry to list. For example, A.B.C would list the A.B.C entry only.

level: The level of qualification at which to begin listing. For example, A.B would list all entries that have A.B as a level of qualification. You can also code an asterisk as a wild card character to indicate any name at that level: A.*.C. The asterisk should not be used at the lowest level (A.B.*)—leaving it off does the same thing (A.B).

	options: These are listed following this.
Abbreviation:	LISTC ENT(*entry name*) ...
	LISTC LVL(*level*) ...
Use:	KSDS, ESDS, RRDS, non-VSAM
Required:	No, because of default.
Default:	All entries are listed if just LISTCAT is coded.
Example:	LISTCAT ENTRIES(A.B.C.D)
	LISTCAT LEVEL(A.B)

The use of ENTRIES or LEVEL is often a source of confusion for application programmers new to VSAM, because they have a similar syntax and because they are often confused with the NAME parameter, which limits the output to object names.

The ENTRIES parameter. ENTRIES (ENT) requires you to specify each level of qualification, either explicitly or implicitly, using an asterisk as a wild card character in place of one or more levels. The best way to explain this parameter is to demonstrate with a few examples. The first example lists catalog information about the base cluster, the data component, and the index component, because, if you specify the base cluster name with no other limiting parameters, all three components are listed automatically. (The ALL parameter requests all catalog information and has no logical connection to ENTRIES.)

```
LISTCAT                            -
  ENT(A2000.LIB.KSDS.CLUSTER)  -
  ALL
```

The next example would also work, but it would include entries such as A2000.LIB.KSDS.BACKUP, because the asterisk is used as a wild card character.

```
LISTCAT                            -
  ENT(A2000.LIB.KSDS.*)          -
  ALL
```

The CLUSTER parameter in the following two examples restricts information to the base cluster only.

```
LISTCAT                         -
   ENT(A2000.LIB.KSDS.CLUSTER)  -
   CLUSTER                      - <===
   ALL

LISTCAT                         -
   ENT(A2000.LIB.KSDS.*)        -
   CLUSTER                      - <===
   ALL
```

The DATA parameter in the following two examples restricts information to the data component only—and so on.

```
LISTCAT                         -
   ENT(A2000.LIB.KSDS.DATA)     -
   DATA                         - <===
   ALL

LISTCAT                         -
   ENT(A2000.LIB.KSDS.*)        - <===
   DATA                         -
   ALL
```

The following example lists information for any entry that has A2000.LIB as the first two qualifiers, plus two other lower-level qualifiers (four in all).

```
LISTCAT                         -
   ENT(A2000.LIB.*.*)           -
   ALL
```

However, an entry such as A2000.LIB.KSDS.AUTHNAME.AIX would not be listed because, as you can see, it has five levels of qualification. Similarly, an example such as the one below would not be listed, unless the catalog contains this specific two-level entry. To request entries in this way, you need the LEVEL parameter, which we'll come to in a moment.

```
LISTCAT                         -
   ENT(A2000.LIB)               -
   ALL
```

You can use the wild card character for any level of qualification, even the very highest. The example below would list information for entries in the catalog with the second- and third-level qualifiers of KSDS.CLUSTER, regardless of the high-level qualifier.

```
LISTCAT                          -
   ENT(*.KSDS.CLUSTER)           -
   ALL
```

The LEVEL parameter. The syntax of LEVEL (LVL) doesn't require you to account for every qualifier. Instead, if you specify LEVEL (qualifier), VSAM assumes that qualifier to be the high-level qualifier and lists every entry with that leading qualifier, no matter how many other lower-level qualifiers it may have. You can even narrow the search with as many levels of qualification as you want to specify by using the following format:

```
LVL(qualifier.qualifier)
```

You can code the asterisk as a wild card character to specify all names for a level. However, you don't need the asterisk as the last level, because LEVEL by definition lists all lower levels, so coding the asterisk last wouldn't make sense.

We'll demonstrate LEVEL with a few quick examples, the first of which lists information for any entry that has A2000.LIB as the two leading qualifiers. This would catch entries like A2000.LIB.KSDS. AUTHNAME.AIX.

```
LISTCAT                          -
   LVL(A2000.LIB)                -
   ALL
```

The second example lists information for any entry where A2000 is the leading qualifier, anything is the second-level qualifier, KSDS is the third-level qualifier, and any number of low-level qualifiers follow. You can use the asterisk as a mid-level qualifier with LVL. Entries as diverse as A2000.LIB.KSDS and A2000.TEST.KSDS.AIX would be listed.

```
LISTCAT                          -
   LVL(A2000.*.KSDS)             -
   ALL
```

By the way (and this is an important point), if you specify ENTRIES or LEVEL with no other limiting parameters, the default is to only list the entry *names* that meet the search criteria.

```
LISTCAT                        -
  LVL(A2000.*.KSDS)
```

This is the same as though you had specified:

```
LISTCAT                        -
  LVL(A2000.*.KSDS)            -
  NAME                              <===
```

The bottom line on ENTRIES or LEVEL? Use whatever form you're most comfortable with, but be careful with wild card characters because you may not get what you expect.

10.1.2. Objects to Be Listed

You can specify the NAME parameter followed by the type of entry to list the name and type of entry.

Format:

NAME(*type type ... type*)

type: The type of object. It can be any of the following:

ALIAS		
ALTERNATEINDEX	*or*	AIX
CLUSTER	*or*	CL
DATA		
GENERATIONDATAGROUP	*or*	GDG
INDEX	*or*	IX
NONVSAM	*or*	NVSAM
PAGESPACE	*or*	PGSPC
PATH		
SPACE	*or*	SPC
USERCATALOG	*or*	UCAT

Abbreviation:

As shown.

Use:	KSDS, ESDS, RRDS, non-VSAM
Required:	No, because of default.
Default:	All types.
Example:	LISTCAT LEVEL(A.B) NAME(DATA INDEX)

As an alternative to NAME, you can code one of the following logical groups, the names of which you specify as input parameters. NAME and the four parameters are mutually exclusive.

Format:	HISTORY I VOLUME I ALLOCATION I ALL
Abbreviation:	HIST I VOL I ALLOC I
Use:	KSDS, ESDS, RRDS, non-VSAM
	They can only be coded for CLUSTER, DATA, INDEX, AIX, PATH, GDG, PAGESPACE, and NONVSAM.
Required:	No, because of default.
Default:	ALL
Example:	LISTCAT ENTRIES(A.B.C.D) HIST LISTCAT LEVEL(A.B) ALL

The four parameters specify the following:

- *HISTORY* lists reference information for the dataset (or other object) including name, type of entry, creation and expiration date (if one has been assigned), and release of VSAM under which it was created.
- *VOLUME* lists the device type and one or more volume serial numbers of the storage volumes where the dataset resides. HISTORY information is listed as well.
- *ALLOCATION* provides handy information about the provisions that have been specified for space allocation, including the unit (cylinders, tracks), numbers of allocated units of primary and secondary space, and actual extents. The information is displayed only for data and index component entries. If you specify ALLOCATION, VOLUME and HISTORY information are included as well. (Sort of like, "with three, you get soup and eggroll.")
- *ALL* provides all of the previous groups, everything so to speak. (It differs from ALLOCATION only in that ALL displays the allocation

for all entries, whereas ALLOCATION displays it only for the data and index components.) This is the parameter that you will use most often when doing a detailed analysis of your VSAM cluster.

10.2.   USING LISTCAT FOR ANALYSIS

After defining a VSAM dataset and loading it with data, but before creating any alternate indexes, you should do the following:

1. Use the LISTCAT command to analyze the attributes of your dataset to be sure that the values are what you expect.
2. Use the PRINT command to dump a representative sampling of the data records. (See Chapter 13 for information on how to use this command.)

Assume that you have defined the cluster as shown in the following example and have subsequently loaded the empty cluster with data. (You can approach this in one of two ways: use the REPRO command or write an application program. Chapters 12 and 15 offer more information on both methods.)

```
DEFINE CLUSTER (NAME(A2000.LIB.SAMPLE.CLUSTER)    -
                OWNER(SSMITH)                      -
                INDEXED                            -
                RECORDSIZE(80 80)                  -
                KEYS(8 0)                          -
                SPEED                              -
                VOLUMES(VS0101))                   -
        DATA    (NAME(A2000.LIB.SAMPLE.DATA)       -
                CYLINDERS(2 0))                    -
        INDEX   (NAME(A2000.LIB.SAMPLE.INDEX)))
```

Here is one example of the LISTCAT command to use when you want to perform an analysis on various attributes of your dataset.

```
LISTCAT ENT(A2000.LIB.SAMPLE.CLUSTER)             -
    ALL
```

VSAM categorizes and then lists the cluster, data, and index component attributes by the previously mentioned logical groups. Let's look at each individual group first. Then you can view the entire LISTCAT output in Figure 10.2.

10.2.1. CLUSTER Attributes

The first two lines of LISTCAT output display the name of the cluster and the name of the user catalog (PRGMR here) that contains the entry.

```
CLUSTER ------- A2000.LIB.SAMPLE.CLUSTER
     IN-CAT --- PRGMR
```

For the CLUSTER component, information is divided into the following groups: HISTORY, PROTECTION, ASSOCIATIONS, and SMSDATA (for DFSMS-managed datasets).

The cluster HISTORY. HISTORY provides reference information about the cluster.

```
HISTORY
     OWNER-IDENT-----(SSMITH)    CREATION--------1991.218
     RELEASE----------------2    EXPIRATION------0000.000
```

OWNER-IDENT displays the TSO userid of the person who allocated the cluster if the cluster was allocated under TSO; otherwise this field displays NULL.

RELEASE lists the VSAM release under which the cluster was defined; 2 here.

CREATION displays the date that the cluster was defined in the form YYYY.DDD. DDD is the day of year.

EXPIRATION displays the date that the cluster will expire in the form YYYY.DDD. Once again, DDD is the day of year. If EXPIRATION contains a value other than zeros, the TO or FOR parameter was specified either in the DEFINE command, or later with the ALTER command, in order to assign a retention date to the dataset. In this case, you will have to specify the PURGE option as part of the DELETE command in order to override this retention date.

The cluster PROTECTION. PROTECTION lists password and RACF security. If the cluster is password-protected, the password will display in the PSWD field unless the password is suppressed for security reasons, in which case this field will show a value of SUPP.

```
PROTECTION-PSWD-----(NULL)      RACF---------------(NO)
```

The cluster ASSOCIATIONS. ASSOCIATIONS lists the names of the data and index components as well as the names of any alternate indexes that are tied to the base cluster. (There are none in the following example.)

```
ASSOCIATIONS
     DATA------A2000.LIB.SAMPLE.DATA
     INDEX----A2000.LIB.SAMPLE.INDEX
```

The cluster SMSDATA. SMSDATA names any associated DFSMS classes if the cluster is DFSMS managed. This group displays values only at the cluster level, but that makes sense, because DFSMS classes can only be applied at the cluster level.

```
SMSDATA
     STORAGECLASS--------SWIFT    MANAGEMENTCLASS--VSAMGMT
     DATACLASS--------KSDSDATA    LBACKUP----0000.000.0000
```

The LBACKUP field displays the date and time of the last backup. If this data is not available for some reason, the field is displayed as all Xs: XXXX.XXX.XXXX.

10.2.2. DATA Attributes

Information is more detailed for the DATA component and is divided into the following groups: HISTORY, PROTECTION, ASSOCIATIONS, ATTRIBUTES, STATISTICS, ALLOCATION, and VOLUME. Like the CLUSTER component output, the first two lines of DATA output display the name of the entry and the name of the user catalog (PRGMR here) that contain this entry name.

```
DATA------- A2000.LIB.SAMPLE.DATA
   IN-CAT --- PRGMR
```

HISTORY and PROTECTION redisplay the same information as for the cluster already described.

```
HISTORY
     OWNER-IDENT-----(SSMITH)     CREATION--------1991.218
     RELEASE---------------2      EXPIRATION------0000.000

PROTECTION-PSWD------(NULL)       RACF---------------(NO)
```

ASSOCIATIONS refers to the cluster component. Notice that the index component is not listed here.

```
ASSOCIATIONS
  CLUSTER--A2000.LIB.SAMPLE.CLUSTER
```

The ATTRIBUTES information. ATTRIBUTES lists the data attributes as they were defined when the cluster was created. As a programmer, you need to pay special attention to this output. (Due to page space considerations, the output here appears slightly condensed from the actual printout.) Reading down the first column of ATTRIBUTE information:

```
ATTRIBUTES
  KEYLEN----------------8
  RKP-------------------0
  SHROPTNS(1,3)        SPEED
  UNORDERED           NOREUSE
```

KEYLEN displays the length of the primary key, eight bytes here.

RKP displays the primary key position relative to the beginning of the record (0 because the sample key begins in the first position, and all VSAM records start in position zero).

SHROPTNS lists the data-sharing options that were specified for the dataset. The 1, 3 here are the defaults for cross-system and cross-region sharing respectively.

SPEED indicates that the data was initially loaded with the SPEED parameter, which does not preformat the control areas when the data is initially loaded, and it is faster than RECOVERY, the default.

UNORDERED indicates that the volumes do not necessarily have to be accessed in the order specified in the DEFINE CLUSTER VOLUMES parameter. Since only one volume was specified in the DEFINE command, VSAM has assumed the UNORDERED default. ORDERED is the alternative.

NOREUSE indicates that the cluster is not reusable. That is, it cannot be emptied of records and then reloaded without first deleting the original cluster and then redefining it. NOREUSE is the default. If you specify the alternative, REUSE, the cluster's High Used Relative Byte Address (HURBA) is set to zero when the cluster is opened at reload time. (For more on the HURBA, see the VERIFY material in Chapter 12.)

Reading down the second column of ATTRIBUTE information, we see

```
ATTRIBUTES
    AVGRECL--------------80
    MAXRECL--------------80
    UNIQUE          NOERASE
    NOREUSE      NONSPANNED
```

AVGRECL displays the length of the average record.

MAXRECL displays the length of the longest record. Because the records are fixed length here, AVGRECL and MAXRECL values are the same. For variable-length records, these fields display different values.

UNIQUE indicates that the dataset occupies its own VSAM space. SUBALLOCATION is the default for entries contained in a VSAM catalog. Datasets defined in an ICF catalog can only have UNIQUE space.

NOERASE indicates that the data should not be overwritten with binary zeros as a security measure when the dataset is deleted, and it is the default. ERASE is the alternative.

NONSPANNED indicates that individual data records cannot span control intervals, and it is the default. SPANNED is the alternative, used for very large records (except for linear datasets, where data is stored in 4K pages rather than records).

VSAM displays two additional columns of ATTRIBUTE information:

```
ATTRIBUTES
    BUFSPACE-----------45568    CISIZE--------------22528
    EXCPEXIT----------(NULL)    CI/CA------------------30
    INDEXED      NOWRITECHK     NOIMBED       NOREPLICAT
```

BUFSPACE displays the allocated buffer space in bytes. When this parameter is not specified in the DEFINE command, VSAM has assumed the default, which is two data buffers and one index buffer as shown here.

EXCPEXIT indicates by the NULL value that no EXCEPTIONEXIT routine was specified in the DEFINE command. An EXCEPTIONEXIT routine is a user-written routine that takes control in the event of an I/O error.

CISIZE displays either the control interval size specified in the DEFINE command or the control interval size that VSAM has selected. The value of 22528 here was calculated by VSAM. VSAM calculates the default BUFSPACE value as (control interval CISIZE × 2 + index CISIZE).

CI/CA displays a VSAM-calculated value; the number of control intervals per control area. This value is derived from the CISIZE and CASIZE values, the number of tracks per DASD cylinder (15 for a 3380 device), and certain control information.

INDEXED displays the type of VSAM dataset: INDEXED for a KSDS, NONINDEXED for an ESDS, NUMBERED for an RRDS, and LINEAR for an LDS.

NOWRITECHECK indicates that control interval data should not be compared with buffer data and is the default. WRITECHECK is the alternative.

NOIMBED / NOREPLICATE—NOIMBED indicates that the sequence-set record for each control area is not written on the first track of the data control area but is stored with the other index records. NOIMBED is the default; IMBED is the alternative. NOREPLICATE indicates that the index records are only written once, not replicated on the track as many times as will fit. NOREPLICATE is the default; REPLICATE is the alternative.

The STATISTICS information. STATISTICS provides information on dataset usage that is highly valuable for both application programmers and support people. Reading down the first column of STATISTICS information, we see

```
STATISTICS
      REC-TOTAL------------12
      REC-DELETED-----------0
      REC-INSERTED----------0
      REC-UPDATED-----------0
      REC-RETRIEVED---------0
```

REC-TOTAL displays the total number of data records in the data component. If the dataset has been processed in control interval mode, this number may not be accurate. This is true for all of the fields displayed in this column. This has significance only for LDS, which are processed in control interval mode.

REC-DELETED displays the total number of data records deleted since the dataset was created.

REC-INSERTED displays different values depending upon the dataset type. For a KSDS, this field displays the number of records inserted into the data component. Interestingly enough, records added to the end of the data component are not included in the total. For an RRDS, this field displays the number of records inserted in available slots. For an ESDS, this field is not applicable because all new records are added to the end of the dataset.

REC-UPDATED displays the number of records that have been up-dated with new information and then rewritten. It does not include deleted records.

REC-RETRIEVED displays the number of records that have been accessed in both read and update mode since the dataset was defined.

Reading down the second column of STATISTICS information, we see

```
STATISTICS
     SPLITS-CI--------------0
     SPLITS-CA--------------0
     FREESPACE-%CI----------0
     FREESPACE-%CA----------0
     FREESPC-BYTES-----1329152
```

SPLITS-CI displays the actual number of control interval splits that have occurred in the data component, zero in this case.

SPLITS-CA displays the actual number of control area splits that have occurred in the data component, zero in this case. It is important to monitor these two fields carefully, since control interval and control area splits, especially the latter, are one of the most frequent causes of degraded performance in both sequential batch processing and online CICS applications. If the figure reaches a number that is deemed unac-ceptable for your application, you will have to use REPRO to offload the cluster, DEFINE to specify a larger FREESPACE (FSPC) percentage, and finally REPRO again to reload the cluster.

FREESPACE-%CI displays the percentage of control interval free space allocated by the DEFINE command. The default is zero, as shown in the example.

FREESPACE-%CA displays the percentage of control area free space allocated by the DEFINE command. The default is zero, as shown in the example.

FREESPACE-BYTES displays the actual free space in bytes that exists in totally empty control intervals. If you divide this figure by the data CISIZE value (1329152 / 22528), you get the number of totally empty control intervals.

Reading down the third column of STATISTICS information, we see

```
STATISTICS
     EXCPS----------------17
     EXTENTS---------------1
     SYSTEM-TIMESTAMP:
         X'A4E61E1F33856811'
```

EXCPS (EXecute Channel Program)—this field displays the number of physical I/Os that have been issued for the data component since it was last defined.

EXTENTS displays the total number of primary and secondary dataset extensions, one in the example.

SYSTEM-TIMESTAMP indicates the date and time (in hex) that the data component was last closed after a program opened it for update.

The ALLOCATION information. ALLOCATION provides valuable information about the DASD space allocated for the data component. Reading down the first column of ALLOCATION information, we see

```
ALLOCATION
     SPACE-TYPE------CYLINDER
     SPACE-PRI-------------2
     SPACE-SEC-------------0
```

SPACE-TYPE indicates the unit of space specified in the DEFINE command. Possible values are CYLINDER, TRACK, RECORD, MEGABYTE, and KILOBYTE.

SPACE-PRI displays the primary space allocation for the dataset, in units of CYLINDERs here.

SPACE-SEC displays the secondary space allocation for the dataset, once again in units of CYLINDERs for the example. If the dataset extends into the secondary area, space will be allocated in the amount and unit specified, up to 122 times for datasets cataloged in an ICF catalog or those defined with the SUBALLOCATION parameter in a VSAM catalog, or up to 16 times for datasets defined with the UNIQUE parameter in a VSAM catalog. In the example, no secondary space allocation has been specified.

Reading down the second column of ALLOCATION information, we see

```
ALLOCATION
     HI-ALLOC-RBA------1351680
     HI-USED-RBA-------675840
```

HI-ALLOC-RBA indicates the Relative Byte Address (plus 1) of the last *allocated* data control area. This value reflects the total space allocation for the data component. (The extra byte allows for displacement, because VSAM records begin in position zero.)

HI-USED-RBA indicates the Relative Byte Address (plus 1) of the

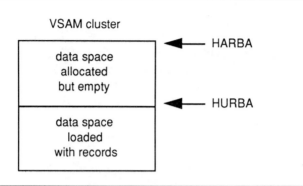

VSAM cluster

data space
allocated
but empty

◀—— HARBA

◀—— HURBA

data space
loaded
with records

Figure 10.1.   The HURBA and HARBA values.

last *used* data control area. This value reflects the portion of the space allocation that is actually filled with data records.

Figure 10.1 depicts the difference between the HI-USED-RBA (HURBA) and the HI-ALLOC-RBA (HARBA). For more information on how the VERIFY command acts on the HURBA, see Chapter 12.

The VOLUME information. VOLUME provides information about the volume (or volumes) where the data component is stored. Reading down the first column of VOLUME information, we see

```
VOLUME
     VOLSER------------VS0101
     DEVTYPE------X'3010200E'
     VOLFLAG------------PRIME
     EXTENTS:
     LOW-CCHH-----X'01AC0000'
     HIGH-CCHH----X'01AD000E'
```

VOLSER lists the volume(s) containing the dataset.

DEVTYPE indicates (in hex code) the device type that holds the storage volume. For example, the value '3010200E' indicates a 3380, and '3050200B' indicates a 3350 device type. Other device type values are shown in a Device Type Translate Table in the Access Method Services reference manual for your operating environment.

VOLFLAG displays the status of the previously named storage volume. Possible values are PRIME (indicating the first volume), OVER-

FLOW (indicating a secondary volume), and CANDIDATE (indicating a potential volume).

EXTENTS provides detailed information on the data component extents, including LOW-CCHH and HI-CCHH. LOW-CCHH displays the device address of the start of the extent, and HI-CCHH displays the device address of the end of the extent.

Reading down the second column of VOLUME information, we see

```
VOLUME
    PHYREC-SIZE---------22528
    PHYRECS/TRK------------2
    TRACKS/CA-------------15
```

PHYREC-SIZE displays the size of the physical record, which is calculated by VSAM and is analogous to the OS block. It's important to note that physical record size is not the same as control interval size. VSAM uses the control interval to calculate the physical record size; there may be multiple physical records per control interval.

The space between each physical record is filled with an interblock gap, which can result in wasted DASD and increased I/O when the control interval is retrieved for processing. For this reason, VSAM chooses the largest physical record size it can, based on the control interval size. One physical record per control interval is the ideal, because then there are no interblock gaps. In this case, CISIZE and PHYREC-SIZE will express the same values.

PHYRECS/TRK displays the number of physical records per track. Once again, this number is calculated by VSAM, taking into consideration the physical record size, the device type, and any necessary control information.

TRACKS/CA displays the number of tracks per control area, 15 here since the storage device is a 3380 type.

Reading down the third and fourth columns of VOLUME information, we get

```
VOLUME
    HI-ALLOC-RBA-----1351680    EXTENT-NUMBER-----------1
    HI-USED-RBA-------675840    EXTENT-TYPE---------X'00'
```

HI-ALLOC-RBA redisplays the same value shown previously in the ALLOCATION group.

HI-USED-RBA redisplays the same value shown previously in the ALLOCATION group.

EXTENT-NUMBER redisplays the total number of primary and secondary dataset extents, one in the example.

EXTENT-TYPE indicates the type of extent. Possible values for a data component include 00, contiguous extents, and 20, unformatted extents.

10.2.3. INDEX Attributes

You can also analyze the various attributes of the index component using the output of the LISTCAT ALL command. Since we've already discussed many of these fields and values for the data component, we'll confine this discussion to those fields that have a different connotation for the index component or those that display different values for various reasons.

LISTCAT names the index component as well as the catalog that contains its entry. HISTORY, PROTECTION, and ASSOCIATIONS are also listed in the same manner as the data component. ASSOCIATIONS names the base cluster but no other components of the dataset.

```
INDEX ------ A2000.LIB.SAMPLE.INDEX
   IN-CAT --- PRGMR
   HISTORY
       DATASET-OWNER---(SSMITH)   CREATION--------1991.218
       RELEASE---------------2    EXPIRATION------0000.000
   PROTECTION-PSWD-----(NULL)     RACF---------------(NO)
   ASSOCIATIONS
       CLUSTER--A2000.LIB.SAMPLE.CLUSTER
```

The ATTRIBUTES information. We'll begin our detailed discussion with the ATTRIBUTES group. Reading down the first column and second columns of information:

```
ATTRIBUTES
   KEYLEN---------------8      AVGRECL---------------0
   RKP-------------------0     MAXRECL-------------505
```

KEYLEN and *RKP* redisplay the length and position of the primary key, which is not too surprising since the index is built on the primary key.

AVGRECL and *MAXRECL* display interesting values. VSAM stores the primary key as a variable-length record, with an AVGRECL of zero and a MAXRECL value that is seven bytes less than the CISIZE value. The seven extra bytes in the control interval are occupied by RDF and CIDF information. See Chapter 3 for more detail concerning these fields.

Reading down the third and fourth columns of ATTRIBUTE information, we see

```
ATTRIBUTES
    BUFSPACE---------------0     CISIZE----------------512
    EXCPEXIT-----------(NULL)     CI/CA-----------------46
```

BUFSPACE displays a zero value because the index buffer space has been folded into the data component BUFSPACE value.

CISIZE indicates a value of 512, calculated by VSAM. Generally, it's better to let VSAM calculate the index CISIZE value. Exceptions are discussed in Chapter 23.

CI/CA displays a VSAM-calculated value, different than its data component counterpart, because the CISIZE is different.

The STATISTICS information. Under STATISTICS we'll look at just a few key fields.

```
STATISTICS
    REC-TOTAL--------------1     SPLITS-CI---------------0
    REC-DELETED-----------0      SPLITS-CA---------------0
    REC-INSERTED----------0      FREESPACE-%CI-----------0
    REC-UPDATED-----------0      FREESPACE-%CA-----------0
    REC-RETRIEVED---------0      FREESPC-BYTES-------23040
```

REC-TOTAL displays a much smaller value than its data component counterpart, because primary key values are stored in sequence set records, each containing multiple key values. See Chapter 23 for more information. The REC-TOTAL value represents one sequence set record per index control interval.

FREESPC-BYTES. Control interval and control area splits do not occur in the index component in the sense that they do in the data component, and so FREESPACE percentages are applied to the data component only. However, VSAM does allow some planned free space in index records, and the value displayed in FREESPC-BYTES represents unused space in bytes.

Here's more STATISTICS information relating to the index:

```
STATISTICS
    EXCPS----------------3        INDEX:
    EXTENTS--------------1        LEVELS----------------1
    SYSTEM-TIMESTAMP:             ENTRIES/SECT----------5
        X'A4E61E1F33856811'       SEQ-SET-RBA-----------0
                                  HI-LEVEL-RBA----------0
```

EXCPS displays the number of I/Os that have been issued for the index component, normally a lower value than that displayed for the data component.

EXTENTS displays the number of index component extents, one here.

SYSTEM-TIMESTAMP—for data integrity, it's important that both the data and index components reflect the same time-stamp value. So, you should only issue the VERIFY command (which closes and time-stamps the dataset and sets HURBA values) against the base cluster.

The following fields display information that relates to the structure of the INDEX:

LEVELS displays important information on the number of levels in the index. If the index has an excessive number of levels, it will operate inefficiently. Because this is a small sample dataset with 12 records, it has only a one-level index—the sequence set. Chapter 23 has a lot more information on the KSDS index.

ENTRIES/SECT—VSAM divides the index record into sections for performance reasons, and this field reflects the number of entries per section. This field is not the same as the PHYREC-SIZE, and it is not normally a concern to application programmers.

SEQ-SET-RBA reflects the Relative Byte Address of the first sequence set record, the level of index closest to the data component.

HIGH-LEVEL-RBA reflects the Relative Byte Address of the highest-level index record. All search efforts begin with this record and travel through the index levels to the data records.

The rest of the fields listed in the ALLOCATION and VOLUME groups may display values different from their data component counterparts, but the information has the same meaning for the index component. If you're interested in these fields, check out the appropriate discussion in the data component section of this chapter and also consult Figure 10.2.

Finally, VSAM displays a list of the number and type of entries processed and the condition codes returned by IDCAMS. If one of the condition codes displayed is greater than zero, you can check out the

```
LISTCAT ENT(A2000.LIB.SAMPLE.CLUSTER) ALL
CLUSTER ------- A2000.LIB.SAMPLE.CLUSTER
     IN-CAT --- PRGMR
     HISTORY
          DATASET-OWNER-----SMITH        CREATION------1991.218
          RELEASE----------------2        EXPIRATION----0000.000
          PROTECTION-PSWD-----(NULL)      RACF------------(NO)
     ASSOCIATIONS
          DATA-----A2000.LIB.SAMPLE.DATA
          INDEX----A2000.LIB.SAMPLE.INDEX
DATA ------- A2000.LIB.SAMPLE.DATA
     IN-CAT --- PRGMR
     HISTORY
          DATASET-OWNER--(SSMITH)         CREATION------1991.218
          RELEASE----------------2         EXPIRATION----0000.000
          PROTECTION-PSWD-----(NULL)       RACF------------(NO)
     ASSOCIATIONS
          CLUSTER-A2000.LIB.SAMPLE.CLUSTER
     ATTRIBUTES
          KEYLEN----------------8    AVGLRECL-------------80    BUFSPACE--------45568   CISIZE---------22528
          RKP------------------0     MAXLRECL-------------80    EXCPEXIT-----(NULL)     CI/CA-------------30
          SHROPTNS(1,3)  RECOVERY   UNIQUE      NOERASE   INDEXED    NOWRITECHK    NOIMBED    NOREPLICAT
          UNORDERED     NOREUSE     NONSPANNED
     STATISTICS
          REC-TOTAL-----------12    SPLITS-CI-------------0    EXCPS-------------17
          REC-DELETED----------0    SPLITS-CA-------------0    EXTENTS------------1
          REC-INSERTED---------0    FREESPACE-%CI---------0    SYSTEM-TIMESTAMP:
          REC-UPDATED----------0    FREESPACE-%CA---------0        X'A4E61E1F3856811'
          REC-RETRIEVED--------0    FREESPC-BYTES--1329152
     ALLOCATION
          SPACE-TYPE-----CYLINDER   HI-ALLOC-RBA----1351680   HI-ALLOC-RBA----1351680
          SPACE-PRI-------------2   HI-USED-RBA------675840   HI-USED-RBA------675840
          SPACE-SEC-------------0
     VOLUME
          VOLSER--------VSO101      PHYREC-SIZE-----22528     EXTENT-NUMBER--------1
          DEVTYPE-----X'3010200E'   PHYRECS/TRK-----------2   EXTENT-TYPE------X'00'
          VOLFLAG--------PRIME      TRACKS/CA------------15
          EXTENTS:
          LOW-CCHH----X'01AC0000'   LOW-RBA--------------0
          HIGH-CCHH---X'01AD000E'   HIGH-RBA------1351679     TRACKS-------------30
```

```
INDEX ------ A2000.LIB.SAMPLE.INDEX
  IN-CAT --- PRGMR
  HISTORY
    DATASET-OWNER--(SSMITH)       CREATION------1991.218
    RELEASE----------2           EXPIRATION----0000.000
    PROTECTION-PSWD----(NULL)     RACF------------(NO)
  ASSOCIATIONS
    CLUSTER--A2000.LIB.SAMPLE.CLUSTER
  ATTRIBUTES
    KEYLEN-----------8      AVGLRECL--------0      BUFSPACE--------0        CISIZE--------512
    RKP--------------0      MAXLRECL------505      EXCPEXIT----(NULL)       CI/CA---------46
    SHROPTNS(1,3)  RECOVERY  UNIQUE    NOERASE     NOWRITECHK   NOIMBED     NOREPLICAT  UNORDERED
    NOREUSE
  STATISTICS
    REC-TOTAL--------1      SPLITS-CI-------0      EXCPS----------3         INDEX:
    REC-DELETED------0      SPLITS-CA-------0      EXTENTS---------1          LEVELS---------1
    REC-INSERTED-----0      FREESPACE-%CI---0      SYSTEM-TIMESTAMP:          ENTRIES/SECT---5
    REC-UPDATED------0      FREESPACE-%CA---0        X'A4E61E1F3856811'       SEQ-SET-RBA----0
    REC-RETRIEVED----0      FREESPC-BYTES-23040                               HI-LEVEL-RBA---0
  ALLOCATION
    SPACE-TYPE-----TRACK    HI-ALLOC-RBA-23552
    SPACE-PRI--------1      HI-USED-RBA----512
    SPACE-SEC--------0
  VOLUME
    VOLSER--------TV4103    PHYREC-SIZE----512     HI-ALLOC-RBA----23552     EXTENT-NUMBER-----1
    DEVTYPE----X'3010200E'  PHYRECS/TRK-----46     HI-USED-RBA-------512     EXTENT-TYPE----X'00'
    VOLFLAG-------PRIME     TRACKS/CA-------1
    EXTENTS:
    LOW-CCHH----X'005C000D'   LOW-RBA--------0      TRACKS----------1
    HIGH-CCHH---X'005C000D'   HIGH-RBA----23551
```

Figure 10.2. Sample LISTCAT listing.

accompanying error message in the *System Messages* manual for your operating environment. The following is displayed.

```
IDCAMS SYSTEM SERVICES
THE NUMBER OF ENTRIES PROCESSED WAS:
                AIX  ------------------0
                ALIAS  ---------------0
                CLUSTER  -------------1
                DATA  ----------------1
                GDG  -----------------0
                INDEX  --------------1
                NONVSAM  ------------0
                PAGESPACE  -----------0
                PATH  ----------------0
                SPACE  ---------------0
                USERCATALOG  ---------0
                TOTAL  ---------------3
THE NUMBER OF PROTECTED ENTRIES SUPPRESSED WAS 0
IDC0001I FUNCTION COMPLETED, HIGHEST CONDITION CODE WAS 0

IDC0002I IDCAMS PROCESSING COMPLETE. MAXIMUM CONDITION CODE
WAS 0
```

10.3. LISTCAT UNDER TSO

You can invoke LISTCAT in native TSO. If you don't specify anything other than the command, TSO assumes that your TSO userid is the highest level of qualification and only lists entries that meet this criteria. It's the same as entering the following:

```
LISTCAT LVL(userid)
```

For example, if your TSO userid is M567923, and you issue the following sequence of commands:

```
LOGON M354789
LISTCAT
```

then TSO returns a list of all the entries in the default catalog where M567923 is the high-level qualifier, in alphabetical order. A random sampling of this output shows:

```
IN CATALOG: TSOCAT
M567923.AIX
M567923.AIX.DATA
M567923.GDG
M567923.GDG.G0001V00
M567923.KSDS.CLUSTER
M567923.KSDS.DATA
READY
```

Chapter 22 discusses the catalog order of search and explains how the default catalog is selected.

You can add parameters to your LISTCAT command. For example, if you enter the following:

```
LISTCAT VOLUME
```

then TSO returns a list of all the entries in the default catalog, where M354789 is the high-level qualifier and includes volume serial information where appropriate. A random sampling of this output shows the following:

```
M567923.AIX
M567923.AIX.DATA
 --VOLUMES--
    VS0101
M567923.GDG
M567923.GDG.G0001V00
 --VOLUMES--
    QS0103
    QS0104
M567923.KSDS.CLUSTER
M567923.KSDS.DATA
 --VOLUMES--
    VS0101
READY
```

Here quickly are some examples of other ways that you can put LISTCAT to work for you using either batch mode or TSO:

- *Need to identify older datasets?* The following LISTCAT command uses the CREATION parameter to scan PRGMR.TESTCAT and list datasets that are more than one year old. The CREATION parameter can only be specified in days, but you can readily see its advantages for both programmers and support people.

```
LISTCAT                             -
    CATALOG(PRGMR.TESTCAT)          -
    CREATION(366)
```

- *Need to see which datasets are ready to expire?* Now we see the LISTCAT command with the EXPIRATION parameter to identify and list datasets in PRGMR.TESTCAT that are due to expire in a specified number of days (30 here), provided they have been assigned a retention period with the TO or FOR parameter either in the DEFINE command or later with the ALTER command.

```
LISTCAT                             -
    CATALOG(PRGMR.TESTCAT)          -
    EXPIRATION(30)
```

It's important to note that expired datasets are not deleted from the catalog automatically, but there's always a possibility that someone may accidentally delete them. Once you've identified the datasets that you want to retain, you can extend the retention period using either the TO or FOR parameter of the ALTER command.

If you do not routinely assign a retention date to your datasets, this command will have limited usefulness because all such unprotected datasets will also be listed in the output. Because such datasets are unprotected by a retention date, they can be deleted at any time. Of course, if your datasets are DFSMS-managed, you don't have to worry about expiration dates, because the MGMTCLAS takes care of that for you.

- *Want to see all entry names in a catalog?* If you want to list every entry in a specified catalog, use the simple form of LISTCAT command shown in the following example:

```
LISTCAT                             -
    CATALOG(PRGMR.TESTCAT)
```

- *Want to see all aliases of an entry?* The example below lists all the aliases of the named qualifier and also displays the name of the catalog containing these entries.

```
LISTCAT                      -
   LVL(A2000)                -
   ALIAS
```

This chapter has provided only a taste of the creative ways you can use the output of LISTCAT to view catalog entries, attributes, and other characteristics of datasets. The more you use this versatile command, the more ways you'll find to use it. The next chapter takes up the subject of alternate indexes.

11

Defining and Building an Alternate Index

In the process of defining a sample KSDS we have discussed two of VSAM's great strengths:

1. A single set of data management facilities (Access Method Services) can manage both VSAM and non-VSAM datasets.
2. Data can be stored and accessed by four different methods depending upon application requirements: key-sequenced (KSDS), entry-sequenced (ESDS), relative record (RRDS), and linear datasets (LDS).

A third great strength of VSAM is its ability to use one or more alternate index keys to provide views of data different from that offered by the primary key. While alternate indexes are usually defined for a KSDS, they can also be defined for an ESDS, even though its internal structure is somewhat different. By the way, it's common to say that an alternate index is "built over" a KSDS or ESDS, and that's the term we'll use.

A commonly used example of an alternate index is a typical personnel dataset. In our example, the primary key is EMP-NUMB and the alternate key is the SOC-SEC-NUMB. In the personnel dataset, the alternate key field is unique, but it doesn't have to be. The unique alternate index has a one-to-one ratio of primary key to alternate key.

```
EMP-NUMB          SOC-SEC-NUMB
354890            376-42-6716
567923            222-46-9872
103248            555-67-9234
```

Now consider this second example of a library dataset, where the alternate key (AUTH-LAST-NAME) is not unique in the dataset, and then we'll look at some considerations that apply to both examples.

```
LIB-NUM         TITLE                      AUTH-LAST-NAME
FICT0025        The Sun Also Rises         Hemingway
FICT8724        For Whom the Bell Tolls    Hemingway
FICT9043        The Old Man and the Sea    Hemingway
```

11.1. ALTERNATE INDEX CONSIDERATIONS

Alternate index keys have the following characteristics:

- They greatly reduce data redundancy. For example, in the personnel example there is no need to keep a separate Social Security dataset for tax reporting. DASD savings can be significant.
- They can have duplicate key values, as seen in the library dataset example. This, of course, greatly enhances the dataset's usability.
- They are easy to define using the IDCAMS DEFINE AIX command. You can use a DATACLAS to implicitly specify some DEFINE AIX parameters, but you can't define an alternate index with JCL statements alone. An alternate index becomes DFSMS-managed if you implicitly (or explicitly) assign a STORCLAS, and optionally, a MGMTCLAS. Usually, you'll want to handle an alternate index the same way you handle its base cluster.
- They allow datasets to be accessed sequentially or randomly, based on the alternate record keys, even for an ESDS.
- They can be updated automatically when the base cluster is updated. Automatic update is an option you choose when defining the alternate index.
- They cannot support a reusable base cluster, but the alternate index itself can be defined with the REUSE parameter unless it is DFSMS-managed. However, you'll usually want to define a base cluster and an alternate index in the same way. See Chapter 7 to review the REUSE parameter.

As you may already suspect, the main disadvantage to using an alternate key is performance degradation. Access by alternate key requires twice as many I/Os because the alternate key must first locate the primary key, which in turn is used to locate the desired record. Updating is also more complex because of this hierarchy of keys.

While it is theoretically possible to have up to 255 alternate keys per dataset, logic and reason dictate that alternate keys be used conservatively. Once again, it's a balancing act among application requirements, DASD usage, and I/O savings.

11.2. STEPS TO CREATE AN ALTERNATE INDEX

Each alternate index has its own separate data and index component. You must build them after the base cluster has been both defined *and* loaded with records. Each alternate index is itself a KSDS. Each record contains the alternate key value, along with the primary key value. For keys that are not unique, several records with different primary keys can have the same alternate key. Creating an alternate index requires three separate steps:

1. Define the alternate index using the IDCAMS DEFINE AIX command.
2. Specify an alternate index path using the IDCAMS DEFINE PATH command. The path forms a connection between the alternate index and the base cluster. While a path is a VSAM object, it does not contain any records. However, the path name becomes a catalog entry.
3. Build the alternate index and populate it with records using the IDCAMS BLDINDEX command. We'll explain each of these steps in turn.

The following example defines an alternate index for our sample KSDS. We'll refer to it as we discuss the various parameters of the IDCAMS DEFINE AIX command.

```
//STEP1 EXEC PGM=IDCAMS
//SYSPRINT DD SYSOUT=*
//SYSIN    DD *
 DEFINE AIX                            -
   (NAME(A2000.LIB.KSDS.AUTHNAME.AIX)  -
    VOLUMES(VS0101)                    -
    RELATE(A2000.LIB.KSDS.CLUSTER)     -
    UPGRADE                            -
    CYLINDERS(2 1)                     -
    KEYS(25 9)                         -
    RECORDSIZE(70 110)                 -
    FREESPACE(20 10)                   -
    SHAREOPTIONS(1)                    -
```

```
    NONUNIQUEKEY                                     -
DATA                                                 -
   (NAME(A2000.LIB.KSDS.AUTHNAME.DATA))     -
INDEX                                                -
   (NAME(A2000.LIB.KSDS.AUTHNAME.INDEX))
```

11.3. STEP 1: DEFINING THE ALTERNATE INDEX

The first step in creating an alternate index is to define it with the DEFINE ALTERNATEINDEX command.

11.3.1. The DEFINE ALTERNATEINDEX Command

This command is analogous to the DEFINE CLUSTER command for the base cluster and informs VSAM that an alternate index is to be created.

Format:	DEFINE ALTERNATEINDEX
Abbreviation:	DEF AIX [commonly used]
Use:	Alternate index over a KSDS, ESDS
Required:	Yes, if an alternate index is defined.
Default:	None
Example:	DEFINE AIX

11.3.2. The NAME Parameter

This required parameter names the alternate index component. It's a good idea to develop a naming convention that conveys some information about the purpose of the alternate index and that, indeed, the named object is an alternate index.

Format:	NAME(*index cluster name*)
Abbreviation:	None
Use:	Alternate index over a KSDS, ESDS
Required:	Yes, if an alternate index is defined.
Default:	None

Example: NAME(A2000.LIB.KSDS.AUTHNAME.AIX)

The previous example uses the fourth-level qualifier to convey that author's last name is the alternate key, and the fifth (or low-level) qualifier to convey that the named object is an alternate index.

11.3.3. The VOLUMES Parameter

This required parameter specifies the volume (or volumes) where the alternate index is to be stored.

Format: VOLUMES(*vol ser*)
                       VOLUMES(*vol ser ... vol ser*)

Abbreviation: VOL [commonly used]

Use: Alternate index over a KSDS, ESDS

Required: Yes, if an alternate index is defined.

Default: None

Example: VOLUMES(VS0101)

Assigning the base cluster and the alternate index to different volumes may be a performance advantage for large datasets, but we have not done so in the previous example. Also, it is possible to assign the alternate index data and index components to different storage volumes, but this is typically not done. Instead, the example assigns storage volume information at the alternate index cluster level. VOLUMES can be part of an implicit or explicit DATACLAS.

11.3.4. The RELATE Parameter

This parameter establishes the relationship between the base cluster and the alternate index via the use of the base cluster name. It is unique to the DEFINE AIX command, and it is required.

Format: RELATE(*base cluster name*)

Abbreviation: REL

Use: Alternate index over a KSDS, ESDS

Required:	Yes, if an alternate index is defined.
Default:	None
Example:	RELATE(A2000.LIB.KSDS.CLUSTER)

If the base cluster name is password-protected, you must specify the password as well as the name.

RELATE(*base cluster name/password*)

11.3.5. The UPGRADE Parameter

UPGRADE specifies that the records in the alternate index are to be updated automatically whenever the records in the base cluster are updated. The use of UPGRADE makes the alternate index part of the cluster's so-called "upgrade set." UPGRADE is the default. Code NOUPGRADE if the records in the base cluster are not to be updated automatically.

Format:	UPGRADE I NOUPGRADE
Abbreviation:	UPG I NUPG
Use:	Alternate index over a KSDS, ESDS
Required:	No, because of default.
Default:	UPGRADE
Example:	UPGRADE
	NOUPGRADE

UPGRADE is the default, but it carries with it a performance penalty, because more I/O is required to update the alternate index as well as the base cluster records.

NOUPGRADE can be coded if your application doesn't require that this alternate index be kept "in synch" with the base cluster. However, it then becomes the programmer's responsibility to see that updates to the alternate index are made in a timely manner; perhaps the alternate index records can be updated in off-peak hours. If you choose NOUPGRADE, the alternate index is not part of the cluster's upgrade set.

If you have multiple alternate indexes built over a single base cluster, it's possible to have some defined with UPGRADE and some with NOUPGRADE. The programmer can choose what is to be done.

UPGRADE is only part of the update picture, however. For more, see the DEFINE PATH command later in this chapter for a description of the UPDATE parameter in the DEFINE PATH command.

11.3.6. Space Allocation

You must allocate space for an alternate index as well as a base cluster. In the preceding example, we've allocated space in units of CYLINDERS, but it can also be in TRACKS, RECORDS, MEGABYTES, or KILOBYTES. Space allocation can be part of an implicit or explicit DATACLAS. For more details on space allocation, refer to that section in Chapter 6.

11.3.7. The KEYS Parameter

The KEYS parameter defines the length and offset of the alternate index key.

Format:	KEYS(*length offset*)
	length is the length of the key in bytes.
	offset is the key's displacement in bytes from the beginning of the record. The first byte is offset 0. KEYS(25 9) specifies a key in bytes 10 through 34.
Abbreviation:	None
Use:	Alternate index over a KSDS, ESDS
Required:	No, because of default, which is the same as the primary key.
Default:	KEYS(64 0)
Example:	KEYS(25 9)

While KEYS can be part of an implicit or explicit DATACLAS definition, this is not the usual case because key position is generally unique to each application.

11.3.8. The RECORDSIZE Parameter

The RECORDSIZE parameter specifies the average and maximum length of each alternate index record.

Format:	RECORDSIZE(*avg max*)
Abbreviation:	RECSZ [commonly used]
Use:	Alternate index over a KSDS, ESDS
Required:	No, because of default.
	But note the size of the default below, which is inappropriate for virtually every application. Accepting the default can result in an alternate index with a large amount of unusable, empty space.
Default:	RECORDSIZE(4086 32600)
Example:	RECORDSIZE(70 110)

If the alternate index is defined with UNIQUEKEY, the record is fixed length and the *avg* and *max* values are the same. On the other hand, if the alternate index is defined with NONUNIQUEKEY, the record is variable length, and the *avg* and *max* values will most likely be different. To see why this is so, we need to look at the structure of an alternate index record. Because the unique (fixed-length) alternate index record is less complex, we'll look at its structure first.

KSDS unique alternate index. Each unique alternate index record built over a KSDS consists of the following:

- Five bytes of VSAM housekeeping information.
- The alternate index key.
- The single primary key pointer that the alternate index key resolves to.

Figure 11.1 illustrates an example of a unique alternate index record with a 9-byte Social Security number as the alternate key and an 8-byte employee number as the primary key, resulting in a 22-byte, fixed-length record.

KSDS non-unique alternate index. A non-unique alternate index key built over a KSDS has a more complex structure. Each non-unique alternate index record built over a KSDS consists of the following:

- Five bytes of VSAM housekeeping information.
- The alternate index key.
- One or more primary key pointers that the alternate index key resolves to.

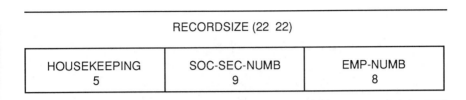

RECORDSIZE (22 22)

HOUSEKEEPING 5	SOC-SEC-NUMB 9	EMP-NUMB 8

Figure 11.1. Example of a unique alternate index record.

Figure 11.2 illustrates an example of a non-unique alternate index key where a 25-character author last name is the alternate key and an 8-character library number is the primary key. For this particular record, AUTH-LAST-NAME points to three different primary index keys.

HOUSEKEEPING 5	AUTH-LAST-NAME 25	LIB-NUM 8	LIB-NUM 8	LIB-NUM 8

Figure 11.2. Example of a non-unique alternate index key.

In Figure 11.3 we've added some values to the non-unique alternate index key. There are three books by author Hemingway in the library KSDS.

To assign average and maximum values for the RECORDSIZE parameter you have to know something about the nature of the application, specifically the average and maximum number of primary keys that the alternate index key can point to—a (average) and m (maximum) respectively in the following calculation.

Let's say that in the library KSDS the average number of titles per author is 5, and the maximum number is 10. (The Hemingway example has only three titles, but that doesn't affect the calculation.) You perform two separate calculations to come up with the values you want to assign to RECORDSIZE here.

HOUSEKEEPING 5	HEMINGWAY 25	FICT0025 8	FICT8724 8	FICT9043 8

Figure 11.3. Non-unique alternate index key with values.

```
1.  Housekeeping + Alternate Key + Primary Key × (a)
         5       +     25       + (8 × 5 = 40)   = 70 avg
2.  Housekeeping + Alternate Key + Primary Key × (m)
         5       +     25       + (8 × 10 = 80)  = 110 max
    Results in: RECORDSIZE(70 110)
```

The alternate index record can contain fewer primary key pointers than the average (consider the Hemingway example), but it cannot contain more than the maximum specified. Thus, if you had a great demand for Hemingway books, you would get an error message when you tried to add the eleventh Hemingway entry. In this case, you could delete the alternate index, redefine it with a larger max RECORDSIZE value, and then rebuild it.

11.3.9. The FREESPACE Parameter

The FREESPACE parameter allocates some percentage of both the control interval and the control area for planned free space. This free space can be used for adding new records.

Format:	FREESPACE(*ci% ca%*)
Abbreviation:	FSPC [commonly used]
Use:	Alternate index over a KSDS, ESDS
Required:	No, because of default.
Default:	FREESPACE(0 0)
Example:	FREESPACE(20 10)

As with the base cluster, FREESPACE for an alternate index applies only to the data component even though you typically code it at the cluster level. It's a good idea to allocate the same FREESPACE values to both the base cluster and the alternate index cluster.

11.3.10. Other DEFINE AIX Parameters

You can also add the following parameters to your DEFINE AIX command if circumstances (and personal preference) warrant. These parameters have been described in previous chapters.

ATTEMPTS(*tries*)

AUTH(*entry point*)

BUFFERSPACE(*bytes*)

CATALOG(*catalog / password*)*

CODE(*code*)

CISZ(*bytes*)

CONTROLPW(*password*)*

ERASE | NOERASE*

EXCEPTIONEDIT(*entry point*)

IMBED | NOIMBED

KEYRANGES(*low key high key*)

KEYS(*length offset*)

MASTERPW(*password*)*

ORDERED | UNORDERED

READPW(*password*)*

REPLICATE | NOREPLICATE

REUSE | NOREUSE*

SHAREOPTIONS

SPEED | RECOVERY

UNIQUEKEY | NONUNIQUEKEY

UPDATEPW(*password*)*

WRITECHECK | NOWRITECHECK*

*Avoid for DFSMS-managed alternate indexes.

You can specify a DATACLAS for any alternate index and an implicit (or explicit) MGMTCLAS and/or STORCLAS to make the alternate index DFSMS managed. See Chapter 9 for more information on these DFSMS constructs.

11.3.11. Building an Alternate Index over an ESDS

The unique and non-unique alternate indexes that we've looked at so far have been built over a KSDS. The following example shows how to define an alternate index over an ESDS. We'll refer to this example as we discuss what's different (not much) and what's the same (almost everything) about an alternate index and an ESDS.

```
//STEP1 EXEC PGM=IDCAMS
//SYSPRINT DD SYSOUT=*
//SYSIN    DD *
 DEFINE AIX                                        -
   (NAME(A2000.LIB.ESDS.TIMESTMP.AIX)             -
    VOLUMES(VS0101)                                -
    RELATE(A2000.LIB.ESDS.CLUSTER)                 -
    UPGRADE                                        -
    CYLINDERS(2 1)                                 -
    KEYS(12 0)                                     -
    RECORDSIZE(21 21)                              -
    FREESPACE(20 10)                               -
    SHAREOPTIONS(1)                                -
    UNIQUEKEY                                      -
   )                                               -
 DATA                                              -
   (NAME(A2000.LIB.ESDS.TIMESTMP.DATA))            -
 INDEX                                             -
   (NAME(A2000.LIB.ESDS.TIMESTMP.INDEX))
```

We'll begin with the main disadvantage to using an alternate index over an ESDS: It is not supported in batch COBOL, either the OS variety or VS COBOL II. However, if your application runs in Assembler or online CICS, an alternate index can provide a fast and efficient means to access ESDS records randomly. You can use IDCAMS commands like PRINT and REPRO to access ESDS records via an alternate index as well.

An ESDS is perfect for any dataset that is built in entry sequence such as a journal file from an IMS or DB2 database. Assume that A2000.LIB.ESDS.CLUSTER is such a journal file and that the alternate index is built over a 12-byte time-stamp, thus enabling your non-COBOL application to access these records randomly.

Note the following items of interest in the previous example:

- Only the self-documenting index cluster, base cluster, data, and index names (all of which use ESDS as a mid-level qualifier) signify that this alternate index is built over an ESDS. The other coding is identical to its KSDS counterpart.
- The RELATE parameter is used to establish the relationship be-

tween the base cluster and the alternate index cluster, just like the alternate index built over a KSDS.

- Since the alternate index is really a KSDS, you can assign the KEYS and FREESPACE parameters. The KEYS default value (64 0) is like that of a base cluster, totally inappropriate, so you should always specify a key here also.
- Like any KSDS, NAME, VOLUMES, and space allocation parameters are required. See Chapter 6 for more information concerning these parameters.
- An alternate index built over an ESDS can be unique (UNIQUEKEY) or non-unique (NONUNIQUEKEY). UNIQUEKEY is the default.
- The example is unique because time-stamps, which consist of date and time data, are by their very nature unique. The RECORDSIZE parameter shows us that this is a fixed-length record. If the alternate index is non-unique, the RECORDSIZE parameter should display average and maximum values instead.
- The RECORDSIZE parameter expresses different values than those of a KSDS, reflecting the RBA of the base cluster rather than its primary key.

The Relative Byte Address revisited. Recall that the Relative Byte Address (RBA) represents the displacement of the record from the beginning of the dataset. Thus, for a 50-byte record, the RBA of the first record is 0, the RBA of the second record is 49, the RBA of the third record is 99, and so on.

In the base cluster record the RBA is just a symbolic address and doesn't occupy any space. However, in the alternate index record it is represented as a four-byte binary field.

ESDS unique alternate index. Each unique alternate index record built over an ESDS consists of the following:

- Five bytes of VSAM housekeeping information.
- The alternate index key.
- The single RBA of the base cluster record that the alternate index key resolves to.

Figure 11.4 illustrates a unique alternate index record where a 12-byte time-stamp is the alternate key and the single RBA that it points to in the base cluster is represented as a 4-byte binary field, resulting in a 21-byte, fixed-length alternate index record, reflected in a RECORDSIZE of (21 21).

RECORDSIZE (21 21)

HOUSEKEEPING 5	TIMESTAMP 12	RBA 4

Figure 11.4. Example of unique alternate index record.

Like its KSDS counterpart, a non-unique alternate index key built over an ESDS has a more complex structure, consisting of the following:

- Five bytes of VSAM housekeeping information.
- The alternate index key.
- One or more RBA pointers that the alternate index key resolves to.

To calculate average and maximum RECORDSIZE values for a non-unique alternate index built over a KSDS, we use the same formula we used for the non-unique alternate index, but we substitute the multiple RBA length of 4 (always) for the primary key length as shown in the following equation.

```
Housekeeping + Alternate Key + RBA × average length
     5                          4
Housekeeping + Alternate Key + RBA × maximum length
     5                          4
```

If your application is written in a language that supports this feature, an AIX built over an ESDS is superior to its KSDS counterpart for two reasons:

1. Because an RBA is always represented as a four-byte binary field, and most primary keys are longer than four bytes, the ESDS alternate index will most certainly occupy less storage space.
2. Access by RBA is faster and more direct than access through the primary key index.

11.4. STEP 2: SPECIFYING THE ALTERNATE INDEX PATH

Once you have defined any alternate indexes, you must define a separate path for each one, using the IDCAMS DEFINE PATH command. This path name is the dataset name that you use in the JCL when processing an alternate index. It is a separate catalog entry and forms a logical connection (path) through the alternate index to the base cluster.

11.4.1. The DEFINE PATH Command

A path is considered a VSAM object even though it doesn't contain any records. The path command has the same format whether the alternate index is built over a KSDS or an ESDS.

Format:	DEFINE PATH -
	(NAME(*path name*) -
	path name: This name becomes the DSN in your execution JCL for any applications that access records via the alternate index. This path name becomes a separate catalog entry.
	PATHENTRY(*entry name / password*) -
	UPDATE	NOUPDATE
	)
Abbreviation:	DEF PATH
Use:	Alternate index over a KSDS, ESDS
Required:	Yes, for an alternate index.
Default:	None
Example:	DEFINE PATH -
	(NAME(A2000.LIB.KSDS.AUTHNAME.PATH) -
	PATHENTRY(A2000.LIB.KSDS.AUTHNAME.AIX) -
	UPDATE)

You must supply the same DSN in your execution JCL as specified with the NAME parameter for any applications that access records via the alternate index.

```
(NAME(A2000.LIB.KSDS.AUTHNAME.PATH)

//JOBA     JOB ...
//STEP1    EXEC PGM=MYAPP
//LIBMAST  DD DSN=A2000.LIB.KSDS.CLUSTER ...
//LIBMAS1  DD DSN=A2000.LIB.KSDS.AUTHNAME.PATH
```

11.4.2. The PATHENTRY Parameter

The PATHENTRY parameter specifies the alternate index cluster name. This establishes the path entry between alternate index cluster and the path.

Format:	PATHENTRY(*entry name/password*)
	entry name: The name assigned to the alternate index cluster.
	password: Optional. Specify the password if required.
Abbreviation:	PENT
Use:	Alternate index over a KSDS, ESDS
Required:	Yes, for an alternate index.
Default:	None
Example:	PATHENTRY(A2000.LIB.KSDS.AUTHNAME.AIX)

PATHENTRY connects the alternate index cluster to the path just as the RELATE parameter of the DEFINE AIX command establishes the relationship between the base cluster and the alternate index cluster.

```
DEFINE AIX                                      -
    (NAME(A2000.LIB.KSDS.AUTHNAME.AIX)          -
        RELATE(A2000.LIB.KSDS.CLUSTER)

DEFINE PATH                                     -
    (NAME(A2000.LIB.KSDS.AUTHNAME.PATH)         -
        PATHENTRY (A2000.LIB.KSDS.AUTHNAME.AIX)

DEFINE CLUSTER                                  -
        (NAME(A2000.LIB.KSDS.CLUSTER)
```

11.4.3. The UPDATE Parameter

The UPDATE parameter specifies whether the base cluster's alternate indexes are to be updated automatically when the path is opened for processing. NOUPDATE specifies that the indexes are not to be automatically updated.

Format:	UPDATE | NOUPDATE
Abbreviation:	UPD | NUPD
Use:	Alternate index over a KSDS, ESDS
Required:	Yes, for an alternate index.
Default:	UPDATE
Example:	UPDATE
	NOUPDATE

UPDATE *vs.* NOUPDATE is similar to the UPGRADE *vs.* NOUPGRADE parameter of the DEFINE AIX command. The UPDATE *vs.* NOUPDATE option of DEFINE PATH works in tandem with the UPGRADE *vs.* NOUPGRADE option of DEFINE AIX. However, there's a subtle but important distinction.

UPGRADE specifies that any changes made in the base cluster records will be reflected immediately in the alternate index records. For this to happen the base cluster itself must be opened in the application program. Assuming UPGRADE has been specified, the statement below opens any alternate indexes for update also.

```
OPEN I-O LIBMAST ...
```

[UPGRADE is the default; NOUPGRADE is the alternative.]

UPDATE specifies that any changes made as a result of opening the *alternate index path alone*, without opening the base cluster, will be reflected in the alternate index records.

```
//LIBMAS1 DD DSN=A2000.LIB.KSDS.AUTHNAME.PATH,DISP=SHR
       . . .
     OPEN I-O LIBMAS1
```

[UPDATE is the default; NOUPDATE is the alternative.]

It's important to note that most alternate index processing is done by opening the base cluster. If UPGRADE has been specified, the alternate index records are kept in synch with the base cluster records. Fortunately, UPGRADE and UPDATE are both the default for their respective commands. However, a situation like the following would delete the base cluster record but not the alternate index record. NOUPDATE is the culprit.

```
1. DEFINE AIX -
      UPGRADE

2. DEFINE PATH -
      NOUPDATE

3. OPEN alternate index ddname
      DELETE ...
```

The following example illustrates the use of the DEFINE PATH command for our sample KSDS. Notice it has just three parameters (all important and all required, or defaulted as in the case of UPDATE).

```
//STEP1 EXEC PGM=IDCAMS
//SYSPRINT DD SYSOUT=*
//SYSIN DD *
 DEFINE PATH                                     -
    (NAME(A2000.LIB.KSDS.AUTHNAME.PATH)          -
     PATHENTRY(A2000.LIB.KSDS.AUTHNAME.AIX)   -
     UPDATE)
```

11.4.4. LISTCAT Listing

You can check the LISTCAT fields ASSOCIATIONS and AT-TRIBUTES to see specific information about your alternate index and path entry.

11.4.5. Other DEFINE PATH Parameters

The following parameters described in previous chapters can also be coded on the DEFINE PATH command.

ATTEMPTS(*tries*)

AUTH(*entry point*)

CATALOG(*catalog* / *password*)*

CODE(*code*)

CONTROLPW(*password*)*

MASTERPW(*password*)*

READPW(*password*)*

UPDATEPW(*password*)*

*Avoid for DFSMS-managed alternate indexes.

11.5.   STEP 3: BUILDING THE INDEX

Earlier in the chapter we said that creating each alternate index is a three-step process. So far, we've defined an alternate index over our sample KSDS and also defined and named a path for it. The third and final step in creating an alternate index is to actually build and populate it with records. For this, you use IDCAMS again, this time with the BLDINDEX command.

11.5.1.   BLDINDEX Considerations

The BLDINDEX command performs the following steps when it is executed:

1. The data component of the base cluster is read sequentially, and pairs of key pointers are extracted. These pairs of key pointers consist of the alternate key field and either its corresponding primary key field (if the base cluster is a KSDS) or RBA (if the base cluster is an ESDS). VSAM creates a temporary work file with records that contain these two key fields. Figure 11.5 shows this.
2. This temporary work file is sorted in ascending alternate key sequence. There is now a one-to-one ratio of alternate key to primary key or RBA, whether or not UNIQUEKEY has been specified. If there's enough virtual storage available, VSAM prefers to do an internal sort, but it will resort to an external sort if you have specified two work files in the execution JCL. We'll show you how to do this.

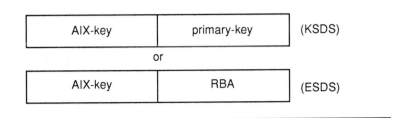

Figure 11.5.   Keys created when building an alternate index.

3. If DEFINE AIX specifies NONUNIQUEKEY, a merge operation takes place at this point. For each non-unique alternate key, a data record is created consisting of the alternate key and each primary key or RBA that the alternate key points to. Figure 11.2 gives an idea of what this record looks like.

   If DEFINE AIX specifies UNIQUEKEY, the data record consists of one alternate key and one primary key or RBA that the alternate key points to.

4. All of the work up to now has been performed on the data component of the alternate index. At this point, VSAM constructs the index component, just as it does for any KSDS. However, unlike a regular KSDS, the index key is not stored in compressed form. And yes, the five bytes of housekeeping information have been added to the data component at this point.

The result is a fully functional, working alternate index.

11.5.2. BLDINDEX JCL

The following JCL example uses BLDINDEX to create and populate the author name alternate index over our sample KSDS.

```
//STEP1    EXEC PGM=IDCAMS
//SYSPRINT DD SYSOUT=*
//DD1      DD DSN=A2000.LIB.KSDS.CLUSTER,DISP=OLD
```

[DD1 names the base cluster as the input dataset. The base cluster is always the input dataset, whether you are building an alternate index over a KSDS or an ESDS. DD1 is our example name, but any valid ddname is acceptable. Even though VSAM datasets usually specify DISP=SHR, when building an alternate index you should assume absolute control of the dataset by specifying DISP=OLD.]

```
//DD2      DD DSN=A2000.LIB.KSDS.AUTHNAME.AIX,DISP=OLD
```

[DD2 names the alternate index cluster as the output dataset. However, the path name is an acceptable substitute. The alternate index cluster name is more efficient because VSAM doesn't need to first resolve the path name to the alternate index cluster name. DISP=OLD is also specified here in order to assume absolute control while the alternate index is being built.]

```
//IDCUT1    DD DSN=A2000.BLDINDEX.WRKFLE1,DISP=OLD,
//          AMP='AMORG',UNIT=3380,VOL=SER=VS0101
//IDCUT2    DD DSN=A2000.BLDINDEX.WRKFLE2,DISP=OLD,
//          AMP='AMORG',UNIT=3380,VOL=SER=VS0101
```

[IDCUT1 and IDCUT2 name two sort work files to be used in case there is not enough virtual storage for VSAM to perform an internal sort (the default and also specified in the INTERNALSORT parameter). By VSAM default, these work files are ESDS, though the JCL doesn't indicate this. IDCUT1 and IDCUT2 are the default ddnames, and you can change them by coding the WORKFILES(*ddname1 ddname2*) parameter (abbreviated WFILE), but it is difficult to conceive why you would do this.]

```
//SYSIN     DD *
  BLDINDEX               -
    INFILE(DD1)          -
    OUTFILE(DD2)         -
    INTERNALSORT
/*
```

Note that the preceding JCL is more complex than that used by most IDCAMS processing because of the optional sort work files, IDCUT1 and IDCUT2, and because both an input dataset (DD1) and an output dataset (DD2) are named.

The minimum coding for the sort work files (IDCUT1 and IDCUT2) is ddname plus AMP, UNIT, and VOL=SER parameters. Even though the sort work files are temporary and are deleted by VSAM upon successful completion of the job, we've taken the precaution of naming them so that we can inspect (and perhaps manually delete) them if the job fails for some reason.

It's a good idea to adopt a naming convention that readily identifies the nature of these datasets, as we have done. Once again, DISP=OLD is required to maintain exclusive control. The AMP parameter designates these datasets as VSAM, and VSAM is smart enough to know that they have an ESDS structure.

Notice that the UNIT specifies 3380, and VOL=SER specifies VS0101, the same volume as the base cluster. However, this can be any high-capacity volume that has a moderate amount of unused VSAM space. Interestingly enough, you don't have to specify the amount of space.

Remember, these datasets will be used only if VSAM can't perform an internal sort for some reason.

11.5.3. The BLDINDEX Command

The BLDINDEX command builds the alternate index.

Format:
```
BLDINDEX                              -
    INFILE(ddname)                    -
    OUTFILE(ddname)                   -
    INTERNALSORT | EXTERNALSORT
```

INFILE and OUTFILE are required parameters that point to DD statements. As an alternative to INFILE and OUTFILE, you can code the INDATASET and OUTDATASET parameters:

```
BLDINDEX                              -
    INDATASET(dataset name)           -
    OUTDATASET(dataset name)          -
    INTERNALSORT | EXTERNALSORT
```

Abbreviation: BIX

Use: Alternate index over a KSDS, ESDS

Required: Yes, for alternate indexes.

Default: None

Example:
```
BLDINDEX                              -
    INFILE(DDA)                       -
    OUTFILE(DDB)                      -
    INTERNALSORT
```

```
BLDINDEX                                            -
    INDATASET(A2000.LIB.KSDS.CLUSTER)               -
    OUTDATASET(A2000.LIB.KSDS.AUTHNAME.AIX)         -
    INTERNALSORT
```

11.5.4. The INFILE/INDATASET Parameters

The INFILE parameter specifies a DD statement that refers to the input dataset. The INDATASET parameter names the dataset and saves having to code a DD statement.

Format: INFILE(ddname) | INDATASET(dataset name)

Abbreviation: IFILE | IDS

Use:	KSDS, ESDS
Required:	Yes, you must code one or the other.
Default:	None
Example:	INFILE(DD1)
	INDATASET(A2000.LIB.KSDS.CLUSTER)

11.5.5.   The OUTFILE/OUTDATASET Parameters

The OUTFILE parameter specifies a DD statement that refers to the output dataset. The OUTDATASET parameter names the dataset and saves having to code a DD statement.

Format:	OUTFILE(*ddname*) | OUTDATASET(*dataset name*)
Abbreviation:	OFILE | ODS
Use:	KSDS, ESDS
Required:	Yes, you must code one or the other.
Default:	None
Example:	OUTFILE(DD2)
	OUTDATASET(A2000.LIB.KSDS.AUTHNAME.AIX)

INDATASET and OUTDATASET dynamically allocate the input and output datasets and ensure that the job obtains exclusive control. You can omit the input and output DD statements in the JCL. The following example shows the same BLDINDEX command using INDATASET and OUTDATASET in place of INFILE and OUTFILE.

```
//STEP1    EXEC PGM=IDCAMS
//SYSPRINT DD SYSOUT=*
//IDCUT1   DD DSN=A2000.BLDINDEX.WRKFLE1,DISP=OLD,
//         AMP='AMORG',UNIT=3390,VOL=SER=VSO101
//IDCUT2   DD DSN=A2000.BLDINDEX.WRKFLE2,DISP=OLD,
//         AMP='AMORG',UNIT=3390,VOL=SER=VSO101
//SYSIN    DD *
 BLDINDEX                                     -
   INDATASET(A2000.LIB.KSDS.CLUSTER)          -
   OUTDATASET(A2000.LIB.KSDS.AUTHNAME.AIX)    -
   INTERNALSORT
/*
```

You can mix and match INFILE/OUTFILE and INDATASET/ OUTDATASET. For example, the following is valid:

```
//DD1     DD DSN=A2000.LIB.KSDS.CLUSTER,DISP=OLD
//SYSIN   DD *
 BLDINDEX                                          -
    INFILE(DD1)                                    -
    OUTDATASET(A2000.LIB.KSDS.AUTHNAME.AIX)  -
    INTERNALSORT
/*
```

Generally, it's the programmer's call to use the combination of these parameters that seems right for the application and the operating environment (unless installation standards dictate otherwise). INFILE and OUTFILE have some advantage from an operations point of view because the dataset names are readily visible in the JCL. However, be aware that because these parameters act like a referback to the JCL, they may cause your job to fail in certain circumstances—for example, if doing a DELETE, DEFINE, and BLDINDEX in the same step. At step initiation time, the volume assignments are dynamically allocated, and if the AIX is deleted and reallocated on a different volume, the allocation (and the job step) will fail.

INFILE/OUTFILE and INDATASET/OUTDATASET are used with other IDCAMS commands like REPRO and PRINT, as you'll see in the next chapter.

11.5.6. The INTERNALSORT or EXTERNALSORT Parameters

These parameters direct VSAM to perform an internal sort (INTERNALSORT, which uses virtual storage) or an external sort (EXTERNALSORT, which uses disk space) during step 2 of building an index. INTERNALSORT is the default and need not be coded, except as documentation.

Format:	INTERNALSORT ⏐ EXTERNALSORT
Abbreviation:	ISORT ⏐ ESORT
Use:	Alternate index over a KSDS, ESDS
Required:	No
Default:	INTERNALSORT
Example:	INTERNALSORT
	EXTERNALSORT

If sufficient virtual storage is not available (not generally the problem in today's XA and ESA operating environments), VSAM will perform an external sort, but only if you have included the IDCUT1 and IDCUT2 DD statements in the JCL for work files.

INTERNALSORT is faster and more efficient, but if you need an external sort performed for some reason (perhaps chronic lack of virtual storage), you should:

- Include the IDCUT1 and IDCUT2 DD statements in your JCL.
- Specify EXTERNALSORT in the BLDINDEX command.

12

Loading Data/Protecting Data and Datasets

This chapter examines the commands used by application programmers and support people to load empty VSAM clusters with data, and to back up and restore existing datasets. We'll also see how to protect the integrity of both data and datasets. We'll begin with a versatile command called REPRO.

12.1. THE REPRO COMMAND

REPRO is an all-purpose load and backup utility command. It is VSAM's version of the old IBM war horse, IEBGENER. Because REPRO can operate on non-VSAM datasets, it can be used in place of IEBGENER.

12.1.1. REPRO Considerations

REPRO performs three basic functions:

1. It loads an empty VSAM cluster with records. The data and index components (for a KSDS) are built automatically.
2. It creates a backup of a VSAM dataset on a physical sequential dataset, and then restores and rebuilds the VSAM dataset using this dataset as input.
3. It merges data from two VSAM datasets.

REPRO has two distinct advantages over IEBGENER: It is extremely easy to use, and you can use it with any type of VSAM dataset, even an LDS.

You can convert an ISAM dataset to VSAM format (but not vice versa) and, as an alternative to IEBGENER, copy a non-VSAM dataset to a physical sequential or partitioned dataset. You can even copy records from one type of VSAM dataset to another type of previously defined, empty VSAM dataset; for example, KSDS to ESDS. Our focus will be on loading, backing up, restoring, and merging VSAM datasets.

Of course, REPRO has a few disadvantages. You have little control over the input data, catalog information is not copied with the data, and a prior DELETE is required before cluster redefinition unless you have specified the REUSE parameter. Keep in mind though that REUSE is not valid for a base cluster that supports an alternate index.

12.1.2. Loading a KSDS

Immediately after defining the base cluster (before defining and building any alternate indexes) you should load the empty cluster with the data records. You can approach this in one of two ways:

1. By writing an application program to load the data. For example, you might want to do this if you needed to edit the input data. (Refer to Chapter 15, if you're interested in this approach.)
2. Perform any editing in a prior step and then use REPRO to load the data. This is the most common approach.

However, if you use REPRO and your output dataset is a KSDS, you must first sort the input data in ascending sequence by the field that will become the primary key in the output dataset.

12.1.3. REPRO JCL

The following example shows a two-step procedure that first sorts the input records and then loads them using REPRO. SORTSTEP performs an external sort and writes a temporary dataset (&&SRTWRK in the example) as the output dataset. You can also catalog the dataset if you wanted to retain it—say, to use in another job.

```
//LOADJOB  JOB ...
//SORTSTEP EXEC PGM=SORT
//SORTLIB  DD DSN=SYS1.SORTLIB,DISP=SHR
//SORTIN   DD DSN=A2000.INPUT.DATA,DISP=OLD
//SORTOUT  DD DSN=&&SRTWRK,DISP=(NEW,PASS,DELETE),
```

```
//              SPACE=(CYL(10,1)),UNIT=SYSDA,
//              DCB=(RECFM=FB,LRECL=80)
//SYSIN    DD *
  SORT FIELDS=(1,8,CH,A)
//LOADSTEP EXEC PGM=IDCAMS
//SYSPRINT DD SYSOUT=*
//DD1      DD DSN=&&SRTWRK,DISP=(OLD,DELETE,DELETE)
```

[DD1 names the input dataset for LOADSTEP, &&SRTWRK, here. In this case, we have specified that the dataset is to be deleted at the end of the job, whether or not the job runs to completion.]

```
//DD2      DD DSN=A2000.LIB.KSDS.CLUSTER,DISP=OLD
```

[DD2 names the base cluster. Notice we have specified DISP=OLD in order retain exclusive control during LOADSTEP.]

```
//SYSIN    DD *
  REPRO                    -
    INFILE(DD1)            -
    OUTFILE(DD2)
/*
```

Notice that SORT FIELDS specifies a sort field starting in position one for eight characters, the length and position of the potential primary key. The remaining subparameters specify character data (CH) and ascending sequence (A). See reference 1 for a complete description of the IBM DFSORT utility.

```
SORT FIELDS=(1,8,CH,A)
```

Contrast this with the KEYS parameter of our sample DEFINE CLUSTER command which specifies the primary key as starting in offset zero for eight characters.

```
KEYS(8 0)
```

Remember that a SORT FIELDS command specifies the absolute byte position of the field (1 to n). This is in contrast to specifying the VSAM record key in which the relative byte position is used (0 to n-1). If you code SORT FIELDS incorrectly, your input records will be out of sequence. Also note that for variable-length records, including VSAM records, you must allow for the four bytes at the beginning of the record that contain the record descriptor word.

The input to LOADSTEP must be in ascending collating sequence by the primary key. VSAM issues an error message for the first few out-of-sequence records encountered (or other logic error) and then it abends the IDCAMS program.

Remember also that duplicate primary keys are not allowed. If necessary, you'll need to edit the input data and physically delete any records where the potential primary key field has duplicate values.

12.1.4.   REPRO Command Syntax

REPRO is coded as follows:

Format:
```
REPRO                                            -
    INFILE(ddname) | INDATASET(dsname)   -
    OUTFILE(ddname)|OUTDATASET(dsname)  -
    optional parameters
```

Abbreviation: None

Use: KSDS, ESDS, RRDS

Required: Yes

Default: None

Example:
```
REPRO               -
    INFILE(DD1)    -
    OUTFILE(DD2)
```

INFILE and OUTFILE are required parameters that point to DD1 and DD2 respectively. As an alternative to INFILE and OUTFILE, you can use the INDATASET and OUTDATASET parameters described in Chapter 11 to dynamically allocate the input and output datasets, but only if the referenced dataset is cataloged. The following is valid:

```
OUTDATASET(A2000.LIB.KSDS.CLUSTER)
```

The following is invalid because &&SRTWRK is not a cataloged dataset:

```
INDATASET(&&SRTWRK)
```

The next example uses REPRO with a combination of INFILE and OUTDATASET. This technique is commonly used for so-called "utility" commands like REPRO and PRINT, covered in the next chapter.

```
//LOADSTEP EXEC PGM=IDCAMS
//SYSPRINT DD SYSOUT=*
//DD1      DD DSN=&&SRTWRK,DISP=(OLD,DELETE,DELETE)
//SYSIN    DD *
 REPRO                              -
   INFILE(DD1)                      -
   OUTDATASET(A2000.LIB.KSDS.CLUSTER)
```

12.1.5.   Loading an ESDS

The next example shows how to use the REPRO command to load an ESDS. Because the records are loaded in entry sequence, the preliminary sort step can be eliminated if your application doesn't require a specific sequence. Except for the input and output dataset names, the coding is the same as for a KSDS.

```
//LOADJOB JOB ...
//LOADSTEP EXEC PGM=IDCAMS
//SYSPRINT DD SYSOUT=*
//DD1      DD DSN=A2000.INPUT.ESDS.DATA,DISP=OLD
//DD2      DD DSN=A2000.MY.ESDS.CLUSTER,DISP=OLD
//SYSIN    DD *
 REPRO              -
   INFILE(DD1)      -
   OUTFILE(DD2)
```

12.1.6.   Loading an RRDS

The following example shows how to use the REPRO command to load an RRDS. The records are loaded in relative record sequence starting with "1," and if there is a field in the dataset that correlates to the relative record number, the input should be sorted on this field first. Except for the input and output dataset names, the coding here is the same as a KSDS.

```
//LOADJOB JOB ...
//LOADSTEP EXEC PGM=IDCAMS
//SYSPRINT DD SYSOUT=*
//DD1      DD DSN=A2000.INPUT.RRDS.DATA,DISP=OLD
//DD2      DD DSN=A2000.MY.RRDS.CLUSTER,DISP=OLD
//SYSIN    DD *
```

```
REPRO                    -
  INFILE(DD1)            -
  OUTFILE(DD2)
```

12.1.7.   Limiting Input and Output Records

While you can't edit the input to REPRO, you can effectively limit it by applying one or more optional parameters to the input dataset. For example, you can count (or skip) a number of records, or specify a range of keys or addresses to be loaded. In the application testing phase, you can use these parameters to easily build a test dataset that contains a representative sampling of your data.

Four mutually exclusive parameters are provided to specify the first input record to copy with the REPRO command: FROMKEY, FROMADDRESS, FROMNUMBER, and SKIP. There are also four corresponding parameters provided to specify the last record to copy: TOKEY, TOADDRESS, TONUMBER, and COUNT. These four parameters are also mutually exclusive. Only SKIP and COUNT can be used with non-VSAM sequential datasets.

The FROMKEY and TOKEY parameters. FROMKEY specifies the key of the input record at which to begin reading. TOKEY specifies the key of the last input record to write. You can code either or both parameters.

Format:	FROMKEY(*key*)
	TOKEY(*key*)
	key: 1 to 255 EBCDIC characters. You can specify generic keys by coding an asterisk (*) as the last character. Copying starts or stops if a record is encountered that matches all the characters up to the *.
Abbreviation:	FKEY, TKEY
Use:	KSDS, ISAM (non-VSAM)
Required:	No
Default:	First record in dataset for FROMKEY and last record in dataset for TOKEY.

Example: FROMKEY(HEMINGWAY)

                           TOKEY(HEM*)

The following example uses the sample library KSDS to load records with keyranges FICT0025 through FICT9043 to a new KSDS. Remember, the input dataset is sequenced logically (but not necessarily physically, depending on split activity) by the primary key.

```
//DD1      DD DSN=A2000.LIB.KSDS.CLUSTER,DISP=OLD
//DD2      DD DSN=A2000.MYNEW.KSDS.CLUSTER,DISP=OLD
//SYSIN    DD *
  REPRO                  -
   INFILE(DD1)           -
   OUTFILE(DD2)          -
     FROMKEY(FICT0025)   -
     TOKEY(FICT9043)
```

If VSAM doesn't find an exact match for the FROMKEY value, it starts loading records at the next higher value. On the other hand, if VSAM doesn't find an exact match for the TOKEY value, it stops loading records at the previous lower value. Thus, given the range of records shown below, VSAM would load key values FICT0026 through FICT0042. (If TOKEY is not specified, VSAM loads the entire remaining dataset, starting with the FROMKEY value.)

```
FICT0024
FICT0026
FICT0027
  . . .
FICT0041
FICT0042
FICT0044
```

You can specify FROMKEY or TOKEY with an asterisk used as a wild card character to load records based on a generic key value. The next example loads records with the string 'FICT' in the first four bytes of the primary key.

```
//DD1      DD DSN=A2000.LIB.KSDS.CLUSTER, DISP=OLD
//DD2      DD DSN=A2000.MYNEW.KSDS.CLUSTER,DISP=OLD
//SYSIN    DD *
```

```
REPRO                     -
  INFILE(DD1)             -
    FROMKEY(FICT*)        -
  OUTFILE(DD2)
```

The FROMADDRESS and TOADDRESS parameters. FROM-
ADDRESS specifies the relative byte address (RBA) value of the key of the
input record at which to begin copying. You can also use FROMADDRESS
to copy KSDS records in physical sequential order, but this is rarely
done. TOADDRESS specifies the relative byte address (RBA) value of
the key of the last input record to copy. You can code either or both
parameters.

Format:	FROMADDRESS(*address*)
	TOADDRESS(*address*)
	address: The RBA address of the first or last record to copy.
Abbreviation:	FADDR, TADDR
Use:	KSDS, ESDS
Required:	No
Default:	First record in dataset for FROMADDRESS and last record in dataset for TOADDRESS.
Example:	FROMADDRESS(6250)
	TOADDRESS(12684)

The output of the PRINT command will tell you the RBA value of
individual records.

```
REPRO                     -
  INFILE(DD1)             -
  OUTFILE(DD2)            -
    FADDR(4124)           -
    TADDR(6250)
```

The FROMNUMBER and TONUMBER parameters. FROM-
NUMBER specifies the relative record number of the first RRDS record

to copy. TONUMBER specifies the relative record number of the last record to copy. You can code either or both parameters.

Format:	FROMNUMBER(*relative number*)
	TONUMBER(*relative number*)
	relative number: The relative record number of the first or last record to copy. The first record is number 0.
Abbreviation:	FNUM, TNUM
Use:	RRDS
Required:	No
Default:	First record in dataset for FROMNUMBER and the last record in the dataset for TONUMBER.
Example:	FROMNUMBER(10)
	TONUMBER(1000)

FROMNUMBER and TONUMBER can also specify ranges of LDS data to copy. Remember, LDSs are not stored in records but in data streams of 4K pages. The output of the PRINT command will tell you the relative record number (RRN) value of individual records.

```
//DD1     DD DSN=A2000.MY.RRDS.CLUSTER,DISP=OLD
//DD2     DD DSN=A2000.MYNEW.RRDS.CLUSTER,DISP=OLD
//SYSIN   DD *
 REPRO                 -
   INFILE (DD1)        -
   OUTFILE(DD2)        -
     FNUM(7)           -
     TNUM(201)
```

The SKIP and COUNT parameters. SKIP specifies the number of input records to skip before beginning to copy. COUNT specifies the number of output records to copy. You can code either or both parameters.

Format:	SKIP(*number*)
	COUNT(*number*)

	number: The number of records to skip or copy.
Abbreviation:	None
Use:	KSDS, ESDS, RRDS, non-VSAM datasets
Required:	No
Default:	SKIP defaults to the first record in dataset, and COUNT defaults to all the records in the dataset.
Example:	SKIP(40)
	COUNT(500)

COUNT and SKIP can be used alone or together to limit the number of records loaded. The following example skips the first 100 records and begins copying at 101. It copies 500 records.

```
REPRO               -
  INFILE(DD1)       -
  OUTFILE(DD2)      -
    SKIP(100)       -
    COUNT(500)
```

12.1.8. Backup Considerations

Here are five good reasons for backing up VSAM datasets on a regular basis. You can probably find many more.

1. To provide security for the dataset.
2. To enable the dataset to be restored from the backup copy, if system failure causes online data to be lost.
3. In order to rebuild the catalog, if it becomes unusable for any reason.
4. In case you want to transport the data to another system or another site.
5. In order to rebuild and restore the VSAM cluster from the backup copy. This is where REPRO shines. More on this later.

Backing up a VSAM dataset to a physical sequential dataset (like magnetic tape) only requires one step. The next example shows a typical backup step for a KSDS, but the coding would be the same for another type of VSAM dataset, even though some of the JCL subparameter values might be different.

```
//LOADJOB   JOB ...
//LOADSTEP  EXEC PGM=IDCAMS
//SYSPRINT  DD SYSOUT=*
//DD2       DD DSN=A2000.LIB.KSDS.BACKUP(+1),
//             DISP=(NEW,CATLG,DELETE),UNIT=TAPE,
//             VOL=SER=954789,LABEL=(1,SL),
//             DCB=(RECFM=FB,LRECL=80)
//SYSIN     DD *
  REPRO                                  -
    INDATASET(A2000.LIB.KSDS.CLUSTER) -
    OUTFILE(DD2)
```

As you can see, the backup step is straightforward and uses garden-variety JCL statements for tape backup. We need to point out only the following:

- We have specified INDATASET to dynamically allocate the input KSDS and assure exclusive control of the dataset while it is being backed up. Of course, you could also substitute the following for the input dataset:

```
//DD1     DD DSN=A2000.LIB.KSDS.CLUSTER,DISP=OLD
   :
  REPRO          -
    INFILE(DD1)  -
    . . .
```

- The output tape dataset is part of a generation data group (GDG) (specified by +1). It's a good idea to build a GDG and keep multiple generations of backup in case you need data that goes back further than the current version.
- Catalog information is not copied with the dataset. For this, you need to use the EXPORT command, covered later in this chapter.

Backing up a VSAM dataset involves only one step; restoring and rebuilding it from the backup copy involves one step with three parts (unless you specify the REUSE option, which we'll discuss in a bit).

1. Delete the original cluster using the IDCAMS DELETE command. (We haven't discussed DELETE yet, but its format is simple.)
2. Redefine the cluster using the IDCAMS DEFINE CLUSTER command. You now have an empty cluster with the HURBA (High Used Relative Byte Address) set to zero. *Note:* If your VSAM dataset is

DFSMS managed, you can use JCL statements to accomplish steps one and two with an application program.
3. Load the empty cluster with data using the IDCAMS REPRO command.

The following example shows you the entire three-part job described previously.

```
//REPOJOB   JOB ...
//STEP1     EXEC PGM=IDCAMS
//SYSPRINT  DD SYSOUT=*
//DD1       DD DSN=A2000.LIB.KSDS.BACKUP(+0),
//             DISP=OLD,UNIT=TAPE,LABEL=(1,SL)
//SYSIN     DD *
 DELETE A2000.LIB.KSDS.CLUSTER
 /***************************************************/
 DEFINE CLUSTER                                    -
    (NAME(A2000.LIB.KSDS.CLUSTER)                  -
     CYLINDERS(5 1)                                -
     VOLUMES(VSO101)                               -
     RECORDSIZE(80 80)                             -
     KEYS(8 0)                                     -
     SHAREOPTIONS(1)                               -
     INDEXED                                       -
     )                                             -
     DATA                                          -
     NAME(A2000.LIB.KSDS.DATA)                     -
     CISZ(4096)                                    -
     FREESPACE(20 10)                              -
     )                                             -
     INDEX                                         -
     (NAME(A2000.LIB.KSDS.INDEX)                   -
     )
 /***************************************************/
 REPRO                                             -
    INFILE(DD1)                                    -
    OUTDATASET(A2000.LIB.KSDS.CLUSTER)
```

Using one EXEC statement, IDCAMS does the following:

- Uses a simple DELETE command to delete the KSDS. The previous KSDS cluster definition doesn't exist at this point. DELETE has a domino effect, so any alternate indexes are deleted also. (Be careful!)

- Redefines the basic cluster. Notice we've used the same basic parameters discussed in previous chapters. The cluster is empty at this point and the HURBA is set to zero.
- Uses the previously created backup to load the empty cluster with records.

When you delete, redefine, restore, and rebuild a VSAM dataset using a procedure like the one shown in the previous example, it has the following effects for a KSDS (all good):

1. Control interval and control area splits are eliminated and records are reordered logically and physically by primary key. Access time is improved for both random and sequential access.
2. Free space is redistributed throughout the dataset according to the original specifications of your FREESPACE parameter. In fact, if you reorganize often, you don't have to allow as much free space because it is used so much more efficiently.
3. The primary index is rebuilt. However, you'll have to define any associated alternate indexes separately.

Of course, there's a downside to frequent reorganization. IDCAMS may fail for some reason, and this will require manual intervention by support personnel. In the meantime, the KSDS is not available for online or batch processing. For this reason, you may want to limit reorganizations to off-peak hours.

An ESDS or RRDS doesn't need to be reorganized because the record position is fixed permanently by sequence of entry or record number relative to the beginning of the dataset. However, from a security and operational standpoint, it's a good idea to back up these datasets as application needs dictate. If the dataset becomes damaged, you can use REPRO to restore it from the backup copy.

12.1.9.   The REUSE Parameter with REPRO

If the VSAM cluster (KSDS, ESDS, or RRDS) has been originally defined with the REUSE parameter, you can specify REUSE (again) with the REPRO command when restoring it.

```
DEFINE CL            -        REPRO             -
   other parameters  -           INFILE(DD1)    -
   REUSE             -           OUTFILE(DD2)   -
                                 REUSE
```

REUSE sets the HURBA to zero whenever the dataset is opened for OUTPUT by an application program, or if REPRO is executed. This has the effect of logically deleting the existing records in the cluster. For the KSDS example shown in the previous example, the DELETE and DEFINE CLUSTER commands could be eliminated. When REUSE is specified (NOREUSE is the default), the cluster is said to be "reusable."

A reusable cluster is good to use for a test KSDS, because you don't have to go through all the hassle of repeatedly deleting and redefining the cluster. However, there are a few caveats concerning the use of REUSE:

- A reusable KSDS does not support an alternate index.
- You cannot use the ALTER command to change reusability.
- You cannot specify keyranges for a reusable KSDS.

12.1.10. The REPLACE Parameter for Merge Operations with REPRO

Besides loading, and backup and restore operations, you can also use the REPRO command to merge two datasets into one. The target (output) dataset can be a nonempty KSDS, ESDS, or RRDS. KSDS to KSDS is probably the most common application of this merge technique. The source (input) dataset can be any organization if the target dataset is a KSDS or ESDS. If the target dataset is an RRDS, the source dataset must also be an RRDS.

You specify the REPLACE option as part of the REPRO command to replace records with duplicate primary keys (in the case of a KSDS) or duplicate relative record numbers (in the case of an RRDS).

Format:	REPLACE
Abbreviation:	REP
Use:	KSDS, ESDS, RRDS
Required:	No
Default:	Matching records are not replaced.
Example:	REPLACE -
	COUNT(500)

If the target dataset is an ESDS, the merged records (duplicate or not) are added to the end of the existing dataset. REPLACE is not appropriate in this case. The next example does a KSDS-to-KSDS merge. It is really just a copy, because the source dataset is left intact.

```
//DD1     DD DSN=A2000.LIB.KSDS.CLUSTER,DISP=OLD
//DD2     DD DSN=A2000.MYNEW.KSDS.CLUSTER,DISP=OLD
//SYSIN   DD *
 REPRO                 -
   INFILE(DD1)         -
   OUTFILE(DD2)        -
   REPLACE
```

12.2. THE EXPORT/IMPORT COMMANDS

The EXPORT/IMPORT commands can be used for backup and recovery, as well as exporting a dataset, an alternate index, or a catalog to a different (but compatible) system.

12.2.1. EXPORT/IMPORT Considerations

As an alternative to REPRO, the EXPORT/IMPORT duo has several significant advantages:

- Catalog information is exported along with the data.
- DFSMS classes are preserved during the export/import process.
- Cluster deletion and redefinition are not necessary during the import step because the input dataset already contains catalog information.
- Also, because the dataset contains catalog information, it can be more easily ported to other systems. We say that an exported dataset has "cross-system portability" if the source and target systems have compatible releases of MVS/DFP.

As with REPRO, key-sequenced datasets are reorganized, and you can change certain (but by no means all) dataset attributes during the IMPORT step.

Of course, there's a downside to all of this. EXPORT and IMPORT can only be used for VSAM datasets, and the dataset created by the EXPORT command can only have a sequential organization. In addition, the dataset created by the EXPORT step is not processable until it has gone through a corresponding IMPORT step. As you may suspect,

there is generally more overhead involved in running EXPORT/IM-
PORT than in REPRO. For example, it is slower than REPRO.

Still, the advantages for VSAM datasets used by online systems are
obvious: The dataset is more readily available to users because cluster
delete and redefinition are eliminated, and there is less chance that the
dataset will be "clobbered" during restoration because three steps (for
REPRO) are reduced to one (for IMPORT).

12.2.2. The EXPORT Command

The EXPORT command exports a VSAM dataset.

Format:	EXPORT *entry name / password* -
	entry name / password: The name of the cluster or alternate index to be exported.
	The *password* is coded only if needed.
	OUTFILE(*ddname*) I OUTDATASET(*dsname*) -
	optional parameters
Abbreviation:	EXP
Use:	KSDS, ESDS, RRDS
Required:	Yes
Default:	None
Example:	EXPORT A2000.LIB.KSDS.CLUSTER -
	OUTFILE(DD2)

The following example shows the coding needed to use the EXPORT
command to back up the KSDS to tape.

```
//EXPOJOB  JOB ...
//STEP1    EXEC PGM=IDCAMS
//SYSPRINT DD SYSOUT=*
//DD2      DD DSN=A2000.LIB.KSDS.BACKUP(+1),
//            DISP=(NEW,CATLG,DELETE),UNIT=TAPE,
//            VOL=SER=954789,LABEL=(1,SL),
//            DCB=(RECFM=FB,LRECL=80)
//SYSIN    DD *
```

```
EXPORT A2000.LIB.KSDS.CLUSTER
   OUTFILE(DD2)
```

There's nothing remarkable about the JCL for EXPORT, so let's turn our attention to the command itself, which has several unusual parameters. First notice that EXPORT refers directly to the KSDS cluster name. OUTFILE points to DD2, which is a tape dataset. Remember, the output (target) dataset from an EXPORT command must always be a sequential dataset.

The ERASE parameter. The ERASE parameter causes the exported item to be overwritten with zeros when it is deleted. NOERASE causes the item to not be overwritten. ERASE I NOERASE override whatever was specified for the item when it was created.

Format:	ERASE I NOERASE
Abbreviation:	ERAS I NERAS
Use:	KSDS, ESDS, RRDS
Required:	No, because of default. (Not valid for DFSMS-managed datasets.)
Default:	Whatever was specified when the item was created.
Example:	ERASE NOERASE

The INHIBITSOURCE parameter. INHIBITSOURCE specifies that the source dataset can be accessed in read-only mode. Use this parameter to keep the records in your source dataset in synch with the exported copy. This is a clear advantage over REPRO, which offers no such facility. NOINHIBITSOURCE (the default) allows the source dataset to be updated after the EXPORT operation is complete.

Format:	INHIBITSOURCE I NOINHIBITSOURCE
Abbreviation:	INHS I NINHS
Use:	KSDS, ESDS, RRDS
Required:	No, because of default.

Default:	NOINHIBITSOURCE
Example:	INHIBITSOURCE
	NOINHIBITSOURCE

You can use the ALTER command to change INHIBITSOURCE to NOINHIBITSOURCE, and vice versa, if circumstances change.

The INHIBITTARGET parameter. INHIBITTARGET specifies that the target dataset can be accessed in read-only mode after the corresponding IMPORT operation is complete. You may want to do this if you're importing a dataset to another system for the purpose of querying only, with no updates intended. NOINHIBITTARGET is the default and specifies that the target dataset will be fully updatable after the IMPORT operation.

Format:	INHIBITTARGET I NOINHIBITTARGET
Abbreviation:	INHT I NINHT
Use:	KSDS, ESDS, RRDS
Required:	No, because of default.
Default:	NOINHIBITTARGET
Example:	INHIBITTARGET
	NOINHIBITTARGET

Once again, you can use the ALTER command to change this parameter.

The TEMPORARY parameter. The TEMPORARY parameter directs VSAM to retain the source dataset after the EXPORT operation completes. PERMANENT (the default) directs VSAM to delete the source dataset after the EXPORT operation completes. (It's kind of crazy, but that's just the way it is.)

Format:	TEMPORARY I PERMANENT
Abbreviation:	TEMP I PERM
Use:	KSDS, ESDS, RRDS
Required:	No, because of default.
Default:	PERMANENT

Example: TEMPORARY

                    PERMANENT

When using this and other EXPORT parameters, you need to think carefully about your objectives for the source and target datasets. For example, you may do the following:

1. Back up the source for security only, with no IMPORT intended for the target dataset unless the source dataset is corrupted.
2. Back up the source in order to reorganize and rebuild the dataset using the target dataset as input to the IMPORT command. In this case, the source dataset is actually deleted and replaced by the target dataset.
3. Back up the source in order to import the target dataset on another system, in which case you may (or may not) want to delete the source after the IMPORT operation has completed successfully.

Whatever the objectives, it's a good idea to document them as well as the function of these parameters, because their unusual syntax can easily cause confusion among your support people.

Another parameter that you may want to apply to an ESDS or an LDS is CIMODE, which allows you to process the target dataset (after importing it, of course) in control interval rather than in record mode, a clear processing advantage for the ESDS and a must for the LDS. RECORDMODE is the default for KSDS, ESDS, and RRDS, while CIMODE is the default for LDS. However, in the case of the LDS, you may want to explicitly code CIMODE in order to provide documentation.

```
//SYSIN    DD *
 EXPORT dataset name            -
   OUTFILE(ddname)              -
   CIMODE
```

12.2.3.   The IMPORT Command

IMPORT is used to load in a dataset created by the EXPORT command.

```
Format:          IMPORT                                -
                   INFILE (ddname)|INDATASET(dsname)   -
                   OUTFILE(ddname)|OUTDATASET(dsname)  -
                 optional parameters
```

Abbreviation:	IMP
Use:	KSDS, ESDS, RRDS
Required:	Yes
Default:	None
Example:	IMPORT A2000.LIB.KSDS.CLUSTER -
	INFILE(DD1) -
	OUTFILE(DD2)

The previous example showed the coding necessary to EXPORT the sample KSDS in order to reorganize and rebuild it. The next example shows the corresponding IMPORT command needed in order to complete the procedure. As you can see, it has a very simple structure.

```
//IMPOJOB  JOB ...
//STEP1    EXEC PGM=IDCAMS
//SYSPRINT DD SYSOUT=*
//DD1      DD DSN=A2000.LIB.KSDS.BACKUP(+0),
//           DISP=OLD,UNIT=TAPE,VOL=SER=954789
```

[INFILE points to DD1, the sequential tape dataset created by the previous EXPORT example. It is not really necessary to specify DCB information for the source dataset, but if you do, it must be the same as that specified on the target dataset for the EXPORT command, because the former target is now the source. (Got that?)]

```
//SYSIN    DD *
 IMPORT                                  -
   INFILE(DD1)                           -
   OUTDATASET(A2000.LIB.KSDS.CLUSTER)
```

[OUTDATASET dynamically allocates the new target dataset.]

IMPORT deletes the old dataset and defines a whole new one using the sequential dataset created by EXPORT, even though this is transparent to the programmer.

The INTOEMPTY parameter. INTOEMPTY allows you to import a previously exported dataset into an empty, previously defined cluster. In fact, this parameter is required if the cluster is devoid of records.

Format: INTOEMPTY

Abbreviation: IEMPTY

Use: KSDS, ESDS, RRDS

Required: Yes, if output dataset is empty.

Default: Nonempty dataset

Example: INTOEMPTY

The OBJECTS parameter. OBJECTS allows you to change some of the attributes of the new target dataset, including STORCLAS, MGMTCLAS, VOLUMES, and KEYRANGES.

Format: OBJECTS(*entry name*)

[Names the cluster, alternate index, or path that is to be changed.]

KEYRANGES(*low key high key*)

[Specifies the range of keys to place on the different VOLUMES as described in Chapter 7.]

NEWNAME(*new dataset name*)

[Renames the item.]

ORDERED|UNORDERED

[Associates the keys with the VOLUMES as described in Chapter 7.]

VOLUMES(*vol ser ... vol ser*)

[Specifies the VOLUMES on which to import the dataset.]

Abbreviation: OBJ

Use: KSDS, ESDS, RRDS

Required: No

Default: Same attributes as exported dataset.

Example: OBJECTS(A2000.LIB.KSDS.CLUSTER)
                   NEWNAME(A2000.YOUR.KSDS.CLUSTER)

Other IMPORT parameters. You can also code the CATALOG and ERASE | NOERASE parameters for the imported dataset, but not if it's managed by DFSMS.

12.3. DFHSM AND DFDSS FOR BACKUP AND RESTORE

If your installation uses Data Facility Product (DFP), you can take advantage of the dump and restore functions of two of its components, Data Facility Hierarchical Storage Manager (DFHSM) and Data Facility Dataset Services (DFDSS). Both of these components provide data management services that include backup and recovery for individual datasets or entire volumes of VSAM and non-VSAM datasets cataloged in ICF catalogs. For datasets cataloged in the older VSAM catalog structure, DFDSS provides only volume-level backup and recovery services.

The dump and restore services of both DFHSM and DFDSS are of the "plain wrap" variety; they do not reorganize a VSAM dataset during the restore process. However, DFHSM can be used to invoke the Access Method Services EXPORT and IMPORT commands.

DFHSM is a command-driven procedure, and DFDSS is typically invoked in batch with JCL statements. Both can be accessed via Interactive Storage Management Facility (ISMF), a series of panels based on ISPF/PDF.

For more information on DFP and its related data management components, see Chapter 25 of this book. And, if you're interested in using DFDSS and DFHSM to complement REPRO and EXPORT/IMPORT, see references 2, 3, and 4.

12.4. THE VERIFY COMMAND

Judicious use of the VERIFY command is important for preserving data integrity. VERIFY verifies and updates the catalog with information from the physical end of the data in the cluster via a field called the HURBA (High Used Relative Byte Address). The HURBA reflects the ending RBA (Relative Byte Address) of the highest (used) control area in the data component. VERIFY verifies that the catalog HURBA field stores the true values from the control block HURBA field.

Format: VERIFY FILE(*ddname* / *password*)

                                   or

                         VERIFY DATASET(*entry name* / *password*)

Abbreviation:	VFY
Use:	KSDS, ESDS, RRDS (not valid for an LDS)
Required:	No
Default:	None
Example:	VERIFY A2000.LIB.KSDS.CLUSTER

There are actually two HURBAs: one in the VSAM control block of the cluster and one in the catalog entry for the cluster. The danger is that if the catalog HURBA field is incorrect, there's a possibility that previously added records may be overwritten, especially in the event of subsequent control area splits. Figure 12.1 is a graphic illustration of this relationship.

It's actually more complicated than this and involves more fields, but since this is just an awareness issue for programmers, this simplified explanation is sufficient for our purposes.

VERIFY can be issued from TSO or within JCL statements using either the FILE or DATASET parameter. All three formats are shown in the following examples. In the first, FILE (not INFILE) points to DD1, which specifies the name of the base cluster. DISP=OLD assures exclusive control of the dataset for the duration of the VERIFY step.

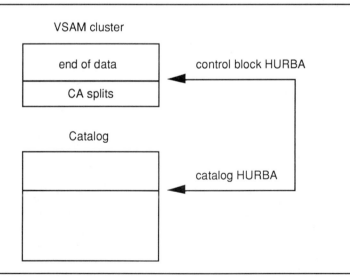

Figure 12.1.   Relationship between HURBA in catalog and cluster.

```
//REPOJOB   JOB ...
//STEP1     EXEC PGM=IDCAMS
//SYSPRINT  DD SYSOUT=*
//DD1       DD DSN=A2000.LIB.KSDS.CLUSTER,DISP=OLD
//SYSIN     DD *
 VERIFY FILE(DD1)
```

In the next example, DATASET (not INDATASET) allocates the cluster dynamically and assures exclusive control of it for the duration of the VERIFY step. This second example is the most widely used form of the command.

```
//REPOJOB   JOB ...
//STEP1     EXEC PGM=IDCAMS
//SYSPRINT  DD SYSOUT=*
//SYSIN     DD *
 VERIFY DATASET(A2000.LIB.KSDS.CLUSTER)
```

VERIFY has no parameters other than password if the cluster is password protected. You can VERIFY a base cluster or an alternate index, but not the data or index components of the base cluster or the path name. Thus, either of these are correct and could be entered directly through TSO:

```
VERIFY A2000.LIB.KSDS.CLUSTER
VERIFY A2000.LIB.KSDS.AUTHNAME.AIX
```

These are incorrect:

```
VERIFY A2000.LIB.KSDS.DATA
VERIFY AS000.LIB.KSDS.INDEX
VERIFY A2000.LIB.KSDS.AUTHNAME.PATH
```

It's downright dangerous to VERIFY data and index components because the time-stamp for each component will then be set to different values, thus compounding your out-of-synch problems. However, you must VERIFY the base cluster and any alternate indexes separately. VSAM doesn't care about the different time-stamps because they're different catalog entities. VERIFY comes in two flavors, explicit and implicit.

12.4.1.   Explicit VERIFY

The explicit verify (as shown in the previous examples) actually performs three steps:

1. It opens the dataset, thus establishing the VSAM control blocks. It also senses if the open-for-output indicator is on, signifying that a previous job may have terminated without closing the dataset.
2. It invokes a VERIFY macro, which compares EOD (End Of Data) values between the dataset and the catalog HURBA. If there is a difference, the macro updates the control block HURBA field but not the catalog HURBA field. This is an important point, as you'll see in a moment.
3. It closes the dataset, which turns off the open-for-output indicator and updates the catalog HURBA with the values contained in the control block HURBA. Everything is now in synch, and the dataset is once again ready for processing by an application program.

12.4.2.   Implicit VERIFY

When VSAM runs under Data Facility Product (DFP), it does an implicit VERIFY if it detects an open-for-output indicator already on when a dataset is opened by a program. This sounds like a heaven-sent solution to the out-of-synch problem, but it is not a total panacea. Consider this: Because the implicit VERIFY is a subset of its explicit counterpart, it only invokes the VERIFY macro (step 2 in the previous discussion), which updates the control block HURBA field. The catalog HURBA field is not updated with the correct information, and the open-for-output indicator is not reset.

Once the implicit VERIFY has been invoked and the dataset has been opened, processing continues; when the program closes the dataset, the catalog HURBA field is updated with the correct values and reflects the true physical end of the dataset, and the open-for-output indicator is turned off.

That's the normal sequence of events, but if processing is interrupted before the dataset is closed, once again the catalog HURBA field is not updated, and the open-for-output indicator light is not reset. It will be more difficult (perhaps impossible) to recover any records lost as a result of the first failure. Of course, any intervening control area splits will add to the debacle—need we say more?

VERIFY is a fairly resource-intensive operation because VSAM must read the entire dataset in order to determine the true physical end of the data. This can have an effect on performance if a large number of datasets (or a number of very large datasets) are being verified simultaneously. Because of this, to prevent a lot of redundant verifying operations, and to minimize the type of problem escalation described previously, some shops have disabled the implicit VERIFY feature and returned responsibility for explicit dataset verification to the programmers and support people. You need to ask your systems programmer what the policy is at your shop.

12.4.3. VERIFY Guidelines

In order to minimize your chances of having catalog information that is out of synch and to reduce the possibility of lost records, refer to the following general guidelines for use of the VERIFY command:

1. When opening a dataset in a COBOL program, always check the return code for a greater-than-zero condition. If the return code is greater than zero, stop processing immediately. *Do not close* the dataset. Immediately issue an explicit VERIFY command. Document this well for your support people.
2. Since CICS opens its datasets, always issue an explicit VERIFY command before passing these datasets to the CICS application.
3. Always issue an explicit VERIFY command before opening any datasets that are shared across systems.
4. Do not attempt to verify an empty cluster or a cluster that is only partially filled with records due to failure during the load step. In the event of a load-mode failure, it's best to delete the cluster, redefine it, and attempt the load from scratch.

12.5. THE EXAMINE COMMAND

The EXAMINE command is used by both systems and application programmers to inspect and report on structural errors within datasets. KSDS, VSAM catalogs, and the BCS (Basic Catalog Structure) component of an ICF catalog can be examined in this way. You cannot use this command with an ESDS, RRDS, or LDS.

Format:	EXAMINE NAME(*cluster name / password*) *optional parameters*
Abbreviation:	None
Use:	KSDS

Required: No

Default: None

Example: EXAMINE NAME(A2000.LIB.KSDS.CLUSTER)

EXAMINE is different from LISTCAT because it attempts to analyze any problems encountered and issues informational messages directing the user to possible recovery techniques.

12.5.1.   The INDEXTEST Parameter

INDEXTEST (the default) examines the vertical and horizontal pointers of the index component and reports any structural problems. NOINDEXTEST does no examination.

Format: INDEXTEST I NOINDEXTEST

Abbreviation: ITEST   I NOITEST

Use: KSDS

Required: No

Default: INDEXTEST

Example: INDEXTEST

                 NOINDEXTEST

12.5.2.   The DATATEST Parameter

DATATEST reads all control intervals of the data component sequentially and reports on record and control interval integrity, free space, and other conditions as well. DATATEST uses more resources and runs longer than INDEXTEST. NODATATEST performs no testing and is the default.

Format: DATATEST I NODATATEST

Abbreviation: DTEST   I NODTEST

Use: KSDS

Required: No

Default: NODATATEST

Example: DATATEST

                              NODATATEST

12.5.3.   The ERRORLIMIT Parameter

ERRORLIMIT specifies the number of errors for which detailed EXAM-
INE error messages are to be printed. Application programmers will
generally want to set this parameter to zero to suppress the plethora of
details that EXAMINE produces. You'll still receive structural information about the examined component.

Format: ERRORLIMIT(*number*)

                              number: Values from 0 through 2147483647.

Abbreviation: ELIMIT

Use: KSDS

Required: No

Default: 2,147,483,647

Example: ERRORLIMIT(0)

    The following example uses EXAMINE to test the primary index of
the sample KSDS for structural errors.

```
//REPOJOB  JOB ...
//STEP1    EXEC PGM=IDCAMS
//SYSPRINT DD SYSOUT=*
//SYSIN DD *
 EXAMINE                                -
 NAME(A2000.LIB.KSDS.CLUSTER)           -
 INDEXTEST                              -
 NODATATEST                             -
 ERRORLIMIT(0)
```

    Notice first that the required NAME parameter specifies the cluster
name explicitly. The JCL does not require the use of ddnames such as
DD1. Exclusive control of the cluster is maintained for the duration of the
EXAMINE step. If the cluster is password-protected, you must specify
the password also. You must have the proper RACF authority to EXAM-
INE a dataset.

REFERENCES

1. "DFSORT Application Programming Guide," Program No. 5740-SM1, San Jose, CA: IBM Corporation, 1985.

2. "DFHSM: User's Guide," Order No. SH35-0093, San Jose, CA: IBM Corporation.

3. "DFDSS: User's Guide," Order No. SC26-4388, San Jose, CA: IBM Corporation.

4. "MVS/ESA SML: Managing Datasets and Objects," Order No. SC26-4408, San Jose, CA: IBM Corporation.

Using ALTER, PRINT, and DELETE

In this chapter we're going to take a look at three IDCAMS commands used by application programmers and systems people to manage VSAM datasets. ALTER changes certain dataset attributes. DELETE purges datasets. PRINT prints dataset records in one of several formats.

13.1. THE ALTER COMMAND

The general form of the ALTER command is as follows:

Format:	ALTER *entry name* / *password parameters*
	entry name: The name of the entry to alter.
	password: The password for the entry if there is one. Omit the */password* if the entry doesn't have a password.
	parameters: These are described on the following pages.
Abbreviation:	None
Use:	KSDS, ESDS, RRDS, non-VSAM
Required:	No
Default:	None
Example:	ALTER A2000.KSDS.DATA FREESPACE(30 30)

You can use this powerful command to change certain (but by no means all) attributes of a previously defined VSAM object. These objects include a base cluster and its data or index component, an alternate index cluster and its data or index component, and even a VSAM or ICF catalog, if you are properly authorized. You can ALTER non-VSAM dataset attributes as well, but we'll confine our discussion to VSAM-related issues.

With ALTER you can revise FREESPACE percentages, change passwords, temporarily INHIBIT updates, and ADDVOLUMES for storage. However, you cannot ALTER internal attributes such as space allocation, CISZ, IMBED, or REPLICATE (all of which makes perfect sense, if you think about it). Use ALTER with extreme caution on all DFSMS-managed datasets.

For example, you cannot use ALTER to change non-DFSMS-managed datasets into DFSMS-managed ones because you can't store DFSMS-managed data on a volume that is not controlled by DFSMS. However, you could REPRO the dataset into a sequential dataset, DELETE the cluster, then redefine it with DFSMS constructs and use REPRO again to load the original data into the newly defined DFSMS-managed cluster. Similarly, you cannot change a VSAM dataset type, say from a KSDS to a RRDS. However, if an ESDS has previously been assigned a CISZ of 4096, you can change it to an LDS, but not vice versa. (Once an LDS, always an LDS, so to speak.)

The following is a list of common attributes that are completely alterable. They are fully described in the *Access Method Services* reference manual.

- ADDVOLUMES(*volumes*) or AVOL
  Specifies the volumes to add from the list of candidate volumes.
- ATTEMPTS(*number*) or ATT*
  Changes the number of times an operator can try to enter a password.
- AUTHORIZATION(*entry string*) or AUTH*
  Specifies that a user-security-verification routine is used.
- BUFFERSPACE(*size*) or BUFSP or BUFSPC
  Specifies the minimum space for buffers.
- CODE(*code*)*
  Specifies a password code name.
- CONTROLPW(*password*) or CTLPW*
  Specifies the control password.
- EMPTY | NOEMPTY or EMP | NEMP

EMPTY specifies that when the maximum number of generations of a generation group is exceeded, all generations are to be uncataloged. NOEMPTY uncatalogs only the oldest generation.

- ERASE | NOERASE or ERAS | NERAS*
  ERASE specifies that the data component is to be erased when the catalog entry is deleted.
- EXCEPTIONEXIT(*entry*) or EEXT
  Specifies the name of a routine to receive control when an I/O error occurs.
- FILE(*ddname*)
  Names a DD statement pointing to the object to alter.
- FREESPACE(*ci% ca%*) or FSPC
  Specifies the percentage of control interval and control area free space.
- INHIBIT | UNINHIBIT or INH | UNINH
  INHIBIT specifies that the item can be accessed for a read.
- MASTERPW(*password*) or MRPW*
  Specifies the master password.
- NEWNAME(*newname*) or NEWNM
  Specifies a new name to give the item.
- NULLIFY(*list*) or NULL*
  Specifies one or more attributes—AUTHORIZATION, CODE, CONTROLPW, EXCEPTIONEXIT, MASTERPW, OWNER, READPW, RETENTION, or UPDATEPW—to nullify.
- OWNER(*ownerid*)
  Specifies the owner id of the item.
- READPW(*password*) or RDPW*
  Specifies the read password.
- REMOVEVOLUMES(*volumes*) or RVOL*
  Specifies volumes to remove from list of candidate volumes.
- SCRATCH | NOSCRATCH or SCR | NSCR*
  SCRATCH specifies that generation datasets are to be scratched when they are uncataloged.
- SHAREOPTIONS(*crossregion crosssystem*) or SHR
  Specifies the cross-region and cross-system share options.
- TO(*date*) | FOR(*days*)*
  Specifies the retention date.
- UPDATE | NOUPDATE or UPD | NUPD
  UPDATE specifies that an AIX upgrade set is to be allocated when the path is allocated.
- UPDATEPW(*password*) or UPDPW*

Specifies the update password.

- UPGRADE | NOUPGRADE or UPG | NUPG
  UPGRADE specifies that an AIX is to be automatically upgraded.
- WRITECHECK | NOWRITECHECK or WCK | NWCK*
  WRITECHECK specifies that hardware write-check is to be performed for a data or index component.

* Avoid for DFSMS-managed datasets.

Remember from our discussions in Chapters 8 and 12 respectively that you can use ALTER to override the ERASE or NOERASE attributes of the DEFINE CLUSTER command and the INHIBITSOURCE or INHIBITTARGET parameters of the EXPORT command.

The following attributes are alterable but with significant restrictions, which means that you should ALTER them with caution.

- CATALOG(*name*/*password*) or CAT
  Specifies the catalog containing the entry to be altered. Not needed if the high-level qualifier is an alias for the catalog containing the entry. Avoid for DFSMS-managed datasets.
- KEYS(*length offset*)
  Specifies the length and offset of record keys. Can only be coded for empty clusters.
- RECORDSIZE(*avg max*) or RECSZ
  Specifies the average and maximum record size. Can only be coded for empty clusters.
- UNIQUEKEY | NONUNIQUEKEY or UNQK | NUNQK
  Specifies whether the AIX has unique keys. Can only be coded for an empty AIX.
- ESDS to LDS
  Can only be done if the CISZ is 4096.

The following attributes are unalterable. You have to DELETE the cluster and redefine it with the new attributes.

- CISZ
- Cluster type, except as previously noted.
- DATACLASS
- IMBED/REPLICATE
- REUSE/NOREUSE
- Variable-length RRDS to fixed-length and vice versa.

Each parameter used to alter attributes has a slightly different format. Most require that you specify the data or index component (if appropriate) as the entry name. You can combine several *parameters* under one ALTER command, but each *entry name* requires its own ALTER command. Let's look at a few typical examples.

13.1.1. ALTER with DFSMS Classes

The following example adds a DFSMS DATACLAS to the sample KSDS. If the DFSMS class has not been previously defined, or if DFSMS is not active for some reason, the ALTER command will fail.

```
//ALTJOB    JOB ...
//STEP1     EXEC PGM=IDCAMS
//SYSPRINT DD SYSOUT=*
//SYSIN     DD *
 ALTER                          -
    A2000.LIB.KSDS.CLUSTER     -
    [FILE or DATASET parameters are not required.]
    DATACLAS(KSDATA)
```

Note: Most installations prohibit programmers from using ALTER to add or remove STORCLAS and MGMTCLAS constructs because of the inherent danger of an inappropriate allocation.

Notice that ALTER refers directly to the cluster name. This format is similar to the DELETE command that we first saw in Chapter 12 in that neither the FILE nor the DATASET parameter is required.

```
DELETE A2000.LIB.KSDS.CLUSTER
```

13.1.2. ALTER with ADDVOLUMES/REMOVEVOLUMES

The following example adds a volume (VS0102) to the dataset's storage volume grouping. Note that the data and index component names must be specified, rather than the cluster name, and each component has its own ALTER command. More than one volume can be added by coding the following:

```
ADDVOLUMES (volser1 volser2 ... volsern)

//ALTJOB    JOB ...
//STEP1     EXEC PGM=IDCAMS
//SYSPRINT DD SYSOUT=*
//SYSIN     DD *
```

```
ALTER                           -
   A2000.LIB.KSDS.DATA          -
   ADDVOLUMES(VS0102)

ALTER                           -
   A2000.LIB.KSDS.INDEX         -
   ADDVOLUMES(VS0102)
```

The advantage of using ALTER with ADDVOLUMES is that you can do this on the fly if you're having space problems with a dataset (say, one used in a CICS application) in the midst of a business day. The dataset is unavailable to users only while the ALTER step is executing.

If the entry for the dataset is contained in a VSAM catalog, that catalog must also own the volume being added. This requirement doesn't apply in an ICF catalog environment. For more on both VSAM and ICF catalogs, see Chapter 22.

You can remove one or more storage volumes with the following format:

```
ALTER                           -
   dataset name                 -
   REMOVEVOLUMES(vol ser)   -
   FILE(ddname)
```

13.1.3.   ALTER with FREESPACE

The FREESPACE parameter changes the percentage of planned free space used to add new records or to increase the size of existing ones (if the dataset has variable-length records). The basic format of this parameter is FREESPACE (*ci% ca%*). Altering the FREESPACE attribute in this manner has no effect on existing CI and CA splits. To eliminate these, you need to redefine the cluster. For more on FREESPACE considerations, see Chapter 7.

The following example alters FREESPACE and uses UNINHIBIT to remove a previous read-only restriction from the dataset.

```
//ALTJOB    JOB ...
//STEP1     EXEC PGM=IDCAMS
//SYSPRINT DD SYSOUT=*
//SYSIN     DD *
   ALTER                        -
```

[Each component requires its own ALTER command.]

```
    A2000.LIB.KSDS.DATA            -
```

[Must specify component name that you want to ALTER, rather than the cluster name.]

```
    FREESPACE(30 30)               -
    UNINHIBIT
```

[Overrides a previous INHIBIT parameter.]

```
ALTER                              -
    A2000.LIB.KSDS.INDEX           -
    FREESPACE(30 30)               -
    UNINHIBIT
/*
```

13.1.4.   ALTER with INHIBIT and UNINHIBIT

The UNINHIBIT parameter overrides a previous INHIBIT. You can only specify INHIBIT or UNINHIBIT with the ALTER command; they are not part of the DEFINE CLUSTER syntax. INHIBIT can be used whenever you want to give users temporary read-only access to a dataset for some reason. Later, you can reinstate full update privileges with UNINHIBIT on the fly, without bringing the entire system down.

13.1.5.   ALTER with NEWNAME

The following example uses the NEWNAME parameter to assign a new cluster component name and the TO parameter to extend the cluster retention date to January 1, 2001.

```
//ALTJOB    JOB ...
//STEP1     EXEC PGM=IDCAMS
//SYSPRINT DD SYSOUT=*
//SYSIN     DD *
 ALTER                             -
    A2000.MY.KSDS.CLUSTER          -
    NEWNAME(A2000.LIB.KSDS.CLUSTER)   -
```

[The dataset name must be enclosed in parentheses.This changes only the cluster component.]

```
    TO(2001001)
/*
```

There are two approaches to renaming datasets: conservative and brave. The following example represents the conservative person's approach to renaming all the components of a KSDS with the NEWNAME parameter using three ALTER statements to explicitly state both the old and new names.

```
//ALTJOB    JOB ...
//STEP1     EXEC PGM=IDCAMS
//SYSPRINT DD SYSOUT=*
//SYSIN     DD *
 ALTER                                       -
    A2000.MY.KSDS.CLUSTER                     -
    NEWNAME(A2000.LIB.KSDS.CLUSTER)
 ALTER                                       -
    A2000.MY.KSDS.DATA                        -
    NEWNAME(A2000.LIB.KSDS.DATA)
 ALTER                                       -
    A2000.MY.KSDS.INDEX                       -
    NEWNAME(A2000.LIB.KSDS.INDEX)
/*
```

On the other hand, the example that follows represents the "no guts, no glory" approach to renaming all components of a KSDS; one ALTER statement with an asterisk used as a wild card character for each level. Using this method, all strings of 'A2000.MY.*something.something*' will be replaced with 'A2000.LIB.*something.something*'. Use this if you like, but be careful. The results may not be what you want.

```
//ALTJOB    JOB ...
//STEP1     EXEC PGM=IDCAMS
//SYSPRINT DD SYSOUT=*
//SYSIN     DD *
 ALTER                                       -
    A2000.MY.*.*                             -
    NEWNAME (A2000.LIB.*.*)
/*
```

13.1.6. ALTER with TO/FOR

You can specify values for TO in one of two formats:

1. You can do so with a two-byte year and a three-byte day of year starting with January 1. For example, 92015 assumes January 15,

1992; 98365 assumes December 31, 1998, and so on. You can see the inherent minefield here as we approach the year 2000.

2. You can use a four-byte year and a three-byte day of year starting with January 1. For example, 1992015 assumes January 15, 1992; 2001001 assumes January 1, 2001, and so on. This format offers more safety as we approach the year 2000.

As an alternative to the TO parameter, you can also ALTER retention using the FOR parameter with the value specified in days, for example

- FOR(9998) directs VSAM to retain the dataset for 9,998 days.
- FOR(9999), the highest value allowed, directs VSAM to retain the dataset indefinitely.

You can specify days in decimal, hexadecimal, or binary format. However, we suggest you make it easy on yourself and stick with decimal format. (If you find yourself wanting to enter the days in hex or binary, you should think about getting out of computing before it is too late.)

Note: Avoid ALTER with TO or FOR under DFSMS. The MGMTCLAS assigns these values.

13.2.   THE DELETE COMMAND

The IDCAMS DELETE command can be used to delete both VSAM and non-VSAM objects. It has a very simple syntax, requiring only an entry name as shown:

Format:	DELETE *entry name*
	DELETE *entry name* / *password options*
	entry name: The name of the entry to delete. An asterisk can be coded as a wild card character in place of a *name*.
	password: The password for the entry if there is one. Omit the */password* if the entry doesn't have a password.
	options: These are described on the following pages.
Abbreviation:	DEL
Use:	KSDS, ESDS, RRDS, non-VSAM
Required:	No

Default: All objects having the name.

Example: DELETE A2000.KSDS.DATA

The options for DELETE are the following:

- ALIAS
  Requests that only the alias of that name be deleted.
- ALTERNATEINDEX or AIX
  Requests that only the alternate index of that name be deleted.
- CATALOG(*name / password*) or CAT
  Specifies the name in which the item is cataloged and any password. This is not needed if the highest-level qualifier for the item is an alias for the catalog name. Don't code for DFSMS-managed datasets.
- CLUSTER or CL
  Requests that only the cluster of that name be deleted.
- GENERATIONDATAGROUP or GDG
  Requests that only the generation data group of that name be deleted.
- NONVSAM or NVSAM
  Requests that only the non-VSAM dataset of that name be deleted.
- PAGESPACE or PGSPC
  Requests that only the page space of that name be deleted.
- PATH
  Requests that only the path of that name be deleted.
- SPACE or SPC
  Requests that only the empty data spaces of that name be deleted.
- USERCATALOG or UCAT
  Requests that only the user catalog of that name be deleted.
- ERASE | NOERASE or ERAS | NERAS
  ERASE specifies that the deleted item is to be overwritten with binary zeros.
- FILE(*ddname*)
  Names a DD statement pointing to the object to delete.
- FORCE | NOFORCE or FRC | NFRC
  FORCE allows the item to be deleted even if it is not empty.
- PURGE | NOPURGE or PRG | NPRG
  PURGE allows the item to be deleted even if its expiration date has not arrived.
- SCRATCH | NOSCRATCH or SCR | NSCR
  SCRATCH scratches non-VSAM datasets. NOSCRATCH just uncatalogs the dataset.

Usually you won't need a FILE parameter, and you can also omit a DD statement referring to the entry name from your IDCAMS JCL. As with all IDCAMS commands, DELETE supports a full complement of options, and we'll look at some of the more popular ones.

In all of our examples in this chapter we make the assumption that the high-level qualifier of the dataset represents an alias for the catalog that contains its entry, so no CATALOG parameter would be required.

A2000.LIB.KSDS.CLUSTER   (cluster name)
↓
A2000   (user catalog alias)
↓
PRGMCAT   (user catalog name)

If this is not the case with your dataset, you will also have to specify a CATALOG parameter in the following format:

CATALOG(*catalog name/password*)

In the JCL you will also have to specify a JOBCAT or STEPCAT statement. Remember however, that JOBCAT and STEPCAT statements are not valid with DFSMS-managed datasets, and CATALOG parameters are actually discouraged.

VSAM objects that can be deleted using this command include a base cluster and all of its components, an alternate index and all of its components, an alternate index path, dedicated VSAM space, or a VSAM or ICF catalog. Because they all have basically the same syntax, we confine our discussion to the VSAM objects generally managed by application programmers; that is, the base cluster, alternate index, and alternate index path.

There are several compelling reasons to use the DELETE command both in the testing stage and as part of regular production maintenance; for example, if the dataset (or other object) has become obsolete or redundant, or needs to be redefined because it is damaged, because non-ALTERable attributes need to be changed (or added), or because control interval and/or control area splits have made it inefficient to process.

Unless you specify the ERASE parameter, VSAM performs a logical delete on the selected object. That is, it only removes the catalog entry. The data still exists on disk, but now it can be overwritten by new data.

DELETE has a domino effect on subordinate objects, which can have dire consequences for the hapless person who is not aware that if you delete a base cluster (say, a KSDS), all of its related objects including the data and index components, any alternate indexes, and the path are automatically deleted in one fell swoop.

Here are the messages that IDCAMS returns from the successful delete of a KSDS base cluster and all of its components. (PURGE is a DELETE option that overrides any previous retention date assigned by either the TO or FOR parameters. NOPURGE is the default.)

```
DELETE (A2000.LIB.KSDS.CLUSTER) PURGE
OIDC0550I ENTRY (R) A2000.LIB.AUTHNAME.PATH DELETED
OIDC0550I ENTRY (D) A2000.LIB.AUTHNAME.DATA DELETED
OIDC0550I ENTRY (I) A2000.LIB.AUTHNAME.INDEX DELETED
OIDC0550I ENTRY (G) A2000.LIB.AUTHNAME.AIX DELETED
OIDC0550I ENTRY (D) A2000.LIB.KSDS.DATA DELETED
OIDC0550I ENTRY (I) A2000.LIB.KSDS.INDEX DELETED
OIDC0550I ENTRY (C) A2000.LIB.KSDS.CLUSTER DELETED
OIDC0001I FUNCTION COMPLETED, HIGHEST CONDITION CODE
  WAS 00
OIDC0002I IDCAMS PROCESSING COMPLETE. MAXIMUM CONDITION
  CODE WAS 0
```

If you delete an alternate index, the path is also deleted, but the base cluster remains untouched. Similarly, if you delete the path, both the alternate index and the base cluster remain untouched. Also, you cannot delete data and index components separately.

Your DELETE step will fail if the dataset is already open for processing by another application on the same system. Across systems it's another story entirely. Your DELETE may succeed, leaving the other application high and dry. You need to take extra precautions when deleting objects that are used by different systems. See your systems people for advice here.

13.2.1.   DELETE with ERASE

The following example deletes the base cluster and all subordinate objects and specifies that the data is to be overwritten with binary zeros as a security precaution. If the cluster was previously defined or altered with NOERASE, the ERASE parameter is ignored. You would have to ALTER the cluster and then DELETE it.

```
//DELJOB    JOB ...
//STEP1     EXEC PGM=IDCAMS
//SYSPRINT DD SYSOUT=*
//DD1       DD DSN=A2000.LIB.KSDS.CLUSTER,DISP=OLD
//SYSIN     DD *
 DELETE                           -
   FILE(DD1)                      -
   ERASE
```

13.2.2.   Deleting Multiple Clusters

The following example deletes two named clusters and all of their subordinate objects. Notice that the entry names are enclosed in parentheses, with the plus sign used as a continuation character.

```
//DELJOB    JOB ...
//STEP1     EXEC PGM=IDCAMS
//SYSPRINT DD SYSOUT=*
//SYSIN     DD *
DELETE                           -
  (A2000.LIB.KSDS1.CLUSTER       +
   A2000.LIB.KSDS2.CLUSTER)
```

13.2.3.   Deleting an Alternate Index

The following example deletes an alternate index cluster and all of its subordinate objects: the alternate index data and index components and the alternate index path. The base cluster and its data and index components remain untouched, however.

```
//DELJOB    JOB ...
//STEP1     EXEC PGM=IDCAMS
//SYSPRINT DD SYSOUT=*
//SYSIN     DD *
 DELETE                           -
   A2000.LIB.KSDS.AUTHNAME.AIX
```

13.2.4.   Deleting a Dataset via JCL

If the dataset is DFSMS managed, you can delete it in the JCL that executes your application program by specifying DISP=(OLD,DELETE).

However, if DFSMS is not active for some reason or if the dataset has been deleted previously, the request (and possibly the job) will fail. For this reason, we recommend that you use IDCAMS and the DELETE command instead. In this case, an unsuccessful DELETE will only result in a bad return code, not a job failure that could affect other steps.

If your installation is converting to DFSMS, you need to review all of your JCL carefully, because previous careless coding of DISP= (OLD,DELETE) may cause valid datasets to be accidentally deleted. Needless to say, this could play havoc with your production datasets.

13.3. THE PRINT COMMAND

If you want to view your data, you can use the IDCAMS PRINT command to print it in one of several formats. The basic form is quite simple:

Format:

PRINT INDATASET(*entry name/password*) *options*

PRINT INFILE(*ddname/password*) *options*

entry name: The name of the entry to print.

password: The password for the entry if there is one. Omit the */password* if the entry doesn't have a password.

ddname: The name of a DD statement included in the JCL that names the object to print.

options: These are described on the following pages.

Abbreviation: PRINT IDS(*entry name/password*)

Use: KSDS, ESDS, RRDS, non-VSAM

Required: No

Default: None

Example: PRINT A2000.KSDS.DATA

The following options are allowed:

- CHARACTER | DUMP | HEX or CHAR
  Specifies the format in which to print.
- COUNT(*number*)
  Specifies the number of logical records to print.

- FROMADDRESS(*rba*) or FADDR
  Specifies the relative byte address at which to begin printing.
- FROMKEY(*key*) TOKEY(*key*) or FKEY TKEY
  Specifies the first key to print.
- FROMNUMBER(*rrn*) or FNUM
  Specifies the relative record number at which to begin printing.
- OUTFILE(*ddname*) or OFILE
  Specifies the name of a DD statement describing where to write the output.
- SKIP(*number*)
  Specifies the number of logical records to skip before beginning to print.
- TOADDRESS(*rba*) or TADDR
  Specifies the relative byte address at which to end printing.
- TOKEY(*key*)
  Specifies the key of the last record to print.
- TONUMBER(*rrn*) or TNUM
  Specifies the relative record number of the last record to print.

You can use PRINT to print VSAM and non-VSAM objects. As we discuss PRINT options, note that PRINT has a syntax similar to RE-PRO in that it uses INFILE or INDATASET to refer to the entry name and parameters like SKIP, COUNT, FROMKEY, and TOKEY to limit the input.

If you want the printed output directed to other than SYSPRINT, such as another dataset, you can add the OUTFILE parameter.

Format:	OUTFILE(*ddname*)
	ddname: The name of a DD statement specifying where the output is to be written.
Abbreviation:	OFILE
Use:	KSDS, ESDS, RRDS, non-VSAM
Required:	No, because of default.
Default:	OUTFILE(SYSPRINT)
Example:	PRINT A2000.KSDS.DATA OFILE(TEMPDD)

13.3.1. PRINT Formats

Depending upon the nature of your input data, you can specify one of three formats.

Format:	CHARACTER ∣ HEX ∣ DUMP
Abbreviation:	CHAR ∣ ∣
Use:	KSDS, ESDS, RRDS, non-VSAM
Required:	No, because of default.
Default:	DUMP
Example:	PRINT A2000.KSDS.DATA CHAR

The three formats are as follows. (Note that we have shortened all of our PRINT examples (denoted by . . .) to fit on the printed page.)

1. *CHARACTER* (CHAR) prints as EBCDIC, 120 characters per line. Key fields also print in character format. Periods denote nonprintable characters. You can use this format for mostly alphanumeric data.

```
   PRINT   INFILE(OUTDD)     CHAR                          00102005
1IDCAMS  SYSTEM SERVICES          TIME: 14:27:54           12/05/91
-LISTING OF DATA SET -A2000.LIB.SAMPLE.CLUSTER
0KEY OF RECORD - 01019601
 01019601409ALL.REGS0106DISCOVER RE MGRS LTD301     1135C09199101...
0KEY OF RECORD - 01019711
 01019711409ALL.REGS0106DISCOVER RE MGRS LTD352     1135C09199101...
```

2. *HEX* prints each character as 2 hexadecimal digits, side by side, 120 hex characters per line. Key fields are also printed in hex. You can use this format for numeric data that you need to analyze for some reason.

```
   PRINT   INFILE(OUTDD)     HEX                           00103005
1IDCAMS  SYSTEM SERVICES          TIME: 14:27:54           12/05/91
-LISTING OF DATA SET -A2000.LIB.SAMPLE.CLUSTER
0KEY OF RECORD - F0F1F0F1F9F6F0F1
 F0F1F0F1F9F6F0F1F4F0F9C1D3D34BD9C5C7E2F0F1F0F6C4C9E2C3D6E5C5D940...
 F9F1F0F1000000000C000000000C000000000C00
```

3. *DUMP* prints records in both hexadecimal and character format. DUMP is the PRINT default.

```
   PRINT   INFILE(OUTDD)     DUMP                          00101004
1IDCAMS  SYSTEM SERVICES          TIME: 14:27:54           12/05/91
```

```
-LISTING OF DATA SET -A2000.LIB.SAMPLE.CLUSTER
OKEY OF RECORD - F0F1F0F1F9F6F0F1
  000000 0F1F0F1 F9F6F0F1...*01019601409ALL.REGS0106DISCOVER *
  000020 9C540D4 C7D9E240...*RE MGRS LTD301     1135C09199101*
  000040 0000000 0C000000...*................             *
```

13.3.2.   Limiting PRINT Output

You can limit the PRINT output by specifying where to begin and end printing in several ways.

Limiting PRINT with SKIP and COUNT. The SKIP parameter specifies a number of logical records to skip before beginning to print. For example, if you code SKIP(99), printing begins with the one hundredth logical record. COUNT specifies the number of logical records to list. Don't use SKIP or COUNT if you access records through a path.

Format:	SKIP(*number*) COUNT(*number*)
	number: The number of logical records to skip before beginning to print (SKIP) or the number of logical records to print (COUNT). Either or both can be coded.
Abbreviation:	None.
Use:	KSDS, ESDS, RRDS, non-VSAM, but not a path.
Required:	No, because of default.
Default:	SKIP(0), COUNT(infinity)
Example:	PRINT A2000.KSDS.DATA SKIP(199) - COUNT(100)

Limiting PRINT with FROMKEY and TOKEY. If the entry name specifies a KSDS, you can print a range of records using the FROMKEY and TOKEY parameters and named key values.

Format:	FROMKEY(*key*) TOKEY(*key*)
	key: The first (FROMKEY) or last (TOKEY) key at which to begin printing. Either or both can be coded.

Abbreviation:	FKEY
Use:	KSDS, alternate index, catalog
Required:	No, because of default.
Default:	First key for FROMKEY and last key for TOKEY.
Example:	PRINT A2000.KSDS.DATA CHAR - FROMKEY(ALASKA)

The following example prints records with the keyranges FICT0025 through FICT9043. Remember, the input dataset is sequenced logically (but not necessarily in physical sequence because of split activity) by the primary key.

```
//PRIJOB   JOB . . .
//STEP1    EXEC PGM=IDCAMS
//SYSPRINT DD SYSOUT=*
//DD1      DD DSN=A2000.LIB.KSDS.CLUSTER,DISP=SHR
//SYSIN    DD *
 PRINT              -
   INFILE(DD1)        -
     FROMKEY(FICT0025) -
     TOKEY  (FICT9043)
```

Notice in the JCL that we've requested DISP=SHR. Normally you don't need exclusive control when you are merely printing records. As an alternative to INFILE you can specify INDATASET.

```
INDATASET(A2000.LIB.KSDS.CLUSTER)
```

This parameter causes the dataset to be allocated dynamically and obtains exclusive control for VSAM. The output is directed to SYSPRINT, so you don't need an output dataset.

Limiting PRINT with FROMADDRESS and TOADDRESS. If the input dataset is a KSDS or ESDS, you can print a range of records using the FROMADDRESS and TOADDRESS parameters with their respective RBA values.

Format: FROMADDRESS(rba) TOADDRESS(rba)

	rba: The first (FROMADDRESS) or last (TOADDRESS) relative byte address at which to begin printing. Either or both can be coded.
Abbreviation:	FADDR(*rba*) TADDR(*rba*)
Use:	KSDS, ESDS
Required:	No, because of default.
Default:	First relative byte address for FROMADDRESS (0) and last relative byte address for TOADDRESS (the HURBA value).

Example:	PRINT -
	   INFILE(DD1) -
	     FADDR(RBA-value) -
	     TADDR(RBA-value)

Limiting PRINT with FROMNUMBER and TONUMBER. If the input dataset is an RRDS, you can print a range of records using the FROMNUMBER and TONUMBER parameters with their respective relative record number (RRN) values. Only slots in which records have been written are printed.

Format:	FROMNUMBER(*rrn*) TONUMBER(*rrn*)
	rrn: The first (FROMNUMBER) or last (TONUMBER) relative record number at which to begin printing. Either or both can be coded.
Abbreviation:	FNUM(*rrn*) TNUM(*rrn*)
Use:	RRDS
Required:	No, because of default.
Default:	First relative record number for FROMNUMBER and relative record number for TONUMBER.
Example:	PRINT A2000.KSDS.DATA CHAR - FNUM(200)

For more about the FROMKEY and TOKEY, FADDR and TADDR, or FNUM and TNUM parameters, which are also used with the REPRO command, you may want to review the REPRO material in Chapter 12.

13.3.3. Printing a KSDS

If you specify the cluster name when printing a KSDS, base records print in primary key order. Notice that the primary key appears on a separate line before the detail of the record.

```
  PRINT   INFILE(OUTDD)     CHAR                    00102005
1IDCAMS  SYSTEM SERVICES           TIME: 14:27:54   12/05/91
-LISTING OF DATA SET -A2000.LIB.SAMPLE.CLUSTER
0KEY OF RECORD - 01019601
 01019601409ALL.REGS0106DISCOVER RE MGRS LTD301     1135C09199101...
0KEY OF RECORD - 01019711
 01019711409ALL.REGS0106DISCOVER RE MGRS LTD352     1135C09199101...
```

On the other hand, if you specify the data component as the entry name, records print in RBA order. Notice that the RBA appears on a separate line before the detail of the record.

```
-LISTING OF DATA SET -A2000.LIB.SAMPLE.DATA
ORBA OF RECORD - 0
000000   F0F1F0F1 F9F6F0F1 F4F0F9C1 D3D34BD9   C5C7E2F0 F1F0F6C4...
000020   D9C540D4 C7D9E240 D3E3C4F3 F0F14040   404040F1 F1F3F5C3...
000040   00000000 0C000000 000C0000 00000C00

ORBA OF RECORD - 80
000000   F0F1F0F1 F9F7F1F1 F4F0F9C1 D3D34BD9   C5C7E2F0 F1F0F6C4...
000020   D9C540D4 C7D9E240 D3E3C4F3 F5F24040   404040F1 F1F3F5C3...
000040   00000000 0C000000 000C0000 00000C00

ORBA OF RECORD - 160
000000   F0F1F0F1 F9F7F1F2 F4F0F9F0 F9404040   404040F0 F1F0F6C4...
000020   D9C540D4 C7D9E240 D3E3C4F4 F2F34040   404040F1 F1F3F5C3...
000040   00000000 0C000000 000C0000 00000C00
```

If you specify the index component of a KSDS as the entry name, the compression algorithm that is applied to the index key by VSAM can make interpretation of the output difficult. We suggest you avoid this option.

```
-LISTING OF DATA SET -A2000.LIB.SAMPLE.INDEX
ORBA OF RECORD - 0
000000   01F90301 00000000 00000000 00000000   01000035 01F601F6...
000020   15141312 11100F0E 0D0C0B0A 09080706   05040302 01000000...
```

13.3.4.   Printing an ESDS

When the entry name you specify is an ESDS, records also print in RBA order, with the RBA appearing on a separate line.

```
-LISTING OF DATA SET -A2000.LIB.SAMPLE.ESDS
ORBA OF RECORD - 0
000000  F0F1F0F1 F9F6F0F1 F4F0F9C1 D3D34BD9   C5C7E2F0 F1F0F6C4...
000020  D9C540D4 C7D9E240 D3E3C4F3 F0F14040   404040F1 F1F3F5C3...
000040  00000000 0C000000 000C0000 00000C00

ORBA OF RECORD - 80
000000  F0F1F0F1 F9F7F1F1 F4F0F9C1 D3D34BD9   C5C7E2F0 F1F0F6C4...
000020  D9C540D4 C7D9E240 D3E3C4F3 F5F24040   404040F1 F1F3F5C3...
000040  00000000 0C000000 000C0000 00000C00

ORBA OF RECORD - 160
000000  F0F1F0F1 F9F7F1F2 F4F0F9F0 F9404040   404040F0 F1F0F6C4...
000020  D9C540D4 C7D9E240 D3E3C4F4 F2F34040   404040F1 F1F3F5C3...
000040  00000000 0C000000 000C0000 00000C00
```

13.3.5.   Printing an RRDS

When the entry name you specify is a fixed-length RRDS, records print in relative record number order. Nothing is printed for an empty slot, because no record exists there. (There are no empty slots depicted in the following example.)

```
-LISTING OF DATA SET -A2000.LIB.SAMPLE.RRDS
ORELATIVE RECORD NUMBER - 1
000000  F0F1F0F1 F9F6F0F1 F4F0F9C1 D3D34BD9   C5C7E2F0 F1F0F6C4...
000020  D9C540D4 C7D9E240 D3E3C4F3 F0F14040   404040F1 F1F3F5C3...
000040  00000000 0C000000 000C0000 00000C00

ORELATIVE RECORD NUMBER - 2
000000  F0F1F0F1 F9F7F1F1 F4F0F9C1 D3D34BD9   C5C7E2F0 F1F0F6C4...
000020  D9C540D4 C7D9E240 D3E3C4F3 F5F24040   404040F1 F1F3F5C3...
000040  00000000 0C000000 000C0000 00000C00
```

13.3.6.   Printing an AIX

You can print an alternate index in one of two ways: by specifying the alternate index cluster as the entry name (remember each alternate index is really a KSDS) or by specifying the path name. The following example displays the output when the alternate index cluster name has been specified. Notice that only the key and other internal information is printed. This option would be helpful only if you wanted to examine specific key values.

```
-LISTING OF DATA SET -A2000.LIB.SAMPLE.AIX
OKEY OF RECORD - F3F0F1
 000000 01080001 03F3F0F1 F0F1F0F1 F9F6F0F1

OKEY OF RECORD - F3F5F2
 000000 01080001 03F3F5F2 F0F1F0F1 F9F7F1F1

OKEY OF RECORD - F4F2F3
 000000 01080001 03F4F2F3 F0F1F0F1 F9F7F1F2
```

If the alternate index key has been defined as NONUNIQUE, duplicate index keys will be printed (none in the example here). On the other hand, when the alternate index path name has been specified, the full base cluster records print in order by the alternate index key. This feature can be extremely handy for viewing data in an alternate way and helps to demonstrate graphically the logical connection made by the path between the base cluster and the alternate index. (While the path is considered a real VSAM object, it does not contain records. However, there is a catalog entry for the path.)

```
-LISTING OF DATA SET -A2000.LIB.SAMPLE.PATH
OKEY OF RECORD - F3F0F1
 000000  F0F1F0F1 F9F6F0F1 F4F0F9C1 D3D34BD9   C5C7E2F0 F1F0F6C4...
 000020  D9C540D4 C7D9E240 D3E3C4F3 F0F14040   404040F1 F1F3F5C3...
 000040  00000000 0C000000 000C0000 00000C00

OKEY OF RECORD - F3F5F2
 000000  F0F1F0F1 F9F7F1F1 F4F0F9C1 D3D34BD9   C5C7E2F0 F1F0F6C4...
 000020  D9C540D4 C7D9E240 D3E3C4F3 F5F24040   404040F1 F1F3F5C3...
 000040  00000000 0C000000 000C0000 00000C00

OKEY OF RECORD - F4F2F3
 000000  F0F1F0F1 F9F7F1F2 F4F0F9F0 F9404040   404040F0 F1F0F6C4...
 000020  D9C540D4 C7D9E240 D3E3C4F4 F2F34040   404040F1 F1F3F5C3...
 000040  00000000 0C000000 000C0000 00000C00
```

13.3.7.   Printing an LDS

You can use the FADDR and TADDR parameters to print portions of an LDS. Our last PRINT example prints the first three (4K) pages of a Linear Dataset (LDS). FADDR specifies a relative byte address of zero, the beginning of the data stream. (This also defaults if you omit FADDR.) TADDR specifies the relative byte address of the third 4K page.

Remember that an LDS consists of 4096-byte pages, so (4096 * 3 - 1) yields a value of 12287. For more on the LDS structure see Chapter 27.

```
//PRIJOB    JOB ...
//STEP1     EXEC PGM=IDCAMS
//SYSPRINT DD SYSOUT=*
//DD1       DD DSN=A2000.LIB.LDS.SAMPLE,DISP=SHR
//SYSIN     DD *
 PRINT                 -
   INFILE(DD1)         -
     FADDR(0)          -
     TADDR(12287)
```

13.4. SUMMARY

In this section of the book we've looked at the basic commands and parameters used by Access Method Services to define and manage VSAM datasets and alternate indexes. In the next section, we'll show you how to use VSAM datasets in COBOL programs.

PART 3

Using VSAM Datasets in COBOL Application Programs

This part of the book explains with words (as few as possible) and examples (many) how to process VSAM datasets using VS COBOL II for batch applications, and CICS embedded in COBOL for online applications. We'll take you through loading a KSDS, accessing it both sequentially and randomly in the same program. We'll also show you how to process a COBOL application using an ESDS and an RRDS, and how to use both a unique and non-unique alternate index. Finally we'll show considerations for using a KSDS in a CICS online application.

This section assumes that you have basic COBOL skills—at least the ability to read a COBOL program. The intent is not to make you proficient in COBOL, only to point out the differences in processing COBOL programs with VSAM datasets as opposed to other access methods.

This book concerns itself with the following COBOL versions:

- The 1985 version of American National Standard Programming Language (ANSI COBOL 85).[1]
- The VS COBOL II compiler including Version 3, used by MVS/ESA.[2,3] ESA stands for Enterprise Systems Architecture. VS COBOL II is a subset of ANSI COBOL 85. (The ANSI version includes the report writer and communications modules, which are not in VS COBOL II.) VSAM is not a part of the ANSI Standard, but the standard does specify the COBOL statements for processing all datasets. VS COBOL II implements direct and indexed datasets with VSAM, but the COBOL statements themselves are those of the ANSI Standard.

Almost all of ANSI COBOL is included in VS COBOL II, except for the communications module, the report writer module, and (at present) intrinsic functions.[4] VS COBOL II does contain some non-ANSI Standard statements that are a carryover from older IBM compilers, such as the GOBACK statement. Generally these should not be used because there is a risk that IBM will discontinue supporting them.

- The Microsoft[5] and the Micro Focus[6] COBOL compilers. (The Microsoft and Micro Focus compilers are the same. Microsoft markets the Micro Focus COBOL compiler.) These compilers contain all of the ANSI Standard and almost all of VS COBOL II, except for CICS. They also contain extensive screen handling functions not available in either VS COBOL II or the ANSI Standard. They run on the PC and can be used to develop mainframe applications.

The same statements also are used for the PC in Microsoft/Micro Focus COBOL, even though VSAM does not exist on the PC. The result is that COBOL programs can be written that are compatible with the mainframe and PC despite VSAM existing only on the mainframe.

You may do all of your development on the mainframe or part on the PC if you use a product like Microsoft/Micro Focus COBOL. Development on the PC is likely to become the environment of choice as we approach the year 2000, because of the flexibility it provides the programmer and because all mainframes run close to capacity, and this is unlikely to change anytime soon, even with ESA. Just like Los Angeles with its freeways, the more you build, the more you use. The availability of the mainframe, like the availability of freeways, doesn't satisfy demand, it creates it.

The new COBOL allows you to write statements in upper or lower case. We'll use upper case for emphasis, because that is how most programmers are used to seeing statements. We'll assume that you are familiar with the following COBOL terms: data item, data name, elementary and group item, identifier, numeric and nonnumeric literal, figurative constant, and table.

14

COBOL and VSAM:
What's New, What's
Different

We'll use this chapter to survey the various COBOL statements and techniques commonly used to process VSAM datasets. In subsequent chapters we'll look at these statements and techniques in more depth as they apply to different application scenarios.

The IDENTIFICATION DIVISION coding to process a VSAM dataset is the same as for a non-VSAM dataset, requiring only the program name, so let's fast-forward to the ENVIRONMENT DIVISION, where the real action begins.

```
IDENTIFICATION DIVISION.
PROGRAM-ID. VDEM01.
****************************************************
* Many helpful comments describing function, but  *
* not implementation, are displayed here.         *
****************************************************
```

14.1. THE SELECT CLAUSE

In the INPUT-OUTPUT SECTION in the FILE-CONTROL paragraph, the SELECT clause for a VSAM dataset has the following format:

```
ENVIRONMENT DIVISION.
INPUT-OUTPUT SECTION.
FILE-CONTROL.
```

SELECT *file name* ASSIGN TO ⎯⎯⎯⎯⎯⎯⎯
```
                              ddname
                              AS-ddname
```

[The *file name* is also specified in the FILE SECTION FD, which is no different from non-VSAM file processing. The *ddname* appears in the JCL. You must prefix the ddname with a prefix of *AS-* for an ESDS, but this is not necessary for a KSDS or an RRDS. If you do name a prefix for a KSDS or RRDS, COBOL treats it as a comment.]

ORGANIZATION IS ⎯⎯⎯⎯⎯⎯⎯
```
                              INDEXED
                              SEQUENTIAL
                              RELATIVE
```

[The ORGANIZATION clause must agree with the dataset type specified in the DEFINE command. The choices are INDEXED for a KSDS, whether accessed sequentially or randomly, SEQUENTIAL for an ESDS, and RELATIVE for an RRDS.]

ACCESS MODE IS ⎯⎯⎯⎯⎯⎯⎯
```
                              SEQUENTIAL
                              RANDOM
                              DYNAMIC
```

[Names the access mode for the program. The choices are SEQUENTIAL for sequential-only access, RANDOM for random-only access, and DYNAMIC for a combination of sequential and random access. Note that the dataset ORGANIZATION never changes, but ACCESS can vary from program to program.]

RECORD KEY IS *primary key data name*

[For a KSDS only. Names the primary index key whose length and offset have been specified with the KEYS parameter in the DEFINE CLUSTER command. This data name must also appear in a record description in the FD clause.]

PASSWORD IS *password data name*

[Names an eight-byte alphanumeric data item defined in WORKING-STORAGE that stores the password for the cluster. If access is for read-only, the READPW must be specified. If access is for update, the UPDATEPW password must be specified. If the program processes records via an alternate index and the alternate index is password-protected, you must specify a PASSWORD clause following each ALTERNATE KEY clause. If the cluster is not password-protected, omit this clause entirely. Note that passwords are not supported by DFSMS.]

ALTERNATE KEY IS *alternate index key data name*

[For a KSDS only. Names an alternate index key whose length and offset have been specified with the KEYS parameter in the DEFINE AIX command. This data name also appears in the FD clause. If the program uses more than one alternate key, you write an ALTERNATE KEY clause for each one.]

WITH DUPLICATES

[Tells COBOL to expect duplicate alternate index keys for the alternate key just specified. If you omit this clause, COBOL expects unique alternate index keys. This clause must agree with the UNIQUEKEY I NONUNIQUEKEY parameter specified in the DEFINE CLUSTER command.]

FILE STATUS IS *status key*.

[Names a two-byte alphanumeric data item that stores a special status key generated by COBOL after every I/O operation. Note that you must enter a period after the last clause in the SELECT to end it.]

The following is a SELECT clause specifying sequential access for the sample KSDS.

```
SELECT LIB-MAST ASSIGN TO LIBMAST
                ORGANIZATION IS INDEXED
                ACCESS MODE IS SEQUENTIAL
                RECORD KEY IS LIB-KEY
                FILE STATUS IS STAT1.
```

14.2.   VSAM I/O ERROR PROCESSING

I/O error handling is one vital area where VSAM dataset processing differs from non-VSAM dataset processing. When processing non-VSAM datasets, most programmers code their application programs to ignore errors, because the access method will abend the program if a serious I/O error occurs. Not so when processing VSAM datasets.

14.2.1.   The COBOL FILE STATUS Key

VSAM places program control in the hands of the programmer, not the operating system. For this reason, it is important to check the COBOL status key designated in the FILE STATUS clause after every I/O operation. You're in the driver's seat here. For some error keys you'll want to abend the program immediately; for others you can just display the key, the record, and an informative message and continue processing. In the ensuing chapters of the book, we'll show you situations and techniques for dealing with both situations.

Here's a list of the most common COBOL status key values. As you can see, the more serious the error, the higher the value. For these status key values, continue processing normally:

00   Successful I/O.

02   Duplicate alternate key encountered (expected).

10   End of file.

But for these status key values, bypass the record, display pertinent information, and continue processing:

21   Input record out of sequence.

22   Duplicate primary key or unique alternate key encountered (unexpected).

23   Record (or key) not found.

You may want to have the program count the number of times these key values are returned and terminate the program if the counter reaches an unacceptable number, which would likely indicate that your input is bad.

```
IF NOT-FOUND
   DISPLAY ...
   ADD 1 TO COUNT-MAX-ERRORS
END-IF
IF COUNT-MAX-ERRORS > 50 ...
```

For the following status key values, terminate the program:

24   Out-of-space condition (KSDS or RRDS).

30   Nonspecific I/O problem.

34   Out-of-space condition (ESDS).

49   REWRITE attempted; dataset not opened for I-O.

90   Dataset unusable or logic error.

92   Logic error.

93   Resource not available.

94   Current record pointer undefined.

95   Nonzero HURBA for OPEN OUTPUT.

96   No corresponding JCL DD statement.

97   If your shop has enabled the implicit VERIFY command, this means that the dataset was opened after an implicit VERIFY, and you can continue processing. Otherwise it means that the dataset was not closed by a previous job, and you should terminate the program without attempting to close the dataset, and issue an explicit VERIFY command.

Table 14.1 contains a complete description of all the status codes and their meanings.

14.2.2.   VSAM Return Code

You can also specify and check a six-byte data item that holds information returned by VSAM whenever the COBOL status key is greater than zero. Use this VSAM return code to get more specific information about your I/O problems. If you want the VSAM return code, code a FILE STATUS clause naming both the COBOL status key and the VSAM return code. Both status keys can also be coded in Microsoft/ Micro Focus COBOL, but the values stored in the VSAM return code may be different from those in VS COBOL II. You code the FILE STATUS as:

```
FILE STATUS IS STAT1, STAT2.
```

TABLE 14.1. FILE STATUS codes.

key-1	key-2	Cause
Successful completion:		
0	0	No further information.
	2	Duplicate key detected.
	4	Wrong fixed-length record.
	5	Dataset created when opened. With sequential VSAM datasets, 0 is returned.
	7	CLOSE with NO REWIND or REEL, for nontape.
End-of-file:		
1	0	No further information.
	4	Relative record READ outside dataset boundary.
Invalid key:		
2	1	Sequence error.
	2	Duplicate key.
	3	No record found.
	4	Key outside boundary of dataset.
Permanent I/O error:		
3	0	No further information.
	4	Record outside dataset boundary.
	5	OPEN and required dataset not found.
	7	OPEN with invalid mode.
	8	OPEN of dataset closed with LOCK.
	9	OPEN unsuccessful because of conflicting dataset attributes.
Logic error:		
4	1	OPEN of dataset already open.
	2	CLOSE for dataset not open.
	3	READ not executed before REWRITE.
	4	REWRITE of different-size record.
	6	READ after EOF reached.
	7	READ attempted for dataset not opened I-O or INPUT.
	8	WRITE for dataset not opened OUTPUT, I-O, or EXTEND.
	9	DELETE or REWRITE for dataset not opened I-O.
Specific compiler-defined conditions:		
9	0	No further information.
	1	VSAM password failure.
	2	Logic error.
	3	VSAM resource not available.
	4	VSAM sequential record not available.
	5	VSAM invalid or incomplete dataset information.
	6	VSAM—no DD statement.
	7	VSAM OPEN successful. Dataset integrity verified.

Then, in WORKING-STORAGE, define a status area something like the example below:

```
01   LIB-STATUS-AREA.
     05   STAT1              PIC X(02) VALUE SPACES.
     05   STAT2.
          10  LIB-RETURN     PIC 9(02).
```

[VSAM return code.]

```
          10 LIB-FUNCTION    PIC 9(01).
```

[VSAM function code.]

```
          10 LIB-FEEDBACK    PIC 9(03).
```

[VSAM feedback code.]

Finally, in the PROCEDURE DIVISION, display the VSAM return code in order to receive more precise information concerning your I/O problem.

```
IF STAT1 > "00"
    DISPLAY STAT2 ...
END-IF
```

For example, after reading a record, LIB-STATUS-AREA might hold the following values:

```
STAT1        =   21
```

[Input record out of sequence.]

```
LIB-RETURN   =   08
```

[The contents of Register 15 stating that the request was not accepted.]

```
LIB-FUNCTION =    0
```

[The value of the function code.]

```
LIB-FEEDBACK = 024
```

[The input record to be inserted does not fall within the key range that was specified for the dataset in the DEFINE CLUSTER command.]

As you can see, the VSAM return code field gives you the level of detail needed to effectively diagnose your I/O problem. We've supplied the interpretation in the preceding example, but if you want to know more about interpreting the values in these VSAM return codes, check out the Request Parameter List (RPL) in references 7 and 8.

14.3. FILE SECTION ENTRIES

In the FILE SECTION, the FD (LIB-MAST in the example) describes the VSAM dataset, just as it does a QSAM or other non-VSAM dataset.

```
FD  LIB-MAST.
```

[Must match the *file name* specified in the SELECT clause.]

```
01   LIB-RECORD.
     05 LIB-KEY          PIC X(08).
     05 LIB-AUTH-LNAME   PIC X(15).
     05 LIB-AUTH-FNAME   PIC X(12).
     05 LIB-AUTH-INIT    PIC X(01).
     05 LIB-TITLE        PIC X(28).
     05 LIB-ISBN-NO      PIC X(13).
     05 LIB-COPIES       PIC 9(03).
```

The following depicts the relationship among the JCL, the SELECT clause, and the FD.

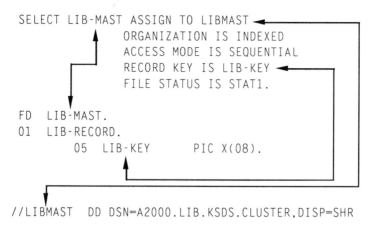

```
SELECT LIB-MAST ASSIGN TO LIBMAST
                ORGANIZATION IS INDEXED
                ACCESS MODE IS SEQUENTIAL
                RECORD KEY IS LIB-KEY
                FILE STATUS IS STAT1.

FD   LIB-MAST.
01   LIB-RECORD.
     05  LIB-KEY        PIC X(08).


//LIBMAST   DD DSN=A2000.LIB.KSDS.CLUSTER,DISP=SHR
```

14.4. WORKING-STORAGE ENTRIES

As stated previously, you define a status area in WORKING-STORAGE. Assuming you're going to define and test both the COBOL status key and the VSAM return code, it will probably look something like the following:

```
01  LIB-STATUS.
    05  STAT1             PIC X(02)  VALUE SPACES.
        88  OK                       VALUE "00" "02".
        88  EOF                      VALUE "10".
        88  DUPLICATE                VALUE "22".
        88  NOT-FOUND                VALUE "23".
        88  VERIFIED                 VALUE "97".
    05  STAT2
        10  LIB-RETURN    PIC 9(02).
        10  LIB-FUNCTION  PIC 9(01).
        10  LIB-FEEDBACK  PIC 9(03).
```

Notice that we've specified condition names for the various conditions (OK, EOF, DUPLICATE) that we're going to test for:

```
IF OK
    THEN CONTINUE . . .
END-IF
```

However, you can "hardcode" the status key values into the program statements themselves:

```
IF STAT1 = "00"
    THEN CONTINUE ...
END-IF
```

We recommend that you always use condition names because they provide so much flexibility for your application program and are easier for the reader of the program to interpret.

If your VSAM dataset is password-protected, you need to code a password area in WORKING-STORAGE, something like the following:

```
01  LIB-PASSWORD.
    05 LIB-READPW         PIC X(08)  VALUE SPACES.
    05 LIB-UPDTPW         PIC X(08)  VALUE SPACES.
```

For both security and program maintenance reasons, you should avoid hardcoding passwords in the program statements. (Anyone reading the listing can learn the password.) A better technique is to enter the password as a parameter on the EXEC statement. The following example shows this:

```
//STEP1 EXEC PGM=program name,PARM='password'
 . . .
01  PARM.
```

```
05  PARM-LENGTH          PIC 9(4) BINARY SYNC.
05  PARM-VALUE           PIC X(100).
.  .  .
    MOVE PARM-VALUE TO LIB-PASSWORD
```

Alternatively, you can enter the password following a SYSIN statement as shown here:

```
//SYSIN DD *
password
/*
.  .  .
    ACCEPT LIB-PASSWORD FROM SYSIN
```

And finally, you could prompt the operator to supply the password, although installations like to minimize operator messages and the operator has no real need to know the password. The following is an example of this:

```
DISPLAY "Please enter the password" UPON CONSOLE
ACCEPT LIB-PASSWORD FROM CONSOLE
```

The following depicts the relationship among the SELECT clause and the WORKING-STORAGE status and password areas.

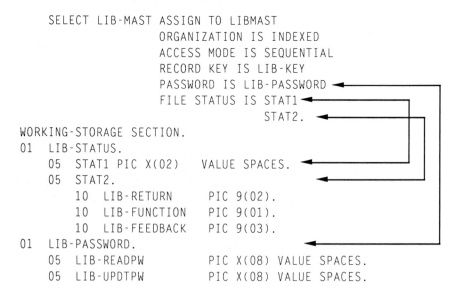

```
    SELECT LIB-MAST ASSIGN TO LIBMAST
                    ORGANIZATION IS INDEXED
                    ACCESS MODE IS SEQUENTIAL
                    RECORD KEY IS LIB-KEY
                    PASSWORD IS LIB-PASSWORD
                    FILE STATUS IS STAT1
                                   STAT2.
WORKING-STORAGE SECTION.
01  LIB-STATUS.
    05  STAT1 PIC X(02)   VALUE SPACES.
    05  STAT2.
        10  LIB-RETURN    PIC 9(02).
        10  LIB-FUNCTION  PIC 9(01).
        10  LIB-FEEDBACK  PIC 9(03).
01  LIB-PASSWORD.
    05  LIB-READPW        PIC X(08) VALUE SPACES.
    05  LIB-UPDTPW        PIC X(08) VALUE SPACES.
```

14.5. PROCEDURE DIVISION PROCESSING

When coding PROCEDURE DIVISION statements, you'll soon see that there's a direct relationship between what you code in the SELECT ORGANIZATION and ACCESS MODE clauses and the form of the COBOL I/O statement you choose. This is especially true for the OPEN statement.

We'll survey the most important I/O statements in this chapter and then discuss them in more depth in later chapters as we examine the different VSAM application scenarios, such as random and dynamic access and alternate index processing.

You code the ORGANIZATION and ACCESS clauses as follows:

```
                 INDEXED      (KSDS)
                 SEQUENTIAL   (ESDS)
                 RELATIVE     (RRDS)
ORGANIZATION IS  _____


                 SEQUENTIAL
                 RANDOM
                 DYNAMIC
ACCESS MODE IS   _____
```

14.5.1.   The OPEN Statement

The OPEN statement has several options:

```
                 EXTEND
                 INPUT
                 OUTPUT
                 I-O
OPEN file name   _____
```

If you want to open a VSAM dataset that has never contained records, and you have specified ACCESS IS SEQUENTIAL, you can only use OPEN OUTPUT or EXTEND. If you have specified RANDOM or DYNAMIC access for a KSDS or RRDS, you can OPEN I-O, but a sequential record load is faster and more efficient.

If you want to open a KSDS, ESDS, or RRDS that currently contains records, you can OPEN INPUT for reading records only. For an ESDS you must specify SEQUENTIAL access, but for a KSDS or an RRDS you can specify either RANDOM or DYNAMIC access. If you want to add and update KSDS or RRDS records and you have specified RANDOM or DYNAMIC access, you can OPEN I-O. If you want to add ESDS records (remember, access is always SEQUENTIAL) you can OPEN EXTEND. If you want to update ESDS records, you can OPEN-IO.

If you OPEN EXTEND and the dataset is a KSDS, each new record added must have a record key whose value is higher than the highest key value currently in the dataset. (This makes perfect sense if you think about it, because you are indeed "extending" the dataset.) If you OPEN EXTEND and the dataset is an ESDS or RRDS, the new records are added to the end of the file. (This also makes perfect sense if you think about it.)

No matter what form of the OPEN statement you choose, you should *always* check the COBOL status key and, optionally (under VS COBOL II), the VSAM return code after opening the dataset.

Chapter 15 covers loading an empty dataset with records in greater depth.

14.5.2. The READ Statement

The format of the READ statement for a VSAM dataset is the same as that of its non-VSAM counterpart:

```
READ file name
```

Like the READ statement for a non-VSAM sequential dataset, the use of this statement for a VSAM dataset retrieves records one at a time for browsing or updating. However, unlike a non-VSAM sequential dataset (or an ESDS), which can only be read sequentially, a KSDS or an RRDS can be read sequentially or randomly.

To read any VSAM record sequentially or randomly you need to open the dataset for INPUT or I-O. And it's important to check the COBOL status key after every READ statement as well.

For an ESDS, you must specify ACCESS IS SEQUENTIAL in the SELECT clause, and read access is always sequential. However, if you specify ACCESS IS SEQUENTIAL in the SELECT clause for a KSDS or RRDS, read access becomes sequential by default. If you specify AC-CESS IS RANDOM in the SELECT clause for a KSDS or an RRDS, read access becomes random by default. However, the DYNAMIC option provides even more flexibility, and this is another area where VSAM shines.

If you specify ACCESS IS DYNAMIC in the SELECT clause for a KSDS or an RRDS, you can switch back and forth between random and sequential access in the same program. You use the START statement to place a conceptual pointer called the File Position Indicator at the next record to be accessed sequentially. Then you use the READ NEXT statement to access records sequentially until you're ready to switch back to random access or until you reach the end-of-file. DYNAMIC access is especially efficient if most of your activity is concentrated in certain areas of the dataset, and we'll cover it in more depth in Chapter 17.

14.5.3.   Other COBOL I/O Statements

The other COBOL statements you will use when processing VSAM records are WRITE, REWRITE, and DELETE. The WRITE statement adds a new record to the dataset. It does not replace the records that are already there. To do that, you need the REWRITE statement, which replaces an existing record in a dataset that has been opened for I/O. If you have specified sequential access, you must read the record before rewriting it. A prior read is unnecessary if you have specified random or dynamic access. No matter which access type of access you specify, you can change the length of a KSDS record by rewriting it, but you cannot change the value of the primary key.

The DELETE statement deletes an existing record and is unique to the VSAM environment. You can delete both a KSDS and an RRDS, but not an ESDS. If you have specified sequential access (remember, the dataset must have an indexed or relative record file structure), you must read the record before deleting it. This is also true for KSDS spanned records. A prior read is unnecessary if you have specified random or dynamic access and your records are not spanned.

You should check the COBOL status key after every WRITE, RE-WRITE, and DELETE statement. For more information you may want to check the VSAM return code as well.

Chapters 15 through 20 examine application-specific issues for the WRITE, REWRITE, and DELETE statements.

14.5.4.   The CLOSE Statement

The format of the CLOSE statement for a VSAM dataset is the same as that of its non-VSAM counterpart:

```
CLOSE file name
```

COBOL automatically closes any open datasets when you terminate the run, but it is best to avoid the vagaries of this by having your program close the dataset. Always check at least the COBOL status key after the close operation. If something goes amiss with the closing, you should immediately issue an explicit VERIFY to update the HURBA pointers before doing any further processing with the dataset.

However, there is an exception to the rule of always closing your VSAM dataset: If COBOL can't open the VSAM dataset for some reason, you should abend the program without closing the dataset, determine the cause of the problem, and issue an explicit VERIFY, if appropriate.

14.6. SUMMARY

In a nutshell, here's what's new or different about processing a VSAM dataset with COBOL:

1. SELECT clause options:
   - In the SELECT clause, you must prefix the ddname with AS for an ESDS; for a KSDS or an RRDS, a prefix is treated as a comment.
   - The ORGANIZATION clause must agree with the file type specified in the DEFINE command (INDEXED, SEQUENTIAL, or RELATIVE). File organization does not change from program to program.
   - The ACCESS MODE clause names the access mode for the program: SEQUENTIAL, RANDOM, or, for a combination of sequential and random access, DYNAMIC. Access mode can change from program to program.
   - The RECORD KEY names the primary key for a KSDS. This data name also appears in the FD.
   - The ALTERNATE KEY clause names the alternate index key for a KSDS. A program can use more than one alternate key.
   - The FILE STATUS clause names the COBOL status key and, under VS COBOL II, the VSAM return code. You should check at least the COBOL status key after every I/O operation and abend the program for a serious I/O problem, for example, an OPEN error.

2. FILE SECTION entries:
   - The FD LABEL RECORDS clause is treated as a comment by VSAM. LABEL RECORDS is an obsolete item in the ANSI Standard and is to be removed in the next update.
   - The FD also describes the primary key and any alternate keys used in processing.

3. WORKING-STORAGE entries:
   - Name a status area to define the COBOL status key and, optionally, the VSAM return code named in the FILE STATUS clause.

4. PROCEDURE DIVISION statements:
- There is a direct relationship between what you code in the SELECT ORGANIZATION and ACCESS MODE clauses and the form of the COBOL I/O statement you choose. This is especially true for the OPEN statement.

REFERENCES

1. "American National Standard for Information Systems—Programming Language—COBOL," ANSI X3.23-1985, New York: American National Standards Institute, Inc., 1985.
2. "VS COBOL II Application Programming Language Reference," Order No. GC26-4047, San Jose, CA: IBM Corporation, 1989.
3. "VS COBOL II Application Programming Guide for MVS and CMS," Order No. SC26-4045, San Jose, CA: IBM Corporation, 1990.
4. "American National Standard for Information Systems—Programming Language—Intrinsic Function Module for COBOL," ANSI X3.23a-1989, New York: American National Standards Institute, Inc., 1985.
5. "Microsoft (R) COBOL Optimizing Compiler Version 3.0 for MS(R) OS/2 and MS-DOS(R)," Redmond, WA: Microsoft Corporation, 1988.
6. "Micro Focus COBOL/2™," Palo Alto, CA: Micro Focus Inc., 1991.
7. "VSAM Administration Guide," Order No. SC26-4518, San Jose, CA: IBM Corporation, 1989.
8. "VSAM Administration: Macro Instruction Reference," Order No. SC26-4517, San Jose, CA: IBM Corporation, 1989.

15

Loading Records

When loading a new VSAM dataset with records, it is generally more efficient to use the IDCAMS REPRO command than a COBOL program. However, if you want to reformat, edit, or validate the input, you may opt for the COBOL program, because REPRO doesn't provide any of these services. For more on using REPRO to load records, see Chapter 12. Of course, another option is to write a COBOL program to "massage" the input data and then use REPRO to load it. In the end, it just comes down to choosing the option that seems right for your application. No matter which method you choose, before actually loading the records, you'll need the following information (which you should gather as part of the program design phase).

For the input data you'll need to know the following:

1. Whether it's to be loaded from just one input dataset or several.
2. The name, file organization, and record length of each input dataset, and where each one is stored. If the detail is stored on a PC, you'll need to consider how you're going to upload it to the mainframe.
3. Whether all of the data is to be loaded, or just a portion of it.
4. Specifications for any validating, editing, and reformatting routines.
5. If it needs to be sorted in primary key order (if the target dataset is a KSDS).

Assuming the output dataset is VSAM, you'll need to know the following:

1. Its name and VSAM file type.
2. Whether it has been previously defined.
3. What its attributes are and where it is stored. (This is not necessary for a DFSMS-managed dataset.)
4. If DFSMS managed, the name of its assigned STORCLAS and, optionally, its DATACLAS and MGMTCLAS as well.
   Note: For items 1 through 4, the LISTCAT command can be used to view catalog entry details. See Chapter 10 for more information.
5. If a KSDS, whether any alternate index processing is planned.
6. Whether it currently contains records, has previously contained records but is now empty, or has never contained records (an unloaded dataset). If you want to add records to a VSAM dataset that currently contains records, refer to Chapters 16 and 17 that cover KSDS processing using random and dynamic access, and Chapters 19 and 20 that cover ESDS and RRDS processing issues. The rest of this chapter will deal primarily with loading a KSDS that has never contained records.

15.1. LOADING A DATASET WITH A COBOL PROGRAM

Now we'll take you though the steps necessary to write a COBOL program to load a dataset.

15.1.1. Unloaded Versus Empty Dataset Considerations

First we need to get some terms straight. When speaking of VSAM datasets, an "unloaded" dataset is one that is empty and has never contained any records. An unloaded dataset has a HURBA value of zero.

On the other hand, an "empty" dataset is one that has previously held records but is now empty because all of the records have been removed with the COBOL DELETE statement or by some other process. An empty dataset has a HURBA value that is greater than zero.

To load an *empty* dataset with records, you must OPEN I-O or EXTEND. You cannot OPEN OUTPUT, because the value of HURBA is greater than zero. If you try, COBOL will set its status key to a value of 95, and the OPEN will fail. The one exception is a KSDS that has been defined with the REUSE option. Even if the dataset contains records and the HURBA value is greater than zero, the REUSE option forces the logical deletion of all existing records before the loading process, and you can OPEN OUTPUT.

To load an *unloaded* KSDS with records, you can OPEN OUTPUT or

EXTEND, but OUTPUT is significantly faster. You can also specify sequential or random access. However, sequential access is faster and it honors the FREESPACE allocation in the DEFINE command, which is ignored by random access loading. The bottom line here is to specify ACCESS IS SEQUENTIAL and OPEN OUTPUT in your load program unless there's some compelling reason for not doing so.

The other thing you need to remember is that to load a KSDS sequentially, the input records must be in primary key order, so you'll probably have to add a separate sort step to your input procedure.

We'll spend the rest of the chapter looking at a simple VS COBOL II program that writes KSDS records to an unloaded dataset using an 80-byte QSAM transaction file as input.

15.1.2.   IDENTIFICATION DIVISION Considerations

The following is the IDENTIFICATION DIVISION for a VS COBOL II load program that loads a KSDS. Note that we've used the structured technique of creating a self-documenting program by adding comments wherever appropriate. To paraphrase the words of a famous duchess, "You can't be too thin, too rich, or have too many comments in your COBOL program."

```
IDENTIFICATION DIVISION.
PROGRAM-ID.    VDEMO1.
****************************************************************
* This program loads a previously unloaded 80-byte KSDS      *
* with records using an 80-byte transaction file as          *
* input. The transaction file must be previously sorted      *
* in ascending sequence by TRAN-KEY, which becomes the       *
* primary key LIB-KEY in the output file. Because the        *
* file is opened for OUTPUT, SEQUENTIAL access is            *
* specified.                                                 *
*                                                            *
*                                                            *
*                                                            *
* Maintenance history:  If you maintain this file,           *
*                       please add name, date, and           *
*                       remarks here.                         *
****************************************************************
```

In the FILE-CONTROL paragraph, ORGANIZATION must be INDEXED because the target dataset is a KSDS, and ACCESS MODE IS

SEQUENTIAL because the dataset is to be loaded sequentially by primary key. The RECORD KEY clause names this primary key.

```
ENVIRONMENT DIVISION.
INPUT-OUTPUT SECTION.
FILE-CONTROL.
    SELECT TRAN-FILE ASSIGN TO          TRANFILE.
    SELECT LIB-MAST  ASSIGN TO          LIBMAST
                     ORGANIZATION IS INDEXED
                     ACCESS MODE  IS SEQUENTIAL
                     RECORD KEY   IS LIB-KEY
                     FILE STATUS  IS STAT1,
                                     STAT2.
```

The FILE STATUS clause names both a COBOL status key and a VSAM return code. The program will test the COBOL status key for an appropriate value after every I/O operation and, depending on the value, either display a message and continue processing or abend the program.

15.1.3. FILE SECTION Considerations

In the FILE SECTION of the DATA DIVISION, the FD for TRAN-FILE names TRAN-KEY. The input has been sorted in ascending sequence by this field, because it becomes the primary key in the output record. (You don't really have to identify this field unless you use it in the PROCEDURE DIVISION, but we've done so in order to point out its significance.)

The FDs for both TRAN-FILE and LIB-REC specify RECORD CONTAINS 80 CHARACTERS. This is for documentation purposes only. VSAM doesn't require this clause. The same is true for the LABEL RECORDS . . . clause.

```
DATA DIVISION.
FILE SECTION.
FD  TRAN-FILE
    LABEL RECORDS ARE STANDARD
    RECORD CONTAINS 80 CHARACTERS.
01  TRAN-REC.
    05  TRAN-KEY          PIC X(08).
*       Input sorted in ascending sequence by this field.
    05  FILLER            PIC X(72).
```

```
FD   LIB-MAST
     LABEL RECORDS ARE STANDARD
     RECORD CONTAINS 80 CHARACTERS.
01   LIB-REC.
     05 LIB-KEY            PIC X(08).
*        The primary key.
     05  LIB-AUTH-LNAME    PIC X(15).
     05  LIB-AUTH-FNAME    PIC X(12).
     05  LIB-AUTH-INIT     PIC X(01).
     05  LIB-TITLE         PIC X(28).
     05  LIB-ISBN-NO       PIC X(13).
     05  LIB-COPIES        PIC 9(03).
```

15.1.4.   WORKING-STORAGE Considerations

In the WORKING-STORAGE SECTION, note that the input record is
read into and the output record is written from a work area called WS-
LIB-REC. This is a common COBOL practice, but you can also read and
write from the buffer (the input area).

```
WORKING-STORAGE SECTION.
01   FILLER                   PIC X(27) VALUE
                              "WORKING STORAGE STARTS HERE".
*******************************************************
* The output record is written from WS-LIB-REC.   *
* WS-LIB-REC is also used for data validation in  *
* 300-VALIDATE-INPUT.                             *
*******************************************************
01   WS-LIB-REC.
     05  WS-LIB-KEY           PIC X(08).
     05  WS-LIB-AUTH-LNAME    PIC X(15).
     05  WS-LIB-AUTH-FNAME    PIC X(12).
     05  WS-LIB-AUTH-INIT     PIC X(01).
     05  WS-LIB-TITLE         PIC X(28).
     05  WS-LIB-ISBN-NO       PIC X(13).
     05  WS-LIB-COPIES        PIC 9(03).
```

LIB-STATUS-AREA further defines the COBOL status key (STAT1)
and the VSAM return code (STAT2) specified in the FILE STATUS
clause. If a serious I/O error occurs, the information in STAT2 can be
displayed and analyzed.

```
01  LIB-STATUS-AREA.
    05   STAT1                 PIC X(02)     VALUE SPACES.
*        The COBOL status key.
         88  OK                              VALUE "00".
         88  OUT-OF-SEQUENCE                 VALUE "21".
         88  DUP                             VALUE "22".
    05   STAT2.
*        The VSAM return code. (Values for VS COBOL II
*        only).
         10  V-RETURN          PIC 9(02).
         10  V-FUNC            PIC 9.
         10  V-FEEDBACK        PIC 9(03).
```

The COBOL status key conditions to check for in an initial load are:

21   Primary key out of sequence

22   Duplicate primary key encountered

Also in WORKING-STORAGE, the FLAGS-AND-SWITCHES-AREA names and defines the following switches. The use of switches and flags to control processing is a common COBOL technique, not a VSAM processing requirement.

```
01  FLAGS-AND-SWITCHES-AREA.
    05   OPEN-SW               PIC X(03)     VALUE "   ".
         88 OPEN-ERR                         VALUE "OPN".
*            Value for an OPEN error.
    05   TRAN-SW               PIC X(03)     VALUE "   ".
         88 TRAN-EOF                         VALUE "END".
*            Transaction end-of-file; an unexpected
*            condition.
    05   ERROR-SW              PIC X(03)     VALUE "   ".
         88 IO-ERR                           VALUE "I/O".
*            Serious I/O error.
    05   INPUT-FLAG            PIC X(03)     VALUE "   ".
         88 INPUT-ERR                        VALUE "INP".
*            Set each time an input record is bypassed
*            due to invalid data.
```

COUNTER-AREA names and defines a series of counters.

```
01  COUNTER-AREA.
    05  TOTAL-GOOD-RECS    PIC 9(04)    VALUE ZEROES.
*         Total output records written.
    05  TOTAL-BYPASSED     PIC 9(02)    VALUE ZEROES.
*         Total input records bypassed.
    05  TOTAL-BAD-RECS     PIC 9(02)    VALUE ZEROES.
*         Count of out-of-sequence or duplicate records.
        88  TOO-MANY-ERRORS            VALUE 3.
*           Number of TOTAL-BAD-RECS to count before
*           abending program. Input file is probably
*           not in proper sort order.
```

15.1.5.   PROCEDURE DIVISION Considerations

The PROCEDURE DIVISION begins with a label of 100-PROCESS routine. VS COBOL II and Microsoft/Micro Focus COBOL don't require that a program begin with a label, but ANSI COBOL does, so we'll include one, even though it isn't used. Then we display a message saying that the program has begun execution.

```
PROCEDURE DIVISION.
100-PROCESS.
    DISPLAY "STARTING VDEMO1 PROGRAM."
```

The OPEN OUTPUT statement. We then open the TRAN-FILE and LIB-MAST datasets. We needn't check that the OPEN was successful for the TRAN-FILE because it is not a VSAM dataset. However, we will verify that the OPEN was successful for the VSAM LIB-MAST dataset. Note that we open LIB-MAST for OUTPUT because the program is loading the data sequentially.

```
OPEN INPUT TRAN-FILE
OPEN OUTPUT LIB-MAST
```

We examine the COBOL status key STAT1 immediately after opening the LIB-MAST dataset. If its value is greater than "00" (error), we set the OPEN-ERR flag, display messages, and drop through without closing the dataset. If it's the standard at your shop, you may want to check for a previous implicit VERIFY here and continue processing if a value of 97 is returned. For other VERIFY considerations, see Chapter 12.

```
IF NOT OK
    SET OPEN-ERR TO TRUE
    DISPLAY "OPEN ERROR ON LIB-MAST"
    DISPLAY "COBOL STATUS KEY IS" STAT1
    DISPLAY "VSAM RETURN CODE IS" STAT2
    DISPLAY "ISSUE EXPLICIT VERIFY AND THEN"
    DISPLAY "RERUN PROGRAM"
ELSE
```

[If there is no OPEN error, we do the processing for the main loop of the program.]

```
    PERFORM 200-READ UNTIL TRAN-EOF OR IO-ERR
END-IF ...
```

If VSAM can't OPEN LIB-MAST for some reason, some other CO-BOL status key values that you may see displayed are as follows, with their most probable cause and what your course of action should be:

30   A serious I/O error has occurred. Since no other information is displayed, the information in the VSAM return code can really help you here. You should check both the IDCAMS DEFINE command and your program logic.

90   The dataset is unusable for some reason. Check to be sure that OPEN OUTPUT is specified, and ACCESS MODE IS SEQUEN-TIAL.

91   The dataset is password-protected and either the password has been incorrectly specified or it has been ignored.

92   The dataset is already open. Terminate the program without closing the dataset and issue an explicit VERIFY.

93   There is not currently enough virtual storage available, or the dataset is not available for some reason. You can increase the JCL REGION parameter in case of the former, and check the DEFINE command SHAREOPTIONS in case of the latter. Another possibility is that another batch job is using the cluster with DISP=OLD coded in the JCL, or an online task may be using the dataset.

95   VSAM detected a non-zero HURBA on OPEN OUTPUT. The dataset may already contain records.

96   There's a problem with the dataset DD statement. Check that
      the program SELECT clause uses the same ddname as in the
      JCL.

```
SELECT LIB-MAST ASSIGN TO ddname
```

//ddname DD DSN= ...

End-of-file processing. When the transaction end-of-file is reached
or a serious I/O error occurs, we always close TRAN-FILE. However, if
the OPEN-ERR switch indicates that LIB-MAST was never successfully opened, we do not attempt to close the dataset but instead fall
through to STOP-RUN.

```
PERFORM 200-READ WITH TEST AFTER
    UNTIL TRAN-EOF OR IO-ERR ...
CLOSE TRAN-FILE
IF NOT OPEN-ERR
    CLOSE LIB-MAST
```

We won't check the CLOSE for TRAN-FILE because it isn't a VSAM
dataset. But we will check the CLOSE for LIB-MAST. If the CLOSE
statement fails for some reason, we first set IO-ERR to TRUE, then
display appropriate messages and both the COBOL status key and the
VSAM return code. Someone should then analyze this display information before rerunning the program.

```
IF NOT OK
    SET IO-ERR TO TRUE
    DISPLAY "CLOSE ERROR ON LIB-MAST"
    DISPLAY "COBOL STATUS KEY IS" STAT1
    DISPLAY "VSAM RETURN CODE IS" STAT2
    END-IF
END-IF
```

If VSAM can't close the dataset, the likely COBOL status key values
are as follows, along with their most probable cause and what your
course of action should be:

30   A serious I/O error has occurred. Since no other information is
      displayed, the information in the VSAM return code can really

help you here. You should check both the IDCAMS DEFINE command and your program logic.

90 A catch-all meaning VSAM logic error. Check your program logic.

92 The dataset is already closed. Check your program logic.

93 Not enough virtual storage available or resource not available.

COBOL status key values 30, 90, 92, and 93 can also be returned for OPEN, WRITE, or CLOSE errors. For this reason, it's important to display appropriate messages along with the COBOL status key.

Finally, if we've made it all the way through the program with no serious errors (NOT IO-ERR), we display appropriate end-of-processing information and end the program in a normal fashion.

```
IF NOT IO-ERR
   DISPLAY "PROGRAM VDEMO1 ENDED OK"
   DISPLAY "NUMBER OF RECORDS ADDED",
        TOTAL-GOOD-RECS
   DISPLAY "NUMBER OF INPUT RECORDS BYPASSED",
        TOTAL-BYPASSED
   DISPLAY "NUMBER OF OUT-OF-SEQUENCE OR"
   DISPLAY "DUPLICATE RECORDS BYPASSED: ",
        TOTAL-BAD-RECS
ELSE
   DISPLAY "TERMINATING BECAUSE OF ERROR"
END-IF
STOP RUN
```

[In COBOL 85, the only requirement for a period is that it end a paragraph. It could be placed on a line by itself here so statements could be added without worrying about it and to also help document that this is the end of a paragraph.

You should carefully analyze this end-of-processing information to be sure that the numbers are what you expect. Then you'll want to use LISTCAT to doublecheck the attributes of your new dataset.

READ and WRITE considerations. Let's step back a moment and look at some READ and WRITE considerations for the initial record load.

We perform 200-READ until the transaction end-of-file or a serious I/O error is encountered. Note we are using the AT END/NOT AT END technique to avoid having multiple READ statements in the program. If 300-VALIDATE-INPUT returns a good record (NOT INPUT-ERR), we write the output KSDS record from the WORKING-STORAGE record.

```
        PERFORM 200-READ WITH TEST AFTER
            UNTIL TRAN-EOF OR IO-ERR
  200-READ.
*          Initialize WS-LIB-REC each time through the
*          loop.
                INITIALIZE WS-LIB-REC
                READ TRAN-FILE INTO WS-LIB-REC
                    AT END
                        SET TRAN-EOF TO TRUE
                    NOT AT END
                        PERFORM 300-VALIDATE-INPUT
                        IF NOT INPUT-ERR
                            WRITE LIB-REC FROM WS-LIB-REC
```

It's very important to check the COBOL status key after every WRITE statement. When this status key is OK (00), we add one to the TOTAL-GOOD-RECS counter, fall through the rest of the routine, and immediately loop through 200-READ again.

```
EVALUATE TRUE
    WHEN OK
        ADD 1 TO TOTAL-GOOD-RECS
    [Loop again.]
```

OUT-OF-SEQUENCE and DUPLICATE records. When the COBOL status key indicates that the previous WRITE statement was unsuccessful due to an out-of-sequence input record (21) or a duplicate input record (22), we display an appropriate message. A few out-of-sequence or duplicate records can be safely bypassed.

```
WHEN (OUT-OF-SEQUENCE OR DUP)
    ADD 1 TO TOTAL-BAD-RECS
```

Monitoring WRITE errors. Each time the COBOL status code indicates an out-of-sequence or duplicate record, we add one to the TOTAL-

BAD-RECS counter. If ten bad records are encountered, we're assuming the input is bad, and we display an appropriate message.

```
IF TOO-MANY-ERRORS
   DISPLAY "INPUT MESSED UP"
   SET IO-ERR TO TRUE
   DISPLAY "ENDING PROGRAM VDEMO1 NOW"
END-IF
```

Serious I/O errors. After the WRITE statement, if the COBOL status key is not OK (00) and not OUT-OF-SEQUENCE (21) and not DUPLICATE (22), OTHER indicates that a serious WRITE I/O error has occurred. If this happens, we display an appropriate error message with both the COBOL status key value and the VSAM return code values.

```
WHEN OTHER
     DISPLAY "OTHER VSAM ERROR"
     DISPLAY "COBOL STATUS KEY IS" STAT1
     DISPLAY "VSAM RETURN CODE IS" STAT2
     SET IO-ERR TO TRUE
     DISPLAY "ENDING PROGRAM VDEMO1 NOW"...
```

If a serious WRITE error has occurred, the COBOL status key values that you may see displayed are as follows, along with their most probable cause and what your course of action should be:

24   The dataset is out of space. You may need to redefine the cluster and increase the space allocation.

30   A serious I/O error has occurred. Since no other information is displayed, the information in the VSAM return code can really help you here. You should check both the IDCAMS DEFINE command and your program logic.

90   A catch-all meaning VSAM logic error. Check your program logic.

92   The dataset is not open. Check your program logic.

93   Not enough virtual storage available, or the resource is not available.

Validating input. After reading each record into the WORKING-STORAGE record WS-LIB-REC, we perform 300-VALIDATE-INPUT. Take some time to examine code for this typical input validation routine.

It is particularly important to examine WS-LIB-KEY, the primary key, and both alternate index keys, WS-LIB-AUTH-LNAME and WS-ISBN-NO (the Library of Congress number), for blank or invalid data.

To be safe, we check each numeric field for zeros (if appropriate) or nonnumeric data and reject any invalid records. We examine WS-LIB-COPIES in this manner to prevent any divide-by-zero or data-exception errors while processing. This, of course, is not a VSAM requirement, just a COBOL coding practice.

```
300-VALIDATE-INPUT.
****************************************************************
* SUBROUTINE TO VALIDATE THE INPUT RECORD.                    *
****************************************************************
      MOVE SPACES TO INPUT-FLAG
      IF WS-LIB-KEY = SPACES
          ADD 1 TO TOTAL-BYPASSED
          SET INPUT-ERR TO TRUE
          DISPLAY "ERROR—BAD RECORD KEY"
      END-IF
      IF (WS-LIB-AUTH-LNAME = SPACES OR
          WS-LIB-AUTH-LNAME(1:1) NOT ALPHABETIC)
          ADD 1 TO TOTAL-BYPASSED
          SET INPUT-ERR TO TRUE
          DISPLAY "ERROR—BAD AUTHOR NAME"
      END-IF
      IF (WS-LIB-AUTH-FNAME = SPACES OR
          WS-LIB-AUTH-FNAME(1:1) NOT ALPHABETIC)
          DISPLAY "WARNING—BAD FIRST NAME"
      FND-IF
      IF  WS-LIB-TITLE = SPACES
          ADD 1 TO TOTAL-BYPASSED
          SET INPUT-ERR TO TRUE
          DISPLAY "ERROR—NO TITLE"
      END-IF
      IF  WS-LIB-ISBN-NO = SPACES
          ADD 1 TO TOTAL-BYPASSED
          SET INPUT-ERR TO TRUE
          DISPLAY "ERROR—BAD ISBN NUMBER"
      END-IF
      IF (WS-LIB-COPIES = ZERO OR
          WS-LIB-COPIES NOT NUMERIC)
```

```
      ADD 1 TO TOTAL-BYPASSED
      SET INPUT-ERR TO TRUE
      DISPLAY "ERROR--INVALID COPIES"
   END-IF
   IF INPUT-ERR
      DISPLAY "TRANSACTION IN ERROR IS: "
      DISPLAY WS-LIB-REC
   END-IF.
```

As part of the input data validation routine, you can also examine each primary key for an out-of-sequence or duplicate condition, but it's generally better to rely on information from the COBOL status key rather than your program logic (which after all may not be perfect) to identify and bypass these "bad apple" records.

Complete processing statements. To see everything in context, turn to Appendix B for the complete COBOL statements to load a previously unloaded KSDS with records. Note in the PROCEDURE DIVISION that the example makes generous use of the EVALUATE statement, AT END/NOT AT END logic, and various scope terminators (END-EVALUATE, END-IF) because of the flexibility they offer.

15.2. LOAD JCL STATEMENTS

Below are the complete JCL statements that you need to load a previously unloaded KSDS with records using a sorted sequential transaction dataset as input.

```
//COBLOAD   JOB ...
//STEP1     EXEC PGM=VDEMO1
//SYSOUT    DD SYSOUT=*
//TRANFILE  DD DSN=A1000.SORTED.LIB.INPUT,DISP=SHR
```

[The ddnames TRANFILE and LIBMAST point back to their respective SELECT statements in the program VDEMO1.]

```
//LIBMAST   DD DSN=A2000.LIB.KSDS.CLUSTER,DISP=OLD,
```

[We've specified DISP=OLD for LIBMAST in order to maintain exclusive control while loading the file.]

```
//          AMP=('BUFND=10')
```

[We've requested extra data buffers with the AMP parameter in order to process this sequential load more efficiently. The default is two data buffers.]

If your VSAM dataset is DFSMS managed, you can create the KSDS dynamically in the COBOL load program without a prior IDCAMS DEFINE CLUSTER command. Here are the equivalent JCL statements for using this technique. Note that in this case the DISP parameter specifies NEW,CATLG. For a further explanation of these parameters, see Chapter 9.

```
//SMSLOAD  JOB ...
//STEP1     EXEC PGM=VDEMO1
//SYSOUT    DD SYSOUT=*
//TRANFILE  DD DSN=A1000.SORTED.LIB.INPUT,DISP=SHR
//LIBMAST   DD DSN=A2000.LIB.KSDS.CLUSTER,
//          DISP=(NEW,CATLG),
//          AMP=('BUFND=10'),
//          SPACE=(CYL(5,1)),
//          LRECL=80,
//          KEYLEN=8,KEYOFF=0,
//          RECORG=KS,
//          DATACLAS=KSDSDATA
```

Assume here that MGMTCLAS and STORCLAS are assigned implicitly through storage administration-controlled ACS routines.

15.3. SUMMARY

To recap, here's what is needed to load a previously unloaded KSDS with records using a sequential dataset sorted in ascending sequence on the potential primary key field:

- Specify SEQUENTIAL in the ACCESS MODE clause.
- Name a COBOL status key in the FILE STATUS clause and define it in WORKING-STORAGE.
- OPEN the KSDS for OUTPUT.
- Check the COBOL status key after the OPEN statement, after each WRITE statement, and after the CLOSE statement.
- Bypass records that have an out-of-sequence (21) or a duplicate (22) primary key.
- Don't attempt to CLOSE the KSDS if you can't OPEN it. Instead, end the program and issue an explicit VERIFY command before rerunning.

16

Accessing and Updating Records in a KSDS

Just as there are 50 ways to leave your lover, there are 3 ways to access a KSDS. This chapter describes two such methods, sequential and random access. We'll look at dynamic access in the next chapter.

16.1. SEQUENTIAL ACCESS

Sequential access for a KSDS has the same meaning that it does for a QSAM dataset: reading records, one after another, from the beginning of the dataset to the end. Straight sequential access is mostly used with batch COBOL programs.

Let's say for our sample application of an audio book service that we need the total number of copies of all the titles for a summary report. This is a simple example, but it serves our purpose nicely. Just to refresh your memory, here's a snapshot view of the LIB-REC record description again.

```
01  LIB-REC.
*     The primary key.
      05  LIB-KEY           PIC X(08).
      05  LIB-AUTH-LNAME    PIC X(15).
      05  LIB-AUTH-FNAME    PIC X(12).
      05  LIB-AUTH-INIT     PIC X(01).
      05  LIB-TITLE         PIC X(28).
      05  LIB-ISBN-NO       PIC X(13).
      05  LIB-COPIES        PIC 9(03).
```

LIB-COPIES is the field to be totaled, and for this application we won't have to use the primary key field (LIB-KEY) at all, even though we identify it in the SELECT clause that follows. The SELECT clause specifies INDEXED organization (always, because the dataset is a KSDS) and SEQUENTIAL access mode (for this application only). This is the same SELECT clause that we used for the sequential record load in the last chapter, except that now the KSDS is used as the input dataset.

```
SELECT LIB-MAST ASSIGN TO       LIBMAST
                ORGANIZATION IS INDEXED
                ACCESS MODE  IS SEQUENTIAL
                RECORD KEY   IS LIB-KEY
                FILE STATUS  IS STAT1,
                                STAT2.
```

The COBOL status key and the VSAM return code (not shown here) are defined in WORKING-STORAGE just as for the sequential load, except that now we have added a value to check for the end-of-file. For sequential access, this is an expected condition and we'll explain further as the need arises.

```
01  LIB-STATUS-AREA.
*   The COBOL status key.
    05 STAT1            PIC X(02)   VALUE SPACES.
       88  OK                       VALUE "00".
       88  END-OF-FILE              VALUE "10".  <===
```

16.1.1. OPEN INPUT Statement

In the PROCEDURE DIVISION, we open LIB-MAST as INPUT. You could also open it as I-O if you were going to rewrite or delete some records. However, you cannot add new records if you specify the combination of sequential access and OPEN I-O. Since we're only reading the records for reporting purposes in this application, there's no reason to open the dataset as I-O.

```
OPEN INPUT LIB-MAST
```

You should check the COBOL status key value immediately after opening the dataset, and if it is greater than 00 (NOT OK), you should terminate the program without attempting to CLOSE the dataset.

```
IF OK
    Continue processing
ELSE
    SET INPUT-ERR TO TRUE
    Terminate program
END-IF
```

However, if your shop supports the implicit VERIFY (status key value 97) you can code a condition for this and continue processing.

```
05  STAT1              PIC X(02)    VALUE SPACES.
    88  OK                          VALUE "00".
    88  VERIFIED                    VALUE "97".
.  .  .
IF OK OR VERIFIED
    Continue processing
ELSE
    SET INPUT-ERR TO TRUE
    Terminate program
END-IF
```

If VSAM can't OPEN the dataset for some reason, the following CO-BOL status key values show the probable cause and what your course of action should be:

30   A serious I/O error has occurred. Since no other information is displayed, the information in the VSAM return code can really help you here.

90   The dataset is unusable for some reason. Check to be sure that the OPEN INPUT is specified and ACCESS MODE IS SEQUEN-TIAL. Another possibility is that the dataset may be empty.

91   The dataset is password-protected and either the password has been incorrectly specified or it has been ignored. For read-only access, the READPW password is sufficient.

92   There is a logic error. Perhaps the dataset is already open. Sta-tus codes 35 through 39 or 41 may also be returned.

93   There is not currently enough virtual storage available, or the dataset is not available for some reason. You can increase the JCL REGION parameter for the former and check the DEFINE

command SHAREOPTIONS for the latter. Another possibility is that another job has obtained exclusive control of the dataset by coding DISP=OLD in the JCL.

96   There's a problem with the DD statement for the dataset. Check the program SELECT clause ddname against the JCL.

16.1.2.   Reading Records Sequentially

Once the KSDS has been opened successfully, the program can begin to read records sequentially. The basic format for the READ statement is the same as that of a sequential dataset:

```
READ file name INTO identifier  or  READ file name
   AT END ...                          AT END ...
   NOT AT END ...                      NOT AT END ...    .
END-READ                            END-READ
```

Both INTO (which reads the record directly into some WORKING-STORAGE area) and AT END/NOT AT END (which handles end-of-file processing logic) are optional, but, of course, you'll always want to test for the end-of-file, for example:

```
READ LIB-MAST
   AT END
      Do end-of-file processing
   NOT AT END
      ADD LIB-COPIES TO COUNT-TOTAL
      . . .
END-READ
```

An even more precise method is to check the COBOL status key for a value of 10, which indicates that the end of the KSDS has been reached. You can use the EVALUATE statement for this as in the following example.

```
READ LIB-MAST
EVALUATE TRUE
   WHEN OK
      ADD LIB-COPIES TO COUNT-TOTAL
      . . .
   WHEN END-OF-FILE
      SET EOF TO TRUE  <===
```

```
WHEN OTHER
    Display appropriate message and status codes
    Terminate program
END-EVALUATE
```

OTHER is a catch-all that captures any condition that passes the previous WHEN tests.

If the COBOL status key returns a value that is higher than 10, the dataset has a serious problem, and you should terminate the program. In this case, you may see status key value 92 displayed, or with COBOL 85 you could see 46 or 47, both of which pertain to the READ statement.

The READ statement can be placed in a paragraph, such as 200-READ, and then performed repeatedly until all the records are read or a serious error is encountered.

```
PERFORM 200-READ WITH TEST AFTER
    UNTIL EOF OR IO-ERR
```

16.1.3.   The CLOSE Statement

Once the program has read all of the records in the dataset, reached an end-of-file, and performed any end-of-file logic, you CLOSE the dataset and check the COBOL status key value to be sure that the CLOSE was successful. Of course, if your OPEN statement fails (INPUT-ERR set to TRUE) you shouldn't CLOSE the dataset. You should issue an explicit VERIFY before processing the dataset again.

```
PERFORM 200-READ WITH TEST AFTER
    UNTIL EOF OR IO-ERR
IF NOT IO-ERR
    Display appropriate message
END-IF
IF NOT INPUT-ERR
    CLOSE LIB-MAST
    IF NOT OK
        Display appropriate message and status codes
    END-IF
END-IF
```

And if VSAM can't CLOSE the dataset for some reason, you should issue an explicit VERIFY command before attempting to use the dataset in other processing.

16.1.4. Recap of Sequential Access Requirements

To recap, here are the statements you should have to read a KSDS sequentially:

- In the SELECT clause, specify sequential access.

```
ACCESS MODE IS SEQUENTIAL
```

- Also in the SELECT clause, name at least a COBOL status key and, optionally, a VSAM return code data item.

```
FILE STATUS IS STAT1, STAT2.
```

- Open the KSDS as INPUT and check the COBOL status key.

```
OPEN INPUT LIB-MAST
IF OK
    Continue processing
ELSE
    Terminate the program without closing the file
END-IF
```

- Perform a paragraph similar to this until all of the records are read or a serious I/O error is encountered.

```
READ LIB-MAST
EVALUATE TRUE
  WHEN OK
    Continue processing
  WHEN END-OF-FILE
    SET EOF TO TRUE
  WHEN OTHER
    Display appropriate message and status codes
    Terminate program
END-EVALUATE
```

- If the KSDS has been opened successfully, CLOSE the dataset and immediately check the COBOL status key.

```
IF NOT INPUT-ERR
   CLOSE LIB-MAST
   IF NOT OK
     Display appropriate message and status codes
     . . .
   END-IF
END-IF
```

16.2. RANDOM ACCESS

The *American Heritage Dictionary* defines random access as "Allowing access to stored computer data without regard to data sequence." This is another area where VSAM shines, especially since under VS COBOL II, VSAM processing is the only way to access data randomly using key-sequenced or relative record datasets. VS COBOL II does not support ISAM (Indexed Sequential Access Method) or BDAM (Basic Direct Access Method) dataset processing. ISAM and BDAM are access methods largely replaced by VSAM.

Just as sequential read-only access of a KSDS is more often done in batch COBOL (say for reporting, like the previous example), random read-only access is more often done in an online CICS application. If we take our example of an audio book mail order business, the order desk people would need to query LIB-MAST to see if a requested title is available for shipping. This is most efficiently done online using CICS and we'll explore this in Chapter 21. However, for the rest of this chapter let's look at some random access techniques for updating a KSDS using batch COBOL.

The new sample application program is to read input transactions from an 81-character sequential input dataset and, based on a TRAN-CODE in position 81, add (A), delete (D), replace (R), or update (U) the 80-character LIB-MAST KSDS. We've added comments to this effect in the IDENTIFICATION DIVISION. (There's a complete listing of a similar program in Appendix C of this book. You can use it as a model for a random or dynamic update program.)

```
IDENTIFICATION DIVISION.
PROGRAM-ID.    VDEMO2.
*************************************************************
* This example supports Titles-On-Tape Audio Library      *
* (TOTAL), a mail-order audio book enterprise.            *
*                                                          *
* The program reads input transactions ...                 *
*                                                          *
* Maintenance history:  If you maintain this file,         *
*                       please add name, date, and         *
*                       remarks here.                      *
*************************************************************
```

To read a KSDS randomly, the SELECT clause specifies random access.

```
SELECT LIB-MAST ASSIGN TO        LIBMAST
                ORGANIZATION IS INDEXED
                ACCESS MODE  IS RANDOM <===
                RECORD KEY   IS LIB-KEY
                FILE STATUS  IS STAT1,
                                STAT2.
```

You can also specify dynamic access, which allows you to read the dataset both sequentially and randomly, and we'll look at that technique in the next chapter.

In the FILE SECTION notice the FDs for both TRAN-FILE (the input transaction dataset) and LIB-MAST. Observe that TRAN-KEY is an eight-byte alphanumeric data item, a mirror image of the primary key, LIB-KEY.

```
FILE SECTION.
FD  TRAN-FILE
    RECORD CONTAINS 81 CHARACTERS.
01  TRAN-RECORD.
    05  TRAN-KEY          PIC X(08).
    05  FILLER            PIC X(73).
FD  LIB-MAST
    RECORD CONTAINS 80 CHARACTERS.
01  LIB-RECORD.
*   The primary key.
    05  LIB-KEY           PIC X(08).
    05  FILLER            PIC X(72).
```

For random access, you indicate the record you want by storing a value in the RECORD KEY identifier. In our case, we move TRAN-KEY to LIB-KEY. Then the READ statement is executed for LIB-MAST.

```
MOVE TRAN-KEY TO LIB-KEY
READ LIB-MAST INTO identifier
```

TRAN-FILE may be unsequenced, but if it is first sorted into key sequence, you can reduce the physical I/O to the random dataset and improve performance considerably. We'll cover the random READ statement in more detail in just a bit. First, let's look at the WORKING-STORAGE COBOL status key values you need to check for.

```
01  LIB-STATUS-AREA.
*   The COBOL status key.
    05  STAT1             PIC X(02)    VALUE SPACES.
        88  OK                         VALUE "00".
        88  EOF                        VALUE "10".
        88  DUP                        VALUE "22".
        88  NOT-FOUND                  VALUE "23".
        88  VERIFIED                   VALUE "97".
```

When updating a KSDS randomly, you'll need to check for duplicate records (when adding new records) and record not found (when rewriting or deleting old records). With random access, you shouldn't encounter the KSDS end-of-file marker, but that's a possibility with dynamic access, and we'll look at that situation in the next chapter.

16.2.1.   OPEN I-O

In the PROCEDURE DIVISION, we open the KSDS for I-O because we're going to both read from and write records to the same dataset.

```
PROCEDURE DIVISION.
100-START-PROGRAM.
    OPEN INPUT TRAN-FILE
    OPEN I-O LIB-MAST <===
```

Writing records to the dataset just read is known as an *update in place,* and it is a technique different from a sequential update where you read the old master and write records to the new master.

```
READ OLD-MASTER INTO OLD-RECORD
WRITE NEW-RECORD FROM OLD-RECORD
```

As always, check the COBOL status key value to be sure that the OPEN statement was successful:

```
OPEN I-O LIB-MAST
IF (OK OR VERIFIED)
    Continue processing
ELSE
    Display error message and terminate
END-IF
```

The following COBOL status key values may occur if VSAM can't open the dataset for some reason. Since values returned for a dataset opened I-O are basically the same as one opened INPUT (except for 90), see the OPEN INPUT paragraph earlier in this chapter to review details concerning them.

30   A serious I/O error has occurred.

90   The dataset is unusable for some reason. Check to be sure that the OPEN I-O is specified and ACCESS MODE IS RANDOM. Another possibility is that the dataset may be empty.

91   There's a password problem.

92   The dataset is already open.

93   There is not currently enough virtual storage available, or the dataset is not available for some reason.

96   There's a problem with the DD statement for the dataset.

97   An implicit VERIFY was issued. In this example we're assuming the implicit VERIFY is supported.

16.2.2.   Processing Logic

After determining that the dataset is successfully opened, the program performs a paragraph like the one that follows until it encounters a serious I/O error or the transaction end-of-file.

```
PERFORM 200-PROCESS WITH TEST AFTER
   UNTIL IO-ERR OR TRAN-EOF
```

Notice that we used the WITH TEST AFTER clause. WITH TEST AFTER always loops through the performed paragraph one time, and then tests the condition. It's the same as the DO UNTIL construct in structured programming. It is used for a read loop because you must always execute the loop at least once to determine if there is an end-of-file.

First, we set up an area in WORKING-STORAGE named TRAN-REC and the program reads each input record into this area. TRAN-CODE (position 81 in the record) contains a one-byte field indicating that the transaction to be applied to LIB-MAST is an add (A), delete (D), replace (R), or update (U).

```
01   TRAN-REC.
     05   TRAN-KEY            PIC X(08).
     05   other data names ...
     05   TRAN-CODE           PIC X(01).
          88  TRAN-ADD                  VALUE "A".
          88  TRAN-DEL                  VALUE "D".
          88  TRAN-REPL                 VALUE "R".
          88  TRAN-UPDATE               VALUE "U".
```

In the 200-PROCESS paragraph, we read each TRAN-FILE record into TRAN-REC using the AT END/NOT AT END clauses to control program flow.

```
200-PROCESS.
    READ TRAN-FILE INTO TRAN-REC
       AT END
          SET TRAN-EOF TO TRUE
       NOT AT END
          ADD 1 TO COUNT-TRAN
          EVALUATE TRUE ...
    END-READ
```

Then we test TRAN-CODE using the EVALUATE TRUE clause, and if "A" we perform the 300-ADD paragraph, if "D" we perform the 400-DELETE paragraph, and so on.

```
EVALUATE TRUE
   WHEN TRAN-ADD
      PERFORM 300-ADD
   WHEN TRAN-DEL
      PERFORM 400-DELETE
   WHEN TRAN-REPL
      PERFORM 500-REPLACE
   WHEN TRAN-UPDATE
      PERFORM 600-UPDATE-COPIES
   WHEN OTHER
      ADD 1 TO COUNT-SKIP
END-EVALUATE
```

Adding records randomly. Let's assume that the first TRAN-CODE has a value of "A." To add the new record, we move TRAN-REC to LIB-

RECORD and write LIB-RECORD. Remember the old adage: You READ datasets and WRITE records.

```
300-ADD.
    MOVE TRAN-REC TO LIB-REC
    WRITE LIB-RECORD
```

Note that you don't need to READ LIB-MAST before writing a new record. The new record is added in logical (but not necessarily physical) primary key order. It is important to note that after the WRITE statement, the record cannot be accessed from the FD area.

Immediately after writing the new record, we check the COBOL status key to be sure that the WRITE statement worked okay.

```
WRITE LIB-RECORD
EVALUATE TRUE
  WHEN OK
    ADD 1 TO COUNT-ADD
```

When adding new records, always check for a duplicate primary key in the transaction and the KSDS. If COBOL detects a duplicate primary key, it returns a COBOL status key value of 22 (DUPLICATE) and the WRITE statement fails. Just as with the sequential load program of the last chapter, you should count input errors and terminate the program if the counter reaches an unacceptable number, because your input is probably bad.

```
WHEN DUP
  DISPLAY "ERROR-ADDED RECORD ALREADY IN"
  DISPLAY "MASTER"
  DISPLAY "TRANSACTION KEY: ", TRAN-KEY
  ADD 1 TO COUNT-SKIP
  Count errors
  Terminate program if too many errors
```

A common cause of bad input is reading the wrong version of a generation dataset. You need to consider that the valid current version (0) may have been accidentally deleted, thus making the minus one (–1) version the current version.

In Chapter 18 you'll see that in certain circumstances a duplicate alternate index key is an expected condition, and a new record can be successfully written to the KSDS.

A COBOL status key value OTHER than 00 or 22 generally indicates a serious condition. Besides 30 (unspecified I/O error) or 90 (VSAM logic error), the KSDS may be out of space, resulting in a value of 24. If this happens, you may have to offload the dataset and reorganize it using the REPRO command. The contents of the VSAM return code can help you determine the proper course of action.

```
WHEN OTHER
    Display appropriate message and status codes
    Terminate program
```

Deleting records. The DELETE statement is unique to indexed and relative datasets and logically deletes the current record. That is, the space occupied by the current record can be written over with new records. The DELETE statement only works with the KSDS and the RRDS. It is not valid for the ESDS, and deleting records from this type of dataset can be somewhat awkward as you will see in Chapter 19.

The format of the DELETE statement is the following:

```
DELETE file name           same as      DELETE file name RECORD
    INVALID KEY ...                          INVALID KEY ...
    NOT INVALID KEY ...                      NOT INVALID KEY ...
END-DELETE                              END-DELETE
```

Both the INVALID and NOT INVALID KEY are optional. END-DELETE is needed only if one of them is coded.

Specifying *file name* rather than *record name* may give you an uneasy feeling that you're about to delete the entire dataset, but that's just the syntax. (Writing the longer form of DELETE *file name* RECORD is perhaps more assuring and certainly a more accurate description.) For this reason, programmers often confuse the IDCAMS DELETE command, which purges the entire cluster and all its components, with the COBOL DELETE statement, which operates on just the current record. And to add to the confusion, entire DFSMS-managed VSAM clusters can be purged by specifying DELETE in the JCL DISP parameter. Think carefully about what you want to accomplish before issuing any form of DE-LETE statement, command, parameter, or whatever.

The DELETE statement is used differently with sequential than it is with random and dynamic access. For sequential access, you must first read the record you want deleted and then execute the DELETE statement after the READ. You should verify the key of the record read to make sure that you are deleting the record you want to delete.

```
READ TRAN-FILE
```

[This tells us the record we want to delete.]

```
READ LIB-MAST
IF TRAN-KEY = LIB-KEY
    DELETE LIB-MAST
ELSE
    Read LIB-MAST again until a match is found or the
    transaction key is greater than the VSAM key or
    until the end-of-file is encountered
END-IF
```

For random and dynamic access, you move the value of the record key you want to delete to the RECORD KEY identifier and then execute the DELETE statement to delete that record. This is the method our sample program will use. In our sample application, when TRAN-CODE contains a value of "D", we perform the 400-DELETE paragraph.

```
    EVALUATE TRUE ...
        WHEN TRAN-DEL
            PERFORM-400-DELETE
        . . .
400-DELETE.
    MOVE TRAN-KEY TO LIB-KEY
    DELETE LIB-MAST
```

The MOVE statement stores the key of the record to delete in the RECORD KEY identifier and makes the KSDS record the current record. This current record is then deleted by the DELETE statement.

But what if the program doesn't find a match? There are several techniques for handling this situation as it turns out. We'll explore two of them.

INVALID KEY. One technique for handling the no-match situation is the INVALID KEY phrase. You code it like this:

```
DELETE LIB-MAST
    INVALID KEY
```

```
      Tell that it is invalid
      Display and bypass transaction record
   NOT INVALID KEY
      Continue processing normally
END-DELETE
```

The only problem with the INVALID KEY option is that it is not precise enough for our purposes here. That is, if the key is invalid, you still need to know *why* it is invalid, and this can lead to some convoluted (and redundant) logic.

```
INVALID KEY
   EVALUATE TRUE
```

[Why is it invalid?]

```
   WHEN NOT-FOUND ...
   WHEN OTHER ...
   NOT INVALID KEY
         Continue processing normally
```

The INVALID KEY option works well when you only need to know that the key *is* invalid, not *why* it is invalid, and we'll show you one such situation in the next chapter. For our purpose, a more straightforward approach is to merely EVALUATE the COBOL status key, STAT1 in the sample program.

```
DELETE LIB-MAST
EVALUATE TRUE <===
   WHEN OK
      ADD 1 TO COUNT-DEL
   WHEN NOT-FOUND
      DISPLAY "ERROR IN LIB-MAST TO DELETE"
      DISPLAY "NOT FOUND"
      DISPLAY "TRANSACTION KEY:   ", TRAN-KEY
      ADD 1 TO COUNT-SKIP
      Count errors
      Terminate program if too many errors
```

NOT-FOUND (COBOL status key value 23) is the condition you need to check for when deleting records. Once again, you can safely bypass one (or several) not-found records, but a large number probably signify bad input.

A COBOL status key value OTHER than 00 or 23 generally indi-

ondition. Besides 30 (unspecified I/O error) or 90
), a value of 92 can indicate that sequential access
no READ statement was executed prior to the DE-
......ent. In this case, you'll have to correct the program logic
and then rerun the job.

```
WHEN OTHER
  Display appropriate message and status codes
  Terminate program
END-EVALUATE.
```

Rewriting records. The REWRITE statement allows you to completely replace a record with new information (except for the primary key, which cannot be changed). You can also replace selected fields, and if the dataset is a KSDS or RRDS, lengthen the record, as long as the new length doesn't exceed the maximum RECORDSIZE specified in the DEFINE CLUSTER command. In the example below, you couldn't lengthen the record beyond 120 bytes.

```
DEFINE CLUSTER ...
  RECORDSIZE(80 120)
```

The format of the REWRITE statement is simply

```
REWRITE record name
  INVALID KEY ...
  NOT INVALID KEY ...
END-REWRITE
```

or

```
REWRITE record name FROM identifier
  INVALID KEY ...
  NOT INVALID KEY ...
END-REWRITE
```

Both the INVALID and NOT INVALID KEY are optional. END-REWRITE is needed only if one of them is coded.

Like the DELETE statement, REWRITE is different for sequential access and for random or dynamic access. For sequential access, the REWRITE statement requires a prior READ statement to first read the record. It is best to check the key of the record read before rewriting it to make sure you read the record you expected.

```
READ TRAN-FILE
```

[This tells us the record we want to rewrite.]

```
READ LIB-MAST
IF TRAN-KEY = LIB-KEY
    REWRITE LIB-RECORD
    Check for successful REWRITE
ELSE
    Read LIB-MAST again until a match is found or the
    transaction key is greater than the VSAM key or
    until the end-of-file is encountered
END-IF
```

For random or dynamic access, you move the value of the key you want to rewrite to the RECORD KEY identifier and then execute the REWRITE statement. You don't have to code a random READ statement with random or dynamic access to first read the record. However, you usually have to first read the record before rewriting it so that you have the record to rewrite. That is, you may be changing only one field in a rewrite, so you need the original record to get all the other fields. To simplify things, the following example replaces every field in LIB-REC with corresponding fields from TRAN-REC.

In the sample update program, if TRAN-CODE contains a value of "R", we perform the 500-REPLACE program, which rewrites the current record with new information.

```
                WHEN TRAN-REPL
                    PERFORM 500-REPLACE


        . . .
500-REPLACE.
    MOVE TRAN-KEY TO LIB-KEY
```

[We store the key of the record we want to rewrite.]

```
    READ LIB-MAST <===
```

[We read the record we want to rewrite.]

```
    EVALUATE TRUE
```

[We always make sure we read it correctly.]

```
        WHEN OK
            REWRITE LIB-REC FROM TRAN-REC <===
```

[We read it correctly. Now we rewrite it with the new record.]

```
EVALUATE TRUE
```

[Then we make sure it was rewritten properly.]

```
    WHEN OK
        ADD 1 TO COUNT-REWRITE
    WHEN OTHER
        Display appropriate message and status codes
        Terminate program
    END-EVALUATE
WHEN NOT-FOUND
    DISPLAY "ERROR—REPLACEMENT RECORD NOT FOUND"
    DISPLAY "TRANSACTION KEY: ", TRAN-KEY
    ADD 1 TO COUNT-SKIP
    Count errors
    Terminate program if too many errors
WHEN OTHER
    Display appropriate message and status codes
    Terminate program...
```

As you can see, checking status is somewhat more complex after a READ/REWRITE combination because you are checking two I/O operations. However, let's analyze each piece. First we evaluate the COBOL status key value returned by the random READ statement, and if it is the record we expected, we REWRITE the record.

```
MOVE TRAN-KEY TO LIB-KEY
READ LIB-MAST
EVALUATE TRUE
WHEN OK
  REWRITE ...
```

After the READ statement, we also check the COBOL status key for a NOT-FOUND condition (value 23). Once again, we can safely bypass one (or several) not-found records, but a large number probably signify bad input.

```
WHEN NOT-FOUND
  DISPLAY "ERROR—REPLACEMENT RECORD NOT FOUND"
  DISPLAY "TRANSACTION KEY:  ", TRAN-KEY
  ADD 1 TO COUNT-SKIP
  Count errors
  Terminate program if too many errors
```

A COBOL status key value OTHER than 00 or 23 generally indicates a serious condition. Besides 30 (unspecified I/O error) or 90 (VSAM logic error), a value of 92 can indicate that the dataset is not open, in which case you'll have to correct your program logic.

```
WHEN OTHER
    Display appropriate message and status codes
    Terminate program
```

Now let's analyze the COBOL status key checking done after the REWRITE statement (on the WHEN OK branch after the READ statement). Things are simpler here because the REWRITE statement is either okay or things are messed up (OTHER). For example, a value of 24 indicates that there is not enough space to REWRITE the record and you should terminate the program before attempting to add or change any more records.

```
WHEN OK
   REWRITE LIB-REC FROM TRAN-REC
   EVALUATE TRUE
     WHEN OK
       ADD 1 TO COUNT-REWRITE
     WHEN OTHER
       Display appropriate message and status codes
       Terminate program
END-EVALUATE
```

Rewriting selected fields. The previous REWRITE example did a full record replace. That is, every field in the master record was replaced with corresponding fields from the transaction record (except the primary key, which can't be changed). However, you often want to update one field, and here is the logic to do that. Assume for the following example that when extra copies of certain titles are acquired, TRAN-COPIES is added to LIB-COPIES, and then the record is rewritten. A common logic error is to attempt the REWRITE before doing the necessary processing (ADD here).

```
MOVE TRAN-KEY TO LIB-KEY
READ LIB-MAST
EVALUATE TRUE
   WHEN OK
     ADD TRAN-COPIES TO LIB-COPIES <===
```

```
REWRITE LIB-REC
EVALUATE TRUE
  WHEN OK
      . . .
```

There are no special CLOSE statement considerations for random processing, but, of course, you should always close the dataset (unless VSAM can't open it in the first place).

```
IF NOT OPEN-ERR
   CLOSE LIB-MAST
   IF NOT OK
      . . .
   END-IF
END-IF
```

16.2.3.   Sample JCL

Here's the JCL you need to run the new sample application. It is the same no matter which access mode your program specifies.

```
//COBPROC  JOB ...
//STEP1    EXEC PGM=VDEMO2
//SYSOUT   DD SYSOUT=*
//TRANFILE DD DSN=A1000.INPUT.TRANS,DISP=SHR
//LIBMAST  DD DSN=A2000.LIB.KSDS.CLUSTER,DISP=SHR
```

16.2.4.   Recapping Random Access Requirements

Here's a brief recap of what is needed to access (and optionally update) a KSDS randomly:

• In the SELECT clause, specify random access.

```
ACCESS MODE IS RANDOM
```

• Also in the SELECT clause, name at least a COBOL status key and, optionally, a VSAM return code data item.

```
FILE STATUS IS STAT1, STAT2.
```

• Open the KSDS for I-O and check the COBOL status key.

```
OPEN I-O LIB-MAST
IF OK
    Continue processing
ELSE
    Terminate the program without closing the file
END-IF
```

- To specify the record to read, move the key value to the RECORD KEY identifier and then read the dataset. In our example, we move the transaction key to the primary key field and then read LIB-MAST.

```
MOVE TRAN-KEY TO LIB-KEY
READ LIB-MAST
```

- Check the COBOL status key after each random READ request and after each I/O operation such as WRITE, DELETE, and REWRITE. Two conditions that you need to be aware of are: NOT-FOUND (23) after a READ, DELETE, or REWRITE; and DUPLICATE primary key (22) after a WRITE statement.

That's the basics of random access techniques. In the next chapter, we'll explore some of the advantages of dynamic processing.

DYNAMIC Access Techniques for a KSDS

To lay the groundwork for this chapter, let's begin with a recap of what we've learned in the last three chapters about ACCESS MODE and the KSDS.

- If you specify ACCESS MODE IS SEQUENTIAL, you can only access records sequentially for reading or updating.
- If you specify ACCESS MODE IS RANDOM, you can only access records randomly for reading or updating.
- If you specify ACCESS MODE IS DYNAMIC, you can access records both sequentially and randomly for reading or updating in the same program—the best of both worlds.

While we're at it, let's also recap the OPEN statement for KSDS.

- To write records into a previously unloaded KSDS (one with a zero-value HURBA), specify sequential access mode and OPEN OUTPUT. New records are written in sequence by primary key, the most efficient way to load a KSDS.
- To add records with key values higher than the highest key value currently in the KSDS, specify sequential access mode and OPEN EXTEND. New records are written at the end of the KSDS, in primary key order. OPEN EXTEND has no meaning for random or dynamic access.

- To read all records, specify sequential access and OPEN INPUT. If you only want to read selected records, specify random access and OPEN INPUT.
- To read all records and, optionally, rewrite or delete them, specify sequential access and OPEN I-O. This combination has limitations, however, because you cannot write new records.
- To read and update selected records and write new records as well, specify random access and OPEN I-O.
- To do a combination of the previous two, processing some records sequentially and others randomly, specify dynamic access and OPEN I-O. You can see that this gives you a great deal of flexibility when processing a KSDS.

The following matrix matches valid KSDS COBOL statements with the form of the OPEN statement required by each access mode.

- ACCESS MODE IS SEQUENTIAL

	READ	WRITE	REWRITE	DELETE	START
OPEN INPUT	Y	N	N	N	Y
OPEN OUTPUT	N	Y	N	N	N
OPEN EXTEND	N	Y	N	N	N
OPEN I-O	Y	N	Y	Y	Y

- ACCESS MODE IS RANDOM

	READ	WRITE	REWRITE	DELETE	START
OPEN INPUT	Y	N	N	N	N
OPEN OUTPUT	N	Y	N	N	N
OPEN EXTEND	N	N	N	N	N
OPEN I-O	Y	Y	Y	Y	N

- ACCESS MODE IS DYNAMIC

	READ	WRITE	REWRITE	DELETE	START
OPEN INPUT	Y	N	N	N	Y
OPEN OUTPUT	N	Y	N	N	N
OPEN EXTEND	N	N	N	N	N
OPEN I-O	Y	Y	Y	Y	Y

This chapter shows you the basic techniques for using this dynamic access mode. First, let's set the scene. In the last chapter we introduced a new COBOL programming example, VDEMO2. This program reads the sample KSDS (LIB-MAST) randomly based on a matching key in the transaction input dataset (TRAN-FILE).

```
FILE SECTION.
FD  TRAN-FILE
    RECORD CONTAINS 80 CHARACTERS.
01  TRAN-RECORD.
    05  TRAN-KEY           PIC X(08).
    05  FILLER             PIC X(73).
FD  LIB-MAST
    RECORD CONTAINS 80 CHARACTERS.
01  LIB-RECORD.
*   The primary key.
    05 LIB-KEY             PIC X(08).
    05 FILLER              PIC X(72).
```

The program reads each input transaction record into a WORKING-STORAGE area named TRAN-REC and, based on a one-byte value in position 81, either adds, deletes, replaces, or updates a matching LIB-MAST record.

```
01 TRAN-REC.
    05  FILLER             PIC X(80).
    05  TRAN-CODE          PIC X(01).
        88 TRAN-ADD                    VALUE "A".
        88 TRAN-DEL                    VALUE "D".
        88 TRAN-REPL                   VALUE "R".
        88 TRAN-UPDATE                 VALUE "U".
```

Suppose that besides the random processing just described, we have a requirement to process a group of LIB-MAST records sequentially by primary key, based on the value of "X" in TRAN-CODE. In CICS jargon, this is called *skip-sequential processing*, and the technique is also valid in batch COBOL processing. Let's see what we need to modify the program VDEMO2 to accommodate this new type of processing.

17.1. DYNAMIC ACCESS SELECT CLAUSE

First, we modify the SELECT clause to specify dynamic access.

```
SELECT LIB-MAST  ASSIGN TO      LIBMAST
                 ORGANIZATION IS INDEXED
```

```
            ACCESS MODE  IS DYNAMIC <===
            RECORD KEY   IS LIB-KEY
            FILE STATUS  IS STAT1,
                            STAT2.
```

In WORKING-STORAGE, we add an additional condition name to TRAN-CODE to accommodate the "X" value programming logic.

```
01 TRAN-REC.
    05  FILLER            PIC X(80).
    05  TRAN-CODE         PIC X(01).
        88  TRAN-ADD                   VALUE "A".
        88  TRAN-DEL                   VALUE "D".
        88  TRAN-REPL                  VALUE "R".
        88  TRAN-UPDATE                VALUE "U".
        88  TRAN-READ                  VALUE "X". <===
```

In the PROCEDURE DIVISION, we still OPEN the dataset for I-O. This is needed for the random update processing, not the skip-sequential processing, because for this application we are only reading the dataset. If you only need to read records either randomly or sequentially, you can specify OPEN INPUT. But so you won't have to think about it, you may always want to specify OPEN I-O with dynamic access.

```
PROCEDURE DIVISION.
100-START-PROGRAM.
    OPEN INPUT TRAN-FILE
    OPEN I-O LIB-MAST    <===
    IF (OK OR VERIFIED)
        Continue processing
          . . .
```

We still perform the 200-PROCESS paragraph until the program encounters a serious I/O error or the transaction end-of-file.

```
PERFORM 200-PROCESS WITH TEST AFTER
    UNTIL IO-ERR OR TRAN-EOF
```

However, we need to add some WHEN logic to the 200-PROCESS paragraph that will perform a new paragraph, 700-START-AND-READ, when a value of "X" is detected in TRAN-CODE.

```
200-PROCESS.
   READ TRAN-FILE INTO TRAN-REC
      AT END
         SET TRAN-EOF TO TRUE
      NOT AT END
         ADD 1 TO COUNT-TRAN
         EVALUATE TRUE
            WHEN TRAN-ADD ...
            WHEN TRAN-DEL ...
            WHEN TRAN-REPL ...
            WHEN TRAN-UPDATE ...
            WHEN TRAN-READ
               PERFORM 700-START-AND-READ <===
            WHEN OTHER
               ADD 1 TO COUNT-SKIP
         END-EVALUATE
   END-READ
```

17.2.   SKIP-SEQUENTIAL PROCESSING

Before examining the logic in this new paragraph, we need to analyze what happens during skip-sequential processing. We'll begin by viewing the structure of the LIB-MAST primary key: four alphabetic characters signifying category of book (BIOG, FICT, HIFI (historical fiction), and so forth) followed by a four-digit sequential number.

```
LIB-KEY     FILLER
PIC X(08)   PIC X(80)
------------------
BIOG0009    ...
BIOG0010    ...
FICT0001    ...
FICT0002    ...
FICT0003    ...
FICT0005    ...
FICT0006    ...
HIFI0001    ...
```

Skip-sequential processing uses a conceptual pointer called the File Position Indicator (also known as the Current Record Pointer) and two COBOL statements, START and READ NEXT. START moves the File Position Indicator to the record where you want to start reading sequentially. READ NEXT reads LIB-MAST sequentially starting with this record.

17.2.1.   START Statement

The START statement is used only for processing records sequentially as part of dynamic processing. It has no meaning for random processing. You move a value to the RECORD KEY identifier that identifies the record at which you want to position and then execute the START statement as follows:

```
START file name
  INVALID KEY ...
  NOT INVALID KEY ...
END-START
```

Both the INVALID KEY and NOT INVALID KEY are optional. END-START is needed only if one of them is coded.

Rather than moving a value to the RECORD KEY identifier, you can supply a data name in the START statement that contains a value to identify the record at which to position. You then use the KEY phrase with a relational operator to tell VSAM that the key at which you want to position is either EQUAL TO (=), GREATER THAN (>), NOT LESS THAN (NOT <), or GREATER THAN OR EQUAL TO (>=) a data name—for example

```
MOVE "FICT0001" TO START-VALUE
START LIB-MAST KEY >= START-VALUE
```

[In case there's not an exact match, we'll specify >=.]

17.2.2.   READ NEXT Statement

READ NEXT is another statement that is used for processing records sequentially as part of dynamic processing. It is invalid for random access, and the format is the following:

```
READ file name NEXT
  AT END ...
  NOT AT END ...
  END-READ
```

   or

```
READ file name NEXT INTO identifier
   AT END ...
   NOT AT END ...
END-READ
```

Both the AT END and NOT AT END are optional. END-READ is needed only if one of them is coded.

With READ NEXT, you can specify either the AT END/NOT AT END clauses, or you can test the COBOL status key for a value of 10, indicating the end-of-file, a more precise method. Whatever method chosen, you should always test for the end-of-file when reading records sequentially. If you read beyond the end-of-file, VSAM will return a COBOL status key value of 46 or 94.

If you wanted to position the File Position Indicator at the record whose primary key value is "FICT0001" and read the following sequentially until you got one with a key greater than "FICT0006", you could code the following.

```
MOVE "FICT0001" TO START-VALUE
START LIB-MAST KEY >= START-VALUE
   NOT INVALID KEY
      PERFORM WITH TEST AFTER
            UNTIL LIB-KEY > "FICT0006"
         READ LIB-MAST NEXT
            AT END ...
         END-READ
      END-PERFORM
END-START
```

Here's a pictorial representation of how the START and READ NEXT statements operate on the KSDS:

```
                              LIB-KEY       FILLER
                              PIC X(08)     PIC X(80)
                              - - - - - - - - - - - - - - - - - - -
                              BIOG0009         ...
                              BIOG0010         ...
START/READ-NEXT               FICT0001         ...
      READ-NEXT               FICT0002         ...
      READ-NEXT               FICT0003         ...
      READ-NEXT               FICT0005         ...
      READ-NEXT               FICT0006         ...
                              HIFI0001         ...
```

17.2.3. More on the File Position Indicator

The File Position Indicator is a concept, not a physical entity that you can see, feel, or taste. It is a very important part of sequential processing, and if it becomes defined for some reason, a sequential READ statement will return a COBOL status key value of 46 or 94. The File Position Indicator is first set to the first record in the dataset by the OPEN statement. It is changed by each START, READ, or READ NEXT statement. It is not reset by WRITE, REWRITE, or DELETE statements. If the File Position Indicator becomes undefined due to faulty program logic, you should do the following:

- Terminate the program and CLOSE the dataset. When you OPEN it again, the File Position Indicator is reset at the first record.
- Modify your program logic to include appropriate START and READ NEXT combinations whenever you want to process records sequentially. You can do this from several places in the same dataset if your application requires it.
- Check for the end-of-file (COBOL status key value 10) after every READ NEXT statement, and if you don't want to read sequentially to the end of the file, limit the scope of READ NEXT by using PERFORM UNTIL the condition you want to meet occurs.

```
PERFORM WITH TEST AFTER
   UNTIL LIB-KEY NOT = TRAN-KEY
READ file name NEXT ...
   . . .
```

If the File Position Indicator becomes undefined because you have reached the KSDS end-of-file (say a transaction key was higher than the highest KSDS key), you need to change your program logic so that the next statement is either a START statement or a random READ request. Either of these statements will reset the File Position Indicator.

```
READ LIB-MAST NEXT
   AT END
     START or READ statement
END-READ
```

17.2.4. Using Generic Keys

The START statement can specify some number of leading bytes of a record key and then position to the first record in the dataset matching these bytes. For example, our LIB-RECORD key has eight bytes, but we could use only the first four for a generic key to position to the first record containing the characters "HIFI" in its record key. Then we could begin reading at this point. Here is an example of this:

```
01   LIB-RECORD.
     05   LIB-KEY.
          10   LIB-CAT          PIC X(04).
```

[This becomes the generic key.]

```
          10   LIB-NUM          PIC X(04).
```

[This can't be used as a generic key because it doesn't begin in the first byte of the record key.]

```
. . .
01   SEARCH-KEY               PIC X(04).
```

Specifying the generic key (LIB-CAT) enables us to read sequentially all records with a certain generic key value, say all titles in the historical fiction (HIFI) category.

```
MOVE "HIFI" TO SEARCH-KEY
START LIB-MAST KEY = SEARCH-KEY
```

The START statement positions to the first record in the dataset in which the left four bytes equal "HIFI" as shown here:

```
       LIB-KEY.
          LIB-CAT  PIC X(04).
          LIB-NUM  PIC X(04).
       - - - - - - - - - - - - - - - - - - - -
          BIOG0009      ...
          BIOG0010      ...
          FICT0001      ...

             .
             .
          FICT0006      ...
===>      HIFI0001      ...
          HIFI0002      ...
          HIFI0003      ...
          HIST0001      ...
```

You can see the obvious advantages of this technique for online processing, but it has its place in batch COBOL reporting as well. For example, perhaps since the release of the *Gone With the Wind* sequel, *Scarlett*, there has been such an upsurge of interest in historical fiction that the marketing and purchasing people need to reevaluate the current library of titles in this category. They can use a batch report like this to help them make a good business decision.

17.2.5. The Example Revisited

Let's return to our example and use the generic key technique to read a group of records sequentially. Recall we modified the sample program (VDEMO2) in the following manner:

- Specified ACCESS MODE IS DYNAMIC in the SELECT clause.
- Added an additional condition name (TRAN-READ) to the WORKING-STORAGE TRAN-CODE item.

```
01 TRAN-REC.
   05  FILLER              PIC X(80).
   05  TRAN-CODE           PIC X(01).
       88  TRAN-ADD                    VALUE "A".
       88  TRAN-DEL                    VALUE "D".
       88  TRAN-REPL                   VALUE "R".
       88  TRAN-UPDATE                 VALUE "U".
       88  TRAN-READ                   VALUE "X".  <===
```

- Specified OPEN LIB-MAST I-O in the PROCEDURE DIVISION.
- Added WHEN phrases to the 200-PROCESS paragraph to accommodate the processing.

```
200-PROCESS.
   READ TRAN-FILE ...
   EVALUATE TRUE
     WHEN TRAN-ADD ...
     WHEN TRAN-DEL ...
     WHEN TRAN-REPL ...
     WHEN TRAN-UPDATE ...
     WHEN TRAN-READ
       PERFORM 700-START-AND-READ  <===
   END-EVALUATE
```

Here's what else is needed:

- First we need to further define both TRAN-KEY and LIB-KEY to handle the generic processing logic.

```
05   TRAN-KEY.
       10   TRAN-CAT        PIC X(04).
       10   TRAN-NUM        PIC X(04).
05   LIB-KEY.
       10   LIB-CAT         PIC X(04).
       10   LIB-NUM         PIC X(04).
```

- Then we code the 700-READ-AND-START paragraph with statements like the following:

```
700-START-AND-READ.
    MOVE TRAN-CAT TO LIB-CAT
    START LIB-MAST KEY = LIB-CAT
    EVALUATE TRUE
      WHEN OK
        DISPLAY "LISTING TITLES IN THIS CATEGORY: ",
                LIB-CAT
        PERFORM 750-READ-NEXT WITH TEST AFTER
                UNTIL EOF OR NOT-FOUND OR
                      NOT OK OR
                      LIB-CAT NOT = TRAN-CAT
      WHEN NOT-FOUND
        Display appropriate message
      WHEN OTHER
        SET IO-ERR TO TRUE
        Display appropriate message and status codes
        Terminate program
    END-EVALUATE
```

These statements may appear daunting at first glance, but let's look at them one at a time. First, we move TRAN-CAT to LIB-CAT (the generic key) and START the KSDS.

```
MOVE TRAN-CAT TO LIB-CAT
START LIB-MAST KEY = LIB-CAT
```

The START statement places the File Position Indicator at the first record of the HIFI generic key.

```
START  ===>  HIFI0001
             HIFI0002
             HIFI0003
             HIST0001
```

Next, we evaluate the COBOL status key, and if we get the thumbs-up sign (OK), we display a message that we are listing titles in the requested category (this is not a very fancy report—in real life you'd probably write all of this to a report dataset) and perform the 800-READ-NEXT paragraph until one of four conditions is encountered. We'll go over each of them in just a bit.

```
EVALUATE TRUE
  WHEN OK
    DISPLAY "LISTING TITLES IN THIS CATEGORY:   ",
            LIB-CAT
    PERFORM 750-READ-NEXT WITH TEST AFTER
            UNTIL EOF OR NOT-FOUND OR
                  NOT OK OR                       <===
                  LIB-CAT NOT = TRAN-CAT
```

Still looking at the START statement logic, if the generic key is NOT-FOUND (status code value 23), we display a message and fall through the paragraph to the next START statement or a random READ request. This logic is necessary because a NOT-FOUND condition renders the File Position Indicator undefined, but it can be reset within the program with a successful START or random READ request.

```
WHEN NOT-FOUND
  Display appropriate message
  Fall through paragraph to random READ or
    START statement
```

In the unlikely event that the status key value is something OTHER than 00 or 23, you have a logic problem serious enough to warrant terminating the program.

```
WHEN OTHER
  Display appropriate message and status codes
  Terminate program
END-EVALUATE
```

17.2.6. START with INVALID KEY

With START, you can use the INVALID KEY/NOT INVALID KEY option, and usually there are no problems. However, with very little extra coding you can check status key values and provide that extra measure of precision that can make all the difference. But it's your decision.

```
START LIB-MAST KEY = LIB-CAT
   INVALID KEY
      Display and fall through
   NOT INVALID KEY
      Perform normal processing
END-START
```

Now let's analyze the coding logic in 750-READ-NEXT, the paragraph we perform if the START statement executes successfully. We begin reading LIB-MAST sequentially starting with the first HIFI record.

```
750-READ-NEXT.
      READ LIB-MAST NEXT

      . . .

READ NEXT ===>     HIFI0001
                   HIFI0002
                   HIFI0003
                   HIST0001
```

After each READ-NEXT statement, we evaluate the COBOL status key for one of four conditions requiring an immediate termination of the read loop. When we encounter the LIB-MAST EOF condition (10) or NOT-FOUND (23), we reinitialize the generic key by moving spaces to it and fall through to the next random READ or START statement, which resets the File Position Indicator.

```
      EVALUATE TRUE
         WHEN EOF OR NOT-FOUND
            MOVE SPACES TO LIB-CAT
            Fall through to random READ or START statement

      . . .

                   HIFI0001 OK
                   HIFI0002 OK
                   HIFI0003 OK
```

```
READ-NEXT ===> HIST0001 NOT EQUAL
```

If we encounter a condition that is NOT OK (that is, other than 10, 23, or 00), it is serious enough to warrant terminating the program. Most likely a previous logic error has caused the File Position Indicator to become undefined.

```
WHEN NOT OK
  SET IO-ERR TO TRUE
  Display appropriate message and status codes
  Terminate program
```

When everything is okay, we continue to display TITLE information for our simple report, as long as LIB-CAT equals TRAN-CAT.

```
        WHEN OK
          IF LIB-CAT = TRAN-CAT
            DISPLAY "NEXT TITLE:  ", LIB-TITLE
            ADD 1 TO COUNT-CAT
          END-IF
        END-EVALUATE
```

```
TRAN-CAT | LIB-CAT
 value   |  value
---------------------------------------------------------------
  HIFI      HIFI  ===>  NEXT TITLE: Gone With the Wind
  HIFI      HIFI  ===>  NEXT TITLE: The Agony and the Ecstasy
  HIFI      HIFI  ===>  NEXT TITLE: The Red Badge of Courage
  HIFI      HIST  ===>  (NOT EQUAL)
```

There are no special CLOSE considerations to check for when processing records dynamically, but always check the COBOL status key after the CLOSE statement, and if it is greater than 00, you should issue an explicit VERIFY to update the HURBA values before processing the dataset again.

```
CLOSE LIB-MAST
IF NOT OK ...
```

17.3. JCL FOR DYNAMIC ACCESS

There are no special JCL considerations for dynamic access, but here's the JCL for our sample application anyway, just to refresh your memory.

```
//COBPROC  JOB ...
//STEP1    EXEC PGM=VDEMO2
//SYSOUT   DD SYSOUT=*
//TRANFILE DD DSN=A1000.INPUT.TRANS,DISP=SHR
//LIBMAST  DD DSN=A2000.LIB.KSDS.CLUSTER,DISP=SHR
```

17.4. DYNAMIC ACCESS/SKIP-SEQUENTIAL RECAP

Here's a brief recap of what's required to use skip-sequential processing as part of dynamic access.

- Specify ACCESS MODE IS DYNAMIC in the SELECT clause.
- Specify OPEN I-O if your processing will include updating records. For reading records randomly or sequentially, you can specify OPEN INPUT.
- Use the START statement to place the File Position Indicator (a conceptual pointer) at the record where you want to start reading, and then read records sequentially from that point with the READ NEXT statement.
- If the File Position Indicator becomes undefined, the COBOL status key displays a value of 46 or 94. If this happens as a result of a NOT-FOUND record, structure program logic so that the next statement is either START or a random READ request.

In the next chapter, we'll see how to apply dynamic processing techniques to accessing records via an alternate index.

18

Alternate Index
Processing Techniques

An alternate index AIX provides a view of data different from the one offered by the primary key. For example, the sample audio tape library dataset might be accessed in sequence by the primary key (LIB-KEY) as in the following example.

```
LIB-KEY          TITLE                    AUTH-LAST-NAME
AUTO0001         Me                       HEPBURN
AUTO0002         A Life on the Road       KURALT
AUTO0003         Out of Africa            DINESEN
```

However, through an alternate index based on AUTH-LAST-NAME you have the ability to browse and even update the same KSDS in logical sequence by the author's last name. In the example that follows, you can browse all titles in stock for author HEMINGWAY, an obvious advantage for both online and batch access.

```
AUTH-LAST-NAME    TITLE                    LIB-KEY
HEMINGWAY         For Whom the Bell Tolls  FICT8724
HEMINGWAY         The Old Man and the Sea  FICT9043
HEMINGWAY         The Sun Also Rises       FICT0025
```

Chapter 11 showed how to define and build an alternate index. This chapter shows how to process that alternate index using COBOL statements. First, let's briefly review the features of an alternate index.

18.1. AIX CONSIDERATIONS REVISITED

An alternate index key has the following characteristics:

- It reduces data redundancy by eliminating (or greatly reducing) the need to keep separate datasets with basically the same information but different reporting needs. Witness the AUTH-LAST-NAME example shown previously.
- It can be accessed sequentially, randomly, or dynamically.
- It can degrade performance, especially if multiple alternate indexes are used in one program. Access by alternate key may require twice as many I/Os because the alternate key must first be used to locate the primary key, which in turn is used to locate the desired record. It's the same never-ending story, a trade-off among application requirements, DASD usage, and I/O savings. Good buffer management can help, though.

Here are the features of an alternate index key:

- It can be updated (upgraded) or not, when the base cluster is updated. Automatic upgrade is an option that you choose for the DEFINE command.

```
DEFINE AIX ...
   UPGRADE | NOUPGRADE
```

Choosing UPGRADE (the default) makes the alternate index part of the *upgrade set* of the KSDS. From an operations point of view, it's important to know if an alternate index is part of the upgrade set. However, the actual COBOL programming statements are the same in any case.

- It can have duplicate key values, as seen in the previous AUTH-LAST-NAME example. Allowing duplicate key values is another option that you choose for the DEFINE command.

```
DEFINE AIX ...
   UNIQUEKEY | NONUNIQUEKEY
```

Choosing UNIQUEKEY (the default) makes the alternate index key unique, just like the primary key. If you specify NONUNIQUEKEY, duplicate alternate index key values are an expected condition. This uniqueness issue can definitely affect your COBOL processing logic, especially when checking the status key.

18.1.1. AIX Run JCL

Let's begin with the run JCL needed to process the sample program using an alternate index. You'll find that it has several interesting features.

```
//COBPROC  JOB ...
//STEP1    EXEC PGM=VDEMO2
//SYSOUT   DD SYSOUT=*
//TRANFILE DD DSN=A1000.INPUT.TRANS,DISP=SHR
//LIBMAST  DD DSN=A2000.LIB.KSDS.CLUSTER,DISP=SHR
//LIBMAS1  DD DSN=A2000.LIB.KSDS.AUTHNAME.PATH,DISP=SHR
```

Notice first that there must be one DD statement for the base cluster and one for each alternate index used by the application program. If the program uses two alternate indexes, the DD statements would look like this:

```
//LIBMAST  DD DSN=A2000.LIB.KSDS.CLUSTER,DISP=SHR
//LIBMAS1  DD DSN=A2000.LIB.KSDS.AUTHNAME.PATH,DISP=SHR
//LIBMAS2  DD DSN=A2000.LIB.KSDS.ISBN.PATH,DISP=SHR
```

You can omit the alternate index DD statements if your application doesn't use alternate key processing, even if one or more AIXs have been defined over the base cluster. However, if alternate key processing is planned, the DD statement for the alternate index must specify the path name rather than the alternate index name. This is an important point—and a frequent source of error. (Finally, the reason for the path becomes clear.)

```
//LIBMAS1  DD DSN=A2000.LIB.KSDS.AUTHNAME.PATH,DISP=SHR
```

Seeing the ddname (LIBMAS1), you would also expect to see an ASSIGN name like this in the SELECT clause:

```
SELECT LIB-MAST ASSIGN TO LIBMAS1
```

But not so. No matter how many alternate indexes you specify in the program, there is only one ASSIGN clause pointing to the ddname of the base cluster.

```
      SELECT LIB-MAST ASSIGN TO LIBMAST

//LIBMAST  DD DSN=A2000.LIB.KSDS ...
```

There's no COBOL standard for assigning ddnames to alternate indexes, so a quasi-standard has emerged whereby a sequential number is appended to the eighth character of the base cluster ddname. Thus for one base cluster and two alternate indexes you would specify the following:

```
//LIBMAST  DD DSN=A2000.LIB.KSDS.CLUSTER,DISP=SHR
//LIBMAS1  DD DSN=A2000.LIB.KSDS.AUTHNAME.PATH,DISP=SHR
//LIBMAS2  DD DSN=A2000.LIB.KSDS.ISBN.PATH,DISP=SHR
```

You are not required by any COBOL or JCL rule to follow this naming standard, and things may very well be different at your shop. But if not, this one is easy for the programmer to remember and easy for support and maintenance people to figure out.

18.1.2. The AIXBLD JCL Parameter

In Chapter 11, we said that there was no way to create an alternate index with JCL statements alone, as you can for a DFSMS-managed base cluster. This is not completely accurate—you *can* use the AIXBLD parameter as part of your initial load program. AIXBLD is a run-time option that dynamically invokes Access Method Services through your application program. However, AIXBLD is so resource-intensive (because IDCAMS and your application program must work together) that even IBM recommends building alternate indexes with the IDCAMS BLDINDEX command instead. The following example demonstrates the use of AIXBLD.

```
//COBLOAD  JOB ...
//STEP1    EXEC PGM=VDEMO1,PARM='/AIXBLD'
//SYSOUT   DD SYSOUT=*
//SYSPRINT DD SYSOUT=*
//TRANFILE DD DSN=A1000.SORTED.LIB.INPUT,DISP=SHR
//LIBMAST  DD DSN=A2000.LIB.KSDS.CLUSTER,DISP=OLD
//LIBMAS1  DD DSN=A2000.LIB.KSDS.AUTHNAME.PATH,DISP=OLD
```

Unless you have a compelling reason for doing so, avoid the AIXBLD run-time option. However, if you must use it, remember to specify OPEN OUTPUT in your COBOL program and include a SYSPRINT DD statement in your JCL.

18.2. COBOL AIX PROCESSING STATEMENTS

In Chapter 16 we introduced a sample COBOL program, VDEMO2, that reads input transactions from an 81-byte sequential input dataset and, based on a TRAN-CODE in position 81, adds (A), deletes (D), replaces (R), or updates (U) the 80-byte LIB-MAST dataset using random access techniques.

Then in Chapter 17, we added a new TRAN-CODE value (X) to process a group of LIB-MAST records sequentially by primary key using a dynamic access technique called skip sequential processing. Now we'll continue using dynamic access and add still another TRAN-CODE value (L) to access a group of LIB-MAST records by a non-unique alternate index key, LIB-AUTH-LNAME.

18.2.1.   The AIX SELECT Clause

The following example shows the SELECT clause needed to specify alternate index processing.

```
SELECT LIB-MAST
       ASSIGN TO        LIBMAST
```

[One ASSIGN clause supports both primary and alternate key access.]

```
       ORGANIZATION IS INDEXED
```

[Always, because COBOL only supports KSDS alternate index processing.]

```
       ACCESS MODE IS DYNAMIC
```

[Application-dependent. SEQUENTIAL and RANDOM access both support alternate key access.]

```
       RECORD KEY IS LIB-KEY
```

[Names the primary key.]

```
       ALTERNATE RECORD KEY IS LIB-AUTH-NAME <===
```

[Names the alternate index key. Code one ALTERNATE RECORD KEY phrase for each alternate index that the program uses.]

```
       WITH DUPLICATES
```

[Specifies that duplicate alternate index keys are an expected condition. The corresponding DEFINE command option is NONUNIQUEKEY. Omit WITH DUPLICATES if the DEFINE command option is UNIQUEKEY (the default)].

```
       FILE STATUS IS STAT1,
                      STAT2.
```

[Same considerations as primary key access.]

It's worth restating that you only need one SELECT clause whether or not your program uses an alternate index. However, if the program specifies more than one alternate index, you must code an ALTERNATE RECORD KEY clause for each one. The example below names two alternate index keys. Only the first specifies duplicate keys; in the second, LIB-ISBN-NO is unique by default.

```
SELECT LIB-MAST
       ASSIGN TO        LIBMAST
       ORGANIZATION IS INDEXED
       ACCESS MODE   IS DYNAMIC
       RECORD KEY    IS LIB-KEY
       ALTERNATE RECORD KEY IS LIB-AUTH-NAME
          WITH DUPLICATES
       ALTERNATE RECORD KEY IS LIB-ISBN-NO
       FILE STATUS   IS STAT1,
                        STAT2.
```

18.2.2.   AIX Passwords

You can password-protect alternate indexes as well as datasets. If your alternate index is password-protected, you'll need to name an up-to-eight-byte alphanumeric data item defined in WORKING-STORAGE that stores the password for the alternate index. For read-only access, the READPW can be specified. If access is for update, the UPDATEPW password must be specified. Avoid passwords for DFSMS-managed alternate indexes.

```
    SELECT LIB-MAST ...
           ALTERNATE RECORD KEY IS LIB-AUTH-NAME
              WITH DUPLICATES
              PASSWORD IS LIB-READPW.
01  LIB-PASSWORD.
    05  LIB-READPW        PIC X(08)  VALUE SPACES.
    05  LIB-UPDTPW        PIC X(08)  VALUE SPACES.
```

18.2.3.   AIX DATA DIVISION Entries

In the DATA DIVISION, you'll want to identify the data names of any alternate index keys.

```
01   LIB-REC.
*    The primary key.
     05   LIB-KEY            PIC X(08).
*    Non-unique alternate key.
     05   LIB-AUTH-LNAME     PIC X(15).
     05   LIB-AUTH-FNAME     PIC X(12).
     05   LIB-AUTH-INIT      PIC X(01).
     05   LIB-TITLE          PIC X(28).
*    Unique alternate index key.
     05   LIB-ISBN-NO        PIC X(13).
     05   LIB-COPIES         PIC 9(03).
```

18.2.4.   AIX WORKING-STORAGE Entries

In WORKING-STORAGE, we've added an additional condition name to TRAN-CODE to check for the "L" value. This accommodates the program logic, but it is not an alternate index processing requirement.

```
01   TRAN-REC.
     05   TRAN-KEY           PIC X(08).
     05   other data names ...
     05   TRAN-CODE          PIC X(01).
          88   TRAN-ADD               VALUE "A".
          88   TRAN-DEL               VALUE "D".
          88   TRAN-REPL              VALUE "R".
          88   TRAN-UPDATE            VALUE "U".
          88   TRAN-LIST              VALUE "L".  <===
          88   TRAN-READ              VALUE "X".
```

We've also added another value (02) to the OK condition code. A COBOL status key value of 02 indicates a duplicate alternate index key, an expected condition if you have specified WITH DUPLICATES in the SELECT clause and specified NONUNIQUEKEY in the DEFINE command.

```
01   LIB-STATUS-AREA.
*    The COBOL status key.
     05   STAT1              PIC X(02)   VALUE SPACES.
          88   OK                       VALUE "00" "02".  <===
          88   EOF                      VALUE "10".
          88   DUPLICATE                VALUE "22".
          88   NOT-FOUND                VALUE "23".
```

```
    88 VERIFIED                          VALUE "97".
```

When reading an alternate index key sequentially, you'll also want to check for an end-of-file condition (status key value 10) on the alternate index, which is, after all, just a KSDS.

18.2.5.   Opening an AIX

In the PROCEDURE DIVISION, one OPEN statement opens both the base cluster and any alternate indexes as well. Always check the CO-BOL status key value immediately after opening the dataset, and if it is greater than zero, terminate the program without attempting to CLOSE it. Then issue an explicit VERIFY command before processing the dataset again.

```
PROCEDURE DIVISION.
100-START-PROGRAM.
    OPEN INPUT TRAN-FILE
    OPEN I-O LIB-MAST     <===
    IF (OK OR VERIFIED)
       Continue processing
       . . .
```

Notice we've opened the dataset for I-O because the application does random update processing through the primary key. It is not an alternate index processing requirement. You can open the dataset as INPUT if you only want to read records using both the primary and any alternate index keys. However, if you want to update records using the primary key and read records using the alternate key, (or vice versa) you would need to specify OPEN I-O. In the unlikely event you are using the AIXBLD run-time option to build alternate index records as you load base cluster records, you must specify OPEN OUTPUT.

18.2.6.   Key of Reference

The key that is currently being used to access records is called the *key of reference*. When the program opens the dataset, the primary key becomes, by default, the key of reference. The primary key remains the key of reference when accessing records until it is changed. To start accessing records by an alternate index key, you merely change the key of reference. You do this by using the KEY phrase as part of one of the following statements:

- A random READ statement, for example

```
READ LIB-MAST
  KEY IS LIB-AUTH-LNAME
```

- A sequential READ statement, for example

```
READ LIB-MAST NEXT
  KEY IS LIB-AUTH-LNAME
```

- A START statement, for example

```
START LIB-MAST KEY = LIB-AUTH-LNAME
```

With the START statement, you can use the relational operators EQUAL TO (=), GREATER THAN (>), NOT LESS THAN (NOT <), or GREATER THAN OR EQUAL TO (>=) to position the File Position Indicator at the key of the alternate index record where you want to begin reading. The KEY phrase cannot be specified in a WRITE, REWRITE, or DELETE statement.

18.2.7.   The Default Key of Reference

The following is an important but often overlooked point. When you change the key of reference with a START or sequential READ statement, the new key (say it is the alternate index key) remains the key of reference for all subsequent SEQUENTIAL reads, unless it is physically changed with another START or sequential READ statement. For example, you might change back to the primary key, as this example shows:

```
START LIB-MAST KEY = LIB-KEY
READ LIB-MAST NEXT
```

Or you can change to another alternate index key, as this example shows:

```
START LIB-MAST KEY = LIB-ISBN-NO
READ LIB-MAST NEXT
```

However, by default all reads remain by the primary key, unless physically changed with a random READ statement specifying a new key, as the following example shows:

```
READ LIB-MAST
   KEY IS LIB-AUTH-LNAME
```

Let's return to the example and add some more WHEN phrases to the 200-PROCESS paragraph to perform another paragraph, 800-LIST-AUTHORS, when a value of "L" (TRANS-LIST) is detected in TRAN-CODE.

```
200-PROCESS.
    READ TRAN-FILE INTO TRAN-REC
      AT END
         SET TRAN-EOF TO TRUE
      NOT AT END
         ADD 1 TO COUNT-TRAN
         EVALUATE TRUE
           WHEN TRAN-ADD ...
           WHEN TRAN-DEL ...
           WHEN TRAN-REPL ...
           WHEN TRAN-UPDATE ...
           WHEN TRAN-READ ...
           WHEN TRAN-LIST
              PERFORM 800-LIST-AUTHORS <===
           WHEN OTHER
              ADD 1 TO COUNT-SKIP
         END-EVALUATE
    END-READ
```

If we examine the statements in the 800-LIST-AUTHORS paragraph, we see that its structure and coding logic are similar to the 700-START-AND-READ paragraph for the skip-sequential processing of Chapter 17. However, this time the START statement designates the alternate index key, LIB-AUTH-LNAME, as the key of reference.

```
800-LIST-AUTHORS.
    MOVE TRAN-AUTH-LNAME TO LIB-AUTH-LNAME
    START LIB-MAST KEY = LIB-AUTH-LNAME        <===
    EVALUATE TRUE
      WHEN OK
         DISPLAY "LISTING TITLES FOR AUTHOR:  ",
                 LIB-AUTH-LNAME
         PERFORM 850-READ-AIX-NEXT WITH TEST AFTER
```

```
                UNTIL EOF OR NOT-FOUND OR
                      NOT OK OR
                      LIB-AUTH-NAME NOT = TRAN-AUTH-LNAME
        WHEN NOT-FOUND
          Display appropriate message
        WHEN OTHER
          SET IO-ERR TO TRUE
          Display appropriate message and status codes
          Terminate program
      END-EVALUATE
```

Let's analyze the coding, one statement at a time. First we move TRAN-AUTH-LNAME (say its value is HEMINGWAY) to LIB-AUTH-LNAME and START the KSDS. This effectively transfers the key of reference from the primary key to the alternate index key named in the START statement. It's that simple.

```
MOVE TRAN-AUTH-LNAME TO LIB-AUTH-LNAME
START LIB-MAST KEY = LIB-AUTH-LNAME
```

The START statement places the File Position Indicator at the first alternate index record with a key value of HEMINGWAY.

```
START ===>  HEMINGWAY
            HEMINGWAY
            HEMINGWAY
            HEPBURN
```

Next, we evaluate the COBOL status key, and if okay, we display a message that we are listing titles for the requested author and perform the 850-READ-AIX-NEXT until one of four conditions is encountered. We'll come back to these conditions.

```
EVALUATE TRUE
  WHEN OK
    DISPLAY "LISTING TITLES FOR AUTHOR:   ",
            LIB-AUTH-LNAME
    PERFORM 850-READ-AIX-NEXT WITH TEST AFTER
            UNTIL EOF OR NOT-FOUND OR   <===
                  NOT OK OR
                  LIB-AUTH-LNAME NOT = TRAN-AUTH-LNAME
```

If the alternate index key is NOT-FOUND (status code value 23), we display a message and fall through the paragraph to the next START statement or a random READ request. This logic is necessary because a NOT-FOUND condition renders the File Position Indicator undefined, but it can be reset within the program with a successful START or random READ request. This works the same way whether using START with a primary or an alternate index key.

```
WHEN NOT-FOUND
  Display appropriate message
  Fall through paragraph to random READ or
    START statement
```

In the unlikely event that the status key value is something OTHER than OK or NOT-FOUND, the problem is serious enough to warrant terminating the program.

```
WHEN OTHER
  Display appropriate message and status codes
  Terminate program
```

As with primary key processing, you can use INVALID KEY/NOT INVALID KEY logic instead of status code testing with alternate key processing, but we've seen that COBOL status code testing is more precise. Since you're dealing with more complex programming logic when switching the key of reference between the primary key and alternate key, it's better to take extra precautions in case your logic isn't perfect.

Now let's analyze the coding logic in 850-READ-AIX-NEXT, the paragraph we perform if the START statement executes successfully. We begin reading LIB-MAST sequentially by the alternate key beginning with the HEMINGWAY record.

```
850-READ-AIX-NEXT.
    READ LIB-MAST NEXT

      . . .
READ NEXT ===>   HEMINGWAY
                 HEMINGWAY
                 HEMINGWAY
                 HEPBURN
```

After each READ NEXT statement, we evaluate the COBOL status code for one of four conditions requiring an immediate termination of the read loop. When we encounter the alternate index dataset end-of-file condition (10) or NOT-FOUND (23), we reinitialize the generic key and fall through to the next random READ or START statement in order to reset the File Position Indicator, the same as for primary key processing.

```
EVALUATE TRUE
   WHEN EOF OR NOT-FOUND
      MOVE SPACES TO LIB-CAT
      Random READ or START statement
   . . .
                              Status key value
                              - - - - - - - - - - - - - - - -
                HEMINGWAY      02
                HEMINGWAY      02
                HEMINGWAY      00
READ-NEXT ===> HEPBURN
```

There is a most important point to remember when processing duplicate alternate keys. Each time the program reads a record, whether sequentially as in our current example, or randomly, if VSAM senses that another record with a duplicate alternate key value follows, it returns a COBOL status key value of 02, meaning "a successful hit, but more records are coming." When VSAM senses that there are no more records with this key value, it returns a COBOL status key value of 00, meaning, "a successful hit, and this is the last record with this value." You can build this logic into your programming statements, as in the following example.

```
IF STAT1 = "02"
   Do print routine
   . . .
IF STAT1 = "00"
   Do total routine
   . . .
```

If we encounter a condition that is NOT OK (that is, other than 10, 23, or 00 or 02), it is serious enough to warrant terminating the program. Most likely a logic error has caused your File Position Indicator to become undefined and the COBOL status key value will be 46 or 94.

```
WHEN NOT OK
  SET IO-ERR TO TRUE
  Display appropriate message and status codes
  Terminate program
```

When everything is okay, we continue to display TITLE information while LIB-AUTH-NAME = TRAN-AUTH-NAME.

```
WHEN OK
  IF LIB-AUTH-LNAME = TRAN-AUTH-LNAME
    DISPLAY "NEXT TITLE:  ", LIB-TITLE
    ADD 1 TO COUNT-LIST
  END-IF
END-EVALUATE
```

Records are processed as follows:

```
LIB-KEY    LIB-AUTH-LNAME                 LIB-TITLE
- - - - - - - - - - - - - - - - - - - - - - - - - - - - - - - - - - - - - - - -
FICT0025  HEMINGWAY      NEXT TITLE:  The Sun Also Rises
FICT9043  HEMINGWAY      NEXT TITLE:  The Old Man and the Sea
FICT8724  HEMINGWAY      NEXT TITLE:  For Whom the Bell Tolls
AUTO0001  HEPBURN        (NOT-EQUAL)
```

The example just shown illustrates another important point when processing records with duplicate alternate keys. Duplicate alternate key records are not necessarily retrieved in primary key (LIB-KEY) order. They may be, if the AIX has been recently reorganized, but don't take it for granted. And if it's necessary for the retrieved records to be written or printed in primary key within alternate key order, you need to build a mechanism in your program for ordering the records by this (or any other) field that will accommodate the application. Needless to say, this can make alternate key processing logic more complex.

To see why alternate key records are not necessarily retrieved in primary key order, we need to look at the structure of an alternate index record. Suppose that when the alternate index is first built, the AIX record reflects information that there are only two HEMINGWAY titles in stock with primary key values of FICT0025 and FICT9043 respectively as shown.

housekeeping info ...	HEMINGWAY	FICT0025	FICT9043

Later, another HEMINGWAY title is added to the KSDS with a value of FICT8724. The primary key pointers in the alternate index record are now out of order, since the new pointer is added to the end of the record.

housekeeping info ...	HEMINGWAY	FICT0025	FICT9043	FICT8724

If we access the records through the alternate index at this point, they will be retrieved in this order:

```
LIB-KEY     LIB-AUTH-LNAME   LIB-TITLE
- - - - - - - - - - - - - - - - - - - - - - - - - - - - - - - - - - - - - - -
FICT0025   HEMINGWAY        The Sun Also Rises
FICT9043   HEMINGWAY        The Old Man and the Sea
FICT8724   HEMINGWAY        For Whom the Bell Tolls
```

However, if we reorganize and rebuild the alternate index at this point, the records will be retrieved in primary key order within alternate key. This is certainly desirable for programming, and from a performance standpoint it will result in more efficient retrievals.

housekeeping info ...	HEMINGWAY	FICT0025	FICT8724	FICT9043

18.3. THE UPGRADE SET

As an awareness issue, when modifying records in a KSDS that has one or more alternate indexes, you need to know if each alternate index has been defined with UPGRADE, thus making it part of the dataset's *upgrade set*. If so, any modifications to the base cluster (additions, deletions, and rewrites) will be automatically and immediately made to the alternate index record as well as the base cluster record. No extra programming logic is involved.

Thus, if you add a record to the base cluster, VSAM dynamically creates an alternate index record for you. If you rewrite a base cluster record, it automatically modifies the alternate index record to reflect any new information. If you delete a base cluster record, it dynamically deletes the alternate index record.

And that's only part of the story. If during the add, rewrite, or delete operation, VSAM detects an error, it automatically backs out any changes just made and restores synchronization between the base cluster and alternate index records. If VSAM detects an error, the WRITE, REWRITE, or DELETE statement fails and a COBOL status code value of 22 or 23 is set, depending on the program logic. However, data integrity is maintained.

If all this sounds too good to be true, rest assured it can be. For large datasets with multiple alternate indexes or much updating activity, the performance degradation can be considerable.

If for any of these reasons you decide to exclude an alternate index from the upgrade set by coding NOUPGRADE in the DEFINE command, you need to be aware that it will be your complete responsibility to keep the alternate index records in synch with the base cluster records. To do this, you can run a separate procedure, perhaps nightly in off-peak hours. The most common method of upgrading an alternate index is to first delete it with the IDCAMS DELETE command, then redefine it with DEFINE AIX, and finally rebuild it with BLDINDEX. If you decide on this method, be sure to document it clearly, and make sure your operations and support people are aware of the documentation.

18.3.1. Updating Records via the Alternate Index Key

You can update records through the alternate index key instead of the primary key if you use a READ or START statement to designate the alternate index key as the key of reference.

```
READ LIB-MAST
   KEY IS LIB-AUTH-LNAME
```

The syntax of the REWRITE and DELETE statements is exactly the same whether access is made through the primary or the alternate key. However, from a performance standpoint, it's generally more efficient to update by accessing the primary key. Updates through the alternate key may require twice as many I/Os because the alternate index key must first access the primary key in the index component, which in turn accesses the desired data record.

Let's reexamine the WRITE, REWRITE, and DELETE statements in light of what we now know about alternate index processing.

18.3.2. AIX WRITE Considerations

When you WRITE a new record to a base cluster with an alternate index that is part of the upgrade set, the new alternate index record is created automatically. If for example we WRITE a new HEMINGWAY title to the base cluster with values like the following:

```
FICT0045   HEMINGWAY       The Dangerous Summer
```

the alternate index record would then look like this, with the new primary key pointer added to the end of record.

. . . . .	HEMINGWAY	FICT0025	FICT8724	FICT9043	FICT0045

When the alternate index is rebuilt, the new primary key pointer will be positioned sequentially between FICT0025 and FICT8724.

After the WRITE statement executes, the COBOL status key is set to a value of 02, meaning that it has created a valid duplicate key on the alternate index. However, if you try to WRITE a new record and VSAM detects a duplicate *unique* alternate index key, the COBOL status key is set to a value of 22, and the WRITE statement will fail—the same as when VSAM detects a duplicate primary key value. The best thing you can do is display the failed record and then perform an analysis later to determine why it failed.

18.3.3. AIX REWRITE Considerations

One of the best features of alternate index processing is the ability to change the alternate key. This applies to both unique and non-unique keys. For example, let's say we need to change the spelling of one LIB-AUTH-LNAME value from HEPBERN to HEPBURN. The following statements, which access the record by the primary key, will do this:

```
MOVE TRAN-KEY TO LIB-KEY
```

    [Contains the value "AUTO0001".]

```
READ LIB-MAST
```

    [Do a random read.]

```
EVALUATE TRUE
```

    [Evaluate the following conditions.]

```
WHEN NOT-FOUND
  Display and bypass ...
WHEN NOT OK
  Display and terminate ...
WHEN OK
  MOVE TRAN-AUTH-LNAME TO LIB-AUTH-LNAME
```

[Contains the correct value "HEPBURN".]

```
REWRITE LIB-MAST
EVALUATE TRUE
  WHEN OK
```

[00 or 02—a duplicate non-unique AIX key—but not here.]

```
    Continue normally ...
  WHEN DUPLICATE
```

[22—duplicate primary key—not likely since record already passed READ test. Could also mean duplicate unique AIX key, but not in this case.]

```
    Display and bypass ...
  WHEN OTHER
    Display and terminate ...
END-EVALUATE ...
```

This example wouldn't work in batch COBOL if we accessed the record by the alternate key, LIB-AUTH-LNAME, because TRAN-AUTH-LNAME contains a different value ("HEPBERN" vs."HEPBURN") and the READ statement will result in a NOT-FOUND condition. You may be able to work around this in an online application, where you could first search for "HEPBERN" and, when not found, enter the new value of "HEPBURN" interactively.

Once again, with random or dynamic access it's not necessary to READ the record before rewriting it, but in practice it's a good idea to do so, because a prior READ will weed out a lot of problems before the actual REWRITE is attempted, such as the NOT-FOUND condition just described.

After the REWRITE statement is executed successfully, the alternate index record for author HEPBURN will look like the following because the alternate index is part of the upgrade set.

housekeeping info ...	HEPBURN	AUTO0001

18.3.4.   AIX DELETE Considerations

There are no special considerations for the syntax of the DELETE statement in alternate index processing. A prior READ is not required if random or dynamic access is specified, and the syntax specifies *file name* even though the statement deletes only the current record.

```
DELETE LIB-MAST
```

If you DELETE a base cluster record, the alternate index record is deleted automatically if the alternate index is part of the upgrade set. If not, it's your responsibility to delete it.

18.3.5.   AIX CLOSE Considerations

Actually, for alternate index processing, there is nothing different between primary and alternate index key processing. The CLOSE statement closes the base cluster and any alternate indexes as well. Always check the COBOL status code after the CLOSE and issue an explicit VERIFY if the CLOSE statement fails.

18.4.   AIX RECAP

Here in rather a large nutshell is what you need to be aware of when processing a dataset that has one or more alternate indexes:

- An alternate index can be accessed sequentially, randomly, or dynamically.
- Access by alternate key may require twice as many I/Os as primary key access, depending on the buffering specified. (Good buffer management is the subject of Chapter 24.)
- If you chose the UPGRADE option in the DEFINE command, the alternate index becomes part of the cluster's upgrade set, and an update to the base cluster is also made automatically in the alternate index record. UPGRADE is the default. If you choose NOUPGRADE instead, upgrading the alternate index records to maintain data integrity is your responsibility.
- If you choose the UNIQUEKEY option in the DEFINE command, duplicate alternate index records are invalid, and if you try to add one, the WRITE statement fails and the COBOL status code is set to a value of 22. UNIQUEKEY is the default. If you choose NONUNIQUEKEY instead, duplicate alternate index keys are an expected condition. The COBOL status code is set to 02 when VSAM

detects a valid duplicate alternate key as part of a READ, WRITE, REWRITE, or DELETE statement. The value is set to 00 when the last duplicate alternate key has been processed.

- In the run JCL, there must be one DD statement for each alternate index used by that particular program. The DD statement for each alternate index named must specify the path name as the DSN.
- In the COBOL SELECT clause, you must code one ALTERNATE RECORD KEY clause for each alternate index used by the program. The WITH DUPLICATES option must match the DEFINE command option of NONUNIQUEKEY.
- The OPEN statement opens both the base cluster and any alternate indexes.
- The key of reference is set to the primary key by the OPEN statement. To change the key of reference, use the KEY phrase as part of a START or sequential READ statement. The new key of reference remains valid for all subsequent sequential access until it is physically changed. By default, the key of reference for all random reads remains the primary key until physically changed by a random READ statement with the KEY phrase.
- When access is by a duplicate alternate key, records are not necessarily retrieved in primary key order.
- With REWRITE, you can change the value of a non-unique or unique alternate key. However, changing a unique alternate key can result in a DUPLICATE condition and the REWRITE statement will fail.
- The CLOSE statement closes the base cluster and any alternate indexes as well.

19

ESDS Processing

So far in this part of the book, we've concentrated on processing a VSAM key-sequenced dataset, popularly known as a KSDS. This chapter introduces the processing of quite a different VSAM animal, the entry-sequenced dataset, or ESDS. These datasets are indeed sequenced by their order of entry.

The ESDS is not as popular as its KSDS cousin because it has more limitations. For example, because an entry-sequenced dataset has no key field, it can only be accessed sequentially. The program must read every record, just like a QSAM dataset—no skip-sequential processing allowed. Also, because there's no key field, an ESDS does not support alternate index processing in batch COBOL, although you can construct an alternate index on the Relative Byte Address (RBA) and use it for online CICS applications. (We discussed this in Chapter 11.)

Finally, you can't use the DELETE statement to physically delete an ESDS record. To delete a record, you must go through a cumbersome procedure of either copying the dataset and dropping the records to delete, or marking the candidate record in some way, usually by moving high values to a designated field, and then rewriting the record in place.

Still, for some applications an ESDS is a fast and efficient means of storing and processing data. For example, an ESDS is often used for journal logging of transactions from online applications like CICS and IMS. The fact that the ESDS is sequenced by order of entry makes it perfect for this function, because a journal file must, by its nature, be built in time sequence. Another thing—CICS and IMS are more compatible with a VSAM ESDS structure than with that of its QSAM counterpart. Finally, this becomes the most compelling reason of all to use an ESDS in conjunction with CICS and IMS.

Let's see the basics needed to construct a simple program that reads an ESDS log file as input and writes an output backup tape dataset. We could accomplish the same thing with REPRO, except that, say, we want to edit the input records and rewrite certain ones. This ability to rewrite records in place is a major strength of the ESDS.

19.1. ESDS SELECT CLAUSE

The following example shows a sample ESDS SELECT clause.

```
SELECT LOG-TRAN ASSIGN TO AS-LOGTRAN
```

[The AS prefix for the ddname signifies Addressed-Sequential and should be included for an ESDS.]

```
    ORGANIZATION IS SEQUENTIAL
```

[Can be omitted because it's the default, but good to supply for documentation.]

```
    ACCESS MODE IS SEQUENTIAL
```

[You can only access an ESDS sequentially in batch COBOL.]

```
    PASSWORD IS LOG-UPDATEPW
```

[If password-protected, specify the password data name here and define it in WORKING-STORAGE. To rewrite records, specify the UPDATEPW. For read-only operations, the READPW is sufficient.]

```
    FILE STATUS   IS STAT1,
                     STAT2.
```

[You should check COBOL status key (STAT1 here) after every I/O operation, the same as for a KSDS. The VSAM return code (STAT2 here) can also be displayed.]

19.1.1. ESDS FILE SECTION Entries

In the FILE SECTION, the FD (LOG-TRAN in the example) describes the ESDS, just as it does for a KSDS or non-VSAM dataset.

```
FD   LOG-TRAN.
```

[Must match the *file name* specified in the SELECT clause.]

```
01   LOG-RECORD.
       05   LOG-DEL-BYTE        PIC X.
       05   LOG-TIMESTAMP       PIC X(24).
       05   FILLER              PIC X(100).
```

19.2.   ESDS WORKING-STORAGE ENTRIES

In WORKING-STORAGE, a smaller set of condition names will suffice to check the COBOL status key value after each I/O operation. Basically, it's either OK (00), the end-of-file has been reached (10), or OTHER, and you should probably terminate the program.

```
01   LOG-STATUS-AREA.
*      The COBOL status key.
       05   STAT1               PIC X(02)    VALUE SPACES.
             88   OK                         VALUE "00".
             88   EOF                        VALUE "10".
```

Since an ESDS has no keys, a value of 02 (valid duplicate alternate index key) is not returned. Other key-based status codes like 22 (invalid duplicate key), and (23 key not found) are also not returned. If you EVALUATE the OTHER condition, you may also see: out-of-space (34, as opposed to 24 for a KSDS) and invalid REWRITE (49). You can also display the VSAM return code for more detailed status information in case of serious problems.

```
05   STAT2
       10   V-RETURN        PIC 9(02).
       10   V-FUNC          PIC 9.
       10   V-FEEDBACK      PIC 9(03).
```

19.3.   ESDS PROCEDURE DIVISION STATEMENTS

The programming logic needed to process an ESDS is remarkably similar to that of its QSAM counterpart. However, you should pursue COBOL status key checking vigorously after every I/O operation that uses an ESDS (or other VSAM dataset) because VSAM will not abend the program for a serious error as will QSAM in a similar situation. Your ESDS could easily become corrupted if allowed to limp along after a serious I/O problem has occurred.

19.3.1. ESDS OPEN Statement

The rules for opening an ESDS are less complex than those for opening a KSDS, mainly because you have fewer options with the ESDS. An ESDS can be opened as INPUT if you are only going to READ records from it. It must be opened I-O if you are going to READ and optionally REWRITE records. If you are going to WRITE records to an ESDS, the dataset must be opened OUTPUT (if it has never contained records or has been defined with the REUSE option) or EXTEND (if you are adding new records to the end of the file). If you open an ESDS as either OUTPUT or EXTEND, you cannot READ records from it. The matrix that follows matches valid ESDS COBOL statements with the form of the OPEN statement required by each one.

	READ	WRITE	REWRITE
OPEN INPUT	Y	N	N
OPEN OUTPUT	N	Y	N
OPEN EXTEND	N	Y	N
OPEN I-O	Y	N	Y

Because we're planning to REWRITE selected records, the sample application must OPEN the dataset for I-O.

```
PROCEDURE DIVISION.
100-START-PROGRAM.
   OPEN I-O LOG-TRAN <===
   IF OK ...
     Continue
   ELSE
     Terminate the program without closing the file
   END-IF
```

Always check the COBOL status key after the OPEN statement and if it is not OK (00), terminate the program, and issue an explicit VERIFY command before processing the dataset again.

19.3.2. ESDS READ Statement

All READ statements against an ESDS are, by definition, sequential. The first READ statement retrieves the first record, and records are read, one after another, until the end-of-file is reached. Because no skip-sequential processing is allowed, the START statement is not supported. An ESDS has no keys, so the INVALID KEY option is not supported, but you need to check each READ operation for the end-of-file indicator, either by using AT END logic or the more precise COBOL status key test. Note that both methods are used in the two examples that follow.

We have specified the INTO option with READ because we want to rewrite the record in WORKING-STORAGE, but this is not a VSAM requirement, merely an accepted COBOL practice.

```
1.   READ LOG-TRAN INTO WS-LOG-TRAN
        AT END
            Do end-of-file processing
        NOT AT END
            IF OK
                Do normal processing
            ELSE
                Terminate read loop
            END-IF
        END-READ

2.   READ LOG-TRAN INTO WS-LOG-TRAN
        EVALUATE TRUE
        WHEN OK
            Do normal processing
        WHEN EOF
            Do end-of-file processing
        WHEN OTHER
            Terminate read loop
        END-EVALUATE
```

The EVALUATE statement gives more control over the exact condition, but both methods do the same thing.

19.3.3. ESDS WRITE Statement

You cannot WRITE new ESDS records and REWRITE existing ones in the same program. This will become more clear if we again look at the OPEN matrix seen earlier:

	READ	WRITE	REWRITE
OPEN INPUT	Y	N	N
OPEN OUTPUT	N	Y	N
OPEN EXTEND	N	Y	N
OPEN I-O	Y	N	Y

To WRITE new records to an ESDS that has never held records, you must OPEN the dataset as OUTPUT. To WRITE new records to an ESDS that currently has records, you must OPEN the dataset as EX-TEND.

To WRITE new records to an ESDS that has been defined with the REUSE option, you can use OPEN OUTPUT or OPEN EXTEND, but remember that if you select OPEN OUTPUT, all existing records are deleted first. This may not be what you want. To REWRITE records, you must OPEN the dataset for I-O.

Check the COBOL status key value after every WRITE statement. Remember, duplicate keys (status key value 22) will not occur here.

```
WRITE ESDS record
IF OK
    Do normal processing
ELSE
    Terminate read loop
END-IF
```

To WRITE records from an ESDS to a QSAM dataset, as in our example, you merely use the old dataset/new dataset technique.

```
WRITE BACKUP-REC FROM WS-LOG-TRAN ...
```

You could check the COBOL status key after the WRITE, but because we're writing to a QSAM dataset, the access method will abend the program if something goes wrong at this point. However, if the program abends repeatedly here, you might want to insert logic to check the COBOL status key as it will offer you more information about what's going on.

19.3.4.   ESDS REWRITE Statement

One big advantage of an ESDS over a QSAM dataset is the ability to REWRITE records in place; that is, write them back to the same data-set, not a new one, However, you cannot change the record length of variable-length records in this way.

To use REWRITE, the ESDS must be opened for I-O, and a prior READ statement is required. Since an ESDS does not support the use of the DELETE statement, one popular use of REWRITE is to mark candidate records for deletion in some way (say by moving high values to some designated field) and then rewriting them back to the ESDS. Later, they

can be physically deleted using a routine that checks the designated field
for high values and bypasses those records when a new ESDS is written
as output.

This is the logic we're going to use in our sample application. The
following statements do this:

```
READ LOG-TRAN INTO WS-LOG-TRAN
EVALUATE TRUE
  WHEN OK
    IF WS-LOG-TIMESTAMP < PARM-TIMESTAMP
       MOVE HIGH-VALUES TO WS-LOG-DEL-BYTE
       REWRITE LOG-TRAN FROM WS-LOG-TRAN
       IF NOT OK
          Terminate read loop
        ELSE
          Continue processing
        END-IF
  WHEN EOF
    Do end-of-file processing
  WHEN OTHER
    Terminate read loop
END-EVALUATE
```

We need to point out a couple of things about the coding. For example, you can assume here that we're marking records for deletion
whose time-stamp value is less than some time-stamp value that we
enter at run-time.

```
IF WS-LOG-TIMESTAMP < PARM-TIMESTAMP
   MOVE HIGH-VALUES TO WS-LOG-DEL-BYTE
   REWRITE LOG-TRAN FROM WS-LOG-TRAN
     . . .
```

Also, we check for a valid REWRITE statement, and if it failed (no
space is one reason, dataset not OPEN for I-O is another), we need to
terminate the program. With REWRITE, so-called "key logic" COBOL
status codes (duplicate, not found) are never returned for an ESDS.

```
REWRITE LOG-TRAN FROM WS-LOG-TRAN
IF NOT OK
    Terminate read loop
ELSE
```

```
Continue processing
END-IF
```

Assume for our application that the marked records will be deleted in another application and our output tape dataset will have all ESDS records written to it.

19.3.5.   ESDS CLOSE Statement

When the end-of-file is encountered for the input ESDS, we CLOSE the dataset, just as we did for a KSDS (unless of course, we couldn't open it in the first place). If the COBOL status code returned by the CLOSE statement is NOT OK (00), you need to find out why by displaying appropriate messages, and then issue an explicit VERIFY against the dataset.

```
IF NOT IO-ERR
    CLOSE LOG-TRAN
    IF NOT OK
        Display ...
    END-IF
END-IF
STOP RUN
```

In the next chapter, we'll see how to use VS COBOL II statements to process a relative record dataset (RRDS).

20

RRDS Processing

A relative record dataset (RRDS) has many similarities to its key-sequenced cousin, the KSDS. However, there are major differences:

- The records have no primary key. Instead, records are stored and accessed by a relative record number (RRN)—just as the elements of a table are stored and accessed by a subscript.
- There is no physical index component.
- Alternate indexes are not supported either for batch COBOL or online CICS applications.
- Access is considerably faster because VSAM does not have to search an index; it can determine the relative byte address of each record and retrieve it directly.

An RRDS is similar to a KSDS in the following ways:

- The dataset can be accessed sequentially, randomly, or dynamically.
- The DELETE and REWRITE statements are fully supported.
- As with a primary key, you cannot change the value of a relative record number. (Of course, you can always delete a record and write it with a new relative record number, just as you can move an element of a table to another subscript and zero out in the original element.)

We discussed the structure of relative record datasets in Chapter 4, but a little review is in order, starting with an explanation of the term

RECORD1	RECORD2	RECORD3	. . .	RECORD999
RRN=1	RRN=2	RRN=3	. . .	RRN=999

Figure 20.1.   Relative record dataset.

relative record number. The idea is simple. The relative record number is the value that resolves to a particular record's position in the dataset, relative to the beginning of the dataset as shown in Figure 20.1.

An RRDS is analogous to a COBOL table in which the records correspond to the elements of the table as shown in Figure 20.2.

So, in Figure 20.1, the first record in the dataset has an RRN value of 1, record 999 has an RRN value of 999, and all records in between are—well—relative. If you use the IDCAMS PRINT command to dump some RRDS records, you can view the RRN value of each record.

The RRDS comes in two flavors, fixed-length and a newer hybrid-type that supports variable-length records and is defined as a KSDS but processed like an RRDS. The analogy with the table makes it clear why variable-length records are more difficult to implement. With fixed-length records, one can easily calculate the byte position of each record in the table, given its relative record number. With variable-

RRN	
1	RECORD1
2	RECORD2
3	RECORD3
	. . .
n	RECORDn

Figure 20.2.   Comparison of an RRDS to a COBOL table.

length records, it gets messy. The processing of this type of esoteric RRDS is not discussed in this book.

The relative record number in an RRDS is not a key. It is (or is used to calculate) the location of the record—unlike the KSDS, where the key is part of the record. This means that you either write the records randomly, assigning the RRN through programming logic, or you write the records sequentially, in which case VSAM assigns an RRN starting with a value of 1 for the first record, as shown in the preceding example.

Once assigned, the RRN value cannot be changed. However, if the record is later deleted, a new record can occupy the slot and assume its RRN value. This is exactly the same as with a table. If you want to insert a record, you must either leave an empty slot for it or move all records down in the dataset following where you want to insert—a resource-burning operation.

To aid in understanding the concept of the RRDS, consider how a demographics dataset used by the planners of some mythical nations might look. (Any resemblance to real nations is purely coincidental.) Assume that to dispel nationalistic problems they have changed the names of the new Commonwealth nations so that Russia becomes Republic 1, the Ukraine becomes Republic 2, and Belarus becomes Republic 3. Notice that slots are left empty in the dataset for adding republics.

		RRN	
Republic 1	demographic info.	1	
Republic 2	demographic info.	2	
Republic 3	demographic info.	3	<===
Empty slot		4	
Empty slot		5	
Empty slot		6	

The dataset works fine until Siberia decides to secede from Republic 1. If they chose to call the new nation "Republic 4," a new record could be written for it because there is an empty slot for it. Then the revised demographics record for Republic 1 can be rewritten.

		RRN	
Republic 1	demographic info.	1	
Republic 2	demographic info.	2	
Republic 3	demographic info.	3	
Republic 4	demographic info.	4	<===
Empty slot		5	
Empty slot		6	

Now suppose Republic 2 and Republic 3 decide to recombine into a single nation. Of course, neither would agree to take on the name of the other so they might choose the name "Republic 5." We could then delete the records for Republic 2 and Republic 3 and write a new record as Republic 5.

		RRN	
Republic 1	demographic info.	1	
Empty slot		2	
Empty slot		3	
Republic 4	demographic info.	4	
Republic 5	demographic info.	5	<===
Empty slot		6	

Now we must consider the inevitable. Republic 4 will also want to split into two countries, and the splitting country (probably East Siberia) will want to be called Republic 4.5 for reasons of nostalgia. Now things begin to fall apart. There is no way to insert a new record between Republic 4 and Republic 5. If you should need to insert records where there is no slot for them, you could recreate the entire dataset so that Republic 4.5 is located physically between Republic 4 and Republic 5 as shown here:

		RRN
Republic 1	demographic info.	1
Empty slot		2
Empty slot		3
Republic 4	demographic info.	4
Republic 4.5	demographic info.	5 <===
Republic 5	demographic info.	6

Of course, the relative record numbers are no longer the same as the name of the republic, leaving the problem of how one derives the relative record number from the republic numbers. To solve this problem, you could create another dataset containing the republic numbers and the relative record number in the demographics dataset:

Republic Number	RRN in Demographics Dataset
1	1
4	4
4.5	5
5	6

Then to look up a record in the demographics dataset given the republic number, you would go to the second dataset and search for the republic number. The record for it also contains the relative record number of the demographics dataset. Great! We have just reinvented the indexed dataset. The natural question arises of why not just simplify everything and make the original dataset a KSDS? And in fact we should.

The most effective use of an RRDS is when new records can be added in empty slots. If this isn't possible, one should probably use a KSDS instead. The problem isn't how many times records are deleted or added.

The main consideration is whether you can know in advance what slots to leave empty for inserting records. If you can't know in advance which ones to leave empty, you should probably choose a KSDS.

For this reason, the relative record structure is most efficient when coupled with fixed-length records having a numeric, sequential identification. (However, as the name implies, variable-length, relative record datasets can support variable-length records.) The secret to a successful RRDS implementation is in finding some straightforward way of obtaining the relative record number for the record. This might be the day of the week, the month, or the year for a schedule, bin number for inventory control, zip code for a zip code directory, and so on. If you can find that logical hook, an RRN provides the fastest access of all the VSAM dataset types, because there is always just one I/O per access request.

For our RRDS example, we'll construct a simple RRDS from the demographic data example. We'll assume that there is enough central control in the republics that they can be forced to choose unique, integer, ascending numbers for their names.

Let's now take a look at the basic COBOL clauses and statements needed to initially load the RRDS and then to process it. Note that you could also load a simple RRDS such as this using the IDCAMS REPRO command, and we'll show you the statements for this at the end of the chapter. However, since the key to understanding the relative record access technique lies in the relationship between one unique field and the relative record number, studying the following loading technique should help in this endeavor.

20.1.   RRDS SELECT CLAUSE

The following SELECT clause is used to fill an unloaded RRDS with records. Because we've been over this "territory" (no pun intended) several times in the last few chapters, we'll only point out what's needed for an RRDS.

```
FILE-CONTROL.
    SELECT REPUBLIC-FILE
          ASSIGN TO        REPFILE
```

> [A prefix is not required before the assignment name, REPFILE.]

```
          ORGANIZATION IS RELATIVE
```

> [Required because SEQUENTIAL is the default.]

```
          ACCESS MODE IS RANDOM
```

[Required because the program (rather than VSAM) assigns the RRN value. DYNAMIC is okay also. SEQUENTIAL is the default.]

```
RELATIVE KEY IS REPUBLIC-RRN
```

[Names a data item that will contain the RRN. Further defined in WORKING-STORAGE.]

```
FILE STATUS  IS STAT1,
                  STAT2.
            . . .
FD REPUBLIC-FILE ...
01 REPUBLIC-REC
   05  REPUBLIC-DEMOGRAPHICS PIC ...
```

20.2. RRDS WORKING-STORAGE ENTRIES

In WORKING-STORAGE, you must define a data item to match the one named in the RELATIVE KEY clause.

```
01 REPUBLIC-RRN          PIC 9(02).
```

[The data item that contains the RRN. Must be defined as an unsigned integer item that can contain the maximum RRN value (99 for this application).]

The following diagram shows the relationship between the RELATIVE KEY clause and the WORKING STORAGE data item.

```
SELECT REPUBLIC-FILE
       ASSIGN TO REPFILE
       ORGANIZATION IS RELATIVE
       ACCESS MODE IS SEQUENTIAL
       RELATIVE KEY IS REPUBLIC-RRN  ◄─────────┐
       FILE STATUS IS STAT1,                    │
                     STAT2.                      │
WORKING-STORAGE SECTION.                         │
01  REPUBLIC-RRN          PIC 9(02).  ◄─────────┘
```

Contrast this with the diagram that shows the relationship between the RECORD KEY clause and the record FD for a KSDS. Note that for the RRDS the data item containing the relative record number is external to the record, unlike the KSDS where the primary key field is part of the record.

```
SELECT REPUBLIC-MAST
        ASSIGN TO REPMAST
        ORGANIZATION IS INDEXED
        ACCESS MODE IS SEQUENTIAL
        RECORD KEY IS REPUBLIC-KEY ◄──────────┐
        FILE STATUS IS STAT1.                  │
                                               │
FD  REPUBLIC-MAST.                             │
01  REPUBLIC-RECORD.                           │
    05  REPUBLIC-KEY        PIC X(08). ◄───────┘
```

20.3.   RRDS COBOL STATUS KEY CHECKING

For an RRDS, you check for the same COBOL status key values as for a KSDS. However, the value returned refers to the relative record number rather than the primary or alternate index key for values 20 through 24. For example, when loading records you should check for a slot-not-empty condition (22). Recall that for a KSDS, this value is returned if you attempt to WRITE a record with a duplicate primary or unique alternate key.

```
01  REPUBLIC-STATUS-AREA.
    05  STAT1              PIC X(02)    VALUE SPACES.
        88  OK                          VALUE "00".
        88  EOF                         VALUE "10".
        88  SLOT-NOT-EMPTY              VALUE "22".
```

Here's a list of the status key values that pertain to RRDS processing:

00   Successful I/O operation. (Status value 02, valid duplicate alternate index key, has no meaning for an RRDS.)

10   READ statement end-of-file.

22   Slot not empty on WRITE statement.

23   Record not found on READ statement.

24   No-space condition on WRITE or REWRITE statement.

Relative record size error on WRITE statement.

30   A serious I/O error with no further information.

90   A logic error with no further information.

93   Resource not available.

94   File Position Indicator undefined.

95   Invalid dataset information exists.

96   Missing DD statement.

97   Dataset opened successfully after implicit VERIFY.

You may also see status codes 35, 37, 38, 39, and 41, which pertain to the OPEN statement; 42, which indicates a CLOSE error; and 43 through 49, which indicate a READ, REWRITE, or DELETE error.

20.4. RRDS OPEN STATEMENT

The rules for opening an RRDS are the same as for opening a KSDS, and like the KSDS, depend largely on the access method specified by the program. An RRDS can be opened as INPUT if you are only going to READ records from it. It must be opened I-O if you are going to READ, and optionally REWRITE, records. If you are going to WRITE records to an RRDS, the dataset must be opened OUTPUT if it has never contained records, or EXTEND if you are writing new records and sequential access is specified.

If you open an RRDS as either OUTPUT or EXTEND, you cannot READ records from it. The following matrix matches valid RRDS CO-BOL statements with the form of the OPEN statement required by each access method.

1. ACCESS MODE IS SEQUENTIAL

	READ	WRITE	REWRITE	DELETE	START
OPEN INPUT	Y	N	N	N	Y
OPEN OUTPUT	N	Y	N	N	N
OPEN EXTEND	N	Y	N	N	N
OPEN I-O	Y	N	Y	Y	Y

2. ACCESS MODE IS RANDOM

	READ	WRITE	REWRITE	DELETE	START
OPEN INPUT	Y	N	N	N	N
OPEN OUTPUT	N	Y	N	N	N
OPEN EXTEND	N	N	N	N	N
OPEN I-O	Y	Y	Y	Y	N

3. ACCESS MODE IS DYNAMIC

	READ	WRITE	REWRITE	DELETE	START
OPEN INPUT	Y	N	N	N	Y
OPEN OUTPUT	N	Y	N	N	N
OPEN EXTEND	N	N	N	N	N
OPEN I-O	Y	Y	Y	Y	Y

In our example, we'll assume we are reading a sequential IN-FILE dataset containing the republic number and the demographic information.

```
FD IN-FILE ...
01 IN-REC
   05  IN-REPUBLIC PIC 9(2).
   05  IN-DEMOGRAPHICS PIC ...
```

Because we are performing an initial record load, the sample program specifies OPEN OUTPUT for REPUBLIC-FILE, checks the CO-BOL status key value for a value greater than 0, and sets a switch to terminate the program without closing the dataset if that occurs.

```
OPEN INPUT IN-FILE
OPEN OUTPUT REPUBLIC-FILE
IF NOT OK                                <===
   SET OPEN-ERROR TO TRUE
   DISPLAY "OPEN ERROR ON REPUBLIC-FILE"
   DISPLAY "COBOL STATUS KEY IS" STAT1
   DISPLAY "VSAM RETURN CODE IS" STAT2
   DISPLAY "ISSUE EXPLICIT VERIFY AND THEN RERUN
           PROGRAM"
ELSE
   PERFORM 200-READ UNTIL IN-EOF OR IO-ERR
END-IF
```

20.5. ASSIGNING THE RRN

If we had specified ACCESS MODE IS SEQUENTIAL, VSAM would assign consecutive relative record numbers automatically as each successful WRITE statement is executed, starting with a value of 1. (The same thing happens when you load an RRDS with the REPRO command, but either way VSAM controls the value of the RRN.) The following statements show how the RRN would be assigned if the dataset were written sequentially.

```
READ IN-FILE ...
MOVE IN-DEMOGRAPHICS TO REPUBLIC-DEMOGRAPHICS
WRITE REPUBLIC-REC ...
```

However, for our application, the IN-FILE record contains the republic number (IN-REPUBLIC), so we specified ACCESS MODE IS RANDOM and physically move IN-REPUBLIC to the WORKING-STORAGE data item, REPUBLIC-RRN. When we WRITE the record, this RRN is used to store the record.

```
200-READ.
    READ IN-FILE ...
    MOVE IN-DEMOGRAPHICS TO REPUBLIC-DEMOGRAPHICS
    MOVE IN-REPUBLIC TO REPUBLIC-RRN   <===
    WRITE REPUBLIC-REC ...
```

Here's a recap of all the pieces needed write a RRDS, assigning the relative record numbers.

```
1.    ACCESS MODE IS RANDOM

2.    SELECT REPUBLIC-FILE ...
            RELATIVE KEY IS REPUBLIC-RRN ...

3.    FD IN-FILE ...
      01 IN-REC
         05  IN-REPUBLIC       PIC 9(2).
         05  IN-DEMOGRAPHICS   PIC ...

      FD REPUBLIC-FILE ...
      01 REPUBLIC-REC
         05  REPUBLIC-DEMOGRAPHICS PIC ...

4.    WORKING-STORAGE SECTION.
      01 REPUBLIC-RRN           PIC 9(02).
```

```
5.   PROCEDURE DIVISION.
          OPEN OUTPUT REPUBLIC-FILE      <===
          READ IN-FILE ...
          MOVE IN-DEMOGRAPHICS TO REPUBLIC-DEMOGRAPHICS
          MOVE IN-REPUBLIC TO REPUBLIC-RRN   <===
          WRITE REPUBLIC-REC ...
```

20.6. RRDS WRITE STATEMENT

After writing a record to an RRDS, we check for a COBOL status key value of 22, which means VSAM did not find the designated slot empty and so the WRITE statement failed. Any value OTHER than 00 or 22 indicates a serious error and the program should be terminated.

```
WRITE REPUBLIC-REC
EVALUATE TRUE
  WHEN OK
    Continue processing
  WHEN SLOT-NOT-EMPTY
    DISPLAY "SLOT NOT EMPTY"
    DISPLAY IN-REC
  WHEN OTHER
    DISPLAY "OTHER VSAM ERROR"
    DISPLAY "COBOL STATUS KEY IS" STAT1
    DISPLAY "VSAM RETURN CODE IS" STAT2
END-EVALUATE
```

One serious error that you probably can't recover from in the program is indicated by the example that follows. The WORKING-STORAGE relative record data item has been defined with two bytes, and if you attempt to move a value of 100 to REPUBLIC-RRN, the MOVE would truncate the high-order position. REPUBLIC-RRN would contain 00 and the WRITE statement would fail.

```
01  REPUBLIC-RRN           PIC 9(02).
     . . .
    MOVE 100 TO REPUBLIC-RRN ...
```

That's the basics for writing new RRDS records. We'll spend the rest of the chapter looking at READ, REWRITE, DELETE, and START considerations for the RRDS.

20.7. RRDS READ STATEMENT

READ statement considerations for an RRDS are basically the same as for a KSDS; if you specify ACCESS MODE IS SEQUENTIAL, read access is, by default, sequential, and read access begins with the first full slot. For a sequential READ statement, you can specify the AT END option. However, checking the COBOL status key value for a value of 10 (end-of-file) is a more precise method.

```
READ REPUBLIC-FILE
EVALUATE TRUE
    WHEN OK
      Do normal processing
    WHEN EOF
      Do end-of-file processing
END-IF
```

If you specify ACCESS MODE IS RANDOM (or DYNAMIC), read access becomes random by default and you must physically move the value of the RRN of the desired record to the relative key data item to initiate READ access. For example, if you were reading records based on an input transaction dataset, the statements might look something like this:

```
MOVE IN-REPUBLIC TO REPUBLIC-RRN
READ REPUBLIC-FILE
```

Contrast this with the equivalent READ statement for a KSDS. The only difference is that here the primary key (REPUBLIC-KEY) is part of the record, whereas REPUBLIC-RRN is external to the record, being defined in WORKING-STORAGE.

```
MOVE IN-KEY TO REPUBLIC-KEY
READ REPUBLIC-MAST
```

And like a KSDS random READ request, a NOT-FOUND record (status key value 23) is a real possibility, and you need to check for it.

```
READ REPUBLIC-FILE
EVALUATE TRUE
    WHEN OK
```

```
    Do normal processing
  WHEN NOT-FOUND
    Bypass input record
END-EVALUATE
```

20.8. RRDS REWRITE STATEMENT

Like both the KSDS and the ESDS, the RRDS fully supports the RE-WRITE statement. The rules are identical to the KSDS REWRITE. That is, the RRDS must be opened for I-O, and if sequential access has been specified, a prior READ is required; if random or dynamic access has been specified, a prior READ is not required. However, in practice most programmers READ the record first before rewriting it, because this weeds out potential problems like a NOT-FOUND condition.

You can't change the RRN of a record when you rewrite it because it isn't a part of the record. However, you can achieve the same thing by writing it with a new RRN and deleting the record pointed to by the old RRN.

The following is a sample of REWRITE logic for an RRDS record. The prior READ checks for the NOT-FOUND condition, and the RE-WRITE statement is then either OK or it's not out-of-space—status key value 24 is one possibility.

```
MOVE IN-REPUBLIC TO REPUBLIC-RRN
READ REPUBLIC-FILE
EVALUATE TRUE
  WHEN OK
    MOVE IN-DEMOGRAPHICS TO REPUBLIC DEMOGRAPHICS
    REWRITE REPUBLIC-FILE FROM IN-REC
    IF OK
      Continue normal processing
    ELSE
      Terminate program due to serious error
    END-IF
  WHEN NOT-FOUND
    Bypass input record
END-EVALUATE
```

20.9. RRDS DELETE STATEMENT

The DELETE statement works like its counterpart for the KSDS, that is, it deletes the current record. The slot occupied by the current record can be filled by a new record, and the new record can assume the RRN value of the old record.

If sequential access is specified, a prior READ statement is required to make the record available. If random or dynamic access is specified, a prior READ is not required, but you can certainly code one if you prefer. Assuming random access, the following statements make the current REPUBLIC-FILE record available and then DELETE it.

```
MOVE IN-REPUBLIC TO REPUBLIC-RRN
DELETE REPUBLIC-FILE
```

For example, to delete Republic 5, you could code

```
MOVE 5 TO REPUBLIC-RRN
DELETE REPUBLIC-FILE
```

Later, you could write another record in slot 05.

```
MOVE 5 TO REPUBLIC-RRN
MOVE some-data TO REPUBLIC-DEMOGRAPHICS
WRITE REPUBLIC-REC
```

20.10. RRDS START/READ NEXT STATEMENTS

The use of skip-sequential processing is also supported for the RRDS. Recall from Chapter 17 that this type of processing allows you to access records both sequentially and randomly in the same program, using the START statement, which uses a conceptual pointer called the File Position Indicator to indicate where the first sequential READ NEXT statement should begin. You may want to review the material in Chapter 17, keeping in mind the following differences for the RRDS:

- All retrievals are based on the use of the data name specified by the RELATIVE KEY clause rather than the primary key as for a KSDS.
- Because retrieval is by RELATIVE KEY, generic keys are not used in RRDS skip-sequential processing.

20.11. RRDS JCL

Here are the basic JCL statements needed to load records into the sample RRDS described earlier:

```
//RRLOAD    JOB ...
//STEP1     EXEC PGM=VDEMO3
//SYSOUT    DD SYSOUT=*
//INFILE    DD DSN=A1000.INPUT.TRANS,DISP=SHR
//REPFILE   DD DSN=A2000.REPUBLIC.RRDS.FILE,DISP=OLD
```

Here is the equivalent REPRO command that will build an RRN automatically beginning with a value of 1:

```
//LOADJOB   JOB ...
//LOADSTEP  EXEC PGM=IDCAMS
//SYSPRINT  DD SYSOUT=*
//DD1       DD DSN=A1000.INPUT.TRANS,DISP=SHR
//DD2       DD DSN=A2000.REPUBLIC.RRDS.FILE,DISP=OLD
//SYSIN     DD *
REPRO                   -
  INFILE(DD1)           -
  OUTFILE(DD2)
/*
```

The bottom line for RRDS processing? It is almost identical to KSDS processing, but keep in mind that all retrievals are based on the data name specified by the RELATIVE KEY phrase.

In the next chapter, we'll look at some basic considerations when using VSAM datasets in CICS applications.

21

Using VSAM Datasets with CICS

"Is there a seat on Flight 451 to Dallas?" "May I have $40 from my checking account?" "Did that check clear the bank already?" "Do you have Youngblood Hawke in stock?"

Immediate answers to questions such as these are available because of CICS (Customer Information Control System), the most widely used online business transaction processing system in the world today. (In the United States, CICS is pronounced by spelling it out. In England, where it was developed, it is pronounced "kicks.")

Each of the previous questions represents a quick business transaction, and online processing means that a computer, one or more large databases, and telecommunications are involved in these transactions. Just about everyone gets involved with CICS at some time or other. Systems people define terminals, datasets, and other resources to CICS. Application programmers develop programs to run under CICS, and we've already seen that users (including systems people and application programmers) invoke CICS just about every day of their lives to conduct business transactions.

21.1. ONLINE VS. BATCH PROCESSING: A COMPARISON

To gain some CICS perspective, we'll begin by looking at some basic procedural differences between online and batch processing.

Job initiation. In the online environment a user initiates a transaction by typing some form of an identifier from a terminal. In effect, he or she has started an online job.

Batch jobs are initiated by JCL, which assigns each job a priority by class, and may even schedule a job to run at a certain time. Steps (programs) execute in the sequence specified in the JCL stream.

The nature of input. Online input comes from multiple sources, is generally unsequenced, and may be unpredictable in format and time of arrival. Online applications must take this into account.

Batch input has a single source, or at the most, a few datasets, and it may be sorted as well.

File access. Online programs access datasets at the record level, or in the case of VSAM, the control interval level. Because datasets are shared among users, good programming techniques dictate that the record be released as soon as the program is done with it.

Batch programs generally have access to the entire dataset for the duration of the step that uses it and perhaps for the entire job, if it is reused by a different step.

Program output. Online programs provide output in the form of an immediate response to the user, usually as a screen message.

Batch programs write results to reports or update datasets. Either way, the response to the user is delayed.

Notice that the online environment is characterized by words like "immediate," "unsequenced," and "unpredictable." Given the nature of online processing, one might start to think that online systems must be terribly complex. And they are, at least internally. But although online programs have to handle events that are unstructured (when compared to batch), the processing they perform is pretty much the same: read a record, change the record, report (display) the results. The rules are different, but the game is the same. Some things, such as retrieving or updating a specific record, are even simpler.

Internally, CICS consists of a plethora of system tables, control programs, and its own datasets, to say nothing of a set of acronyms and initialisms that can make even the most dedicated computer aficionado beg for mercy. A full depiction of all the bells and whistles of CICS is not the intention of this chapter. What we want to accomplish is to show you just how CICS interfaces with VSAM, and give you some idea of how to use VSAM datasets in your CICS applications.

21.2.   CICS FUNCTIONAL AREAS

Before stepping into the world of CICS programming, you should have a basic understanding of the functional organization of CICS and also be familiar with some of its many terms.

CICS runs as a job in its own address space within the computer. Just like any other job, somebody has to start up CICS when it's time to go live and shut it down at day's end. Once started, CICS continually monitors all the terminals connected to it, just waiting for some user to enter a request for processing—one of those business transactions we told you about earlier. When a transaction comes in, things really start popping.

One of the major problems of CICS derives from the fact that it runs as a single job in its own address space, and many individual CICS applications are executed in the same address space under the control of CICS. There is only so much address space on a mainframe computer, and the XA and ESA versions of the hardware and operating system have all been attempts to increase this limitation. In addition, one program can clobber another. Or if one program abends, it can take down the entire CICS system. This has implications for system reliability and debugging. Most installations run both a production and a test CICS system as an ad hoc solution to the problem.

The real problem is that the MVS operating system was designed as a batch system. Online subsystems such as CICS and TSO just grew. They must run as batch systems that support online applications. As a consequence, online systems in MVS are neither elegant nor clean. Remember, the basic design for MVS was done in the early 1960s. But let's get back to CICS functional areas.

21.2.1. Terminal Management

It is the *terminal management* function that is responsible for getting the transaction in the first place. This is the part of CICS that, working with a telecommunications access method such as VTAM (Virtual Terminal Access Method), monitors the terminals, accepts incoming transactions, and passes them on to task control—where processing actually begins. And when your program wants to say something to the terminal user, terminal management takes care of getting the message where you want it to go.

In your CICS application programs, you will be using a close companion of terminal management, *Basic Mapping Support* (BMS), which makes it easy to send and receive screens full of data to and from terminals. With BMS, you can define the format that display screens will take and process incoming and outgoing data symbolically in your program using that format.

CICS terminal communications transmit a full screen of data. Unlike terminal I/O on a PC in which the PC, having no other users to service, can look at each keystroke, CICS operates by having the user at the terminal fill in an entire screen's worth of information. It then transmits this to the application program for processing.

21.2.2. Task Control

CICS is designed to support the online environment where multiple users can execute the same program or different programs at the same time. This is known as multitasking and CICS task control coordinates the simultaneous execution of multiple jobs. To understand task control, we need to see how applications are organized.

In CICS, a user at a terminal initiates a task by typing a four-character transaction identifier on the screen. We'll assume that a transaction type is analogous to a program, even though more than one program may be involved. A task represents one execution of that program. There can be multiple users executing the same transaction (program) at the same time, but they will each have a different, unique task. Figure 21.1 illustrates the relationship of various tasks to one CICS transaction (whose identifier is LIBR).

21.2.3. Program Control

We just said that a CICS transaction consists of an identifier and one or more application programs. The function of *program control* is to man-

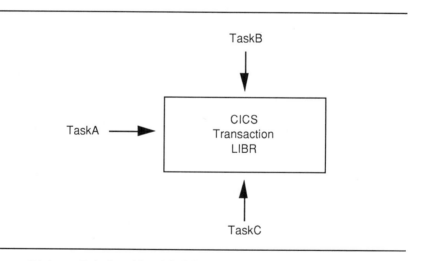

Figure 21.1. Relationship of CICS tasks.

age requests for the execution of CICS programs. Program control locates and executes all the programs that may be needed to process a transaction. It oversees searching the processing program table (PPT) where all programs that will run under CICS must be defined.

Besides programs, tasks also share data. If an update is made by User A to a record in a control interval, the control interval is available to User B as soon as User A's task releases it. This is known as *concurrency* and is also managed by CICS. However, you can aid concurrency by good programming practices, some of which you'll learn in this chapter, with more in Chapter 24, which deals with buffering.

Though tasks may share application programs and datasets, each task has its own copy of WORKING-STORAGE in which to process the data currently retrieved. This is the bailiwick of the *Command Level* (EXEC) *Interface* that also provides services such as interpreting CICS commands within a program.

21.2.4. File Control

As VSAM practitioners, we'll be concerned with CICS *file control*. In the early days of CICS, file control was basically one huge control program that, working with a file access method such as VSAM, handled all file accesses for CICS application programs.

More recently, file control functions have been allocated among a group of smaller system modules. But some CICS old-timers still refer to it as the file control program (FCP for short). Together with the file control table (the FCT, where datasets are defined to CICS), file control enables CICS to access all types of VSAM datasets. Most of this chapter will be concerned with file control techniques. Figure 21.2 illustrates how file control exists today.

Since the subject of this book is VSAM and not CICS, we can't offer

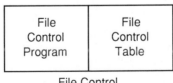

File Control

Figure 21.2. File control.

a complete overview of CICS, which would occupy an entire book in itself. Accordingly, for more information we suggest IBM's *CICS General Information* manual.[1]

And if you're going to write CICS programs, try to get a copy of the following manuals. (In fact, if you're only going to adopt one suggestion in this entire chapter, get these manuals.)

- *CICS Application Programming Guide*[2]
- *CICS Application Programming Primer (VS COBOL II)*[3] (New with CICS/ESA Version 3)
- *CICS Application Programming Reference*[4]

21.3. CICS PROGRAMMING: GENERAL CONSIDERATIONS

Most of this chapter will be devoted to the details of file control, but before we get into that, let's explore some general programming considerations that the application programmer needs to be aware of.

In batch COBOL programs you code COBOL statements like READ and START to access VSAM datasets. These statements invoke COBOL routines, which, in turn, request VSAM to perform the services your program requires. The situation is similar in CICS programs. Instead of COBOL statements, you code CICS commands, which break down to a series of calls to CICS to perform services. (You'll see what a command looks like in just a moment.)

These commands, or "calls," are embedded within traditional language programs such as OS/VS COBOL, VS COBOL II, PL/I, or Assembler for the mainframe. If your installation has moved to the ESA environment using CICS/ESA Version 3, you can also write CICS programs in C. And if you're developing programs on a workstation, you can use the Microsoft/Micro Focus COBOL compilers to write CICS programs, which can run on the workstation (using CICS OS/2) or, alternately, can be uploaded to the mainframe to run on CICS there.

Since your program talks to CICS using commands, CICS application programming is called (quite logically) *Command Level Programming*. If you have a batch COBOL background you probably have the skills to read and understand a good part of a COBOL program with embedded CICS calls. Because it is so widely used in business programming, we're assuming that you have been exposed to batch COBOL at some point. If not, Chapters 14 through 20 of this book should help.

A CICS call begins with EXEC CICS, specifies a CICS command

(such as READ), one or more options (such as UPDATE), and in COBOL programs, ends with END-EXEC in the following format:

```
EXEC CICS command
    option(value)...
    option(value)
END-EXEC
```

The CICS call is embedded within traditional COBOL statements that implement other program logic as in the following example:

```
1200-READ
    PERFORM VARYING X FROM 1 BY 1 UNTIL X > 9
      MOVE SPACES TO MAP-LINE(X)
    END-PERFORM

    EXEC CICS READ FILE ('LIBMAST')
        INTO(WS-LIB-AREA)
        RIDFLD(WS-LIB-KEY)
        UPDATE
        RESP(WS-RESPONSE)
    END-EXEC

EVALUATE WS-RESPONSE ...
```

If you're wondering how the COBOL compiler deals with these embedded calls, the answer is, in their native state, not very gracefully. For this reason, CICS has a facility called the Command Level Translator that translates each CICS command into a series of COBOL-executable MOVE statements, followed by a CALL statement to the CICS EXEC Interface Program (EIP). The EIP provides an interface between the application program and various CICS control programs. Here's an example of typical compiler output. Notice that the CICS command has been commented out by the translator.

```
*     EXEC CICS WRITE FILE('LIBMAST')
*               FROM(WS-LIB-AREA)
*               RIDFLD(WS-LIB-KEY
*               RESP(WS-RESPONSE)
*     END EXEC
      MOVE "..0......00668 " TO DFHEIV0
```

```
MOVE 'LIBMAST' TO DFHC0080
MOVE LENGTH OF WS-LIB-AREA TO DFHB0020
CALL 'DFHEI1' USING DFHEIV0 ...
MOVE EIBRESP TO WS-RESPONSE
```

The translation adds an extra step to the compile and link-edit procedure. First, you receive output from the translator, which identifies syntax errors in CICS commands and other CICS-related diagnostics. You don't even want to see the compiler output until the translator output is clean.

Another major difference in a traditional COBOL program versus the CICS command level program is the total absence of the INPUT-OUTPUT SECTION and FILE SECTION. This means that there are no SELECT clauses and no FDs, the lack of which tends to leave batch COBOL programmers aghast upon first exposure to CICS programs. In a CICS program you go straight from the ENVIRONMENT DIVISION to WORKING-STORAGE with only a brief pause for the DATA DIVISION header.

```
ENVIRONMENT DIVISION.
DATA DIVISION.
WORKING-STORAGE SECTION.
01  FILLER.
    05  WS-PROGRAM-ID         PIC X(08) VALUE "LIB000 ".
```

So how does a CICS program describe and process its data? Well, in CICS, this is mostly the domain of CICS file control. The majority of data that is accessible to CICS is stored as VSAM or BDAM (Basic Direct Access Method) datasets. BDAM datasets, which store and access records by their physical address, are beyond the scope of this book. Data that is organized sequentially (other than the ESDS) is handled not by file control but by the CICS transient data facility, and it also is not within the scope of this book.

If the data in a VSAM dataset has a relationship with other data in other datasets, it is most likely part of a database, such as DATA-BASE2 (DB2), which views data as a series of tables, or Information Management System (IMS), whose DL/I databases view data in hierarchical segments. VSAM is the underlying access method for both DB2 and IMS, but the database manager (especially in the case of DB2) assumes control when managing data. CICS programs access DB2 via the EXEC SQL interface, which returns for each access request a logical set of records rather than individual ones. The DL/I environment offers two interfaces—EXEC DLI, which fully supports command level programming, and the lower-level CALL DL/I. But, let's return to the components of file control.

21.4. CICS PROGRAMMING

21.4.1.   File Control Processing

CICS file control has powerful processing capabilities that handle CICS file I/O. That is, file control processes dataset access requests from CICS application programs to the access method, which is VSAM in this case. This is shown in Figure 21.3.

File control verifies and opens ENABLED datasets the first time they are accessed by a CICS application program. The ENABLED status means the dataset can be opened. Its counterpart status is DISABLED, set by systems people to indicate that the dataset temporarily cannot be used (opened) for some reason.

File control also handles the closing of VSAM datasets and the resulting VSAM status key checking, so your application program doesn't have to deal with those functions either. Additionally, concurrency issues (multiple tasks accessing data in the same control interval at the same time) are managed by file control. (Nice, since let's face it, you've got enough to worry about.)

21.4.2.   File Control Table

To process file access requests, file control uses the file control table (FCT), which describes the VSAM dataset to CICS in much the same way that the catalog entry describes a dataset to VSAM. The FCT has one entry for each dataset described to CICS. (Data stored in DB2 and DL/I databases don't require FCT entries.) Figure 21.4 illustrates the function of the file control table.

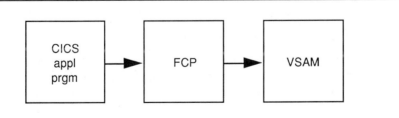

Figure 21.3.   File control processing.

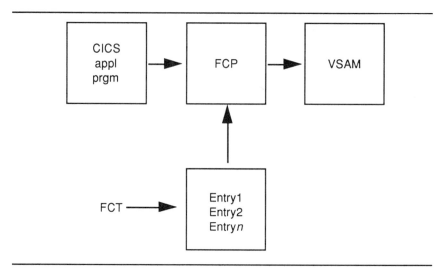

Figure 21.4.   The function of the file control table.

Generally, systems people create and maintain the FCT, but since input for each table entry comes from the application programmer, he or she needs to know the dataset attributes that are described there. With that in mind, we'll browse a typical Resource Definition Online (RDO) entry, which is the interactive CICS facility that uses CEDA, an IBM-supplied transaction, to create and maintain FCT entries and other resources.

RDO's batch counterpart is the DFHFCT macro. However, RDO is superior to the macro definition process because FCT changes can be implemented without bringing CICS down, as is necessary to get macro definitions installed on a running system.

21.4.3.   RDO Entries Described

The following composite depiction of an RDO panel describes only the parameters and attributes that affect application programmers. The CICS choices are displayed on the right side of each line item.

```
OBJECT CHARACTERISTICS                    CICS RELEASE = 0321
CEDA View
```

[CEDA is an online CICS-supplied transaction.]

File   : SAMPLREC

[The internal file name, analogous to the internal name specified in the SELECT clause for batch COBOL.]

Group   : LIB

[Each file must be assigned a group name—functions as an application ID.]

DEScription   : SAMPLE VSAM KSDS

[Optional reference information.]

VSAM PARAMETERS
DSNAme   : A2000.LIB.SAMPLE.CLUSTER

[The fully qualified dataset name.]

Password   :   PASSWORD NOT SPECIFIED

[VSAM password, if assigned.]

Lsrpoolid   : 1   1-8 | None

[Local Shared Resource (LSR) buffer pool. LSR is the default. For Non-Shared Resources (NSR) specify None here. Buffering is covered in Chapter 24.]

DSNSharing   : Allreqs   Allreqs | Modifyreqs

STRings   : 003   1-255

[Specifies the number of concurrent access requests.]

Nsrgroup   :

[For NSR buffering.]

REMOTE ATTRIBUTES ...

[Remote attributes that need to be specified for distributed processing. Beyond the scope of this book.]

INITIAL STATUS
STATUS   : Enabled   Enabled | Disabled | Unenabled

[Specifies the file status, Enabled here. Disabled means the file has been made unavailable for some reason; Unenabled signifies a null status.]

```
Opentime        : Firstref    Firstref | Startup
```

[The file is opened upon first reference, not at CICS startup time.]

```
DIsposition     : Share       Share | Old
```

[Analogous to the JCL DISP parameter.]

```
BUFFERS
DAtabuffers     : 00004       2-32767
```

[The default is one per string, plus one more for split activity.]

```
Indexbuffers    : 00003       1-32767
```

[The default is one per string.]

```
DATA FORMAT
RECORDFormat    : F           V | F
```

[Specifies fixed-length record format. Variable-length is the default.]

```
OPERATIONS
```

[Specifies the type of I/O operations that can be performed on the file. We'll cover the basics of each one.]

```
Add             : Yes         No | Yes
BRowse          : Yes         No | Yes
DELete          : Yes         No | Yes
REAd            : Yes         No | Yes
Update          : Yes         No | Yes
```

```
RECOVERY PARAMETERS
RECOVery        : Backoutonly None | Backoutonly | All
```

[Specifies dataset recovery. Depends on how critical the data is. "All" provides the CICS-supplied "heavy guns" but is resource-intensive. For most datasets, you'll want "Backoutonly", which restores the dataset to its original status in case an update fails.]

21.5. CICS I/O OPERATIONS

The FCT entry takes the place of the batch COBOL SELECT clause and the FD entry, neither of which is required in a CICS command level program. However, it's important to remember that the FCT entry describes the dataset for all applications that access it, not just one application as in the case of a batch COBOL program.

Let's take a brief look at the basic I/O operations that are performed in CICS command level programs. Using a COBOL base program, CICS calls can be embedded as program logic dictates. Remember that each call begins with EXEC CICS, specifies a CICS command (such as READ), one or more options (such as UPDATE), and in COBOL programs ends with END-EXEC.

21.5.1. Reading Records in CICS

As in batch COBOL, CICS command level programs can read VSAM records in one of three ways:

- Directly, with access by primary or alternate key for a KSDS, or RBA for an ESDS, or RRN for an RRDS. (Batch COBOL doesn't support access by RBA for an ESDS, but CICS does.)
- Sequentially as a browse operation.
- Skip-sequentially as a browse operation.

21.5.2. CICS Random READ

The following explains the format of a CICS READ command for random access. Data names or values following options are enclosed in parentheses. Mutually exclusive options are delineated with |.

EXEC CICS READ

[EXEC CICS is the call to CICS. A command is required, and READ is the command in this case.]

DATASET | FILE('internal file name')

[The internal file name specified in the FCT, enclosed in single quotes. Required.]

INTO(ws data area) | SET

[INTO specifies a storage area defined in WORKING-STORAGE. SET specifies storage acquired by file control. INTO is the more popular option, also used in batch COBOL.]

RIDFLD(*ws key name*)

[For a KSDS, specifies the WORKING-STORAGE data name of the primary (or alternate) key. For an ESDS, you move an RBA value to the *ws key name* search argument. For an RRDS, you move an RRN value to the *ws key name* search argument. RIDFLD is required for a random read and is analogous to the RECORD KEY clause of the batch COBOL SELECT clause.]

LENGTH(*ws data name longest record*)

[Specifies the WORKING-STORAGE data name of the longest record for variable-length records. Can be omitted for fixed-length records. If specified, it must match the IDCAMS maximum RECORDSIZE value specified in the DEFINE command.]

UPDATE

[Used to indicate that the record is being read for the purpose of updating it. Do not specify for read-only requests.]

RBA | RRN

[Used to specify an ESDS or RRDS respectively. If omitted, a KSDS is assumed. *Note:* The remaining discussion assumes a KSDS.]

END-EXEC

[Ends the CICS call and returns control to the program. It is required.]

CICS WORKING-STORAGE considerations. WORKING-STORAGE is a very important part of each CICS program because the data names that are specified as part of the command options are defined there, as in the random read request of a KSDS dataset like this:

```
EXEC CICS READ
   FILE('LIBMAST')
   INTO(WS-LIB-AREA)
   RIDFLD(WS-LIB-KEY)
   LENGTH(WS-MAX-REC-LENGTH)
END-EXEC
```

The WORKING-STORAGE entries might look like this, given a variable-length record of 80 bytes (maximum) and a primary key of 8 bytes. The data names can be elementary or group level items.

```
01  WS-LIB-AREA          PIC X(80).
01  WS-LIB-KEY           PIC X(08).
01  WS-MAX-REC-LENGTH    PIC X(80).
```

Alternatively, these work areas can be set up in the LINKAGE SEC-TION, in which case you would use SET rather than the INTO option. This means that you process the record in the CICS buffer rather than in your own WORKING-STORAGE. WORKING-STORAGE record processing is known as move mode; buffer processing is known as *locate mode*.

Remember that even though multiple tasks may share the same program and the same dataset, each task has its own copy of WORK-ING-STORAGE.

CICS generic key processing. You can specify generic key searching and processing for both random read requests and sequential browse operations in CICS. For sequential browse operations, the following options are used with the STARTBR and RESETBR commands, whereas in a random read request they are included as options of the READ command.

- *KEYLENGTH*. Specifies the length of the RIDFLD key to be used as the generic search argument. KEYLENGTH must specify the leftmost positions of the key.
- *GENERIC*. Used with KEYLENGTH to specify generic processing.
- *GTEQ*. Returns records where the generic key is greater than or equal to the generic key search argument. It is the default. For a random read request, only one record is returned. In a sequential browse operation, multiple records may be returned.
- *EQUAL*. Returns records where the generic key is equal to the generic key search argument. For a random read request, only one record is returned. In a sequential browse operation, multiple records may be returned. BGTEQ and BEQUAL are mutually exclusive.

Chapter 17 discusses the concepts of generic key searches and processing. You may want to review the material that is applicable to CICS, as well as batch COBOL programming.

CICS sequential browse considerations. Sequential browse operations can be utilized in CICS programs in much the same way as their batch COBOL counterparts, and they offer two additional commands that make browsing even more flexible in this environment. However, from a performance point of view, you should limit extended browse operations because they tend to lock out other applications. (The evil twins, lockout and deadlock, are discussed in Chapter 24.) These are the CICS browse commands:

- *STARTBR.* Initiates the browse operation by placing the File Position Indicator (also known as the current record pointer) at the record to be read.
- *READNEXT.* Reads the record signified by the File Position Indicator. After the first read, the next sequential record is read. (The File Position Indicator also moves to the next sequential record.)
- *READPREV.* Reads the previous record. This enables you to browse the dataset in reverse order. (The File Position Indicator also moves to the previous record.)
- *ENDBR.* Explicitly ends the browse operation. It is important to always issue an ENDBR before doing a READ with UPDATE intent in order to avoid deadlocks.
- *RESETBR.* Reinitiates the browse operation. It is the same as ENDBR followed immediately by a STARTBR.

The following shows the basic format of each of these commands. We've commented only on the options that are new or have different meanings.

The STARTBR Command

STARTBR begins the browse operation.

```
EXEC CICS STARTBR
   FILE('internal file name')

   RIDFLD(ws key name)
```

[If you move low values to RIDFLD, the browse operation starts at the beginning of the dataset. If you move high values to RIDFLD, you can browse the dataset backwards, but you cannot use the GENERIC option.]

```
   KEYLENGTH(value) GENERIC
```

[KEYLENGTH specifies a value in bytes to indicate the length of the GENERIC key. Generic keys can also be used for random read requests.]

```
   GTEQ | EQUAL
```

[GTEQ retrieves records whose generic key is greater than or equal to the generic key value. GTEQ is the default. EQUAL retrieves records only whose key is equal to the generic key value.]

```
END-EXEC
```

The following example illustrates the use of STARTBR to initiate a sequential browse operation using a generic key of four bytes.

```
EXEC CICS STARTBR
    FILE('LIBMAST')
    RIDFLD(WS-LIB-KEY)
    KEYLENGTH(4)
    GENERIC
    GTEQ
END-EXEC
```

If the value "HIFI*nnnn*" is moved to RIDFLD, the browse operation starts with records that have a value equal to or greater than "HIFI".

```
        BIOG0009
        BIOG0010
        FICT0001
        FICT0006
===>    HIFI0001
        HIFI0003
        HIST0001
```

The READNEXT Command

READNEXT reads the next sequential record.

```
EXEC CICS READNEXT
```

[Only valid after a successful STARTBR.]

```
    FILE('internal file name')
    INTO(ws data area)
    RIDFLD(ws key name)
    LENGTH(ws data name longest record)
END-EXEC
```

The READPREV Command

READPREV reads the previous sequential record.

```
EXEC CICS READPREV
```

[Only valid after a successful STARTBR.]

```
    FILE('internal file name')
    INTO(ws data area)
    RIDFLD(ws data name)
    LENGTH(ws data name longest record)
END-EXEC
```

The ENDBR Command

ENDBR explicitly ends a browse operation.

```
EXEC CICS ENDBR
    FILE('internal file name')
END-EXEC
```

The RESETBR Command

RESETBR reinitiates a browse operation with different criteria.

```
EXEC CICS RESETBR
    FILE('internal file name')
    RIDFLD(ws key name)
    KEYLENGTH(value) GENERIC
    GTEQ | EQUAL
END-EXEC
```

CICS Skip-Sequential Processing

You can use a combination of STARTBR, ENDBR, RESETBR, READNEXT, and READPREV to do skip-sequential processing through the dataset, thus reducing index search time. You simply move the key where you want to start to the RIDFLD of the STARTBR command and then increment the key value in the RIDFLD of the READNEXT or READPREV command. Don't forget that you can start browsing with the first record by moving low values to the RIDFLD option of the STARTBR command. You can also use STARTBR with a generic key for browsing forward using READNEXT but not with READPREV to browse backward.

RESETBR is used to change the characteristics of the browse operation—for example, GTEQ to EQUAL or generic to full-key browsing.

21.5.3. CICS WRITE Command

In CICS programs, you use the WRITE command to add new records to a VSAM dataset. The basic format for the WRITE command for a KSDS is as follows:

```
EXEC CICS WRITE
   FILE('internal file name')
   FROM(ws data area)
```

[FROM specifies a WORKING-STORAGE data area. Required for WRITE.]

```
   RIDFLD(ws key name)
```

[Specifies the data name that contains the new key value. Required for WRITE.]

```
   LENGTH(ws data name longest record)
```

[Required for variable-length records. If specified, it must match the maximum RECORDSIZE value specified in the DEFINE command.]

```
   MASSINSERT
```

[Allows you to write multiple input records that must be in ascending key order. You should issue an UNLOCK command after a MASSINSERT in order to free the affected control intervals.]

```
END-EXEC
```

21.5.4.   The CICS UNLOCK Command to Unlock Records

The following is the basic format of the UNLOCK command, used to explicitly free control intervals so that other processing can continue, say at the end of a MASSINSERT operation.

```
EXEC CICS UNLOCK
   FILE ('internal file name')
END EXEC
```

21.5.5.   The CICS REWRITE Command

In order to REWRITE a record you need to first READ it with UPDATE intent. Because the RIDFLD of the READ command locates the record, it is not necessary to respecify RIDFLD with the REWRITE command. For a KSDS, you cannot change the value of the primary key field. If the KSDS has variable-length records, you can change the length of the record as long as you don't tamper with the primary key field. The following are the basic formats used for the READ UPDATE and RE-WRITE commands.

```
EXEC CICS READ
   FILE('internal file name')
   INTO(ws data area)
   RIDFLD(ws key name)
   LENGTH(ws data name longest record)
```

[Required for variable-length records.]

```
END-EXEC
```

```
EXEC CICS REWRITE
   FILE('internal file name')
   FROM(ws data area)
```

[Generally the same area as specified by INTO in the READ command.]

```
   LENGTH(ws data name longest record)
```

[Required for variable-length records.]

```
END-EXEC
```

If you decide not to REWRITE the record for some reason, you should issue an explicit UNLOCK command to release the control interval.

21.5.6.   The CICS DELETE Command

While it is possible to delete a record by specifying the RIDFLD option with the DELETE command, in most cases you (or your users) will want to inspect the record before deleting it, and so you should READ it first with UPDATE intent. Like REWRITE, it is not necessary to specify RIDFLD with DELETE because it has been specified as part of the READ command. The following format deletes a single record.

```
EXEC CICS READ
   FILE('internal file name')
   INTO(ws data area)
   RIDFLD(ws key name)
   LENGTH(ws data name longest record)
```

[Required for variable-length records.]

```
END-EXEC
```

```
EXEC CICS DELETE
   FILE('internal file name')
```

```
END-EXEC
```

Alternately, you can specify a generic key as part of the DELETE command and use the NUMREC option to specify a number of records to delete. Either way, if you decide not to DELETE the record (or records) for some reason, you should issue an explicit UNLOCK command to release the control interval.

21.5.7.   CICS AIX Considerations

Most of the principles that apply to reading, writing, and updating KSDS records via a primary key apply to alternate key processing as well. However, there are a few things that you should be aware of.

To access records by an alternate key, there must be an FCT entry defined for that alternate index path. For example, here is the RDO entry specifying the internal ddname for the base cluster.

```
OBJECT CHARACTERISTICS            CICS RELEASE = 0321
  CEDA  View
    File          : LIBMAST
```

Here is another RDO entry specifying a different internal name for the alternate index path. (Each path that you want defined to CICS must have its own FCT entry.)

```
OBJECT CHARACTERISTICS            CICS RELEASE = 0321
  CEDA  View
    File          : LIBMAS1
```

And here is a side-by-side view comparing a READ command for the base cluster and the alternate index path. Notice that the example on the left specifies the file name of the base cluster. The example on the right specifies the file name of the alternate index path. The example on the left specifies the data name assigned to the RIDFLD primary key. The example on the right specifies the data name assigned to the RIDFLD alternate index key. Remember that RIDFLD is defined in your program's WORKING-STORAGE and you can call it anything you want.

```
EXEC CICS READ            |     EXEC CICS READ
   FILE('LIBMAST')        |        FILE('LIBMAS1')
   RIDFLD(WS-LIB-KEY)     |        RIDFLD(WS-AUTH-LNAME)
END-EXEC                  |     END-EXEC
```

Another thing—when updating a record via the primary key or a different alternate index key, be aware that other alternate index keys will be updated only if they are part of the upgrade set of the KSDS. Chapter 11 has a full discussion of alternate index considerations, including paths and the upgrade set.

The GENERIC, GTEQ, and EQUAL options may be applied to alternate index key retrieval, but if the alternate index key has been defined as non-unique, the DUPKEY condition will be returned for each record accessed (except for the last, indicating there are no more duplicate keys.) A random read command will access only the first duplicate record. To access all records with the same duplicate key, you must initiate a sequential browse operation.

21.6. CICS EXCEPTION CONDITION HANDLING

We haven't said much about exception handling with CICS, but it should be an integral part of each CICS program. CICS has extensive error and exception checking capabilities, and unlike native VSAM, it will terminate your task (or put it in a wait state) if it senses a serious error from which it can't recover. There are basically two ways to handle errors in a CICS program: HANDLE CONDITION or the RESP option.

21.6.1. The HANDLE CONDITION Command

HANDLE CONDITION is a separate CICS command that checks the command return code and branches to an error routine in your program. You place it before the condition to which it applies, and it applies to all commands that follow until delimited by another HANDLE CONDITION or RESP option. Here is an example that explains the logic of HANDLE CONDITION.

```
EXEC CICS HANDLE CONDITION
    DUPKEY(900-BROWSE)
```

[If this condition occurs during the READ, control is transferred to the 900-BROWSE paragraph.]

```
END-EXEC
EXEC CICS READ ...
END-EXEC
```

[If the condition does not occur, processing continues with the next statement.]

HANDLE CONDITION generates an implicit GO TO when the specified error condition is encountered, thus violating one of the cardinal rules of structured programming: *No GO TOs*. Because of this inherent structural weakness, it is better to avoid HANDLE CONDITION and stick with the RESP option, described next. The only reason you may want to code a HANDLE CONDITION is to invoke a routine that will terminate the application if an unexpected error is encountered (HANDLE CONDITION ERROR).

21.6.2.   The RESP Option

The RESP option is an integral part of each CICS command, as you can see by the example that follows:

```
EXEC CICS READ FILE ('LIBMAST')
    INTO(WS-LIB-AREA)
    RIDFLD(WS-LIB-KEY)
    UPDATE
    RESP(WS-RESPONSE)   <===
END-EXEC
```

WS-RESPONSE represents a data name of your own choosing defined in WORKING-STORAGE as a full-word BINARY (or COMP for OS/VS COBOL) data item. For example, the WORKING-STORAGE entry might be

```
01  WS-RESPONSE            PIC S9(08)  BINARY.
```

Here's another example illustrating the use of RESP with the READNEXT command:

```
EXEC CICS READNEXT FILE('LIBMAST')
          RIDFLD(WS-LIB-KEY)
          INTO(WS-LIB-AREA)
          RESP(WS-RESPONSE)
END-EXEC

EVALUATE WS-RESPONSE
```

[The program evaluates the contents of WS-RESPONSE using the keyword DFHRESP and various CICS-supplied condition names, appropriate for the I/O operation just performed. This is similar to checking the status key in batch COBOL.]

```
WHEN DFHRESP(NORMAL)
     Do something.
WHEN DFHRESP(NOTFND)
WHEN DFHRESP(ENDFILE)
     Do something else.
WHEN OTHER
     Do something entirely different.
END-EVALUATE
```

Here are some CICS-supplied condition names that you may want to evaluate after performing a CICS I/O operation. Notice that most of the condition names are self-explanatory.

READ	READNEXT	READPREV
DFHRESP(NORMAL)	DFHRESP(NORMAL)	DFHRESP(NORMAL)
DFHRESP(NOTFND)	DFHRESP(NOTFND)	DFHRESP(NOTFND)
DFHRESP(NOTOPEN)	DFHRESP(ENDFILE)	DFHRESP(ENDFILE)
DFHRESP(NOTAUTH)	DFHRESP(DUPKEY)	DFHRESP(INVREQ)
DFHRESP(DUPKEY)		DFHRESP(DUPKEY)

[*Note:* DUPKEY applies to alternate indexes only.]

WRITE	DELETE (no READ)	STARTBR
DFHRESP(NORMAL)	DFHRESP(NORMAL)	DFHRESP(NORMAL)
DFHRESP(DUPREC)	DFHRESP(NOTFND)	DFHRESP(NOTFND)
DFHRESP(NOTOPEN)	DFHRESP(NOTOPEN)	
DFHRESP(NOSPACE)	DFHRESP(NOTAUTH)	

REWRITE(prior READ)

```
DFHRESP(LENGERR)
DFHRESP(NOSPACE)
```

[*Note:* LENGERR can appear elsewhere for commands that specify a data area, but it is more likely to appear when rewriting a record.]

21.7. CICS/ESA FEATURES

Let's spend the rest of this chapter looking at some of the features that are available for CICS in the ESA environment. However, in order to do that we need to gain some historical perspective by looking at the features of some prior releases to see how CICS has evolved along with the MVS operating system.

21.7.1. CICS/OS/VS

CICS/OS/VS Version 1.7 first became available in the mid-1980s and, at this writing, is functionally stabilized (a euphemism for dead but not buried), meaning that no new enhancements will be made to the product. CICS 1.7 offered many performance and usability enhancements such as making Local Shared Resource (LSR) buffer pools the default for CICS strings. (LSR buffer pools are covered in Chapter 24.)

Also under CICS 1.7, the file control program was completely revamped to make dataset handling more efficient. For the first time, VSAM datasets defined to CICS could be opened upon first program access. Previously, all VSAM datasets defined to CICS were opened when CICS was initialized. Overall, the basic command level interface hasn't changed much since CICS 1.7. For application programs, the 1.7 look still prevails today. If your shop operates in the non-XA or non-ESA environment, you're probably using CICS 1.7.

21.7.2. CICS/MVS Version 2

CICS/MVS Version 2 has been available since 1988, and at this writing Version 2.1.2 is currently offered. CICS/MVS offers support for the MVS/XA environment, which uses 31 bits for addressing and gives an address space of 2 gigabytes. This significantly larger address space aided CICS, which is designed to run all online applications in the same address space. Another real enhancement in Version 2 was the XRF (eXtended Recovery Facility), the ability to have a standby CPU waiting in the wings, so to speak.

Data Tables—CICS Version 2.1.1 also introduced data tables as a special feature. Data tables are work areas containing VSAM datasets that CICS copies into extended virtual storage controlled by CICS above the 16-megabyte line, thus providing quicker access to heavily accessed data because VSAM doesn't have to get involved as long as the data is used in read-only operations. If operating in the MVS/XA environment, you're undoubtedly using some release level of CICS/MVS Version 2.

21.7.3. CICS/ESA Version 3

CICS/ESA Version 3 has been available since 1990, and at this writing Version 3.2.1 is currently offered. As you might expect, CICS/ESA supports the MVS/ESA environment and permits 31-bit addressing as well as multiple address spaces of 2 gigabytes each. CICS/ESA Version 3 has enabled more system programs and user applications to move above the 16-megabyte line, thus offering some virtual storage constraint relief for applications that still must run with 24-bit addressing, or "below the line."

With CICS/ESA, each application's data can be placed in a separate data space (which contains only data and buffers, not programs) where it is protected from other applications and other programs. Hiperspaces, similar to data spaces but residing in either expanded or external storage, can be used as large work areas. There's more on both data spaces and hiperspaces in Chapter 26.

Domains—Internal restructuring for performance is a big part of Version 3. CICS service requests that used to be handled by individual control programs (formerly called *management modules*) are now said to be *domain-based*. A *domain* is just a collection of control programs, access routines, and storage areas that together handle a given function within CICS. For instance, all messages that CICS itself produces (such as task abend messages) are created and displayed in the message (ME) domain. Requests for storage in the CICS address space (for things like WORK-ING-STORAGE) are handled by the storage manager (SM) domain. And the dispatcher (DS) domain, which is part of the task control function, handles the multitasking we told you about earlier in this chapter.

Domains enable stricter control of the resources they manage, which won't affect you much as an application programmer, except that you need to know that file control, terminal control, program control, and the CICS command level (EXEC) interface are now in the application (AP) domain. You also need to be aware of the kernel (KE) domain that acts as an overall gatekeeper by handling the interfaces among the different domains. If you want to know more about domains, see the IBM manual *CICS/ESA Processing Overview*.[5]

Another issue affecting application programmers is that macrolevel programs are no longer supported under CICS/ESA, meaning that any remaining macrolevel programs in COBOL or Assembler will have to be converted to command level before they can run in the new environment. However, the good news is that CICS/ESA is mostly compatible with CICS/OS/VS Version 1.7 and CICS/MVS Version 2, for older applications that you may want to keep around for a while but not convert. However, currently IBM recommends using CICS/MVS 2.1.2 as a *coexistence base*.

The final word? If you want to keep an older version of CICS hanging around, let it be CICS/MVS 2.1.2, at least at this writing.

Data Tables—Data tables, introduced as a special feature in CICS/ MVS Version 2.1.1, are alive and well in CICS/ESA. If you think your application could benefit from the use of data tables (great for read-only applications), talk to your systems people because each data table needs an FCT entry. Also, you should be aware that data tables come in two flavors, the CICS-maintained variety, where CICS keeps the data in the data table in synch with what's stored under VSAM, and the user-maintained variety, where the programmer or operations people are responsible for upgrades to data in the data table. It depends on how critical the data table data is to the application. Sometimes users can live with data that may not reflect the most current changes, and sometimes they can't. Only you and your user can make that decision. (If the application concerns "hot" credit cards or closed checking accounts, users need the most current data.)

One last thing you need to keep in mind if considering data tables: While data tables are fully updatable by an application, they lose a lot of their effectiveness for update-intensive applications because VSAM has to get involved and this, of course, means extra I/O.

The goal of this CICS evolution? To provide continuous availability for critical online systems. (This is one reason why you can withdraw $40 quick cash from a bank teller machine at midnight if you need to.)

21.7.4. CICS OS/2

One last awareness issue and then we'll be done with CICS. An almost fully functional version of CICS is available for the OS/2 workstation, called, not surprisingly, CICS OS/2. At this writing, Version 1.2 is the current offering. CICS OS/2 has its own VSAM dataset access method with IMPORT and EXPORT capability. It can be used (along with CO-BOL/2 or C/2) as a program development tool, with CICS applications developed and tested on the workstation and then imported to the mainframe for production.

The disadvantages? Both workstations and the CICS product are somewhat expensive, and currently basic mapping support is minimal, plus DL/I databases are not supported directly. Still, if you and your installation can live with these constraints, CICS OS/2 can free up a lot of DASD currently used for test datasets, offer dramatic relief to the mainframe CICS test region, and most importantly, offer application programmers some autonomy in their working environment.

The bottom line on CICS? Across different systems the internals may be different, but CICS application programming interfaces will look the same to developers in line with the contemporary direction of things.

REFERENCES

1. "CICS General Information," Order No. GC33-0155, Mechanicsburg, PA: IBM Corporation, 1990.
2. "CICS Application Programming Guide," Order No. SC33-0675, Mechanicsburg, PA: IBM Corporation, 1991.
3. "CICS Application Programming Primer (VS COBOL II)," Order No. SC33-0674, Mechanicsburg, PA: IBM Corporation, 1991.
4. "CICS Application Programming Reference," Order No. SC33-0676, Mechanicsburg, PA: IBM Corporation, 1991.
5. "CICS/ESA Processing Overview," Order No. SC33-0673, Mechanicsburg, PA: IBM Corporation, 1991.

PART IV

VSAM "BURNING ISSUES"

Part 1 of the book introduced the world of VSAM, most especially the VSAM that is evolving today as we approach the twenty-first century, within SAA (Systems Application Architecture), MVS/ESA (Enterprise Systems Architecture), and DFSMS (Data Facility Storage Management Subsystem).

Then, Part 2 demonstrated how to use IDCAMS, the Access Method Services processor, to define and manage various VSAM datasets, including those that are entry-sequenced (ESDS), key-sequenced (KSDS), and the relative record variety (RRDS).

Continuing on, Part 3 expanded on the concepts and techniques of VSAM presented earlier to demonstrate the use of VS COBOL II statements and techniques to process VSAM datasets in batch COBOL programs, and online CICS applications.

Finally, here in Part 4 we're ready explore some VSAM burning issues that application programmers need to be aware of in today's VSAM environment in order to make sound judgments when faced with performance and tuning decisions. We'll wind up by looking at VSAM as it is evolving within the ESA framework, including an overview of both MVS/DFP (Data Facility Product) and the newest kid on the VSAM block, the Linear Dataset (LDS).

ICF vs. VSAM Catalogs

There can be no doubt that VSAM is the ultimate catalog-driven system. By this we mean that every VSAM dataset must be cataloged, the catalog acts as a central repository for dataset information, and any and all access to the dataset must be through the catalog. The same is true for other VSAM objects as well. Chapter 2 listed the advantages of VSAM as a catalog-driven system. You might want to refresh yourself on the advantages if any doubt remains.

22.1. THE CATALOG ORDER OF SEARCH

When VSAM receives an access request, it searches for the catalog entry in a strict order, based on the IDCAMS and JCL parameters that you have specified as follows:

1. First VSAM searches any catalog that may have been specified with the IDCAMS CATALOG parameter.

```
ALTER CLUSTER          -
  CATALOG(PRGMCAT) ...
```

Note: The CATALOG parameter is not supported for DFSMS-managed datasets.
2. If not found, VSAM searches the catalog (or catalogs, if concatenated) specified on the JCL STEPCAT statement.

```
//REPOSTEP EXEC PGM=IDCAMS
//STEPCAT   DD DSN=PRGMCAT1,DISP=SHR
```

3. If not found, VSAM searches the catalog (or catalogs, if concatenated) specified on the JCL JOBCAT statement.

```
//DEFJOB JOB ...
//JOBCAT DD DSN=PRGMCAT2,DISP=SHR
```

Note: STEPCAT and JOBCAT statements are also not supported by DFSMS.

4. If not found, VSAM checks the high-level qualifier of the named dataset to see if it is either a true catalog name or an alias for a catalog name (in MVS only). Here you can assume that A2000 is a valid alias for a VSAM user catalog named PRGMCAT.

```
NAME(A2000.LIB.KSDS.CLUSTER)
```

5. Finally, VSAM searches its own master catalog for the entry. If the entry is still not found, then VSAM gives an error message for an access request.

In the case of a catalog request, VSAM tries to catalog the entry in the master catalog, which may or may not be allowed, depending on the type of security that's in place for the master catalog. Also, this may not be what you want.

The same order is maintained when a catalog entry is created, say with the DEFINE CLUSTER command. There is an inherent minefield here. For example, if you specify a high-level qualifier that is a valid alias for the catalog that you want to contain the entry, and you also have a JOBCAT or STEPCAT statement in your JCL, VSAM will catalog the entry in the catalog specified in the JOBCAT or STEPCAT statement. This may not be what you intended.

```
//DEFJOB  JOB ...
//JOBCAT  DD DSN=PRGMCAT2
```

[VSAM catalogs the entry in PRGMCAT2.]

```
//STEP1  EXEC PGM=IDCAMS
//SYSIN  DD *
 DEFINE CLUSTER                        -
   (NAME(A2000.LIB.KSDS.CLUSTER)  -...
```

The bottom line here? If your shop uses the high-level qualifier technique, try to avoid using JOBCAT and STEPCAT statements when processing VSAM datasets. Within DFSMS, the whole thing is a nonissue, because these statements, as well as the IDCAMS CATALOG option, are not supported.

22.2. GENERIC CATALOG STRUCTURE REVISITED

In Chapter 2 we looked at the generic catalog structure of VSAM, which consists of one master catalog and (usually) multiple user catalogs. The master catalog contains pointers to the various user catalogs. The various user catalogs are usually allocated by enterprise or function, say for testing, accounting, whatever. The catalog structure contains entries for both VSAM and non-VSAM datasets. While a VSAM dataset must be cataloged in either the master or a user catalog, a non-VSAM dataset can be cataloged in either the master or a user catalog, or in an OS catalog (CVOL), which can coexist in the catalog structure.

There are two types of VSAM catalogs: so-called *VSAM* catalogs, which have been in use since the 1970s, and ICF (Integrated Catalog Facility) catalogs, a product of DFP (Data Facility Product)/VSAM, which supports the XA and ESA environments, including, of course, DFSMS. Many installations operate in a mixed mode, meaning they support ICF, VSAM, and OS catalogs simultaneously. DFSMS-managed datasets (VSAM or not) must be cataloged in ICF catalogs, but typically VSAM and OS catalogs support older applications where no conversion to DFSMS is planned.

That's the generic catalog structure of VSAM. Let's now examine the structure of the individual types of catalogs, starting with the older structure, aptly named VSAM catalog.

22.3. VSAM CATALOG STRUCTURE

A VSAM catalog, whether the master or user variety, is itself a KSDS, though it is not processable as a KSDS. The CISZ is fixed at 512 bytes, and no free space may be specified. Buffering options are also somewhat limited, thus effectively rendering this type of catalog untunable.

A VSAM master or user catalog actually owns the storage volume where it resides and may own other storage volumes as well. The relationship is "one to many" with the catalog acting as the landlord for the datasets (both VSAM and non-VSAM) stored on the owned volumes. The VSAM datasets that are stored on the owned volumes must be cataloged in the owning catalog, and the dataset names must be unique. No other

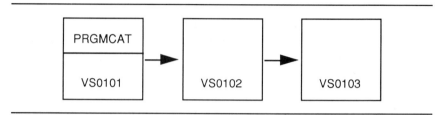

Figure 22.1. Multiple catalogs.

catalog can store its VSAM datasets on a volume owned by another catalog. If it has occurred to you that this constraint can result in inefficient
space utilization among storage volumes, you're absolutely right. Figure
22.1 shows how it all looks pictorially.

In Figure 22.1, the user catalog PRGMCAT is itself cataloged on
storage volume VS0101 and owns volumes VS0102 and VS0103. All
VSAM datasets stored on these volumes must have a catalog entry in
PRGMCAT. This constraint does not apply to non-VSAM datasets; they
can be cataloged in other catalogs. Non-VSAM datasets that are cataloged in a VSAM catalog are defined through Access Method Services.
This includes Generation Data Groups.

Alternately, non-VSAM datasets can be cataloged in an OS CVOL,
in which case the VTOC (Volume Table of Contents) for the storage
volume contains the attribute information that the VSAM user catalog
contains for those datasets defined through Access Method Services.

22.3.1.   VSAM Catalog Definition

In MVS systems, the VSAM master catalog is the system catalog and it
is defined as part of the SYSGEN (System Generation) process. In other
environments, it is defined using the IDCAMS DEFINE MASTER-
CATALOG (abbreviated MCAT) command. User catalogs are always
defined using the IDCAMS DEFINE USERCATALOG (abbreviated
UCAT) command. When defining an ICF catalog, you must specify an
additional parameter, ICFCATALOG, but the following example specifies the default, which is VSAMCATALOG, for a VSAM user catalog.

```
//DEFCAT   JOB ...
//STEP1    EXEC PGM=IDCAMS
//SYSOUT   DD SYSOUT=*
//SYSIN    DD *
 DEFINE UCAT           -
```

```
(VSAMCATALOG       -
   NAME(PRGMCAT)   -
   VOL(VSO101)     -
   CYL(25 1)       - [You can code CYL, REC, or TRK.]
   RECOVERABLE)
```

22.3.2.   VSAM Catalog Recoverability

Note the RECOVERABLE option, which uses a technique called *duplex recovery* to provide recoverability should the catalog become corrupted. Essentially, this entails writing all catalog transactions twice, once to the catalog itself and once to a Catalog Recovery Area (CRA) from which they can be recovered, if the catalog entries become corrupted. RECOVERABLE can be abbreviated RVBL.

RECOVERABLE is an effective means of ensuring catalog integrity, but a price is paid in performance: twice as many I/Os for every catalog transaction. For this reason, RECOVERABLE is not the default, since many shops cannot handle the performance hit that duplex recovery imposes. If the catalog is allowed to default to NONRECOVERABLE (abbreviated NRVBL), maintaining catalog integrity is the responsibility of the person who defines the catalog. Frequent backups is one method employed. RECOVERABLE is not an option for ICF catalogs.

This completes the discussion of the VSAM catalog. Now we will move on to describe other information about ICF catalogs.

22.4.   ICF CATALOG STRUCTURE

When IBM introduced Data Facility Product (DFP) in the early 1980s, it also introduced a new catalog type called the Integrated Catalog Facility (ICF), designed to correct some of the inherent weaknesses of the VSAM catalog. Every ICF catalog (both master and user type) is divided into discrete components consisting of one Basic Catalog Structure (BCS) and one or more VSAM Volume Datasets (VVDS), as shown in Figure 22.2.

The Basic Catalog Structure is actually a variable-length KSDS and each VSAM Volume Dataset is an ESDS. Since the Basic Catalog Structure component is a KSDS, it can be tuned like a KSDS. Quite sensibly, the Basic Catalog Structure contains the more stable information about each catalog entry, including attributes such as component names and storage volume information.

On the other hand, the VSAM Volume Datasets are reserved for the more volatile information about each catalog entry, such as total records,

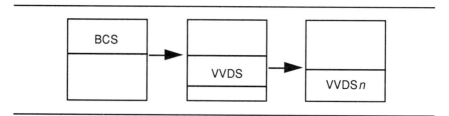

Figure 22.2. ICF catalog structure.

split activity, and HURBA value. This segregation of information results in fewer I/Os against the component containing the stable information and provides a definite performance advantage over the older VSAM catalog structure where all entry information, both stable and volatile, was stored together in one logical entity. (Of course, this segregation of information in the ICF catalog is transparent to the user.)

It's important to note, however, that in the case of non-VSAM datasets, all information is stored in the Basic Catalog Structure component.

The VSAM Volume Dataset resides on the storage volume with the datasets that it describes. On the other hand, the Basic Catalog Structure may or may not co-reside on the same storage volume as the VSAM Volume Dataset. Whereas in the older VSAM catalog structure the catalog owns the volume where it resides, with ICF catalogs we speak of volume *control* rather than ownership. Actually, it is a shared control, since each volume can be shared by multiple ICF catalogs (up to 36). This usually results in more efficient space utilization on a given volume. Figure 22.3 shows user catalogs PRGMCAT and PRGMCAT1 both controlling datasets stored on storage volume VS0101.

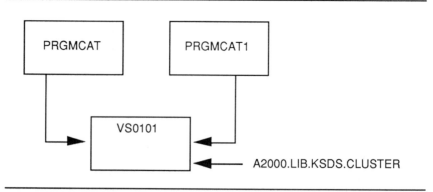

Figure 22.3. Multiple catalogs controlling one volume.

However, each dataset stored on a given volume may have an entry in only one catalog that shares control of that volume. For example, A2000.LIB.KSDS.CLUSTER, which is stored on volume VS0101, can be cataloged in PRGMCAT, but not PRGMCAT1. Interestingly enough, some system datasets have entries in more than one catalog, which can provide a performance advantage.

22.4.1.   Basic Catalog Structure Entries

Each Basic Catalog Structure entry for a VSAM object (let's say it is the sample dataset) always consists of one or more variable-length KSDS records that may span control interval boundaries if necessary. The Basic Catalog Structure primary key always consists of the qualified dataset name (44 characters), plus a one-byte field indicating the number of extension records needed to describe the stable catalog information for the dataset, plus that of all its associations (data and index components and any alternate indexes). Figure 22.4 is a high-level view of a Basic Catalog Structure entry that consists of one record. Because there are no extension records in this case, the one-byte field is blank.

In VSAM catalogs, the associations of a dataset or other object each have a separate catalog entry. You can readily see the performance advantage in having all the associations stored in one or more extended KSDS records as they are in the Basic Catalog Structure component of an ICF catalog.

22.4.2.   VSAM Volume Dataset Structure

Each VSAM Volume Dataset contains two control records: one that has backward pointers to all of the Basic Catalog Structure components that control datasets on the volume, and another that holds catalog information for the VSAM Volume Dataset itself, like a table of contents (described in Figure 22.5 as c/r1 and c/r2).

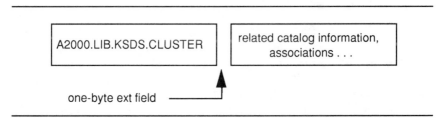

Figure 22.4.   Basic Catalog Structure entry consisting of one record.

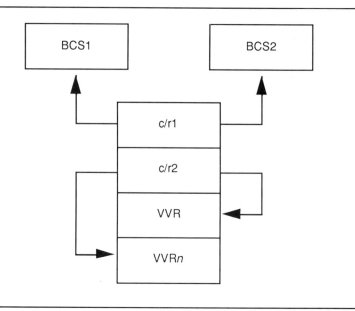

Figure 22.5.   VSAM Volume Dataset structure.

There is also at least one VSAM Volume Record (VVR) for each component on the storage volume. (For example, a KSDS would have at least two VVRs, one each for the data and index components and, under certain circumstances, additional ones as well, but that level of complexity is beyond the scope of the material presented here.) The VVR contains detailed catalog information about the component such as HURBA, CISZ, and so on.

22.4.3. ICF Catalogs: The Big Picture

Figure 22.6 is a high-level diagram showing how the ICF catalog structure fits within a given storage volume. While the Basic Catalog Structure may reside on another volume, the VSAM Volume Dataset must coreside with the data it describes. Also, on a storage volume controlled by one or more ICF catalogs, there is no such concept as suballocated space. Each VSAM dataset resides within its own unique space, which is handled, interestingly enough, not by VSAM at all, but by the OS DADSM (Direct Access Data Space Manager).

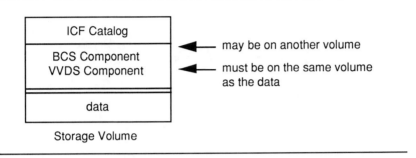

Figure 22.6.   Overview of ICF catalogs.

ICF provides a recovery facility that has made catalog recovery much easier, but there's still a performance hit attached to catalog recovery.

22.4.4.   ICF Recap

ICF catalogs offer the following advantages over their VSAM counterparts:

- Better space utilization because more than one catalog can share control of a given volume, and each can have datasets stored on that volume.
- Better performance due to separation of stable and volatile catalog information stored on the Basic Catalog Structure and VSAM Volume Dataset components respectively.
- Ability to performance-tune the Basic Catalog Structure component as a variable-length KSDS.

In the MVS/ESA environment, ICF catalogs can be kept in data spaces, which are blocks of virtual storage holding only data, and which enable ultra-high-speed catalog access. This facility is called, appropriately enough, Catalog in Data Space. Data spaces are also discussed in Chapter 26.

Next we'll take up the subject of the KSDS index component, which goes hand in hand with buffering management, always a VSAM burning issue.

23

More on the KSDS Index

The KSDS was designed as a functional replacement for the Indexed-Sequential Access Method (ISAM) dataset, which is reluctantly supported by MVS/DFP only for its compatibility with other operating environments. Not surprisingly, ISAM datasets cannot be managed by DFSMS.

While both ISAM and KSDS datasets support random access, the KSDS is superior to its ISAM counterpart because it has a simplified index structure, a better method of accessing records (by RBA rather than physical address), and less storage overhead because there are no pointers attached to individual KSDS records—unlike ISAM records, which can have both backward and forward pointers forming an elaborate chain. ISAM is obsolete today.

In this chapter, we'll look at the structure of a KSDS index, see how it accesses data records, and survey some basic techniques for improving performance by tuning this index component.

23.1. KSDS INDEX STRUCTURE

The index component of a KSDS is itself a subset of a KSDS, with one index record (with multiple entries) per index control interval. An index component has no control area organization, and an index record entirely fills the control interval. In this sense, the terms *index record* and *index control interval* are often used interchangeably.

Each index control interval contains a header field with a pointer to the next logical control interval, multiple entries that point to the values in the next level of index, plus one CIDF and one RDF, which to-

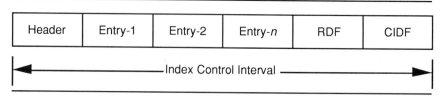

Figure 23.1. KSDS control interval.

gether occupy 7 bytes. This is shown in Figure 23.1. Previous to the release of MVS/DFP, an index CISZ could only have one of four values: 512 bytes, 1K, 2K, or 4K. However, with MVS/DFP, an index CISZ can have the same range of values as the data CISZ. However, for all but the largest KSDS, one of the four original values will suffice. In fact, it's a common practice to allow VSAM to calculate an optimal index CISZ.

The index structure consists of two types of records—unless the data itself occupies only one control area. Then it consists of only the sequence set record. Otherwise, it contains the following:

- *Sequence set records,* one per data control area, that point to the individual data control intervals where data records are stored.
- *Index set records* that contain pointers to the sequence set records (only if the dataset occupies more than one control area). There may be more than one level of index set records depending upon the number of sequence set records, but the top level index will always consist of one record. In this respect the index resembles a tree structure as shown in Figure 23.2.

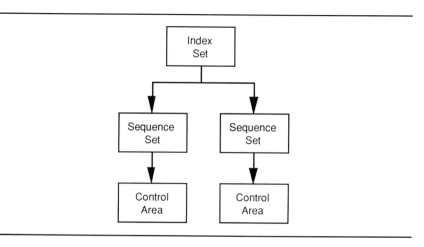

Figure 23.2. KSDS index structure.

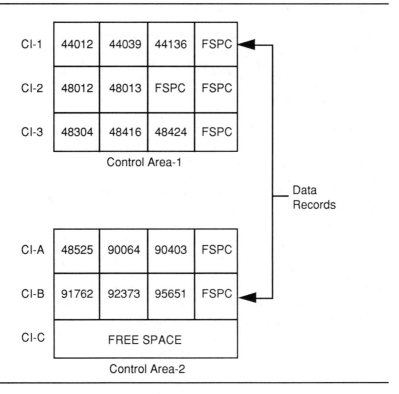

Figure 23.3.   Data component structure.

23.2.   DATA COMPONENT STRUCTURE

In order to lay the groundwork of understanding for the index structure, we need to take a bottom-up approach and start by looking at the structure of the data component. In Figure 23.3, you see two data component control areas labeled CONTROL AREA-1 and CONTROL AREA-2. Notice the following:

1. Each of the control intervals (labeled CI-1 through CI-B) has some free space and CI-C consists of totally free space.
2. The values in the various control intervals (44012, 44039, and so on) represent the primary key value of a KSDS record. (The example represents a zip code directory for Michigan, Ohio, and California.)

23.3.   SEQUENCE SET RECORD STRUCTURE

Now let's add to this structure the two sequence set records. Remember, there is always one sequence set record per data control area. Its entries relate to the highest possible value within each data control interval. Upon first glance, the values may have little meaning, but we'll explain. See Figure 23.4.

We'll begin with SS-REC-1, which contains a header field with a lateral pointer to SS-REC-2. This pointer is used for accessing records in sequential and skip-sequential processing. Even though we don't show it here, SS-REC-1 also contains a field that points to any control intervals in the data component that contain totally free space (none in CONTROL-AREA-1) and may contain some free space of its own that will be used as new records in the data component need to be referenced in the sequence set record.

Additionally, SS-REC-1 contains three entries, one for each control interval in the control area (CONTROL-AREA-1) that it represents. The values in these entries reflect the highest values that the data control interval can contain—one less than the first value of the next index entry. Thus, the highest value that CI-1 can contain is 48011, because the first primary key value in CI-2 is 48012. The highest primary key value that CI-2 can contain is 48303, because the first primary key value stored in CI-3 is 48304, and so on. The highest primary key value that CI-3 can contain is 48524, because the first primary key value in CI-A of CONTROL AREA-2 is 48525.

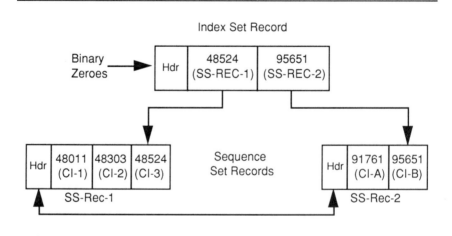

Figure 23.4.   Sequence set record structure.

Of course, if there's no room to add new records, a control interval split takes place and the data records are no longer in sequence within the control area. However, the sequence set entries maintain their logical sequence no matter what's going on in the data component as far as split activity is concerned. That's why VSAM uses the sequence set records when accessing records sequentially.

Let's fast-forward this whole business to SS-REC-2, which represents CONTROL-AREA-2. Notice that the highest primary key value that CI-B can contain is 95651, the logical end of the data component at this time, though more records could be added later. For illustrative purposes, we've shown you the entire primary key value, but VSAM actually stores these keys in a compressed form, the fundamentals of which we'll cover as soon as we explain the structure of the index set record.

23.4. INDEX SET RECORD STRUCTURE

The index set record in our example represents the top of the tree, since this is only a two-level index. Each index set record has the same structure as that of its sequence set counterpart. The header field contains a lateral pointer to the next index set record, or in the case of the high-level index set record as in our example, the header field contains binary zeroes. The index set entries contain references to the highest values contained in each sequence set record that the index set record points to. This is shown in Figure 23.5.

23.4.1. Key Compression

In order to conserve storage space, VSAM compresses the primary key in the index records using its own sophisticated algorithm. This may allow hundreds of entries to be stored on each sequence set record. Of course, this depends on the length of the primary key and how efficiently it compresses. The lurid details of key compression are beyond the scope of this book, but the general technique is to compare the leading bytes of a key value string with the preceding key value string and strip it of duplicates. Thus, in SS-REC-1, most likely the leading characters 48 would be stripped in this manner, resulting in compressed key values of 011, 303, and 524 (Figure 23.6). Here, each compressed value contains three bytes, but that is not always the case. Theoretically, it is possible to compress the key to zero bytes.

If possible, duplicate trailing values are stripped in much the same manner (not possible here). The index entry stores enough information

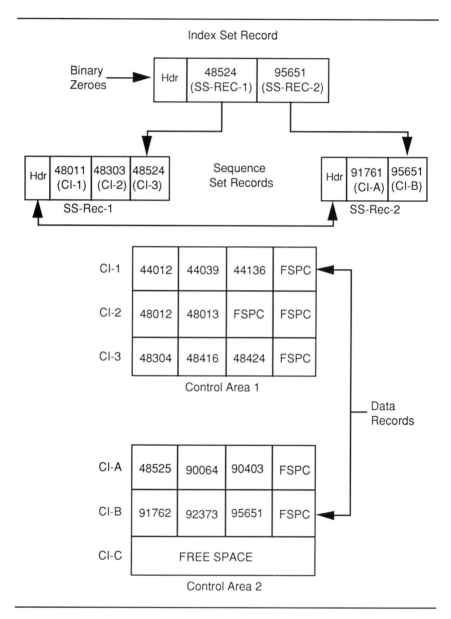

Figure 23.5. Index set record structure.

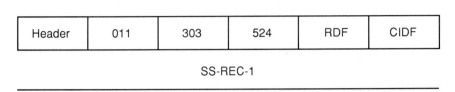

SS-REC-1

Figure 23.6. Compression of keys for SS-REC-1.

about the complete key value to reconstruct it at processing time and the whole process is entirely transparent to the user.

23.4.2. Index Search Techniques

When VSAM receives an access request for a specific KSDS record from an application program or from IDCAMS, it searches the index records to locate the control interval where the requested record is stored. (Remember, retrieval in VSAM is by control interval rather than individual record.) This is done by locating the first index entry with a key less than or equal to the key of the record we are searching for.

If the program specifies sequential access, a horizontal search is undertaken using the sequence set records only. On the other hand, if the program specifies random access, a vertical search is undertaken starting at the highest level of the index set.

If the program specifies dynamic access, and the START and READ NEXT statements are issued, VSAM treats this as a sequential request and mounts a horizontal search; other access requests are treated as random requests and initiate a vertical search.

Horizontal search. Using Figure 23.5 as a guide, let's trace through a horizontal search request. Say a program has issued a sequential request for the record with primary key value 92373. Since this is a sequential request, VSAM bypasses the index set and starts searching the sequence set entries sequentially. Remember, the sequence set entries are in order by the primary key, even though the actual data records may not be in order due to split activity.

VSAM compares each value in SS-REC-1 for a value greater than or equal to the search argument 92373. Since no match is found, it follows the lateral pointer in the header field of SS-REC-1 to SS-REC-2. A match is finally found in the second entry (95651), which has a value greater than 92373, indicating that the requested record might be located in control interval CI-B. There's a field in the sequence set entry for value 95651 that tells VSAM the exact control interval to retrieve. This pointer field is an important part of each sequence set entry in the sequence set record.

VSAM then moves from the index component to the data component and searches the named control interval (CI-B) sequentially until a match is found or a "no match" condition is issued. VSAM makes this decision at the data component level.

Vertical search. Now let's trace through the vertical search of both the index set and the sequence set that is initiated by a random access request. Once again, we're looking for the value 92373.

This time VSAM starts at the very highest-level index set record and looks for a value equal to or greater than the search argument. It finds a match in the second entry of the index set record (95651) and follows the downward pointer contained in this entry to the appropriate sequence set record, SS-REC-2. Then it reads each sequence set record of SS-REC-2 (bypassing SS-REC-1, a big savings of time for a large dataset) until a value equal to or greater than the search argument is found.

Once again a match is found in the second entry (95651), which has a greater value than 92373 and the pointer in the sequence set entry tells VSAM that the record belongs in CI-B. If the requested record is not found in the data control area, only then does VSAM indicate a "not found" condition.

23.4.3.   Index LISTCAT Parameters

You can monitor the performance of your KSDS index component in several ways. One is to check the output of the LISTCAT command, which has quite a few index-only fields. They are listed separately from the data component fields and carry the suffix of "I" as in LEVELS (I). We covered the most important of these fields in Chapter 10, and you may want to review that material in light of what you now know about the index structure.

When checking LISTCAT output, there are three index-only fields that application programmers can usually ignore:

1. *CI/CA (I)*. Since the index component has no control area organization, this field is not a true depiction of control intervals per control area.
2. *SPLITS-CI -CA(I)*. There is no split activity in the sense that there is in the data component.

3. *FREESPACE (I).* Even though index records do contain free space, it is not administered in the same way that data component free space is.

23.4.4.   Index Performance

In most cases it's best to let VSAM calculate the index component control interval size (CISZ), which it does taking into consideration primary key length, the data control area size (one cylinder is optimal), the data control interval size, and the amount of key compression that it's able to achieve.

Data control interval density (the number of control intervals per control area) is also a consideration because a larger index control interval is required to hold the pointers for the numerous data control intervals that equate to a large control interval density. The LISTCAT field CI/CA will give you the control interval density of your data component. (See the previous caveat concerning CI/CA (I).)

An index control interval that is too large results in a lot of wasted DASD space in each index record (remember, one record per control interval), but a too-small index control interval size has several inherent minefields. It can cause excessive data control area splits because there may not be enough room in the sequence set record to hold the data control interval pointers, especially those to the free control intervals, which may never be used. These CA splits also cause increased DASD utilization and can result in slower sequential processing because data records that should be stored together may actually reside in another control area entirely.

Even VSAM can goof when assigning an index control interval size. If you suspect a problem, first use LISTCAT to check the CISZ (I) field to see the value VSAM has assigned. Then you can try redefining the dataset with a larger CISZ value. Better yet, define and load a small subset of data (about one cylinder's worth) with the new CISZ, using DEFINE CLUSTER and REPRO. If you receive an out-of-space message during the REPRO step, select a larger CISZ and repeat the process until the load is successful. At each iteration, check the LISTCAT statistics.

With MVS/DFP there's an even more precise method. You can use the EXAMINE command with the INDEXTEST option to check the structural consistency of your index component. (You can also check the data component in this way.) A message such as the following indicates missing index control interval pointers:

```
IDC11760I MISSING SEQUENCE SET ENTRIES
```

Once again, try increasing the CISZ value (remember with MVS/ DFP the index control interval size can have the same range of values as the data control interval size) and then rerun EXAMINE. Repeat the process until EXAMINE indicates that all is well. Chapter 12 covered the EXAMINE options.

Index and data on separate volumes. For a very large dataset, you can assign the index component and the data component to separate storage volumes. The index component can also be assigned to a faster DASD device than the data component, which sustains fewer I/Os. Ask your systems people if either or both of these are viable options in your operating environment.

Cache controllers and IMBED/REPLICATE. In Chapter 8 we saw that IMBED and REPLICATE (two DEFINE command options) can be used in certain circumstances to improve overall performance. Briefly, IMBED causes sequence set records to be stored in the control area with the data records they reference, not with the index set records, and duplicated as many times as will fit on the first track of the control area they reference. REPLICATE causes index set records to be duplicated on their assigned DASD tracks as many times as will fit.

These two options are generally (but not always) used together to increase performance by reducing both seek time and rotational delay (the time it takes for the DASD unit to complete one revolution under the read/write head). However, IMBED and REPLICATE should never be used with today's cache DASD controllers. These are high-speed disk control units with their own storage buffers capable of holding entire tracks of DASD—the goal is to speed up I/O requests in order to have frequently used data always available. Two examples of cache controller models are the IBM 3880-23 and the 3990.

Cache controllers are most effective when the maximum amount of *unique* index records are packed into each track, and IMBED and REPLICATE with their built-in redundancy defeat this purpose. Not only that—cache is solid state memory with no moving parts, so the effect of REPLICATE in reducing rotational delay is nullified.

The bottom line here? If cache controllers are used in your environment, avoid using IMBED and REPLICATE when specifying DEFINE command options for your KSDS index component.

To recap, here are some basic techniques that you can use to performance-tune the index component of a KSDS:

- Use IMBED and REPLICATE, but never in a cache environment.
- Assign the index and the data components to separate volumes. You can also assign the index to a faster DASD device than the data component.
- If you suspect, because of increased DASD usage, slow sequential processing, or excessive control area splits, that a too-small CISZ is at fault, load a small subset of data with a larger CISZ and check LISTCAT statistics. With MVS/DFP, the EXAMINE command will tell you if the index CISZ is too small.

If no virtual storage constraint exists in your environment, you can also allocate enough index buffers to keep all index set records in virtual storage. Buffer management techniques are the subject of the next chapter.

24

More on VSAM Buffering

The last chapter discussed the structure and function of the index in processing KSDS records. This chapter continues that discussion and demonstrates how good buffering techniques can help keep critical index records continually available to the processor, thus reducing physical I/O, one of the primary goals of performance tuning.

Good buffer management may be the best way to reduce physical I/O, but it is not easily achieved. For example, if your shop doesn't operate in the MVS/XA or MVS/ESA environments, CICS runs below the now famous 16-megabyte line of addressability. CICS components, such as its management modules and indigenous storage area, and VSAM buffers as well, all need to coexist in the available virtual storage. Most likely this imposes upon your operating environment some measure of virtual storage constraint, which means that you won't be able to allocate all the buffers you need to achieve optimum performance.

MVS/XA and MVS/ESA offer virtual storage constraint relief because VSAM buffers can reside above the 16-megabyte line with Release 1.7 and above of CICS. However, some vendor and user applications may still run below the line, and so you may have some measure of virtual storage constraint.

Buffering is fairly simple in the batch COBOL environment and is usually specified by programmers via the AMP parameter in the JCL DD statement for the VSAM dataset.

```
//ddname  DD DSN=dataset name,...,
          AMP=('STRNO=n','BUFNI=n','BUFND=n')
```

Buffering is more complex in the online world of CICS and is specified in the File Control Table (FCT) online using an RDO (Resource Definition Online) routine or in batch using the DFHFCT macro. The RDO or DFHFCT also describes to CICS other dataset characteristics such as the ddname. FCT entries are normally specified by the systems programmers.

```
DFHFCT TYPE=DATASET,DATASET=name,....,
    BUFNI=n,BUFND=n
```

However, *specifications* for the FCT entry generally come from the application programmer, either formally through written specifications, or casually via a conversation. (For our purposes we'll assume the latter.) Once a task is in production, if you, as the application programmer, suspect a buffering problem may be impeding performance, you'll need to have another conversation with your systems people.

While the material in this chapter won't make you an expert in CICS buffering, it will provide you with the concepts and the language of buffer management techniques, and thus enable you to have these conversations. You'll soon discover that buffer management has a language all its own. Let's start with the definition of just a few terms that should see us through batch COBOL buffering. Later, we'll add some more that are more relevant to online CICS buffering.

24.1. DEFINITION OF A BUFFER

A *buffer* is a temporary work area in virtual storage that is used for moving data from the DASD device into central storage where it can be processed. A buffer holds the contents of one control interval—the VSAM unit of work. Therefore the size of the buffer is equal to the control interval size. This is shown in Figure 24.1.

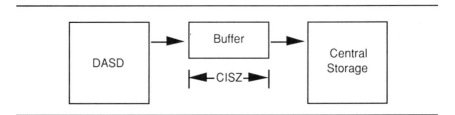

Figure 24.1.   VSAM buffers.

Generally, we speak of data buffers and index buffers, but in contemporary CICS processing, buffer size may be more important than whether the buffer in question is a data or index buffer. (More on this later.) However, it's important to note that since data control intervals and index control intervals are normally different sizes (the same is true of data buffers and index buffers), a buffer size always equates to its respective control interval size.

24.2. STRINGS

Strings play an important part in buffer management, and understanding the concept of the string is vital to being able to communicate your application's buffering requirements. A *string* is a logical entity that provides a placeholder for an access request. Physically, each string is made up of at least one index buffer (for a KSDS), one or more data buffers, and various VSAM control blocks.

VSAM uses a string to process file requests, one string for each request. Batch jobs usually require only one string, but in a CICS environment there can be several concurrently executing tasks each requiring a separate string that accesses the same dataset. The number of strings equates to the number of concurrent access requests that can be issued against that VSAM dataset, two as shown in Figure 24.2.

When all strings are busy, tasks have to wait for one to become available, known in buffering terms as a *string wait*. The CICS shutdown statistics provide statistics on string waits for each dataset that has been defined to CICS. Ask your systems people to check this out for you if you suspect a string wait problem with your VSAM dataset.

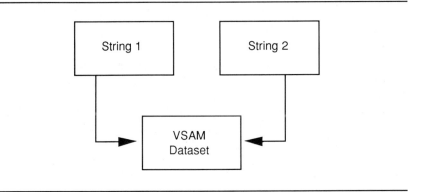

Figure 24.2.   Concurrent accesses to a VSAM dataset.

Strings are allocated via the STRNO parameter in one of three ways:

1. In the Access Method Control Block (ACB) macro for an Assembler program. (*Note:* The ACB is equivalent to the OS Data Control Block (DCB).)

```
ACB     AM=VSAM,
        BUFND=n,
        BUFNI=n,
        DDNAME=ddname,....,
        STRNO=n
```

2. In the AMP parameter of JCL for COBOL programs.

```
//ddname  DD DSN=dataset name, ...
            AMP=('STRNO=n','BUFNI=n','BUFND=n')
```

3. In the FCT entry for CICS applications. We show the DFHFCT macro in the example below, but it could also be an RDO:

```
DFHFCT TYPE=DATASET,DATASET=ddname,....,
    STRNO=n,BUFNI=n,BUFND=n
```
(*Note:* In each example, BUFNI refers to index buffers, and BUFND refers to data buffers.)

Let's put strings aside for now and look at more detail of how both index and data buffers are specified to VSAM.

24.3. HOW BUFFERS ARE SPECIFIED TO VSAM

Buffer space represents the amount of storage needed to process the contents of one control interval of data records or index entries. The VSAM default is to allocate two data buffers for all types of datasets, plus one additional index buffer for a KSDS. VSAM uses one data buffer for processing and reserves the other for potential split activity.

Besides the ACB macro of an Assembler program (which doesn't concern us here), additional buffer space can be specified with the BUFFERSPACE (BUFSP) option in the DEFINE command, in the AMP parameter of JCL for COBOL programs, or in the FCT entry for CICS applications. (We first covered this in Chapter 7, and you may want to review this material in light of what you now know about the index and data components of a KSDS.)

24.3.1. The BUFFERSPACE Option Revisited

Usually you'll want to avoid the IDCAMS DEFINE command BUFFER-SPACE option, which in effect hard-codes buffer space values into the catalog entry for the dataset, because all applications that use the dataset are stuck with this buffer allocation, unless it is overridden with the JCL AMP parameter (for COBOL) or the FCT entry (for CICS). The one exception to this guideline is dynamically allocated VSAM datasets. (We'll explain.)

Consider a KSDS with an alternate index. When only the alternate index is used in an application it is opened via the path, but the base cluster is dynamically allocated, even though no DD statement is required for the base cluster. However, in the example that follows, the BUFNI and BUFND subparameters apply to the alternate index only, and buffering for the base cluster may be inadequate.

```
//LIBMAS1  DD DSN=A2000.LIB.KSDS.AUTHNAME.PATH,
             DISP=SHR,AMP=('BUFNI=2','BUFND=6')
```

In this case you could use the IDCAMS ALTER command to change the BUFFERSPACE value of the base cluster to match that of the alternate index.

```
ALTER A2000.LIB.KSDS.CLUSTER -
  BUFFERSPACE(28672)
```

Given an index component CISZ of 2048 and a data component CISZ of 4096, the calculation would be made as follows:

```
(2 × 2048) + (6 × 4096) = 28672 bytes
```

VSAM will automatically apportion the BUFFERSPACE value (expressed in bytes) between index and data buffers. Later, you can re-ALTER the base cluster back to its original default value, 10240 bytes.

```
2048 + (2 × 4096) = 10240 bytes
```

Next let's spend some time looking at index and data buffering requirements for batch COBOL applications. Your best bet here is to use the JCL AMP subparameters BUFNI and BUFND to specify the buffering you want at run-time, or let it default to BUFNI=1 and BUFND=2, respectively.

24.3.2.　Index Buffers for Random Processing

When accessing records randomly, the ideal is to keep all index set records available in the buffers. That way, there is no I/O against these index set records, which are the most frequently used records in random processing. Under normal circumstances, a batch job requires only one processing string, so the default of STRNO=1 is sufficient and can be safely ignored.

Assuming there's some virtual storage constraint in your operating environment, the following is a guideline that should enable you to allocate enough index buffers to significantly reduce I/O:

Use the LISTCAT field LEVELS (I) to determine the number of levels in your index. Allocate enough buffers to equal the number of levels, plus one more. Thus, for a 2-level index, the BUFNI value would be 3, and so on.

For a 2-level index, the AMP parameter would be

```
AMP=('STRNO=1','BUFNI=3','BUFND=2')
```

If you have a large dataset (more then three index levels), or a large dataset with IMBED or REPLICATE used in a noncache environment, see your systems programmer for a formula to determine the optimum index buffers for batch random access.

If you don't have a virtual storage constraint in your operating environment, you can allocate index buffers with impunity, because starting with MVS/DFP 2.3, extra buffers do not increase the amount of CPU usage due to improved hashing techniques for searching buffers. However, if yours is a cache environment, always see your systems people for buffering guidelines. The cache environment is discussed in Chapter 26.

24.3.3.　Data Buffers for Random Processing

One data buffer per string and one for split activity are required for random access, so the default of two data buffers (BUFND=2) will normally be sufficient for purely random processing.

24.3.4.　Index Buffers for Sequential Processing

Index buffers have no meaning for sequential access, which ignores the index set records and uses only those of the sequence set for processing.

The default value of one index buffer (BUFNI=1) to hold sequence set entries can safely be used for purely sequential access.

24.3.5.   Data Buffers for Sequential Processing

When accessing records sequentially, the ideal is to process one entire track of records at a time, and the number of data buffers allocated will depend on the DASD device type and the data control interval size. Fortunately, all of the information you need is readily available in the LISTCAT output for the data component.

You need to calculate the number of control intervals per track (which becomes the BUFND value). The fields that you use are PHYSRECS/ TRK (which varies with the device type), PHYREC-SIZE, and data CISZ. The formula is as follows:

```
(PHYSRECS/TRK × PHYREC-SIZE) / CISZ   = number of control
                                        intervals per track
```

Given a data CISZ of 2048 on a 3390 DASD device, here is a sample calculation:

```
21 × 2048 / 2048 = 21 (number of control intervals per
                       track)
```

Note: This calculation may appear redundant, but PHYREC-SIZE and CISZ are not always the same value.

For sequential processing you need to allow one extra data buffer for split activity, even if only reading records as input. For writing records as output, an additional buffer for overlap (concurrently moving data to the output buffers as data is written on the track) will enhance performance. Thus, for reading records sequentially, the BUFND value is calculated as

```
number of control intervals per track + 1 = BUFND

completing the previous example: 21 + 1 = 22

AMP=('STRNO=1','BUFNI=1','BUFND=22')
```

And, for writing records sequentially as part of an initial load operation (program specifies OPEN OUTPUT), the BUFND value is calculated as

```
number of control intervals per track + 2 = BUFND

completing the previous example: 21 + 2 = 23

AMP=('STRNO=1','BUFNI=1','BUFND=23')
```

24.3.6.   Buffering for Dynamic Processing

When allocating buffers for dynamic processing (both random and sequential processing in the same program), you'll have to add extra buffers for both index and data buffers according to the guidelines presented previously.

24.3.7.   Buffering for Alternate Index Processing

When processing records through an alternate index, you can safely use the guidelines just presented for specifying index and data buffers. However, there are two situations you need to be aware of:

1. When the application program uses both the base cluster and the alternate index records in the same program, the respective DD statements in the JCL each need their own BUFNI and BUFND values. (They do not have to specify the same values if the base cluster and the alternate index are to be processed differently—for example, if the base cluster is to be read randomly and the alternate index sequentially.)

```
//LIBMAST   DD DSN=A2000.LIB.KSDS.CLUSTER,
//            DISP=SHR,AMP=('BUFNI=3','BUFND=2')
//LIBMAS1   DD DSN=A2000.LIB.KSDS.AUTHNAME.PATH,
//            DISP=SHR,AMP=('BUFNI=1','BUFND=22')
```

2. As discussed previously, when an alternate index is to be accessed only through its path, the base cluster is allocated dynamically, even though no DD statement is required (or permitted) for the base cluster in the JCL. In this case, your only option is to specify buffering for the base cluster with the BUFFERSPACE option of the IDCAMS ALTER command.

24.4.   CICS BUFFERING—GENERAL CONSIDERATIONS

Experts agree that the most common cause of performance degradation in the CICS environment is poorly administered VSAM datasets, especially improper buffer management, which as we have seen causes excessive I/O.

Within CICS there exist two buffering strategies called the Non-Shared Resource (NSR) technique and Local Shared Resource (LSR) buffer pools. In the NSR environment, each VSAM dataset has a pool of buffers for its exclusive use, meaning it does not share these buffers with another dataset. Batch COBOL applications always use NSR buffers, and in the online environment, they are most efficiently utilized for datasets with heavy I/O activity. Because buffers are not shared among datasets, string waits can be a problem in the NSR environment.

In the LSR environment, various VSAM datasets share a pool of buffers. The size of the buffer is more important than whether it is a data or an index buffer. That is, data and index components may use the same buffer (at separate times) if they share a common control interval size. With LSR buffer pools, string waits are normally (but not always) diminished, but deadlocks (unresolvable contentions) can be a problem.

24.4.1.   Global Shared Resources

LSR and NSR buffering can coexist within the same address space, but individual datasets are defined with either LSR or NSR buffering. Global Shared Resources (GSR) is an extension of LSR that shares buffers and other resources across address spaces. GSR is beyond the scope of this book, but if your installation operates in the GSR environment, you need to discuss the buffering considerations that pertain to GSR with your own systems people. Let's go back to LSR buffering.

Starting with Release 1.7 of CICS/OS/VS, LSR became the buffering default, although this is easily overridden. Before looking at the individual characteristics of NSR and LSR buffering, let's define some new terms that mostly apply to buffer management in CICS.

Read-Ahead. The ability to forward-read multiple data-control intervals without incurring extra I/O in a sequential browse operation is called the *read-ahead* feature. If NSR buffering is specified, a read-ahead is performed if there are data buffers remaining after data buffers have been allocated to each string. However, this method is unreliable from an application point of view, because it's impossible to predict when extra data buffers will be available if multiple strings are active.

In the LSR environment, read-ahead is never executed in order to ensure that tasks performing sequential browse operations do not lock out those performing random operations.

Buffer Refresh. The purpose of a buffer refresh, which involves re-reading records from DASD rather than the buffer area, is to preserve data integrity across different systems (CPUs). For example, if a KSDS is assigned share option 4 with the DEFINE command, its index buffers will be refreshed at each I/O request. The goal is to preserve data integrity (updates may have occurred against the requested data elsewhere) at the expense of increasing I/O activity.

Both the NSR and the LSR environments will perform buffer refresh if share option 4 has been specified for a VSAM dataset. Since this results in more I/O activity, you'll want to be especially conservative about specifying share option 4 in the DEFINE command.

Buffer Lookaside. The purpose of a buffer lookaside is to save I/O through the ability of VSAM to first search for a requested control interval in its buffers to see if it is already there before attempting a physical I/O to DASD. VSAM will do a lookaside at the index buffers for random access requests if you have allocated enough index buffers to keep the index set continuously in the buffer area. One of the strongest features of LSR buffering is its extensive lookaside capabilities. With LSR buffering, VSAM will *always* do a lookaside.

Lookaside capabilities for NSR buffering are more limited. For example, if NSR buffering has been specified, VSAM does not do a lookaside at the data buffers.

The following are some other awareness issues for application programmers concerning NSR buffering.

FCT entry for NSR. You code LSRPOOL=NONE in the FCT entry to specify NSR buffering. Starting with CICS/VS Release 1.7, LSR is the default. Also with NSR, the minimum number of buffers that should be allocated is one index buffer per string, plus one more to hold the high-level index record, and one data buffer per string, plus one data buffer that is reserved for split activity.

Sequence set records are allocated by VSAM to the dedicated string buffers (the first three in the following example). They can never be read into any extra index buffers. The best performance (fewest I/Os) can be derived from defining enough index buffers to contain the entire index set.

```
DFHFCT TYPE=DATASET,DATASET=LIBMAST,
    ACCMETH=VSAM,LSRPOOL=NONE,
```

[Specifies NSR buffering.]

```
STRNO=3,BUFNI=4,BUFND=4
```

[Allocates 3 strings and 4 each of index and data buffers. A random access request would require 2 or 3 physical I/Os depending upon whether the entire index set is contained in the buffers.]

With NSR, the strings defined in the FCT represent actual VSAM strings and each acquires control blocks. Lookaside is performed only in extra index buffers.

NSR buffering is especially effective for datasets with a high level of I/O activity because the buffers are not shared with other datasets (though they may be shared with other tasks using the same dataset). For this reason, the allocation of extra data buffers to take advantage of read-ahead capabilities is not recommended, because the specific task that needs the extra buffers may not always get them.

NSR buffering is also more effective for datasets that historically have a lot of control area split activity because dedicated NSR buffers use chained I/O to reduce physical I/O in control area splits. This enables them to move a large amount of data faster than shared LSR buffers.

NSR alternate index considerations. In the FCT entry, the STRNO value for the base cluster is inclusive. That is, it includes STRNO values for the base cluster and all alternate indexes being defined to CICS in the FCT. Also, it is best to use the BASE parameter in each alternate index entry to specify the DD name of the base cluster. This parameter is effective in the NSR environment only and ensures read integrity between the base cluster and the alternate index paths.

```
DFHFCT TYPE=DATASET,DATASET=LIBMAST,
    STRNO=6,BUFNI=8,BUFND=8
```

[Includes STRNO, BUFNI, and BUFND values for the base cluster and the alternate index.]

```
DFHFCT TYPE=DATASET,DATASET=LIBMAS1,BASE=LIBMAST,
```

[Refers to the base cluster ddname.]

```
    STRNO=3,BUFNI=4,BUFND=4
```

[Includes values for the alternate index only.]

LSR buffer pools. In the LSR environment, various VSAM datasets share a pool of buffers and buffers that are allocated by size rather than by the designation of index buffer or data buffer. Beginning with CICS Release 1.7, up to eight pools can be defined, but only in the MVS/XA or MVS/ESA environment. Otherwise, you are restricted to one pool. Here are some other awareness issues for programmers concerning LSR buffer pools:

LSR Lookaside. Within the LSR environment, datasets that are part of the pool are assigned to buffers on a least-recently-used basis (of the buffer, that is.) As each control interval (index or data) is requested by the processor, a lookaside is always performed to see if it is already in the buffer area before doing an I/O to DASD. The bigger the pool, the greater the chance for a successful lookaside. Because buffers can reside above the 16-megabyte line in MVS/XA and MVS/ESA, it's possible to define large LSR buffer pools that exploit this lookaside capability.

LSR Strings. Under LSR, the number of strings defined in the FCT represent a CICS control to limit concurrent access requests. They are not actual VSAM strings as are NSR-defined strings. A goal of LSR fine-tuning is to increase strings to eliminate (or greatly reduce) string waits. CICS shutdown statistics provide information on both LSR string waits and the ratio of lookasides to access requests.

LSR Deadlocks. Due to the way control intervals are queued in an LSR buffer pool, deadlocks can be more of a problem than they are in the NSR environment. One way to minimize deadlocks is when dealing with multiple VSAM datasets, all tasks should update these datasets in the same order. Also, there's good news to report: Starting with CICS/MVS 2.1.1, a task will not wait but will suspend when an exclusive deadlock occurs.

Another way to minimize deadlocks is by observing the following programming guidelines that can be safely implemented whether operating in the NSR or LSR environment. Following these guidelines will also reduce the time a string is held, which can also improve performance significantly.

24.4.2. General Programming Guidelines

- An explicit ENDBR should follow each browse operation before issuing other commands such as READ, UPDATE, DELETE, or WRITE to the same dataset.
- A REWRITE, DELETE, or UNLOCK should follow every READ UPDATE command.
- Always issue the READ command in the *move,* not the *locate,* mode. Locate does not release the string until the end of the task for read-only access. (In case you missed it, there's more on move versus locate in Chapter 21.)

LSR tuning guidelines. The following techniques may be used by the systems people in your shop to fine-tune LSR pools. They only represent a general guideline. Circumstances may preclude the use of some of them in your computing environment.

- In the MVS/XA and MVS/ESA environments, exploit the use of multiple buffer pools by isolating datasets with certain characteristics. For example, put all datasets with heavy browses in one pool.
- Use LSR for datasets with low to medium activity, NSR for high-activity datasets.
- Define pools for all control interval sizes, because if its size is not explicitly defined, a control interval will use the next higher pool, thus wasting precious buffer space.
- Define buffer pools on a 4K boundary. That is, be sure the size is a multiple of 4K.
- Unless operating in a cache environment, use IMBED and REPLICATE to increase the likelihood that index set and sequence set records will be retained in the buffers.
- Establish and enforce standards for defining totally different data and index control interval sizes so they will be self-segregating in LSR pools.
- Above all, monitor LSR buffer pools with CICS shutdown statistics.

NSR buffering recap.

- Each dataset has a dedicated set of buffers.
- Best for datasets with heavy I/O activity.
- Handles control area splits more efficiently than LSR buffering.
- Achieves the best performance when enough index buffers are defined to contain the entire index set.
- Strings defined in the FCT are real VSAM strings and each acquires control blocks.
- Lookaside is limited to that which is done in extra index buffers.
- Read-ahead capability is available but not reliable.

LSR buffering recap.

- All datasets share pools of buffers allocated by size.
- Best for datasets with low to medium activity.
- Strings represent a CICS control to limit concurrent access request but are not actual VSAM strings. Strings should be increased to eliminate string waits.
- Provides virtual storage constraint relief because with MVS/XA and MVS/ESA up to eight pools can be defined and buffers can reside above the 16-megabyte line.

- Deadlocks can be a problem due to the way buffers are queued.
- Read-ahead for sequential browsing is never performed.
- Lookaside is always done before a DASD I/O, even for sequence set and data control intervals.
- Large pools can be defined to exploit lookaside capabilities.

24.4.3.   Buffers in Hiperspace

In the MVS/ESA environment, LSR buffers can also reside in hiperspaces, which are special data spaces that use a hardware mechanism, expanded storage, as an extremely high-speed cache device. Hiperspaces are discussed in Chapter 26, and the next chapter presents an overview of the MVS/DFP, where VSAM lives these days.

25

Data Facility Product Overview

In the MVS/XA and ESA operating environments, VSAM has a new "address." (And yes, the pun is intended.) It now lives within a family of components called Data Facility Product (hereafter known as DFP).

Why is it important for programmers to know this? Well, for one thing DFP manuals now contain reference information for both VSAM and non-VSAM datasets. Also, you create and manage VSAM and non-VSAM datasets differently under DFP. Another thing—the DFP world assumes that if you are not currently using system-managed storage, you soon will be.

System-managed storage means different things to different people, but to IBM it means "an approach to storage management in which the system determines data placement and an automatic data manager handles data backup, movement, space, and security."[1]

IBM's product for system-managed storage is known as Data Facility Storage Management Subsystem (hereafter known as DFSMS). DFSMS in turn consists of an alphabet soup of complementary products that implement automated data placement and management services. They include, in addition to DFP, Data Facility Dataset Services (DFDSS), Data Facility Hierarchical Storage Manager (DFHSM), DFSORT, and RACF, which supports the whole shebang with security services. (If the similarity of names and acronyms is causing you some angst, rest assured you are not alone.) Figure 25.1 shows how DFSMS looks pictorially.

DFP and its system-oriented counterpart, System Product (SP), actually form the foundation for both the MVS/XA and MVS/ESA operating

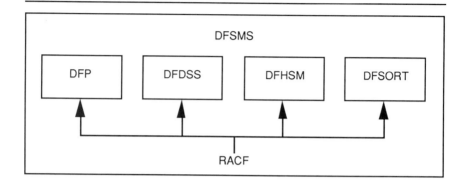

Figure 25.1. A pictorial view of DFSMS.

environments. In the old days (prior to MVS/XA), things were more straightforward. An installation licensed an operating system—say, OS/VS2—and system and data products like JES and VSAM had their own identity. Figure 25.2 shows a partial "olden days" configuration.

The advent of MVS/XA and MVS/ESA changed all of that. Now system components like JES are bundled under the rubric of System Product (SP). Data components like VSAM and system-managed storage routines come under DFP. Figure 25.3 shows a typical MVS/XA or MVS/ESA configuration. (Of course, it's more complicated than this, and there's a lot of crossover among products and functions, but we're just trying to give you an overall view of things.)

It's important to note that the MVS/XA environment includes system-managed storage facilities that are not as fully functional as those in ESA. Here's a brief thumbnail sketch of both operating environments:

- *Extended Architecture (XA)*. MVS/XA implemented 31-bit (as opposed to MVS/370 24-bit) real and virtual storage addressing. Under XA, the size of addressable real and virtual storage has made a

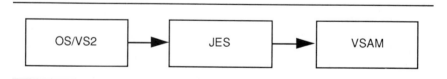

Figure 25.2. Pre-XA, pre-ESA configuration.

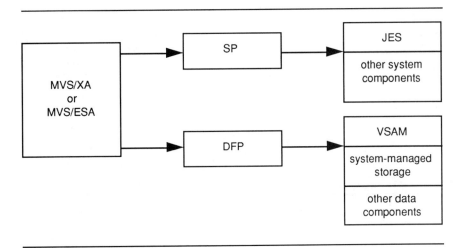

Figure 25.3.   Typical MVS/XA or MVS/ESA configuration.

quantum leap from a maximum of 16 megabytes (million bytes) to 2 gigabytes (billion bytes)—resulting in a real breakthrough in storage capacity plus significant performance gains.

* *Enterprise System Architecture (ESA).* MVS/ESA refined extended architecture to include support for ESA/370, still another architecture, this one hardware oriented. ESA/370 supports data space enhancements and hiperspaces. (If you're curious about these ESA/370 features, see Chapter 26.)

ESA also introduced the Data Facility Storage Management Subsystem (DFSMS), a series of routines designed to further refine the process of system-managed storage. Figure 25.4 illustrates a typical MVS/ESA configuration.

Since our focus here is DFP in the MVS/ESA environment, let's pinpoint some of the storage and data management problems that it addresses. These include the following:

* The vagaries of manual storage management, including the duplication of effort expended to repeatedly code DCB information in JCL.
* Inefficient or wasteful use of DASD due to programmers estimating space allocations and making inappropriate volume assignments for datasets.
* The difficulties involved in enforcing dataset standards.

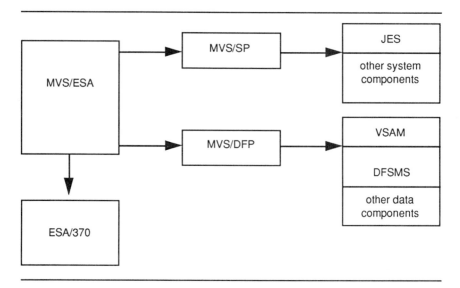

Figure 25.4.   Typical MVS/ESA configuration.

- The general complexities of organizing, cataloging, and accessing both VSAM and non-VSAM datasets, such as frequency of backup, migration standards, and so on.

DFP, through its storage and data management services, provides solutions for the foregoing problems. (DFP also provides program and device management services, and we'll look at these briefly.)

25.1.   SYSTEM-MANAGED STORAGE

The goal of system-managed storage is ambitious but straightforward: to automate the control of DASD. Display Facility Storage Management Subsystem (DFSMS) routines are pressed into service here. Using predefined patterns, DFSMS tells the system where to store the dataset, what it looks like, how and when it will be available, how long it should be retained, what its performance level is, and how often it should be backed up.

DFSMS uses patterns for datasets the same way a garment factory uses different patterns to produce clothing in different sizes. An installation may use different DFSMS patterns for datasets used mostly in batch applications, mostly in online applications, and so on. Thus, DFSMS is highly tailorable (no pun intended here) and can be set up to fit the needs of the installation.

The person who sets up and tailors DFSMS is known in most shops as the storage administrator, and he or she is normally part of the systems group. It is the task of the storage administrator to set up DFSMS so that it reflects the storage needs of the installation, usually no small undertaking. To accomplish that task the storage administrator uses the following tools:

- Interactive Storage Management Facility (ISMF) panels, a series of panels based on ISPF/PDF. ISMF panels are similar to the DB2I panels used in the DB2 environment, but, of course, they offer different options. They also differ in that programmers do not generally have access to ISMF panels.
- Automatic Class Selection (ACS) routines that define, install, and manage DFSMS patterns. In effect, this is the DFSMS software. Storage administrators use ISMF panels to implement ACS routines.

If you want to know more about storage administrator functions and responsibilities, there is a publication available from IBM known as the MVS/ESA *Storage Management Library*.[2]

25.1.1. DFSMS Classes

Actually "DFSMS pattern" is a misnomer. In the DFSMS world these patterns are called *constructs* or *classes*. These concern programmers most directly:

- *DATACLAS*. Assigns dataset attributes including dataset organization, record format and length, allocated space, and retention. VSAM attributes include control interval size, key length and offset, free space, and share options.
- *MGMTCLAS*. Works with another DFSMS product, Data Facility Hierarchical Storage Manager (DFHSM) to automate dataset migration and backup as well as deletion of expired datasets. These services can be implemented at the dataset level, thus allowing the storage administrator to manage DASD in a most effective matter.
- *STORCLAS*. Controls both availability and performance attributes for the dataset. A STORCLAS assignment tells the system that the dataset is DFSMS managed.

The storage administrator assigns names to these classes when defining them, just as we assign names to datasets when defining them. Installation defaults can be set to invoke DFSMS classes implicitly, which may be transparent to the programmer. Less commonly programmers code these classes explicitly within IDCAMS, in JCL statements, or with a TSO ALLOCATE command.

The following example illustrates the explicit use of a DATACLAS named DATA1 in an IDCAMS DEFINE CLUSTER command.

```
DEFINE CLUSTER          -
   (NAME(MYOWN.CLUSTER) -
    DATACLAS(DATA1)     -
    . . .
```

Here is a partial list of values that DATA1 might represent:

Type of dataset (KSDS, ESDS, and so on)

Record length

Share options

Freespace

25.1.2.   DFSMS Storage Groups

DFSMS also provides for storage groups (STOGROUPS), which don't concern programmers directly. Instead, storage administrators use STOGROUPS to place datasets within a group of storage volumes pooled by, say, enterprise, function, performance, or security requirements, or whatever installation criteria dictate. The storage administrator can add to or delete volumes from the storage group quite simply using ISMF panel options. And since this procedure doesn't require an IPL (Initial Program Load—starting up the system from scratch), downtime is effectively reduced.

25.1.3.   DFSMS Advantages

System-managed storage with DFSMS constructs can offer the following advantages:

For the programmer:
- Simplifies the definition of datasets.
- Virtually eliminates the need to be aware of individual device characteristics such as how many tracks are on a DASD storage device.
- Can achieve significant performance improvement for applications

due to increased throughput.

For the support staff:

• Provides de facto compliance with installation standards for creating, storing, and accessing both VSAM and non-VSAM datasets.
• Greatly reduces problems such as dataset recovery and lack of space during production runs.

For the storage administrator:

• Provides automated, efficient management techniques for DASD.
• Provides more efficient utilization of storage resources.
• Maintenance procedures reduce the need for IPLs, thus effectively reducing downtime.
• Allows easier conversion to different DASD devices.
• Storage groupings pool datasets logically by enterprise or function.
• Provides more efficient utilization of 3990-CACHE because caching can be provided at the dataset rather than the volume level.
• Facilitates performance tuning because you can define that criteria in the STORCLAS.

25.2.   DATA MANAGEMENT UNDER DFP

DFP also offers industrial-strength data management services. Stated simply, the goal of data management is to offer easy retrieval of data by providing facilities and services that organize and catalog it. VSAM "lives" in DFP under this data management rubric, as do other data access methods, catalogs, and utilities.

The important components of DFP data management fall into three categories: VSAM-related, non-VSAM-related, and those shared by VSAM and non-VSAM datasets. VSAM-related components include the VSAM access method, the IDCAMS utility program, and various VSAM macros. Non-VSAM-related components include other access methods like QSAM, BSAM, BPAM, BDAM, and ISAM. (BDAM and ISAM, while maintained in the DFP environment for compatibility, are not supported by DFSMS.) Utility programs include those of the IEB and IEH variety, such as IEBCOPY and IEHLIST. OS catalogs are maintained in the DFP environment for compatibility with other access methods but do not support DFSMS-managed datasets. OS catalogs should really be converted to ICF catalogs. Other non-VSAM-related components include VIO (Virtual Input/Output) storage groups and various data management macros.

Important data management components that are shared by both

VSAM and non-VSAM datasets include the Integrated Catalog Facility (ICF) that must be used to catalog DFSMS-managed datasets, whether VSAM or not. All DFSMS-managed datasets must be cataloged. VSAM catalogs (like OS catalogs) are maintained for compatibility with datasets created under earlier versions of VSAM, but they do not support DFSMS-managed datasets. Other players here include Open/Close/End-of-volume and catalog management macros, the Common VTOC Access Facility (CVAF), and Direct Access Device Space Management (DADSM).

As you can readily see, DFP offers an impressive list of services to the installation—sort of a "one-stop shopping center" for its basic data management needs. To round out our big picture of DFP, here's a brief synopsis of its program and device management offerings.

25.2.1. Program Management

The goal of program management is to perform some of the functions needed to prepare programs for execution, store them in load libraries, and read them into virtual storage. MVS/SP performs other program management functions that we won't consider here.

Important program management components include AMBLIST, which produces those formatted program listings we've all grown so attached to; checkpoint/restart; IEBCOPY, which also services data management; fetch, to read modules into virtual storage; a high-performance loader; and a linkage editor, which is the designated functional replacement for the OS/VS2 linkage editor.

25.2.2. Device Management

The goal of device management is also simple—to define and use I/O devices. Important device management components include various utilities that support I/O devices, system generation and tape label support, and user exits.

Pictorially then, DFP looks something like Figure 25.5.

25.2.3. Other DFSMS Products

Other important programs that work with DFP include the following:

- *Data Facility Dataset Services (DFDSS).* DFDSS moves and copies data between DASD devices, performs backup and recovery procedures, and provides other DASD services. You might want to think of DFDSS as a "mover and shaker" in the DFP world.

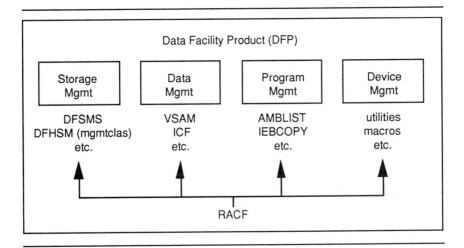

Figure 25.5.   Pictorial view of DFP.

- *Data Facility Hierarchical Storage Manager (DFHSM)*. DFHSM was mentioned previously under storage management, but it is important to reiterate that DFHSM under MVS/ESA provides the capability to manage datasets at the individual (rather than the volume) level, resulting in the most efficient DASD management.
- *Data Facility Sort (DFSORT)*. Provides sorting, merging, and copying services. Under MVS/ESA, DFSORT can be accessed interactively from an ISMF panel.
- *Resource Access Control Facility (RACF)*. While not officially part of the so-called DFSMS family, RACF provides security services for it and for its datasets.

To sum up, DFP, as part of the larger DFSMS picture, provides the following:

- System-managed storage using DFSMS constructs and classes.
- One-stop shopping for data management services supporting both VSAM and non-VSAM datasets.
- Ability to work with MVS/SP to provide program management support.
- Capability of managing I/O devices.
- Comprehensive program and dataset security through RACF.

As you might imagine, DFP has a few shortcomings, most of which relate to system-managed storage, including the following:

- Implementation of system-managed storage requires a top-down commitment of MIS personnel.
- Installation criteria for system-managed storage may be difficult and time-consuming to collect and organize, and it requires a team effort.
- Testing ACS routines to reflect complex "real world" situations can be difficult.
- Maintaining older access methods and catalogs for compatibility purposes can consume storage resources.
- Other than limited availability on VM, DFP does not support different platforms (AS/400, OS/2) at this writing.
- System-managed storage increases the overhead of support staff. (Automated systems that increase the support staff are always suspect.)
- System-managed storage adds another layer of complexity that separates the programmer from the actual process of programming. By the time weary programmers navigate their way through DFSMS, DFP, JES, JCL, MVS/ESA, TSO, CICS, and ISPF/DFP, they may have forgotten what they wanted to do.

Does DFP live up to its promise of providing seamless storage, data, program, and device management in the MVS/XA and ESA environments? Perhaps, but the jury is still out.

REFERENCES

1. "MVS/DFP Using Data Sets," Order No. SC26-4749, San Jose, CA: IBM Corporation, 1991.
2. "MVS/ESA Storage Management Library," Order No. SBOF-3126, San Jose, CA: IBM Corporation, 1991.

26

ESA 370/390 Overview

The past two decades have seen several major new hardware changes to IBM's large family of mainframe computers. To support the new hardware, IBM supplies a new version of the operating system. It often includes new programming features that, since they may depend on the new hardware features, only run in the new version of the operating system that supports the hardware. The cost of developing and maintaining software for old versions of the operating system would be prohibitive.

Besides the inevitable faster I/O and central processing unit, all of the hardware changes of the past two decades have had the same general thrust—to overcome the limitation on the amount of storage that programs and data can use. The computer's memory, within which programs and data must reside to be executed, has been a main bottleneck. The computer's memory was originally called *core storage*, then it evolved to *real storage*, and today it is called *central storage*.

In the early 1970s, central storage was relatively expensive, and virtual storage was introduced to overcome the problem. With virtual storage, a program and its data resided on relatively inexpensive disk storage. The system treated the program and data as contiguous 4K blocks of storage, and special, very fast paging hardware was provided to read and write the 4K blocks on an as-needed basis. This is termed *paging*. The term *virtual storage* means that the programmer can act as if the entire program were in the computer.

When a program executes and accesses data, only the 4K blocks

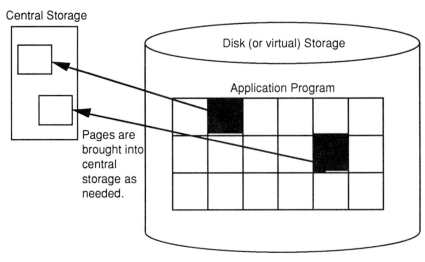

Program is stored on disk and is divided into 4K blocks or pages. Note that the program can be larger than Central Storage.

Figure 26.1. Paging in virtual storage.

containing that portion of the program and the data need actually be in central storage. The remainder of the program and data can continue residing on disk storage. The paging hardware brings in pages and writes them out as needed, so that very large programs can be executed in a limited and even smaller amount of central storage. Virtual storage, by minimizing the amount of central storage required by any one program, also allows many more programs to co-reside in storage for concurrent execution. Figure 26.1 illustrates this.

Today, central storage is so inexpensive that it is not the limitation it once was. However, virtual storage is still important in making effective use of it. Virtual storage is also important to VSAM for two reasons. First, it gave its name to VSAM. There was nothing virtual about VSAM. VSAM was introduced with the version of the operating system that supported virtual storage hardware (MVS for Multiple Virtual System), and, consequently, it was named Virtual Storage Access Method. The second reason virtual storage is important to VSAM is that the newest type of VSAM data organization, Linear Datasets described in Chapter

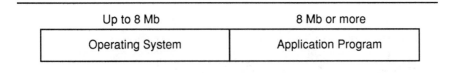

Up to 8 Mb	8 Mb or more
Operating System	Application Program

Figure 26.2.   Address space in MVS.

27, is implemented using virtual storage and the paging hardware. (VSAM finally became virtual.)

While virtual storage solved the problem of limited central storage, it did nothing about increasing the address space of the computer. The System/370 computer was a 32-bit computer with 24 bits used to address memory. This meant that the computer could only address 2^{24} bytes or 16 megabytes of memory. And the operating system could take up as much as 8 megabytes of this address space, as shown in Figure 26.2. Adding more central storage or paging hardware doesn't change this limit.

In the early 1980s, IBM made a hardware change to allow the computer to use 31 bits for the address portion of an instruction. This increased the address space to 2^{31} bytes or 2,048 megabytes, or 2 gigabytes of memory, as shown in Figure 26.3. This increase was coupled with the

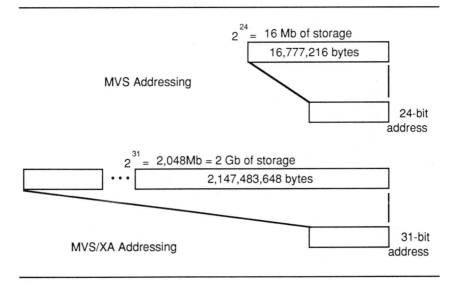

Figure 26.3.   MVS and MVS/XA addressing.

MVS/XA (MVS Extended Architecture) version of the operating system. In addition, much of the system area and common area were moved to the system's own address space.

Except for Assembler language programming, MVS/XA didn't require many programming changes. The main change was in Assembly language and in the linkage editor. Because the number of bits used to address storage above 16 megabytes requires 31 rather than 24 bits, the application programmer must tell the operating system these two things:

- Whether the program addresses storage above the 16-megabyte line. This is done with the linkage editor AMODE (Addressing Mode) parameter. AMODE 24 specifies 24-bit addressing and limits the program to addressing data only below the 16-megabyte line. AMODE 31 specifies 31-bit addressing and allows the program to address data above or below the 16-megabyte line. AMODE ANY specifies both 24-and 31-bit addressing. The 24-bit addressing is used to address storage below the 16-megabyte line and 31-bit addressing is used to address storage above the line.
- Where the program will reside. This is done with the linkage editor RMODE (Residence Mode) parameter. RMODE 24 requires the program to reside below the 16-megabyte line. RMODE ANY allows the program to reside above or below the 16-megabyte line. You must code AMODE 31 or AMODE ANY if you code RMODE ANY.

Unfortunately, the increased address space of MVS/XA didn't quench demand for vast storage by online and database systems. The main problem was with CICS, because all CICS programs must run in the same address space in a CICS system. While 16 megabytes is a considerable amount of storage for any one application, it is a different matter when scores of applications with their buffers and data must share the same address space. To solve this problem, IBM introduced new hardware features with the MVS/ESA (MVS/Enterprise Systems Architecture) version of the operating system to allow multiple address spaces.

MVS/ESA, like MVS/XA, allows each program to have one application space with an address space of 2,048 megabytes. The *application space* can contain programs, data, and system and common areas. The application space is what we used to think of as a job's "region" or address space in the past. In addition—and new in MVS/ESA—a program in an application space can create and use as many as 7,999 more data spaces. *Data spaces* are the same size as application spaces, but they differ in that they can contain only data, as illustrated in Figure

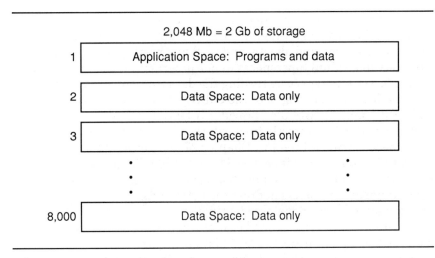

Figure 26.4.   MVS/ESA storage available.

26.4. Programs can't be executed in them, although they can be stored in them as data. Both the application space and data space reside on virtual (disk) storage and can only exist until the job or task controlling them terminates.

For applications such as large databases, the application space is used for the program and data, and one or more data spaces may be used for buffers, tables, or even entire datasets. In a CICS system, all the CICS programs must still co-reside in one application space, but each program can store its data in one or more of its own data spaces, where it is protected from other programs. Because data spaces reside in virtual storage, the paging hardware can be used to read and write them, which is very fast.

As a further refinement, IBM also introduced *hiperspaces* with MVS/ESA. Hiperspaces are somewhat similar to data spaces. They reside on virtual storage (either expanded or external storage). They are created by a job during execution and can exist only until the job or task controlling them terminates. Hiperspaces can be the same size as data spaces, and multiple hiperspaces can be created. (A program can have a total of 7,999 data spaces and hiperspaces.) Unlike data spaces, hiperspaces are not byte addressable. They are divided into 4K blocks, and only the 4K blocks can be accessed. Hiperspaces are also accessed with the paging hardware, but since the hiperspace is organized into the 4K page size the hardware wants, they are very fast.

To create and use either data spaces or hiperspaces, you must write an assembler language program that executes the DSPSERV macro. You can create, expand, delete, and read and write (actually page in or out) data spaces and hiperspaces under program control. You can fill a data space or hiperspace by reading the data from some other medium, such as disk, and storing it in the data space or hiperspace using the DSPSERV macro. IBM also provides a feature called *data-in-virtual* that copies the data directly from external storage to the data space or hiperspace, saving all the I/O. Chapter 27 describes this.

Data in a data space is accessed by assembler language instructions the same as data in an application space—by its byte address. The general-purpose registers address the bytes within the data space, and another set of access registers identify the particular data space. However, data in a hiperspace can't be accessed this way. Data is accessed in a hiperspace by executing the DIV (data in virtual) macro, described in Chapter 27, or the HSPSERV macro. The HSPSERV macro identifies the hiperspace, the 4K blocks within it to read or write, and the application space address into which to read or write the page. The data can then be operated on in the application space. The major functional difference between data spaces and hiperspaces is that data spaces are easier to program and hiperspaces are faster.

Data spaces and hiperspaces are used to contain buffers, large tables, and copies of entire datasets that can be operated on directly without having to read or write records. The operating system also makes use of data spaces and hiperspaces for its internal use, such as ICF catalogs. Data spaces and hiperspaces provide low-level, fast access to data, and they can be used to create specialized data access. Most applications are coded in assembler language, but the data-in-virtual feature provides routines that can be called from high-level languages. The following chapter on Linear Datasets has an example of such use.

MVS/ESA also introduced another important new facility—DFSMS, an optional feature in MVS/ESA, which was described in Chapters 9 and 25.

The hardware changes that speed up the processing, while important, generally have little impact on the programming. Among the hardware features on the newer and larger IBM mainframe computers are the following:

- *Cache instructions.* This feature looks ahead to prefetch instructions and begin interpreting them to speed up CPU execution. Since most instructions execute in sequence or consist of simple branches, it is relatively easy for the computer to look ahead. The application program is totally unaware of this, and the only effect is faster execution.

- *Cache storage controllers.* This feature tries to anticipate and optimize disk I/O by queuing and examining the many requests to read or write disk by all the programs on the system. This has no effect on the application program, except that NOIMBED and NOREPLICATE are more efficient for VSAM datasets on computers having this hardware feature.

- *Expanded storage.* This feature does for paging what cache storage does for computer instructions and I/O. Usually an application program need not be aware of it. However, the linear datasets described in Chapter 27 can use it, and system programs make extensive use of it. Hiperspaces can also be created to utilize it. The expanded storage can be used to keep a single copy of VSAM catalogs and other objects that are being shared by several users. The expanded storage is an address space. (The term real storage now includes both central storage and expanded storage.)

27

Linear Datasets

Linear Datasets (LDS), are the newest and least used of the VSAM data organizations, a very fast, primitive form of data organization. Generally they are used to implement some other type of data access system. For example, DB2, IBM's relational database system, is implemented with them.

A linear dataset consists of a long string of bytes, nothing more. There are no records. The bytes are divided into 4K (4,096 byte) blocks or pages, which enables the paging hardware to be used to access them from disk. Linear dataset access is true VSAM in the literal sense of the words: *virtual storage access method*. They operate very similar to the way virtual storage is used for programs. The linear dataset consists of one long string of data, and the operating system pages 4K blocks in and out of central storage as the data is referenced by the application. Figure 27.1 illustrates this.

Since linear datasets consist logically of a long string of data divided into 4K blocks, there is no record structure. There is also no control interval definition field, no record definition field, no primary index, no alternate index, and the control interval consists of only data.

Linear datasets are generally used for fast random access to data that has no hierarchical structure—that is, for data that is a large flat file, such as a table or array. A relational database is just this.

Linear datasets are defined by IDCAMS commands. The CISZ and any parameters related to it are not coded. The control interval size is automatically 4,096. RECORDSIZE, SPANNED, KEYS, FREESPACE,

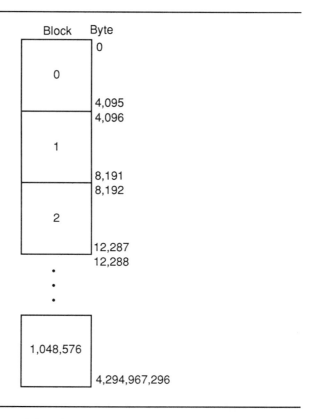

Figure 27.1.   A linear dataset.

and any other parameters related to keys or indexes are also not coded.
This is the command to create a linear dataset.

```
DEFINE CLUSTER                                          -
   (NAME(dataset name)                                  -
   VOLUMES(volume,volume,....,volume)                   -
   LINEAR                                               -
   REC/TRK/CYL(primary secondary)                       -
```

[If you code REC, enter the number of control intervals to allocate.]

```
   SHAREOPTIONS(crossregion crosssystem]               -
   CATALOG(catalog name/password)                       -
```

[If needed. Not for DFSMS-managed datasets.]

```
BUFFERSPACE(bytes)
```

[If needed. When you code this parameter, the bytes must be greater than 8,192, and should be a multiple of 4,096.]

```
)
```

This is the IDCAMS command to print a linear dataset.

```
PRINT                                      -
   INDATASET(dataset name/password)        -
```

[Code the /password only if one is assigned.]

```
CHAR                              -[or DUMP or HEX]
FROMADDRESS(relative byte number)   -
TOADDRESS(relative byte number)
```

[Specify the starting and ending relative byte number of the data to print.]

This is the IDCAMS command to delete a linear dataset.

```
DELETE                            -
   (dataset name/password)  -
   CLUSTER                        -
   ERASE                     - [or NOERASE]
   NOPURGE                   - [or PURGE]
   SCRATCH                     [or NOSCRATCH]
```

The IDCAMS commands describe the linear dataset for disk, called permanent storage. Such a linear dataset is also called a permanent data object, or a data-in-virtual object, or just an object. The linear dataset is called an object in Data Window Services terminology because one can identify either a linear dataset or a hiperspace, and object is a general term that includes both. An object can be as large as 4 gigabytes (4,294,967,296 bytes).

Linear datasets cannot be accessed with VSAM macros. Instead, you must use the Data Window Services DIV (data-in-virtual) macro in Assembler language or use the Data Window Services callable routines for such high-level languages as COBOL, PL/I, FORTRAN, and PASCAL.

The linear dataset can be accessed directly in the permanent data object (on disk), or it can define intermediate storage called a *scroll area* that resides in expanded storage. The scroll area is a hiperspace as described in Chapter 26. It acts as a window into the data and can contain all or part of the data in the permanent data object. You can have multiple scroll areas to look at different parts of the data, but the same block cannot be in more than one scroll area. That is, multiple scroll areas can't overlap. (This temporary data object can be 16 terabytes, 17,592,186,044,416 bytes, because you can have a total of 7999 data spaces or hiperspaces, each containing 2 gigabytes.) When there is a scroll area, the application program treats the scroll area as if it contained the actual data.

The system automatically maps blocks in permanent storage to the scroll area. When data is needed in the application program, the program issues a macro or call to tell which blocks it will need. Blocks are made available in the scroll area but are not brought into application storage until the program actually accesses the data in them. The program also has a choice of canceling any changes or making them permanent by requesting that the system write changed blocks back to the permanent data object.

If the program doesn't request a scroll area, the operation is the same, though slower, since the blocks must be retrieved from the permanent storage object.

The application program, through the macros or calls, identifies the blocks to access by an offset and span. The *offset* identifies the block (0 through n), and the *span* tells how many blocks to transmit (1 to *n*). A span of 0 means to transmit all blocks, starting at the offset to the end of the linear dataset.

To show how a linear dataset is accessed, the DIV macro provides the following services:

IDENTIFY. Identifies the linear dataset by giving the dataset name or a ddname. (It can also identify a hiperspace since hiperspaces are operated on exactly like linear datasets. You can also place the linear dataset in a hiperspace.)

ACCESS. Acts like an open. This specifies read or update access.

MAP. Creates the window or scroll area. (Window is the more general term and it represents a view into the data. With a scroll area, the window is into a hiperspace, and without a scroll area, the view is into the permanent data object.) You specify the following:

• Offset and span of the blocks to be in the window. (You can create multiple windows, but a block can only appear in a single window.)

- Data space or hiperspace—if you want the linear dataset to be in either one of these. The program would first need to create the data space or hiperspace as described in Chapter 26.
- Storage address in the application space where the blocks are to be processed.

Figure 27.2 illustrates two windows used to access a linear dataset. These services make the linear dataset available to an application program. After executing the DIV macro or making the calls to perform the

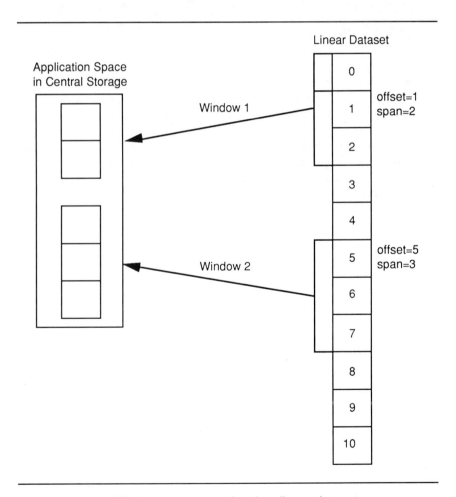

Figure 27.2. Windows to access data in a linear dataset.

services, an application program operates on the blocks using the storage address supplied in the map as if the window were in the program's application space. The system automatically pages blocks in as they are referenced—and only if they are referenced by the program. After processing, the application program can request any of the following DIV macro services to record or ignore changes to the data and to terminate operations on it:

SAVE. Saves a block by writing it from the application space back onto the linear dataset in permanent data object.

RESET. Ignores any changes to the blocks and reloads fresh blocks into the application space from permanent data object.

UNMAP. Gets out of the window.

UNACCESS. Releases access to the linear dataset (the object) on the assumption that the program will later request another ACCESS to use it again.

UNIDENTIFY. Ends the use of the linear dataset (the object) with the assumption that it won't be used again by this program.

The Window Services routines, callable from Assembler language and high-level languages, perform the same services but are easier to use. For example, they automatically create a hiperspace if you request a scroll area.

IDCAMS with DFSMS: Quick Reference Guide

The following is a synopsis of the IDCAMS commands and parameters that require special consideration when your installation uses DFSMS to manage datasets. This guide applies only to VSAM datasets. For other DFSMS-managed objects, consult the AMS reference manual for your operating environment.

ALLOCATE

DATACLASS   Can be specified explicitly or implicitly through ACS routines.

MANAGEMENTCLASS   Is usually specified implicitly through ACS routines.

STORAGECLASS   Is usually specified implicitly through ACS routines.

For more information see Chapter 9.

ALTER

ADDVOLUMES   If explicitly coded, indicate non-specific volume by coding VOLUMES (*).

CATALOG   Avoid altering catalog attributes unless you have proper RACF authority. Avoid JOBCAT and STEPCAT statements.

CONTROLPW   Ignored for DFSMS-managed datasets.

MANAGEMENTCLASS   You must have proper RACF authority to alter the management class.

MASTERPW   Ignored for DFSMS-managed datasets.

NEWNAME   Must be cataloged in the same catalog as the old-name.

REMOVEVOLUMES   Use the wild card character (*) rather than naming specific volume serial numbers.

SHAREOPTIONS   DFSMS-managed datasets cannot share volumes and catalogs with non-DFSMS managed datasets.

STORAGECLASS   You must have proper RACF authority to alter the storage class.

TO/FOR   Do not try to alter values. Specified through MANAGEMENT-CLASS.

For more information see Chapter 13.

BLDINDEX

INFILE/INDATASET   Do not specify the CATALOG sub-parameter for DFSMS-managed datasets. Also, passwords are ignored.

WORKFILES   Specify DFSMS-managed work files.

For more information see Chapter 11.

DEFINE AIX

(Required parameters.)

RELATE   Causes alternate index cluster to assume same MANAGEMENT-CLASS and STORAGECLASS as base cluster.

SPACE   Can be specified with DATACLASS. If explicitly coded, overrides DATACLASS value.

VOLUMES   Can be specified with DATACLASS. If explicitly coded, indicate non-specific volumes by coding VOLUMES (*).

(Optional parameters.)

CATALOG   Do not specify for DFSMS-managed datasets. Also, avoid JOBCAT and STEPCAT statements.

CONTROLPW   Ignored for DFSMS-managed datasets.

DATACLASS   Can specify file attributes for DFSMS- or non-DFSMS-managed datasets.

ERASE   Specify through RACF profile for dataset.

IMBED/REPLICATE   Okay for DFSMS, but avoid in cache environment.

MASTERPW   Ignored for DFSMS-managed datasets.

ORDERED   Ignored for DFSMS-managed datasets.

READPW   Ignored for DFSMS-managed datasets.

SHAREOPTIONS   DFSMS-managed datasets cannot share volumes and catalogs with non-DFSMS-managed datasets.

TO/FOR Avoid coding. Specified implicitly through MANAGEMENT-CLASS.

UPDATEPW Ignored for DFSMS-managed datasets.

For more information see Chapter 11.

DEFINE CLUSTER

(Required parameters.)

SPACE Can be specified with DATACLASS. If explicitly coded, overrides DATACLASS value.

VOLUMES If explicitly coded, indicate non-specific volumes by coding VOLUMES (*).

(Optional parameters.)

CATALOG Do not specify for DFSMS-managed datasets. Also, avoid JOBCAT and STEPCAT statements.

CONTROLPW Ignored for DFSMS-managed datasets.

DATACLASS Can specify file attributes for DFSMS- or non-DFSMS-managed datasets.

ERASE Specify through RACF profile for dataset.

IMBED/REPLICATE Okay for DFSMS, but avoid in cache environment.

KEYS Can be specified with DATACLASS.

MANAGEMENTCLASS Is usually specified implicitly through ACS routines.

MASTERPW Ignored for DFSMS-managed datasets.

ORDERED Ignored for DFSMS-managed datasets.

READPW Ignored for DFSMS-managed datasets.

RECORDSIZE Can be specified with DATACLASS.

SHAREOPTIONS DFSMS-managed datasets cannot share volumes and catalogs with non-DFSMS-managed datasets.

STORAGECLASS Is usually specified implicitly through ACS routines.

TO/FOR Avoid coding. Specified implicitly through MANAGEMENT-CLASS.

UPDATEPW Ignored for DFSMS-managed datasets.

WRITECHECK Avoid coding—too resource-intensive.

For more information see Chapters 6, 7, 8, 9.

DELETE

ERASE Specify through RACF profile for dataset.

For more information see Chapter 13.

EXPORT

OUTDATASET/OUTFILE   Output file can be non-DFSMS-managed, but its entry will be contained in the catalog determined by the catalog search order.

INFILE   Avoid using JOBCAT and STEPCAT statements under DFSMS.

For more information see Chapter 12. (For more on the catalog search order see Chapter 22.)

IMPORT

CATALOG   Do not specify for DFSMS-managed datasets. Also, avoid JOBCAT and STEPCAT statements.

ERASE   Specify through RACF profile for dataset.

MANAGEMENTCLASS   Is usually specified implicitly through ACS routines.

STORAGECLASS   Is usually specified implicitly through ACS routines.

VOLUMES   If coded, indicate non-specific volumes by coding VOLUMES (*).

For more information see Chapter 12.

LISTCAT

LBACKUP   Shows date of last backup or a value of "X."

For more information see Chapter 10.

REPRO

INDATASET/INFILE   Passwords are ignored for DFSMS-managed datasets.

OUTDATASET/OUTFILE   Passwords are ignored for DFSMS-managed datasets.

For more information see Chapter 12.

VERIFY

Passwords are ignored for DFSMS-managed datasets.
For more information see Chapter 12.

VS COBOL II
VSAM Load Program

```
*

       IDENTIFICATION DIVISION.
       PROGRAM-ID.    VDEM01.
       ****************************************************************
       * This program loads a previously unloaded 80-byte KSDS with *
       * records using an 80-byte transaction file as input.  The   *
       * transaction file must be previously sorted in ascending    *
       * sequence by TRAN-KEY, which becomes the primary key,       *
       * LIB-KEY, in the output file.  Because the file is opened    *
       * for OUTPUT, SEQUENTIAL access is specified.                *
       *                                                            *
       * Maintenance history: If you maintain this file, please     *
       *                      add name, date, and remarks here.     *
       ****************************************************************
       ENVIRONMENT DIVISION.
       INPUT-OUTPUT SECTION.
       FILE-CONTROL.
           SELECT TRAN-FILE ASSIGN TO      TRANFILE.
           SELECT LIB-MAST  ASSIGN TO      LIBMAST
                            ORGANIZATION IS INDEXED
                            ACCESS MODE  IS SEQUENTIAL
                            RECORD KEY   IS LIB-KEY
                            FILE STATUS  IS STAT1,
                                            STAT2.
```

```
        DATA DIVISION.
        FILE SECTION.
        FD  TRAN-FILE
            LABEL RECORDS ARE STANDARD
            BLOCK CONTAINS 0 RECORDS
            RECORD CONTAINS 80 CHARACTERS.
        01  TRAN-REC.
            05  TRAN-KEY          PIC X(08).
      *       Input sorted in ascending sequence by this field.
            05  FILLER            PIC X(72).
        FD  LIB-MAST
            LABEL RECORDS ARE STANDARD
            RECORD CONTAINS 80 CHARACTERS.
        01  LIB-REC.
            05  LIB-KEY           PIC X(08).
      *         The primary key.
            05  LIB-AUTH-LNAME     PIC X(15).
            05  LIB-AUTH-FNAME     PIC X(12).
            05  LIB-AUTH-INIT      PIC X(01).
            05  LIB-TITLE          PIC X(28).
            05  LIB-ISBN-NO        PIC X(13).
            05  LIB-COPIES         PIC 9(03).
        WORKING-STORAGE SECTION.
        01  FILLER                PIC X(27)  VALUE
                                  "WORKING STORAGE STARTS HERE".
      ********************************************************************
      * The output record is written from WS-LIB-REC.                   *
      * WS-LIB-REC is also used for data validation in                  *
      * 300-VALIDATE.                                                   *
      ********************************************************************
        01  WS-LIB-REC.
            05  WS-LIB-KEY         PIC X(08).
            05  WS-LIB-AUTH-LNAME  PIC X(15).
            05  WS-LIB-AUTH-FNAME  PIC X(12).
            05  WS-LIB-AUTH-INIT   PIC X(01).
            05  WS-LIB-TITLE       PIC X(28).
            05  WS-LIB-ISBN-NO     PIC X(13).
            05  WS-LIB-COPIES      PIC 9(03).
        01  LIB-STATUS-AREA.
            05  STAT1              PIC X(02)    VALUE SPACES.
      *         The COBOL status key.
                88  OK                          VALUE "00".
```

```
                88  OUT-OF-SEQUENCE              VALUE "21".
                88  DUP                          VALUE "22".
            05  STAT2.
    *           The VSAM return code (COBOL II only).
                10  V-RETURN      PIC 9(02).
                10  V-FUNC        PIC 9.
                10  V-FEEDBACK    PIC 9(03).
        01  FLAGS-AND-SWITCHES-AREA.
            05  OPEN-SW           PIC X(03)    VALUE "   ".
                88  OPEN-ERR                   VALUE "OPN".
            05  TRAN-SW           PIC X(03)    VALUE "   ".
                88  TRAN-EOF                   VALUE "END".
            05  ERROR-SW          PIC X(03)    VALUE "   ".
                88  IO-ERR                     VALUE "I/O".
            05  INPUT-FLAG        PIC X(03)    VALUE "   ".
                88  INPUT-ERR                  VALUE "INP".
        01  COUNTER-AREA.
            05  TOTAL-GOOD-RECS   PIC 9(04)    VALUE ZEROES.
            05  TOTAL-BYPASSED    PIC 9(02)    VALUE ZEROES.
            05  TOTAL-BAD-RECS    PIC 9(02)    VALUE ZEROES.
                88  TOO-MANY-ERRORS            VALUE 3.
        PROCEDURE DIVISION.
        100-PROCESS.
    DISPLAY "STARTING                          VDEMO1 PROGRAM"
            OPEN INPUT TRAN-FILE, OUTPUT LIB-MAST
            IF NOT OK
    ****************************************************************
    * Set the OPEN-ERR flag if OPEN fails.                        *
    * An explicit VERIFY should then be issued                   *
    * before rerunning the program.                              *
    ****************************************************************
                DISPLAY "OPEN ERROR ON LIB-MAST"
                DISPLAY "COBOL STATUS KEY IS," STAT1
                DISPLAY "VSAM RETURN CODE IS," STAT2
                DISPLAY "ISSUE EXPLICIT VERIFY AND THEN"
                DISPLAY "RERUN PROGRAM"
            ELSE
                PERFORM 200-READ WITH TEST AFTER
                    UNTIL TRAN-EOF OR IO-ERR
            END-IF
            CLOSE TRAN-FILE
            IF NOT OPEN-ERR
```

```
            CLOSE LIB-MAST
            IF NOT OK
               SET IO-ERR TO TRUE
               DISPLAY "CLOSE ERROR ON LIB-MAST"
               DISPLAY "COBOL STATUS KEY IS" STAT1
               DISPLAY "VSAM RETURN CODE IS" STAT2
            END-IF
        END-IF
        IF NOT IO-ERR
           DISPLAY "PROGRAM VDEMO1 ENDED OK"
           DISPLAY "NUMBER OF RECORDS ADDED ",
                     TOTAL-GOOD-RECS
           DISPLAY "NUMBER OF INPUT RECORDS BYPASSED ",
                     TOTAL-BYPASSED
           DISPLAY "NUMBER OF OUT-OF-SEQUENCE OR"
           DISPLAY "DUPLICATE RECORDS BYPASSED  ",
                     TOTAL-BAD-RECS
        ELSE
           DISPLAY "TERMINATING BECAUSE OF ERROR"
        END-IF
        STOP RUN
           .
**** EXIT PARAGRAPH
 200-READ.
* Initialize WS-LIB-REC each time through the loop.
     INITIALIZE WS-LIB-REC
     READ TRAN-FILE INTO WS-LIB-REC
         AT END
             SET TRAN-EOF TO TRUE
         NOT AT END
             PERFORM 300-VALIDATE-INPUT
             IF NOT INPUT-ERR
                WRITE LIB-REC FROM WS-LIB-REC
* Evaluate the condition of STAT1.
                EVALUATE TRUE
                  WHEN OK
                     ADD 1 TO TOTAL-GOOD-RECS
                  WHEN (OUT-OF-SEQUENCE OR DUP)
                     ADD 1 TO TOTAL-BAD-RECS
                     IF TOO-MANY-ERRORS
                        DISPLAY "INPUT MESSED UP"
                        SET IO-ERR TO TRUE
```

```
                       DISPLAY "ENDING PROGRAM VDEMO1 NOW"
                  END-IF
               WHEN OTHER
                  DISPLAY "OTHER VSAM ERROR"
                  DISPLAY "COBOL STATUS KEY IS" STAT1
                  DISPLAY "VSAM RETURN CODE IS" STAT2
                  SET IO-ERR TO TRUE
                  DISPLAY "ENDING PROGRAM VDEMO1 NOW"
            END-EVALUATE
         END-IF
    END-READ
         .
**** EXIT PARAGRAPH
 300-VALIDATE-INPUT.
*********************************************************************
* SUBroutine to validate input record.                            *
*********************************************************************
    MOVE SPACES TO INPUT-FLAG
    IF WS-LIB-KEY = SPACES
       ADD 1 TO TOTAL-BYPASSED
       SET INPUT-ERR TO TRUE
       DISPLAY "ERROR—BAD RECORD KEY"
    END-IF
    IF (WS-LIB-AUTH-LNAME = SPACES OR
        WS-LIB-AUTH-LNAME(1:1) NOT ALPHABETIC)
       ADD 1 TO TOTAL-BYPASSED
       SET INPUT-ERR TO TRUE
       DISPLAY "ERROR—BAD AUTHOR NAME"
    END-IF
    IF (WS-LIB-AUTH-FNAME = SPACES OR
        WS-LIB-AUTH-FNAME(1:1) NOT ALPHABETIC)
       DISPLAY "WARNING—BAD FIRST NAME"
    END-IF
    IF WS-LIB-TITLE = SPACES
       ADD 1 TO TOTAL-BYPASSED
       SET INPUT-ERR TO TRUE
       DISPLAY "ERROR—NO TITLE"
    END-IF
    IF WS-LIB-ISBN-NO = SPACES
       ADD 1 TO TOTAL-BYPASSED
       SET INPUT-ERR TO TRUE
       DISPLAY "ERROR—BAD ISBN NUMBER"
```

```
        END-IF
        IF (WS-LIB-COPIES = ZERO OR
            WS-LIB-COPIES NOT NUMERIC)
            ADD 1 TO TOTAL-BYPASSED
            SET INPUT-ERR TO TRUE
            DISPLAY "ERROR—INVALID COPIES"
        END-IF
        IF INPUT-ERR
            DISPLAY "TRANSACTION IN ERROR IS:"
            DISPLAY WS-LIB-REC
        END-IF
        .
 **** END PROGRAM
        .
```

VS COBOL II VSAM Transaction Program

```
*

    IDENTIFICATION DIVISION.
    PROGRAM-ID.    VDEMO2.
    ****************************************************************
    *   This example supports Titles-On-Tape Audio Library (TOTAL)    *
    *   for a mail-order audio book enterprise.                       *
    *                                                                 *
    *   The program reads input transactions from an 81 character     *
    *   input record and based on a TRAN-CODE in position 81, adds (A),*
    *   deletes (D), replaces (R), or updates (U) the fields in the   *
    *   80-character master file.  The transaction can also list (L)  *
    *   the records in the master file.                               *
    *                                                                 *
    *   The files are as follows:                                     *
    *     TRAN-FILE:  Transaction file.  81-byte records,             *
    *                 sequential non-VSAM file.                       *
    *     LIB-MAST:   Master file.  80-byte records, KSDS VSAM file.  *
    *                                                                 *
    *   The transaction records and the master file records have      *
    *   the same format, except for the 81st byte in the transaction  *
    *   file, which contains the transaction code:                    *
    *     A  Add entire transaction                                   *
    *     D  Delete master record                                     *
    *     R  Replace master with entire transaction                   *
```

```
*       U  Update copies field by adding transaction amount to    *
*          master file amount.                                     *
*       L  List titles belonging to an author.                     *
*                                                                  *
******************************************************************
 ENVIRONMENT DIVISION.
 INPUT-OUTPUT SECTION.
 FILE-CONTROL.
     SELECT TRAN-FILE ASSIGN TO    TRANFILE.
     SELECT LIB-MAST  ASSIGN TO    LIBMAST
                      ORGANIZATION IS       INDEXED
                      ACCESS MODE IS        DYNAMIC
                      RECORD KEY IS         LIB-KEY
                      ALTERNATE RECORD KEY IS LIB-AUTH-LNAME
                          WITH DUPLICATES
                      FILE STATUS  IS       LIB-STAT1,
                                            LIB-STAT2.
 DATA DIVISION.
 FILE SECTION.
 FD  TRAN-FILE
     LABEL RECORDS ARE STANDARD
     BLOCK CONTAINS 0 RECORDS
     RECORD CONTAINS 81 CHARACTERS.
 01  TRAN-RECORD        PIC X(81).
 FD  LIB-MAST
     LABEL RECORDS ARE STANDARD
     RECORD CONTAINS 80 CHARACTERS.
 01  LIB-RECORD.
     05  LIB-KEY        PIC X(08).
*          The key is internal to the company.
     05  LIB-AUTH-LNAME PIC X(15).
*          Author's last name.
     05  LIB-AUTH-FNAME PIC X(12).
*          Author's first name.
     05  LIB-AUTH-INIT  PIC X(01).
*          Author's middle initial.
     05  LIB-TITLE      PIC X(28).
*          Title of the tape.
     05  LIB-ISBN-NO    PIC X(13).
*          ISBN number of the tape.
     05  LIB-COPIES     PIC 9(03).
*          Number of copies of the tape in stock.
```

```
WORKING-STORAGE SECTION.
01  TRAN-REC.
    05  TRAN-KEY          PIC X(08).
*           Primary key.
    05  TRAN-AUTH-LNAME    PIC X(15).
*           The last name is an alternate record key.
    05  TRAN-AUTH-FNAME    PIC X(12).
    05  TRAN-AUTH-INIT     PIC X(01).
    05  TRAN-TITLE         PIC X(28).
    05  TRAN-ISBN-NO       PIC X(13).
    05  TRAN-COPIES        PIC 9(03).
    05  TRAN-CODE          PIC X(01).
        88  TRAN-ADD                VALUE "A".
        88  TRAN-DEL                VALUE "D".
        88  TRAN-REPL               VALUE "R".
        88  TRAN-UPDATE             VALUE "U".
        88  TRAN-LIST               VALUE "L".
01  LIB-STATUS.
*    The status is stored here after each I/O.
    05  LIB-STAT1         PIC X(02)  VALUE SPACES.
        88  OK                      VALUE "00" "02".
        88  EOF                     VALUE "10".
        88  DUP                     VALUE "22".
        88  NOT-FOUND               VALUE "23".
        88  VERIFIED                VALUE "97".
*          Following is the VSAM error status code area.
    05  LIB-STAT2.
        10  LIB-V-RETURN   PIC 9(02).
        10  LIB-V-FUNC     PIC 9.
        10  LIB-V-FEEDBACK PIC 9(03).
01  SWITCHES-AREA.
*    This area contains flags indication various events
*    encountered.
    05  TRAN-SW           PIC X(03)  VALUE "   ".
*          End-of-file flag for TRANFILE.
        88  TRAN-EOF                VALUE "END".
    05  ERROR-SW          PIC X(03)  VALUE "   ".
*          I/O error on LIBFILE.
        88  IO-ERR                  VALUE "ERR".
    05  ERROR-CODE        PIC X.
*          Type of error encountered.
*              "1"  Error opening TRAN-FILE.
```

```
*                "2"  Error opening LIB-MAST.
*                "3"  Error closing LIB-MAST.
*                "4"  Bad code in transaction.
*                "5"  Adding transaction already in master.
*                "6"  Can't write addition in master.
*                "7"  Record in master to delete not found.
*                "8"  Can't delete record in master.
*                "9"  Record in master to replace not found.
*                "A"  Can't rewrite master record for replace.
*                "B"  Can't read master record for replace.
*                "C"  Can't find master record for update.
*                "D"  Can't read master record for update.
*                "E"  Can't rewrite master record for update.
*                "F"  Can't find any titles to list for author.
  01  COUNT-AREA.
*        The run statistics are kept here.
       05  COUNT-SKIP       PIC 9(4)     VALUE ZERO.
       05  COUNT-ADD        PIC 9(4)     VALUE ZERO.
       05  COUNT-DEL        PIC 9(4)     VALUE ZERO.
       05  COUNT-REWRITE    PIC 9(4)     VALUE ZERO.
       05  COUNT-UPDATE     PIC 9(4)     VALUE ZERO.
       05  COUNT-LIST       PIC 9(4)     VALUE ZERO.
       05  COUNT-TRAN       PIC 9(4)     VALUE ZERO.
       05  COUNT-ERRORS     PIC 9(4)     VALUE ZERO.
       05  COUNT-MAX-ERRORS PIC 9(4)     VALUE 50.
*            Maximum number of errors to allow before quitting.
  PROCEDURE DIVISION.
  100-START-PROGRAM.
      DISPLAY "STARTING VDEMO2 PROGRAM."
*       Open the transactions file and verify that it was
*       opened correctly.
      OPEN INPUT TRAN-FILE
      IF NOT OK
        THEN MOVE "1" TO ERROR-CODE
             PERFORM 950-DISPLAY-ERROR
*       A simple bail out in case of a serious error.
             GO TO 999-STOP-RUN
      END-IF
*       Do the same for the master file.
      OPEN I-O LIB-MAST
      IF NOT (OK OR VERIFIED)
        THEN MOVE "2" TO ERROR-CODE
```

```
              PERFORM 950-DISPLAY-ERROR
              CLOSE TRAN-FILE
              GO TO 999-STOP-RUN
        END-IF
*        Read all the transactions until no more.
        PERFORM 200-PROCESS WITH TEST AFTER
                UNTIL IO-ERR OR TRAN-EOF
*        Close the files.  Verify that the master file
*        was closed with no problems.
        CLOSE TRAN-FILE, LIB-MAST
        IF NOT OK
           THEN MOVE "3" TO ERROR-CODE
                PERFORM 950-DISPLAY-ERROR
        END-IF
        GO TO 999-STOP-RUN
           .
   200-PROCESS.
   **********************************************************************
   * PROCEDURE TO PROCESS ALL TRANSACTION.                             *
   * PERFORM 200-PROCESS                                               *
   * IN:  LIB-MAST is open.                                            *
   *      TRAN-FILE is open.                                           *
   * OUT: A transaction is read and applied to master file.           *
   *      TRAN-EOF set to TRUE at EOF.                                 *
   *      IO-ERR set to TRUE if I/O error.                             *
   *      COUNT-TRAN contains count of transacations read.            *
   *      COUNT-SKIP contains count of transactions skipped.          *
   **********************************************************************
        INITIALIZE TRAN-REC
        READ TRAN-FILE INTO TRAN-REC
           AT END
               SET TRAN-EOF TO TRUE
           NOT AT END
               ADD 1 TO COUNT-TRAN
               EVALUATE TRUE
                   WHEN TRAN-ADD
                       PERFORM 300-ADD
                   WHEN TRAN-DEL
                       PERFORM 400-DELETE
                   WHEN TRAN-REPL
                       PERFORM 500-REPLACE
                   WHEN TRAN-UPDATE
```

```
                                    PERFORM 600-UPDATE-COPIES
                       WHEN TRAN-LIST
                                    PERFORM 800-LIST-AUTHORS
                       WHEN OTHER
                                    ADD 1 TO COUNT-SKIP
                                    MOVE "4" TO ERROR-CODE
                                    PERFORM 950-DISPLAY-ERROR
                   END-EVALUATE
             END-READ
             .
     300-ADD.
     ******************************************************************
     * PROCEDURE TO ADD TRANSACTION TYPE A TO MASTER FILE.            *
     * PERFORM 300-ADD                                                *
     * IN:  LIB-MAST is open.                                         *
     * OUT: The transaction is written into the master file.          *
     *      COUNT-ADD is bumped up by 1.                             *
     ******************************************************************
             MOVE TRAN-REC TO LIB-RECORD
             MOVE TRAN-COPIES TO LIB-COPIES
             WRITE LIB-RECORD
             EVALUATE TRUE
                 WHEN OK
                         ADD 1 TO COUNT-ADD
                 WHEN DUP
                         MOVE "5" TO ERROR-CODE
                         PERFORM 950-DISPLAY-ERROR
                 WHEN OTHER
                         MOVE "6" TO ERROR-CODE
                         PERFORM 950-DISPLAY-ERROR
             END-EVALUATE
             .
     400-DELETE.
     ******************************************************************
     * PROCEDURE TO DELETE MASTER RECORD MATCHING TYPE D             *
     *   TRANSACTION.                                                 *
     * PERFORM 500-REPLACE                                            *
     * IN:  LIB-MAST is open.                                         *
     * OUT: The master file record matching the transaction is        *
     *      deleted.                                                  *
     *      COUNT-DEL is bumped up by 1.                             *
     ******************************************************************
```

```
      MOVE TRAN-KEY TO LIB-KEY
      DELETE LIB-MAST
      EVALUATE TRUE
          WHEN OK
                  ADD 1 TO COUNT-DEL
          WHEN NOT-FOUND
                  MOVE "7" TO ERROR-CODE
                  PERFORM 950-DISPLAY-ERROR
          WHEN OTHER
                  MOVE "8" TO ERROR-CODE
                  PERFORM 950-DISPLAY-ERROR
      END-EVALUATE

          .
 500-REPLACE.
 **********************************************************************
 * PROCEDURE TO REPLACE MASTER RECORD WITH TRANSACTION TYPE R.    *
 * PERFORM 500-REPLACE                                           *
 * IN:  LIB-MAST is open.                                        *
 * OUT: The master file record is replaced with the transaction  *
 *      record.                                                 *
 *      COUNT-REWRITE is bumped up by 1.                         *
 **********************************************************************
      MOVE TRAN-KEY TO LIB-KEY
      READ LIB-MAST
      EVALUATE TRUE
          WHEN NOT-FOUND
                  MOVE "9" TO ERROR-CODE
                  PERFORM 950-DISPLAY-ERROR
          WHEN NOT OK
                  MOVE "B" TO ERROR-CODE
                  PERFORM 950-DISPLAY-ERROR
          WHEN OTHER
                  REWRITE LIB-RECORD FROM TRAN-REC
                  EVALUATE TRUE
                     WHEN OK
                             ADD 1 TO COUNT-REWRITE
                     WHEN OTHER
                             MOVE "A" TO ERROR-CODE
                             PERFORM 950-DISPLAY-ERROR
                  END-EVALUATE
          END-EVALUATE
```

```
600-UPDATE-COPIES.
**********************************************************************
* PROCEDURE TO UPDATE COPIES FIELD OF MASTER WITH TYPE U      *
*   TRANSACTION.                                              *
* PERFORM 600-UPDATE-COPIES                                   *
* IN:  LIB-MAST is open.                                      *
* OUT: The master file record is updated with copies field    *
*        from the transaction.                                *
*      COUNT-UPDATE is bumped up by 1.                        *
**********************************************************************
     MOVE TRAN-KEY TO LIB-KEY
     READ LIB-MAST
     EVALUATE TRUE
         WHEN NOT-FOUND
                 MOVE "C" TO ERROR-CODE
                 PERFORM 950-DISPLAY-ERROR
         WHEN NOT OK
                 MOVE "D" TO ERROR-CODE
                 PERFORM 950-DISPLAY-ERROR
         WHEN OTHER
                 ADD TRAN-COPIES TO LIB-COPIES
                 REWRITE LIB-RECORD
                    EVALUATE TRUE
                        WHEN OK
                            ADD 1 TO COUNT-UPDATE
                        WHEN OTHER
                            MOVE "E" TO ERROR-CODE
                            PERFORM 950-DISPLAY-ERROR
                    END-EVALUATE
     END-EVALUATE
         .
 800-LIST-AUTHORS.
**********************************************************************
* PROCEDURE TO LIST AUTHOR NAMES WITH TYPE L TRANSACTION.     *
* PERFORM 800-LIST-AUTHORS                                    *
* IN: LIB-MAST is open.                                       *
* OUT: All titles whose author matches the author's last name  *
*        in the transaction are listed.                       *
*      COUNT-LIST counts number of records listed.            *
**********************************************************************
     MOVE TRAN-AUTH-LNAME TO LIB-AUTH-LNAME
     START LIB-MAST KEY IS = LIB-AUTH-LNAME
```

```
          INVALID KEY
              MOVE "F" TO ERROR-CODE
              PERFORM 950-DISPLAY-ERROR
          NOT INVALID KEY
              DISPLAY "LISTING TITLES FOR AUTHOR:  ",
                      LIB-AUTH-LNAME
              PERFORM WITH TEST AFTER
                      UNTIL LIB-AUTH-LNAME NOT = TRAN-AUTH-LNAME
                  READ LIB-MAST NEXT
                      AT END
                          MOVE SPACES TO LIB-AUTH-LNAME
                      NOT AT END
                          IF LIB-AUTH-LNAME = TRAN-AUTH-LNAME
                              THEN DISPLAY "NEXT TITLE:  ", LIB-TITLE
                              ADD 1 TO COUNT-LIST
                          END-IF
                  END-READ
              END-PERFORM
      END-START
          .
 950-DISPLAY-ERROR.
 *********************************************************************
 * PROCEDURE TO PRINT ERROR MESSAGES.                               *
 * PERFORM 950-DISPLAY-ERROR                                        *
 * IN:  ERROR-CODE contains type of error.                          *
 * OUT: IS-ERR  Set to TRUE if it is an I/O error.                  *
 *      An error message is printed.                                *
 *      Message displayed to tell whether skipping transaction      *
 *        or terminating run.                                       *
 *      COUNT-ERRORS bumped up by 1.                                *
 *      COUNT-SKIP bumped by 1 if transaction skipped.              *
 *      Run terminated if COUNT-ERRORS > COUNT-MAX-ERRORS.          *
 *********************************************************************
 *      Set IO-ERR if it is an I/O error.
      EVALUATE ERROR-CODE
          WHEN "1" THRU "3"
          WHEN "6"
          WHEN "8"
          WHEN "A"
          WHEN "B"
          WHEN "D"
              SET IO-ERR TO TRUE
```

```
          END-EVALUATE
     *      Display the error message.
          EVALUATE ERROR-CODE
             WHEN "1"
                  DISPLAY "ERROR—OPENING TRAN-FILE."
             WHEN "2"
                  DISPLAY "ERROR—OPENING LIB-MAST FILE."
             WHEN "3"
                  DISPLAY "ERROR-CANNOT CLOSE LIB-MAST."
                  DISPLAY "JUST NOT YOUR DAY, IS IT!"
             WHEN "4"
                  DISPLAY "ERROR—BAD TRANSACTION CODE."
             WHEN "5"
                  DISPLAY "ERROR—ADDED RECORD ALREADY IN MASTER."
             WHEN "6"
                  DISPLAY "ERROR—CAN'T WRITE LIB-MAST ADDITION."
             WHEN "7"
                  DISPLAY "ERROR—",
                          "RECORD IN LIB-MAST TO DELETE NOT FOUND."
             WHEN "8"
                  DISPLAY "ERROR—CAN'T DELETE LIB-MAST RECORD."
             WHEN "9"
                  DISPLAY "ERROR—REPLACEMENT RECORD NOT FOUND."
             WHEN "A"
                  DISPLAY "CAN'T REPLACE LIB-MAST RECORD."
             WHEN "B"
                  DISPLAY "ERROR—CAN'T READ LIB-MAST RECORD FOR",
                          " REPLACE."
             WHEN "C"
                  DISPLAY "ERROR—TRANSACTION NOT FOUND FOR UPDATE."
             WHEN "D"
                  DISPLAY "ERROR—CAN'T READ LIB-MAST RECORD FOR",
                          " UPDATE."
             WHEN "E"
                  DISPLAY "ERROR—CAN'T REWRITE LIB-MAST RECORD",
                          " FOR UPDATE."
             WHEN "F"
                  DISPLAY "NOTE—NO TITLES FOR AUTHOR."
          END-EVALUATE
     *      Display any other information needed.
          EVALUATE ERROR-CODE
             WHEN "1"
```

```
        WHEN "2"
        WHEN "3"
        WHEN "6"
        WHEN "8"
        WHEN "A"
        WHEN "B"
        WHEN "D"
        WHEN "E"
            SET IO-ERR TO TRUE
            DISPLAY "ERROR CODE: ",          LIB-STATUS
        WHEN "4"
            DISPLAY "TRANSACTION RECORD: ", TRAN-REC
            DISPLAY "TRANSACTION CODE:  ", TRAN-CODE
        WHEN "5" THRU "9"
        WHEN "A" THRU "E"
            DISPLAY "TRANSACTION KEY:  ",   TRAN-KEY
        WHEN "F"
            DISPLAY "AUTHOR: ",             TRAN-AUTH-LNAME
    END-EVALUATE
*   Tell what we are going to do about the error.
    EVALUATE ERROR-CODE
        WHEN "1" THRU "3"
        WHEN "6"
        WHEN "8"
        WHEN "A"
        WHEN "B"
        WHEN "D"
        WHEN "E"
            DISPLAY "TERMINATING RUN."
        WHEN OTHER
            DISPLAY "SKIPPING TRANSACTION."
            ADD 1 TO COUNT-SKIP
    END-EVALUATE
*   Count the errors and quit if too many.
    ADD 1 TO COUNT-ERRORS
    IF COUNT-ERRORS > COUNT-MAX-ERRORS
        THEN DISPLAY "MORE THAN ", COUNT-MAX-ERRORS
            DISPLAY "TERMINATING RUN."
            GO TO 999-STOP-RUN
    END-IF
        .
```

```
 999-STOP-RUN.
*********************************************************************
* PROCEDURE TO PRINT RUN SUMMARY AND TERMINATE.                    *
* PERFORM 999-STOP-RUN                                             *
* IN:   COUNT-AREA identifiers all set.                            *
* OUT: Run summary printed.                                        *
*********************************************************************
     DISPLAY "NUMBER TRANSACTIONS READ:         ", COUNT-TRAN
     DISPLAY "NUMBER TRANSACTION SKIPPED:        ", COUNT-SKIP
     DISPLAY "NUMBER TRANSACTIONS ADDED:         ", COUNT-ADD
     DISPLAY "NUMBER MASTER RECORDS DELETED:     ", COUNT-DEL
     DISPLAY "NUMBER MASTER RECORDS REWRITTEN:   ", COUNT-REWRITE
     DISPLAY "NUMBER MASTER RECORDS UPDATED:     ", COUNT-UPDATE
     DISPLAY "NUMBER MASTER RECORDS LISTED:      ", COUNT-LIST
     IF COUNT-ERRORS > 0
        THEN DISPLAY "NUMBER OF ERRORS:  ", COUNT-ERRORS
        ELSE DISPLAY "NO ERRORS."
     END-IF
     IF IO-ERR
        THEN DISPLAY "!!!! NOTE—THERE WERE I-O ERRORS !!!!"
     END-IF
     DISPLAY "END OF PROGRAM."
     STOP RUN
        .
```

Sample
CICS Program

Note: This program demonstrates the BROWSE function. Refer to
       paragraphs 6200 through 6500. For more on CICS with
       VSAM and COBOL, see Chapter 21.

```
000140*=======================*
000200 IDENTIFICATION DIVISION.
000300*=======================*
000400*
000500 PROGRAM-ID.     VDEMO3.
000600*
000700 AUTHOR.         SMITH & BROWN.
000800*
000900 DATE-WRITTEN.    MARCH 1992.
001000 DATE-COMPILED.
001100*
001400**************************************************************************
001500*                                                                       *
001600*   N O T E S:     ********    COBOL II    *********                     *
001700*                                                                       *
001800*   TRANSACTION USER EXIT FOR TRANSACTION "USYN"                         *
001900*                                                                       *
002000*                 TRANSACTION-STATUS-CODE = 0 ... ALL IS WELL.           *
002100*                 SPRTS   =   2 ... SOME ERROR TO BE DISPLAYED           *
002200*                                  ON THE MENU.                          *
002300*                 TRANSACTION-STATUS-CODE =14 ...  ROLL TO UPDATE D      *
```

```
002400*                                                                *
002500*                                                                *
002600*              ABEND CODE(S)   AND    CONDITIONS:                *
002700*              USYN = UNEXPECTED REQUEST PASSED                  *
002800*                                                                *
002900* PURPOSE:  CHECK ACTION TO BE TAKEN WHEN OPERATOR PRESSES THE   *
003000*           PF10, PF11 OR AFTER PF07 (SAVE). KEYS FROM THE SCREEN*
003100*           ARE STORED IN THE SCRATCH PAD RECD. THIS MODULE LOOKS*
003200*           AT THE SCREEN PAGE AND KEYS, CHECKS THE FILE TO SEE IF*
003300*           THERE ARE MORE RECORDS IN THE "DIRECTION" REQUESTED. *
003400*           IF SO, IT SETS TO "ROLL TO UPDATE", IF NOT IT LETS   *
003500*           THE TRANS FLOW TO COMPLETION                         *
003510*           AFTER A SAVE, IF WE WANT TO GO FORWARD, WE SET PF10  *
003520*           IN THE EIBAID FOR THE NEXT PGM                       *
003600*****************************************************************
003700*                                                                *
003800*                      MODULE CHANGE LOG                         *
003900*                                                                *
004300*****************************************************************
004400*
004500*=====================*
004600 ENVIRONMENT DIVISION.
004700*=====================*
004800*
004900 CONFIGURATION SECTION.
005000*
005100 SOURCE-COMPUTER.     IBM-370.
005200 OBJECT-COMPUTER.     IBM-370.
005300*
005400*==============*
005500 DATA DIVISION.
005600*==============*
005700*
005800*———————*
005900 WORKING-STORAGE SECTION.
006000*———————*
006100*
006200*
006300 01 WS-WORKING-STORAGE.
006400*
006500************************
006600**  PROGRAM CONSTANTS  **
```

```
006700*************************
006800*
006900      WS-FILE-NAME                    PIC X(08) VALUE 'VDEM03    .
007000      05 WS-MAX-SCREEN-LINES          PIC S9(4) COMP    VALUE +15.
007100*
007200*************************
007300**  ADDRESS POINTERS    **
007400*************************
007500*
007600      05 WS-ADDR-COMP                 PIC S9(08) COMP.
007700      05 WS-ADDR-PNTR                 REDEFINES WS-ADDR-COMP
007800                                      USAGE POINTER.
007900*
008000*************************
008100**  KEYS AREA           **
008200*************************
008300*
008400      05  WS-START-KEY.
008500          10 DISTRICT-NUM             PIC  X(02).
008600          10 AI-NUM                   PIC  X(05).
008700          10 STRUCTURE-NUM            PIC  X(11).
008800          10 REST-OF-KEY-TEXT         PIC  X(56).
008900
009000      05  WS-START-BROWSE-KEY.
009100          10 DISTRICT-NUM             PIC  X(02).
009200          10 AI-NUM                   PIC  X(05).
009300          10 STRUCTURE-NUM            PIC  X(11).
009400          10 REST-OF-KEY-TEXT         PIC  X(56).
009500*
009600*************************
009700**  WORK FIELDS         **
009800*************************
009900*
010000      05 WS-SPACES                    PIC X(01)            VALUE SPACE.
010100      05 WS-ABEND-CODE                PIC X(04)            VALUE 'USYN'.
010200
010300      05 WS-RECORD-LENGTH             PIC S9(04) COMP      VALUE ZERO.
010400
010500      05 I                           PIC S9(04) COMP      VALUE ZERO.
010600
010700      05  WS-GETMAIN-LENGTH-F         PIC S9(08) COMP VALUE ZERO.
010800      05  FILLER                      REDEFINES  WS-GETMAIN-LENGTH-F.
```

```
010900            10 FILLER              PIC X(02).
011000            10 WS-GETMAIN-LENGTH   PIC S9(04) COMP.
011100
011200      05   WS-LINK-NAME           PIC X(08)          VALUE SPACES.
011210      05   WS-COMMAREA-LENGTH     PIC S9(04)         COMP VALUE +0.
011220      05   WS-PROGRAM-NAME        PIC X(08).
011300
011400      05   MORE-SYNCHRO-FLAG      PIC X(01)          VALUE 'Y'.
011500           88 MORE-SYNCHRO-RECORDS                   VALUE 'Y'.
011600           88 NO-MORE-SYNCHRO-RECORDS                VALUE 'N'.
011700
011710*01   WS-COMMAREA               PIC X(175).
011800
011900*
012000*************************
012100** MESSAGES          **
012200*************************
012300*
012400      05   RESP-CODE     PIC S9(8) COMP VALUE +0.
012500*
012600      05   CICS-MESSAGE.
012700           10 MSG-COMMAND    PIC X(12) VALUE 'XXXXXXXXXXXX'.
012800           10 FILLER         PIC X(14) VALUE ' ERR ON FILE:
012900           10 MSG-FILE-NAME  PIC X(08) VALUE 'FASYNCN
013000           10 FILLER         PIC X(08) VALUE ', CODE:
013100           10 MSG-CODE       PIC ZZ9.
013200           10 FILLER         PIC X(02) VALUE ' ('.
013300           10 MSG-CODE-TEXT  PIC X(08) VALUE 'XXXXXXXX'.
013400           10 FILLER         PIC X(01) VALUE ')',.
013500*
013600    COPY  DFHAID.
013700*
013800* ————*
013900 LINKAGE SECTION.
014000* ————*
014100*
014120 01 DFHCOMMAREA.
014130    COPY OCEXIT REPLACING ==01 OCEXIT. ==
014140                    BY ==          ==.
014150*
014181****************
014182**  TWA AREA  ** (SCRATCH PAD & MASTER FILE)
```

```
014183****************
014190 01   TWA.
014191      05 SP-ADDR                              PIC S9(08) COMP.
014192      05 SP-ADDR-PTR REDEFINES SP-ADDR USAGE IS POINTER.
014193
014194      05 MF-ADDR                              PIC S9(08) COMP.
014195      05 MF-ADDR-PTR REDEFINES MF-ADDR USAGE IS POINTER.
014196
014900*
015000***********************
015100** SCRATCH PAD RECORD **
015200***********************
015300*
015400     COPY OCSPRSTD.
015500*
015600*****                                      *****
015700**  DPIS'S REDEFINITION OF THE SCRATCH PAD   **
015800*****                                      *****
015900*
016000     COPY FCSPR
016100        REPLACING  ==  OCSPR ==
016200                   BY  ==  GA-SCRATCH-PAD-DATA ==.
016300*
016400*
016500*************************
016600** SYNCHRO RECORD AREA  **
016700*************************
016800*
016900 01 SYNCHRO-RECORD.
017000     COPY FASCHNG.
017100*
017200*==================*
017300 PROCEDURE DIVISION.
017400*==================*
017500*
017600     PERFORM 0100-GET-ADDRESSING.
017700***
017800** CHECK THE PF KEY PRESSED TO GET HERE, LOOK AT KEYS AND
017900** FILE TO DECIDE WHAT TO DO BASED ON WHETHER MORE RECORDS
017910** EXIST
018000***
018100
```

```
018120    EVALUATE  TRUE
018130        WHEN  OCXT-EXIT-POINT-NEXT-ACTION
018140        WHEN  OCXT-EXIT-POINT-PF10
018150        WHEN  OCXT-EXIT-POINT-PF22
018151             MOVE DFHPF10 TO EIBAID
018160             PERFORM 2100-FORWARD
018170        WHEN  OCXT-EXIT-POINT-PF11
018180        WHEN  OCXT-EXIT-POINT-PF23
018190             PERFORM 2200-BACKWARD
018191        WHEN  OTHER
018192             MOVE +2    TO TRANSACTION-STATUS-CODE
018193             MOVE 'INVALID INVOCATION OF EXIT MODULE FTUSI1'
018194                     TO TRANSACTION-TRMNATN-MESG-TEXT
018195    END-EVALUATE.
018196
018197    IF NO-MORE-SYNCHRO-RECORDS
018199      IF OCXT-EXIT-POINT-NEXT-ACTION
018200        MOVE 'UPDATE TRANSACTION COMPLETE'
018201           TO TRANSACTION-TRMNATN-MESG-TEXT
018208      ELSE
018209        MOVE +2    TO TRANSACTION-STATUS-CODE
018210        MOVE 'Y'    TO USER-COMPLETION-MESSAGE-FLAG
018211        MOVE 'NO MORE SCREENS '
018212           TO TRANSACTION-TRMNATN-MESG-TEXT
018214      END-IF
018216    ELSE
018217      SET ROLL-INTO-UPDATE TO TRUE
018218**     MOVE +14 TO TRANSACTION-STATUS-CODE
018220    END-IF.
020700*
020800    EXEC CICS
020900       RETURN
021000    END-EXEC.
021100*
021200    GOBACK.
021300*
021400 0100-GET-ADDRESSING.
021500**************************************************************
021600*** PICK UP ADDRESS OF SCRATCH PAD                       ***
021700**************************************************************
021800
021900    EXEC CICS
```

```
022000          ADDRESS TWA(ADDRESS OF TWA)
022100      END-EXEC.
022200
022300      MOVE SP-ADDR                        TO WS-ADDR-COMP.
022400      SET  ADDRESS OF GA-SCRATCH-PAD-DATA TO WS-ADDR-PNTR.
022500
022600      MOVE ZERO TO TRANSACTION-STATUS-CODE.
022700
022800*
022900 2100-FORWARD.
023000*********************************************************************
023100*** USING LAST KEY, LOOK FOR FORWARD RECDS                    ***
023200*********************************************************************
023300*
023400      IF USYN-RECORD-COUNT-QTY < WS-MAX-SCREEN-LINES
023500        MOVE 'THIS IS LAST PAGE' TO TRANSACTION-TRMNATN-MESG-TEXT
023600        SET NO-MORE-SYNCHRO-RECORDS TO TRUE
023700      ELSE
023800        MOVE USYN-LAST-KEY          TO WS-START-BROWSE-KEY
023900        MOVE USYN-LOWEST-KEY        TO WS-START-KEY
024000
024100        PERFORM 6200-START-BROWSE
024200
024300        IF TRANSACTION-STATUS-CODE = ZERO
024400          PERFORM 6300-READNEXT
024500          PERFORM 6300-READNEXT
024600        END-IF
024700
024800        PERFORM 6500-END-BROWSE
024900      END-IF.
025000
025100
025200*
025300 2200-BACKWARD.
025400*********************************************************************
025500*** IF WE ARE NOT ON FIRST PAGE, THERE WILL BE PREVIOUS RECDS***
025600*********************************************************************
025700*
025800
025900      IF USYN-CURRENT-PAGE-NUMBER = 1
026000        MOVE 'THIS IS FIRST PAGE' TO TRANSACTION-TRMNATN-MESG-TEXT
026100        SET NO-MORE-SYNCHRO-RECORDS TO TRUE
```

```
026200      END-IF.
026300*
026400 6200-START-BROWSE.
026500*********************************************************************
026600*** KEY WILL HAVE BEEN SET UP IN W/S                              ***
026700*********************************************************************
026800      MOVE 'STARTBR' TO MSG-COMMAND.
026900
027000      EXEC CICS STARTBR DATASET (WS-FILE-NAME)
027100                        RIDFLD (WS-START-BROWSE-KEY)
027200                        GTEQ
027300                        RESP   (RESP-CODE)
027400      END-EXEC.
027500
027600      EVALUATE RESP-CODE
027700         WHEN DFHRESP(NORMAL)
027800              CONTINUE
027900         WHEN OTHER
028000              PERFORM 9100-CICS-ERROR
028100      END-EVALUATE.
028200*
028300 6300-READNEXT.
028400*********************************************************************
028500*** UNTIL WE GET OUT OF THE KEY RANGE OR HIT HTE END OF FILE   ***
028600*********************************************************************
028700      MOVE 'READNEXT' TO  MSG-COMMAND.
028800
028900      EXEC CICS READNEXT  DATASET(WS-FILE-NAME)
029000                          RIDFLD (WS-START-BROWSE-KEY)
029100                          SET    (ADDRESS OF SYNCHRO-RECORD)
029200                          LENGTH (WS-RECORD-LENGTH)
029300                          RESP   (RESP-CODE)
029400      END-EXEC.
029500
029600      EVALUATE RESP-CODE
029700         WHEN DFHRESP(NORMAL)
029800**
029900** CHECK THAT  WE ARE STILL IN THE PROPER KEY RANGE
030000**
030100              IF DISTRICT-NUM OF SYNCHRO-RECORD NOT =
030200                  DISTRICT-NUM OF WS-START-KEY
030300              OR AI-NUM OF SYNCHRO-RECORD NOT =
```

```
030400                  AI-NUM OF WS-START-KEY
030500             OR
030600                  (STRUCTURE-NUM OF SYNCHRO-RECORD NOT =
030700                       STRUCTURE-NUM OF WS-START-KEY
030800                  AND STRUCTURE-NUM OF WS-START-KEY > SPACES)
030900                       SET NO-MORE-SYNCHRO-RECORDS TO TRUE
031000             END-IF
031100
031200         WHEN DFHRESP(ENDFILE)
031300             SET NO-MORE-SYNCHRO-RECORDS TO TRUE
031400
031500         WHEN  OTHER
031600             PERFORM 9100-CICS-ERROR
031700
031800      END-EVALUATE.
031900
032000*
032100 6400-READPREV.
032200***********************************************************
032300*** UNTIL WE GET OUT OF THE KEY RANGE OR HIT THE END OF FILE  ***
032400***********************************************************
032500      MOVE 'READPREV' TO KSG-COMMAND.
032600
032700      EXEC CICS READPREV DATASET (WS-FILE-NAME)
032800                         RIDFLD  (WS-START-BROWSE-KEY)
032900                         SET     (ADDRESS OF SYNCHRO-RECORD)
033000                         LENGTH  (WS-RECORD-LENGTH)
033100                         RESP    (RESP-CODE)
033200      END-EXEC.
033300
033400      EVALUATE RESP-CODE
033500         WHEN DFHRESP(NORMAL)
033600**
033700** CHECK THAT WE ARE STILL IN THE PROPER KEY RANGE
033800**
033900             IF FASCHNG-KEY OF SYNCHRO-RECORD <
034000                 USYN-LOWEST-KEY OF FCSPR
034100                 SET NO-MORE-SYNCHRO-RECORDS TO TRUE
034200             END-IF
034300
034400         WHEN DFHRESP(ENDFILE)
034500             SET NO-MORE-SYNCHRO-RECORDS TO TRUE
```

```
034600
034700      WHEN  OTHER
034800            PERFORM 9100-CICS-ERROR
034900
035000      END-EVALUATE.
035100
035200*
035300 6500-END-BROWSE.
035400*********************************************************************
035500*** INSURE IT'S CLOSED                                        ***
035600*********************************************************************
035700
035800
035900      EXEC CICS ENDBR DATASET(WS-FILE-NAME)
036000                  NOHANDLE
036100      END-EXEC.
036200
036300*
036400 9000-LINK.
036500*********************************************************************
036600***                                                           ***
036700*********************************************************************
036800*
036900      EXEC CICS
037000          LINK PROGRAM(WS-LINK-NAME)
037100      END-EXEC.
037200*
037300 9100-CICS-ERROR.
037400*********************************************************************
037500*** FIX UP MESSAGE FOR TERMINATION; FILE CONTROL COMMANDS    ***
037600*********************************************************************
037700*
037800      MOVE    RESP-CODE TO MSG-CODE.
037900      EVALUATE RESP-CODE
038000         WHEN  DFHRESP(NOTFND)
038100               MOVE 'NOTFND' TO MSG-CODE-TEXT
038200         WHEN  DFHRESP(NOTOPEN)
038300               MOVE 'NOTOPEN' TO MSG-CODE-TEXT
038400         WHEN  OTHER
038500               MOVE '??    ' TO MSG-CODE-TEXT
038600      END-EVALUATE.
038700
```

```
038800      MOVE CICS-MESSAGE TO TRANSACTION-TRMNATN-MESG-TEXT.
038900      MOVE +2          TO TRANSACTION-STATUS-CODE.
039000*
039100 9999-ABEND.
039200**************************************************************
039300***                                                        ***
039400**************************************************************
039500*
039600      EXEC CICS ABEND
039700              ABCODE(WS-ABEND-CODE)
039800      END-EXEC.
039900
```

Index